Balasaraswati

Balasaraswati

HER ART & LIFE

Douglas M. Knight Jr.

WESLEYAN UNIVERSITY PRESS

Middletown, Connecticut

Wesleyan University Press
Middletown CT 06459
www.wesleyan.edu/wespress

The publisher gratefully acknowledges the support of the John
Simon Guggenheim Memorial Foundation.

Wesleyan University Press is a member of the
Green Press Initiative. The paper used in this book
meets their minimum requirement for recycled paper.

Library of Congress Cataloging-in-Publication Data
Knight, Douglas M.
Balasaraswati : her art and life / Douglas M. Knight Jr.
    p. cm.
Includes bibliographical references and index.
ISBN 978-0-8195-6906-6 (cloth : alk. paper)
1. Balasaraswati.   2. Dancers — India — Biography.
I. Title.
GV1785.B34K55 2010
792.8028092 — dc22
[B]   2009052105

5 4 3 2 1

The Driftless Series is funded by the
Beatrice Fox Auerbach Foundation Fund
at the Hartford Foundation for Public Giving.

In Memory of Lakshmi Knight

Contents

Illustrations

Notes on Translation, Transliteration, and Dates

WORD AND MEANING

I have written about an individual person, families and communities, events, and a place whose language was Tamil, not English. When people think in a particular language, they think in a particular way; when they communicate in a particular language, they interact in a certain way. This fact is subtly made apparent among peoples who share a language but not a culture — for example, the diverse nations of English speaking people. Any person's or culture's language, with its particular, encoded significance, cannot be translated without an unintended transposition of meaning that may be misleading, especially in print.

My aim has been to capture or preserve the qualities that language contributes to narrative, using translations that have been transcribed into written English. In almost every case, the translators of the recorded interviews and other forms of commentary knew both the person and the subject of the original recording, and this has contributed to my capacity to fulfill this objective. But translations differ in subtle ways; there are various English versions of any one of the public speeches that Balasaraswati presented in Tamil in India, for example. The meaning of the translations may not differ significantly, but the license taken by the translator is clearly apparent, and cannot be avoided. I have had, in the end, to select the translations that best evoke a meaning that corresponds to how *I* understood the spirit of the original statement or document.

Foreign language words and phrases are presented in italics. All italicized words are defined in the text, generally at their first appearance. I have repeated the use of italics throughout so that the reader may recognize that the word is transliterated from a foreign language. Its definition may be located in the text through the index. This approach is at odds with some academic conventions, but I intend this book to be accessible to a broad audience and have presumed that transliterated words, even those considered assimilated into English, are not always clearly or meaningfully understood. Terms that are important for the reader's understanding but may require further explanation or reemphasis are included in a Glossary.

SOUND AND SPELLING

I have transliterated words and names written in various scripts in India using the Roman alphabet, without diacritical marks, and using certain combinations of letters to represent the unique phonetic characteristics of the language. There are many variations of any given representation of a word in transliteration; I have attempted to choose spellings that are among those in most common usage in India today.

I have used the English-language convention of adding an *s* to a word to create a plural form of many Sanskrit and Tamil words used to describe the performance and theory of music and dance (for example, *sangathi* and *sangathis*). The convention often followed in India is to hyphenate the *s* when creating a plural form; I have elected not to follow that practice.

Since I began to learn about this musical system, the common spelling of many transliterated words has changed, and many places have been renamed. In many cases, I use the Anglicized names of places, such as Madras, Bombay, Calcutta, and Delhi, rather than their newer names, Chennai, Mumbai, Kolkatta, and Dilli. When the events in this story occurred, the people associated with it referred to these and other cities and towns by their Anglicized names; to make the narrative consistent with their voices in quotation, I have retained the older names. The one city name that I did not often hear in an Anglicized form was Balasaraswati's *vur*, her place of origin, Thanjavur. Tanjore is the Anglicized form of this city's name, and I learned it that way also. But early in my relationship with Balasaraswati and her family, the city itself, and others who share an ancestral connection to it, I learned to call the place Thanjavur, and so I have used that name in this account.

The music tradition about which I write is transliterated variously as *Carnatic, Karnatak, karnatak, karnatik,* and *karnatic.* I use *karnatic.* The dance form is variously written Bharatanatyam, Bharatnatya, bharat natyam, and bharata natyam, among several other spellings. I use bharata natyam. Because it appears so frequently, I have chosen not to italicize this term.

The spelling of Indian names is also problematic. Balasaraswati's name can be transliterated several other ways, including Balasaraswathi, Bala Saraswati, Balasaraswathy, and so on. Other examples are the subcaste or community names Iyer and Iyengar. Iyer may be spelled Ayyar or Ayyer, and an alternative spelling of Iyengar is Ayyangar. I have chosen for the sake of clarity to standardize the spelling of these two community names as Iyer and Iyengar, and hope that in doing so I will not give great offense. Naturally, some Indians have preferences as to how the English-language versions of their names are handled, and I may have inadvertently violated that preference.

Some dance and music critics I have quoted use the device of a pseudonym, and both the text and the citations in the endnotes identify those. There are also familiar and formal forms of names that may be confusing to the reader; I use several versions of certain names, most notably Balasaraswati, who is called Bala, Balamma, and Sri Balasaraswati. Another example is the familiar form of the name Abhiramasundari, Balasaraswati's cousin, which is Abhirami. I have attempted to be consistent in my acknowledg-

ment of these and other variations and to provide identification where it
seems needed to assist readers unfamiliar with the cast of characters. Some individuals' names are commonly seen in more than one form. I have elected to use names and spellings familiar to me from their use by members of Balasaraswati's family. These variants occasionally disagree with more current academic practice.

One of the consistent ambiguities is in the attachment of Amma (meaning mother) or Ammal, used as either a suffix conveying respect added to an unmarried adult woman's name, or as a contraction with her given name. Examples include Kamakshi Ammal, or Kamakshiammal; or Gauri Ammal or Gauriammal. Both forms appear in print; again I have tried to be consistent with my own usage, but I use the variants Kamakshi Ammal and Kamakshiammal to distinguish between Balasaraswati's great-great-great grandmother and Balasaraswati's aunt. The reader will also note that I have added the suffix Ammal to certain names only when, as the story progresses through time, that individual has progressed from childhood to adulthood (for example, Balasaraswati's aunt is identified as Kamashi when she is referred to as a young girl, and as Kamakshiammal when she is an adult).

In the end, perfect consistency is not always feasible.

DATES

The dating of materials in this biography has also been a challenge. I have, almost without exception, stated a single date for an event, as carefully documented as possible. I have been fortunate that much of Balasaraswati's life was documented by her family and in the Indian and foreign press, but inevitably the reader will discover discrepancies and dates that are recorded differently in other sources. I have attempted to rely, in the end, upon a single source among many, an agreement within the family group recollection. But this story occurs a long time ago and at a time when the dates and places of events meant less to those who lived that history. It is, after all, a story about them and their version of what happened.

Preface

One of the twentieth century's great performing artists was a dancer and musician named Thanjavur Balasaraswati (1918–1984). Her art was a hereditary practice that integrated music, dance, and a stylized dramatic technique into a form called *bharata natyam*, originating in the southern region of India. T. Balasaraswati's art and life defined the heart of a tradition that became the basis for a reconstruction referred to today as one of the "classical" dance forms of India.

A problem that faced the traditional artist in India by the turn of the twentieth century, at least in cities like Madras that had become the new centers of art, was the evolution of a modernized culture and national character in which the reality of the world Balasaraswati inhabited was rejected. That reality became acceptable only in a mythologized form. To visualize Balasaraswati's significance today, we need to free ourselves of the limitations of our perspective, and see with bigger, more easily astonished eyes the world that embraced the tradition of hereditary bharata natyam.

The contemporary reality of India is different from even the recent past; the cultural and social realities of India in 1918, when Balasaraswati was born, are far more remote and therefore very difficult to perceive accurately. A colonized, deeply injured and, seemingly, irreconcilably diverse nation, India faced the rediscovery of itself, overcoming oppression and uncertainty, misperception and misrepresentation, to mature into self-acceptance and pride.

Balasaraswati's biography is drawn in large part from material created, collected, and preserved by various members of her family, among the most celebrated of all of the hundreds of professional families who a century ago were the sole performers of this tradition. This is also the story a family told about itself, seeking to connect with the past, long before Balasaraswati's lifetime — and with the future, since her death.

Balasaraswati's daughter, Lakshmi, considered the perpetuation and documentation of her mother's art to be her own life's work, and she collaborated with others for more than twenty years, until her own death in 2001, to collect the materials that are the foundation for this book. Lakshmi, born when Balasaraswati was twenty-five, was the only person Bala trusted implicitly. Herself a dancer and musician of depth and personal conviction, Lakshmi was Bala's protégée and knew the old art of singing and dancing at the same time. It is her interpretive voice more than any other that brings Bala to life in this biography. Part of Lakshmi's gift to the world of dance was her capacity to distance herself adequately and appropriately from a great artist who was also a totally dependent and devoted parent, to have the insight and artistry to distinguish between the artist and the parent, and to understand both.

It has been my task to create a coherent and compelling narrative from the hundreds of reviews, articles, transcribed interviews, and correspondence collected by Bala's family; from information gathered through my own research; and from many, many hours of conversation with Balasaraswati's family, friends and admirers. In this account I attempt to provide an objective portrayal of the artist and her family. I do not attempt to present a definitive description or history of the entire dance practice that is known as bharata natyam, or of dance in India.

I worked for several years on this manuscript avoiding mention of modernized bharata natyam, in an attempt to avoid the inevitable contention that would arise if I did. But the commentary that I have used as a basis for this book disagrees substantially with popularly accepted accounts. The history of bharata natyam told in the large volume of primary source material that I have woven into the narrative is comprised of Indians' contemporaneous accounts of the history of this practice. One of the most difficult problems I faced writing this book was to be honest about my own assessment, regardless of how I imagined that assessment might be received. I realize that it may raise some eyebrows. I have struggled with the personal realities of what this might mean for me; but I have not hesitated to tell Bala's story with as much integrity and perception as I have been able.

This narrative deliberately does not examine the subject from several points of view that have become concerns of some academic disciplines, including comparative gender studies, dance studies, and ethnomusicology. I am, nonetheless, indebted to scholars, practitioners, critics, and other writers who have addressed subjects that contribute to Balasaraswati's story. I hope this book will be a useful response to the current discourse in each of these, and other, fields.

I have written this book knowing that the audience is very diverse, representing numerous audiences within two distinctly divergent culturally defined groups of people, South Asians and non–South Asians. An objective has been to speak both to readers who are knowledgeable about this particular tradition of music and dance and to readers who are unfamiliar with Indian dance of any form. The Notes on Translation, Transliteration, and Dates following the list of illustrations, as well as an Appendix containing selected biographical sketches and a glossary at the end of the book, are intended to be useful to readers in both groups.

In the narrative there may sometimes be more explanation than those who are well informed will feel they need, and at times there may be more detail than nonspecialist readers will feel they want. But however the book may be judged, the story itself is important for many people from many backgrounds. Over the years since I began work on this book, Balasaraswati's story has continued to amaze and move me, and I hope I have succeeded in communicating the essence and the relevance of that story.

Because this book draws substantially on unpublished interviews, recordings, and personal letters the source and veracity of the quoted material may understandably be questioned. The reader may assume that quotations are taken from a published source, a transcription of a recorded interview, written commentary, or correspondence. All of the material I have used is preserved in its original form, but much of it was also translated. Several people contributed to the translation effort in addition to Balasaraswati's daughter, Lakshmi Knight. They included Balasaraswati's brother T. Viswanathan and cousin T. Shankaran; two distinguished critics, Subbian and P. V. Subramaniam (known as Subbudu); and several of Balasaraswati's friends, including Ra Ganapati and S. Guhan. Among these contributors, T. Shankaran deserves particular note for his translations of many of the reviews, articles, interviews, and letters that inform and bring life to this account.

My relationships with several members of Balasaraswati's family have been at the center of my musical and personal life since the late 1960s. I first met Balasaraswati in 1971, when I was a graduate student at California Institute of the Arts. I was studying with her brothers T. Ranganathan, a drummer, with whom I had begun to learn three years before at Wesleyan University, and T. Viswanathan, a flutist and singer.[1]

I first performed as a drummer with Balasaraswati's daughter, Lakshmi, in 1974, beginning with concerts in the United States and then on several occasions in India when Balasaraswati sang. Lakshmi and I continued to perform together over the next twenty-five years in India and North America. We were married in 1980, and in India we lived in Balasaraswati's home. Our son, Aniruddha, absorbed and learned the family styles of music and dance, which he continues today. Between 1971 and 1981 I attended dozens of Balasaraswati's performances in India and North America, and I attended seven of her residencies in the United States. I observed Balasaraswati teaching classes in the United States and at the Madras Music Academy. I also watched her teach her daughter and coach my son when he was a young boy.

Living within Balasaraswati's family for more than three decades has taught me something about how a hereditary art form endures. Being a household participant in the artistic process, I observed how a hereditary system functioned; how it protected and nurtured a family art; how it enabled the production of revolutionary art; and how it framed hereditary artists' understanding of their position in the community. Writing this book is the fulfillment of a commitment to give voice to that process and to a family of hereditary artists.

Some early readers of this book have cautioned me not to give too much weight to what I perceive as the European and American influence on the history of contemporary dance practice in India. This history was not of particular interest to Balasaraswati, who understood the transmission of the art through the process of inheritance. As I comment on the roots of reconstructed bharata natyam, I do not intend to be critical of the institutions that were created to support or propagate the new practice, or to question the significance of the remarkable individual artists who conceived the new dance. But the fact that modern South Indian dance was directly influenced by a Western social organization and by the echo of British colonial and missionary attitudes is important. That influence contributed directly to the reconsideration and redefinition of the organization and intent of dance, and the renegotiation of who could and should dance. What emerged are two distinctly different performance idioms: the traditional hereditary practice and the reconstructed "classical" form. The distinctions between these two idioms are not well understood; one objective of this book is to more clearly delineate these differences.

Balasaraswati, among many who sought to redefine themselves and their culture, remained true to her heritage, unwilling to subscribe to an effort to define India's greatness through a reconstruction of a mythical ancient past. She embodied that greatness instead through persistence in an artistic practice and system of belief that survived the violence of subjugation and cultural repression.

Balasaraswati's story is set in a community organized according to matrilineal principles. That is, heads of households were women, as is still true today of some families in parts of India and elsewhere in the world. This community, sometimes known by the name *devadasi*,[2] has not had the opportunity to represent itself well, although its members are recognized as the historical bearers of several traditions of music and dance that are currently popular in India.

The term *devadasi* has long been used to refer to a variety of groups of women and their families. In the census published by the British Administration of the Madras Presidency in 1901, seven differentiations of the term *devadasi* are enumerated; one of them is a descriptor of the women who danced and sang as performance practice. That community has become known by other names, including *isai velalar*, and the men of the community sometimes attached suffixes to their family names, commonly *Pillai* and *Mudaliar*. Today the word *devadasi* is often used without discretion, and sometimes misleadingly or reductively. For the sake of clarity, whenever I use the term *devadasi* in this book, I refer exclusively to the hereditary community of musicians and dancers who were the bearers of the tradition of bharata natyam. (Most *devadasi* families supported themselves through farming; only some family members became musicians or dancers.) In English, I refer to the performing artists and families as "hereditary" or "professional." "Professional" refers to the fact that these artists earned their livelihood through the practice of their art. The history of the *devadasi* is tremendously complex and involves various social and socio-religious issues in historical India that are beyond the scope of this work and my scope as an author.

Outside of India, as well as within, Balasaraswati has become something unique in South Indian dance history: a representative of a hereditary art and of a community otherwise almost disappeared. As true as this is, she was first and foremost a passionate revolutionary — an internationally significant, entirely modern artist. Whatever our various interests, and this is a defining qualification, we must accept and understand her and what she did on her terms.

Balasaraswati was a seventh-generation descendant of the musician and dancer Papammal from the eighteenth-century Thanjavur court. Since Papammal's time, music and dance have flowed continuously within the family, from one generation to the next. Twentieth-century members of Balasaraswati's family recognize Papammal's great-great-granddaughter Vina Dhanammal, the seminal musician from Madras, born in 1867 and the matriarch of this family, as the source of its art.

Among the large assortment of people worldwide whose lives were touched by Balasaraswati, each has had a distinct and personal story. Balasaraswati was like that. The multitude of lives she imprinted is one mark of her greatness. Everyone who had a relationship with Balasaraswati felt it to be intensely personal. Bala's vulnerability, from which her daughter would try hard to protect her, grew out of her incapacity to be deliberate in her interactions with people. If she was trustful of someone, she emerged as completely engaging, intensely and profoundly accessible. This meant, of course, that many people who knew Balasaraswati had a particular vision and intuition of who she was. I am aware that my impression is one of many, and I have attempted to reveal this story through the voices of many who knew and admired her, as well as to represent those whose voices I did not use. I have endeavored to be respectful of the multitude of relationships she had, all of which were fully as remarkable as they seemed. There are many relationships that I have been unable to acknowledge.

One of the characteristics of the artists in this family is the energy they devote to teaching and sharing. Balasaraswati and her family made extraordinary investments in the teaching and nurturing of their knowledge and art in India and the United States. Many of the present generation of musicians in India have been influenced by this family's style and repertoire. Since Balasaraswati's brother Viswanathan first visited the United States in 1958, eight members of the family have taught and toured in North America, Europe, and East Asia. The contribution of this one family to the global understanding of the performing arts of India is extraordinary. I am among many who have learned from Balasaraswati's family, though for many years I, at least, did not fully grasp the deprivations and social conditions that surrounded much of their lives. As I worked on this book I was faced with the need to reconcile Balasaraswati's legendary status today with the reality of the strenuousness of the life she led.

I sometimes refer to Balasaraswati as Bala, just as I refer to her brothers Ranganathan and Viswanathan as Ranga and Viswa. It feels awkward, as I write, to refer to them as Bala, Ranga, and Viswa—yet it also feels awkward, when I read, to see their names as Balasaraswati, Ranganathan, and Viswanathan. I think their many friends all over the world may share these complex feelings of respect and lack of familiarity coupled with fondness and a feeling of informality. I have been unable to resolve the ambiguity of awe and friendship, and so in this book I use both the formal and the familiar forms of their names.

Years ago I asked Lakshmi what she thought Bala believed was the most important part of her story, if it were told. Lakshmi responded without hesitation: "The truth."

Balasaraswati

CHAPTER 1 *From the Heart of the Tradition*

The practice of music and dance known as "bharata natyam," which originated in the southern part of India, has now spread, in name, throughout the globe. Its acceptance was not always so widespread. Confined in performance to a professional community of hereditary dancers and musicians until the 1930s, the dance form, its music, and the performers of both became the objects of misperception and derision. By 1950, there remained one dancer from southern India with an intact performing family legacy: Thanjavur Balasaraswati.

THANJAVUR BALASARASWATI

Balasaraswati was a seventh generation performer from a professional matrilineal community with historical roots that reach back at least a millennium. Records show that her ancestors were among the artists who received the patronage of the royal court of Thanjavur in the mid-eighteenth century. The family from which Balasaraswati inherited her art has long been recognized as unique, an irreplaceable repository of the traditions of *karnatic*, or South Indian, music and the practice of bharata natyam. Through the details of Balasaraswati's life and the commentary she offered about her art, we have the opportunity to glimpse the mechanisms and values of an enigmatic artistic community, and an exceptional family from within that community.

Balasaraswati is remembered globally as one of the most significant performing artists of the twentieth century, and as the great exponent of her art form. Narayana Menon, secretary of the Sangeet Natak Akademi (India's National Academy of the Performing Arts), wrote in memoriam after her death in 1984: "Balasaraswati became a legend when she lived. More legends are to come; when at a distance of time we can look back on her life and achievement and realize what she meant to us. But as a critic, in a glowing tribute to her, said, 'What legend could be more luminous than that she was born to us, in our country, in our time?'" The impact of Balasaraswati's performances was felt throughout India as the country moved toward self-definition and independence during the 1930s. She astonished and enlightened audiences who had never seen the traditional dance form, which by then was suppressed from performance, following fifty years of neglect and slander. Through the force of her artistry and personality, she resisted a growing prejudice toward traditional practitioners and propelled her art out of disgrace and ridicule to acclaim and awe. By the 1940s she was recognized as the only performer of a style of bharata natyam that was being overshadowed in the public view by a new, more accessible style of the dance.

She was as great a musician as she was a dancer; she laughed once when an interviewer asked her which she thought was more important. "Ha!" she burst out. "Get the joke?" Music and dance were the same for her. In 1973 she became, and has since remained, the only dancer to receive the title *Sangitha Kalanidhi* ("Treasure of the Art of Music") from the Madras Music Academy.

It was in the early 1960s that Balasaraswati first performed on the international stage, presenting concerts in East Asia, Europe and North America. She was, to my knowledge, the first traditional Indian dancer to appear in Europe since a sensational tour by a troupe of dancers in the 1830s. Charles Reinhart, now director of the American Dance Festival, traveled to India on behalf of Asia Society after Bala's appearance at the East-West Encounter in Tokyo in 1961 to make arrangements for her first tour of America. He later commented in an interview that it was important for Asia Society to show the quality of what existed in Asia—through Bala. Almost forty years later, in 2000, the Dance Heritage Coalition, an alliance of leading American dance performers and teachers, institutions, and dance libraries and collections, published the results of their initiative to identify "America's Irreplaceable Dance Treasures: The First 100." The only artist they included who was neither American nor European was Balasaraswati.

BHARATA NATYAM

Tamil, the language native to the lush tropical Kaveri River Delta in South India, has existed as a written language for two thousand years; at the same time a rich oral tradition of Tamil narrative, poetry, and music also flourished. The composers who created and defined the current practice of South Indian music, which has come to be claimed as "classical," came from villages and towns throughout the Delta. Several other performance traditions also emerged from the Delta, one of which became known as bharata natyam, in which music, dance, and theater were combined as an integrated idiom. The distinctions among dancer, musician, and actor that characterize a modern Western understanding of the performing arts do not apply to the hereditary practice of bharata natyam.

The name *bharata natyam* itself is suggestive of the controversial history of the traditional performing arts. It has been documented to be a two-centuries-old term. Some have argued that it reflects the ancient name for the Indian subcontinent (*bharat*) and the Sanskrit word for the performed arts (*natya*). Others maintain that it is a new name, recently coined to re-flect the evolution of a revived "classical" tradition. Some suggest the name bharata natyam invokes a semi-legendary sage named Bharat Muni as the author of a treatise described as the source of the dance practice.

There has been since the 1930s great power to the notion of the antiquity of the continuity of the arts in South India; it has sometimes been asserted that there is a two-thousand-year continuum of bharata natyam. Balasara-swati categorically denied this. However, a precursor of bharata natyam may have had its roots in a practice that had become established as a tradition during the first pre-Christian millennium. But it was not a direct and con-tinuous practice; it was, rather, an art perpetuated and altered through the same process of evolution that characterizes the history of all the arts.

The poetry of the music of bharata natyam speaks both of the interior world of devotion and human emotions and of the outer world of duty and action. The dancing itself, like most dance-theater forms in India, combines two basic aspects: one narrative and the other abstract. In the narrative aspect the dancer expresses connotative meaning through mime and the-ater, and by using an elaborate associative vocabulary of meaning conveyed through hand gestures. In Balasaraswati's style, as in the style of all heredi-tary dancers, the artist performs music and narrative dance extemporane-ously. Abstract dance is based on form and rhythmic structure, expressed through positions of the torso, limbs, head, and hands, and sounded pat-terns made with the feet, and choreographed using sequences of movement in combination.

The traditional repertoire of music for dance was composed between the sixteenth and twentieth centuries. Practitioners codified the dance form re-peatedly, most notably in the early nineteenth century. At that time, too, composers created a major portion of the musical forms performed today in the traditional style.

Bharata natyam has been described as being at its most sublime a form of Yoga, a discipline that brought the practitioner into the realm of the ex-perience that Balasaraswati described as "communion with Him." It is well known, Balasaraswati argued, that the combined disciplines of music and dance brought the artist into the experience of the Divine. Devotion to art is identical to devotion in the practice and pursuit of spiritual realities, for the dancer's sake and for the sake of the community that benefited from the dancer's pursuit. Through her discipline and humility Balasaraswati became a vessel through which the art flowed, an offering at once to God and to oth-ers who were witness to her offering.

There were other sorts of dance in South India also. Movement per-formed in temples was an essential component of ritual. Dancers, including performers of bharata natyam, offered their art to the presiding deity of the temple and, as well, to kings and invited audiences in the palace. Artists performed for the public on temporary stages erected during festivals, on permanent stages in temples, and in concert halls in the royal courts themselves. Dancers had specialties, such as *abhinaya* (an ancient term dating to a pre-Christian description of the dramatic arts, connoting dance conveying meaning). The early nineteenth century codification in Thanjavur integrated these specialties into a coherent solo concert format.[1] Ritual and secular dance must have been both clearly differentiated and closely related.

Every region had a particular form of ballad singing and tradition of theater in which the performer sang, narrated, acted, and interpreted a story.[2] The *harikathan* was a minstrel found in various forms throughout India who shared with performers of traditional dance a common perspective on their role in the community and on the tools and knowledge required to master their craft. The audience was curious what new life and insight the intellectual singer and dancer would bring to familiar stories. The performing artist was "a bearer, re-enforcer, and interpreter of the myths, images and anecdotes that are the vehicle for that body of beliefs. It was another role filled by women from the hereditary community. In many villages and rural complexes the tradition of singing the *Ramayana* serves the joint purposes of moral education and providing a medium for artistic expressiveness. . . . The individual singer . . . has the fullest liberty to interpolate or paraphrase the text and give it any contemporary validity that he considers fit."[3] The *harikatha* tradition itself, which was popular in the late nineteenth and early twentieth centuries, was an outgrowth of the introduction of Maratha musical and poetic forms from Maharashtra in the Thanjavur court in the mid-eighteenth century.[4]

TRANSMITTING A HERITAGE

The professions of ritual and performing artists in South India were passed on from generation to generation, as were other duties and functions in the community. There were two ways a person might learn the practice of his or her art: the artist might absorb the practice within a birth family of artists bound by a common perception of the art form, or he or she might leave home and become a disciple within the family of a master. In either case, mechanisms within the family and the professional community nurtured and perpetuated the art and maintained the standard of performance. Artists learned the practice and performance of the art through absorption and constant reinforcement — through listening, mimicry, and correction. In this tradition the process of becoming an artist was a process of becoming an extension of one's teacher or family.

Balasaraswati's family is remarkable not only for maintaining a continuous performing arts practice with stylistic continuity, but also for learning from and being influenced by composers, musicians, and dancers from outside of the family, including artists from outside of the regional music culture, and adapting that body of music to the evolving family style. The extended family's vast repertoire of more than one thousand orally retained compositions and intimate knowledge of the performance of more than one hundred musical modes (*ragas*) embraces the core of the South Indian musical tradition.

The family's greatness also is measurable by its artistic persistence during a period of profound cultural shifts. Artists of distinction populated each generation; the style of music was maintained by an extended family that in 1938 boasted more than a dozen artists. No other family is so well represented in the lobby of the Madras Music Academy, where photographs of musicians granted South India's highest honor, *Sangitha Kalanidhi*, as well as other distinctions, are displayed.

The continuously transmitted legacy within Balasaraswati's family was music — and, just as significantly, music as it was understood to be performed with dance. It was through their music that the family survived their transition from Thanjavur to Madras and from the patronage of the court to the modern professional environment. For periods of time family members did not perform dance publicly; it was music that enabled the family dance style to survive and to reemerge in Balasaraswati's art.

At the same time, a process of change characterized this family's artistic depth and persistence, as was common to other families who were hereditary practitioners of many things, not only music and dance. A Sanskrit word that conveys this combination of continuity and evolution is *sampradaya*, or tradition subject to review and redefinition. In keeping with *sampradaya*, Balasaraswati learned how to interpret and expand the extraordinary legacy that she studied, performed, and taught. She was taught how to make art, just as her mother had been taught how to make art, and so on. Balasaraswati did not represent a static historical version of bharata natyam; she embodied an art that was by its very nature going to change.

Balasaraswati most often referred to her art form as bharata natyam, although I also have heard her use the term *chinna melam* (which refers to the dance ensemble). Some scholars, dance practitioners, and others have come to call the hereditary practice *sadir*, *dasiattam*, and several other names.[5]

Sadir is a Tamil word that means, among other things, "beauty," and was used to refer to the activity of dancing. Some artists from the traditional community used this term, but not, I think, as the name of a dance form. It now implies a lesser art than bharata natyam, a crude "country" style of dancing. By the mid 1930s a newly reconstructed form of the dance was given the name "bharata natyam"; there was now a need for a term that distinguished the reconstructed form from the hereditary practice. That term was *sadir*.

Differentiations between the hereditary practice and the "revived" bharata natyam were initially deliberate, reflecting a new perception both of who artists were and of where art fit in the community. An issue fundamental to the reconstruction was whether a person could absorb the traditional practice of an art form simply by learning from a traditional practitioner. In the case of the twentieth-century transition to a modernized practice of bharata natyam, hereditary artists became the sources for reconstructed forms of music and dance. But in fact, an artist could acquire the ability to make stylistically appropriate and consistent alterations only after long experience within the context of a particular family style. A master teacher would adjust both the narrative aspects of the dance form and the formalized abstract shape of the dance to the stature, physique, shape of hands, and facial characteristics of each student. Knowledge of the details of material alone was not adequate as a source for further development. It is a subtle problem not easily understood through learning in an institutional setting or from a teacher not steeped in traditional practice.

New dance has been created as a modern practice. That new dance and its accompanying music and other elements, including staging and the mixing of regional styles, make contributions to the evolution of contemporary dance in India. But the notion that modernized bharata natyam is "based" on the roots of traditional practice can be misleading, minimizing fundamental distinctions between the two.

DEVADASI

It is not the intention of this book to undertake a critique of the social history of India. But to understand this biography, the reader must understand the facts of certain principles of social and family organization in India (among other parts of the world) that changed during the late nineteenth and early twentieth centuries.

Into the twentieth century, families organized according to principles of plural marriage were commonplace and acceptable. There was nothing exceptional about a man having more than one wife. Less common, but still legally sanctioned and acceptable was the presence of matrilineal families, including the *devadasi* community of Tamil Nadu, in which women were heads of household and did not enter into marriage as it is generally understood in a patrilineal social and legal structure.

During the nineteenth century as colonial systems of education, morality, and social convention were established in India, a rising concern among Indians was that their culture was considered primitive, animistic, and immoral. Reform movements emerged with the goal of bringing the social order, including family structure, into line with Western sensibilities. Among the objects of these efforts at reform was the *devadasi* community. Another was the practice of polygamy. The agitation against this structure was the result of the uncomfortable juxtaposition of an existing order that permeated and had defined Indian social systems since antiquity with a modern revised social organization. This realignment became the basis for a movement against the practice of bharata natyam and its traditional performers.

Women in the matrilineal *devadasi* community took partners with whom they bore children and shared emotional attachments, relationships that were arranged and agreed to by family elders and sanctified according to religious rites. Much more often than not, the partnerships remained intact for the lifetime of the individuals. In the *devadasi* family structure, a woman was responsible for the financial well-being of her family. Her mate might well also be a supporter of her art and her family, but she would continue her responsibility to the hereditary property and birth family. She usually would not establish a new home with her mate; she stayed with extended family members in her original home. This was true of Balasaraswati, whose partnership began in 1938 and lasted until her partner's death in 1953.

Balasaraswati was the last nationally significant performer of bharata natyam who was trained and raised in a manner consistent with her antecedents from the *devadasi* community. The question raised when non-hereditary artists first began to perform bharata natyam in 1935 was whether or not the apparent barriers that limited the practice to one community could be transcended. Bala never argued that the hereditary form could not be learned by anyone; she did not argue it needed to be a matter of blood and upbringing. She did believe, however, that it was a matter of discipline, the acceptance of the guidance of a *guru*, and a readiness to learn something that would always remain greater than the student. And Balasaraswati did argue that the art form was compromised by changes imposed by institutionalization and standardization as dancing became popular in pre- and post-Independence India.

The cultural unification of India across barriers of geography, religion, language, and regional difference had become the objective of a newly organized political and social agenda formed at the end of the nineteenth century that was to challenge the domination of the British Raj. However, an irony is that the unification of India through the creation of revivalist concepts of "national" and "modern" identity meant the discrediting and dismantling of some of India's existing cultural and regional social structures, beliefs, and professional communities—in particular, the Thanjavur courtly dance tradition of southern India.

Out of the early Indian independence movement grew efforts of various sorts to redefine and glorify a national history and culture. The movement was founded in the notion of a classical age that was declared a "national" heritage that transcended the tremendous diversity actually existing in India. Sanskrit, with all the nobility and exclusivity it implied as a language with no spoken vernacular, was named the transcendent language of that classical age. The restructuring of the performing arts according to the idea

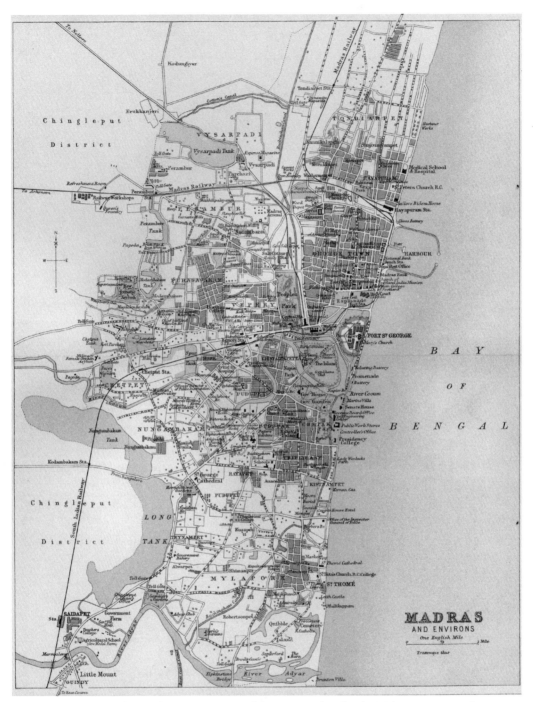

Madras and Environs. *Imperial Gazetteer Atlas of India*, Volume 26, 1909 edition.
Courtesy of the Digital South Asia Library, http://dsal.uchicago.edu/.

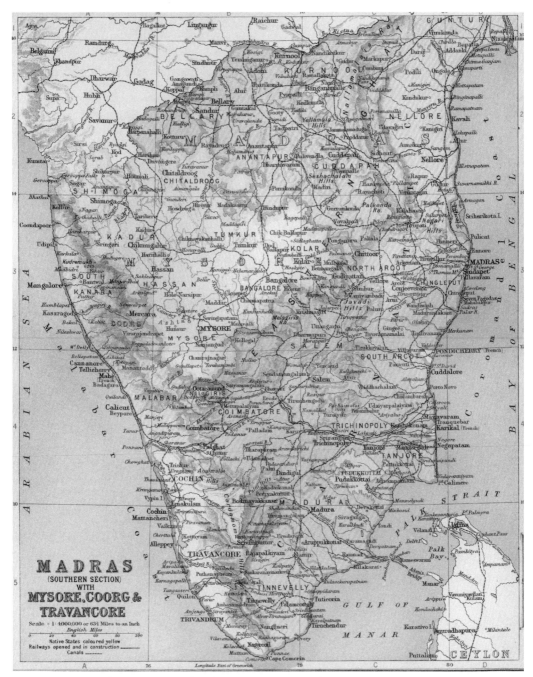

Madras Presidency (southern section) with Mysore, Coorg, and Travancore.
Imperial Gazetteer Atlas of India, Volume 26, 1909 edition. Courtesy of the Digital
South Asia Library, http://dsal.uchicago.edu/.

of a "classical" culture resurrected from obscurity was projected by the body politic as an expression of the renewal of the people and culture of India. There was no argument from Balasaraswati about the importance of raising artistic standards and the significance of participation in the perpetuation and revitalization of India's great heritage.

THANJAVUR

The Kaveri River Delta in the state of Tamil Nadu in southern peninsular India is a level expanse of land with long vistas punctuated by *gopurams*, the towers above temple gateways, and smaller structures that rise above the central shrines of a proliferation of great and small temples. Tributaries of several branches of the river Kaveri lace the landscape, irrigating innumerable squares of paddy of variously intense shades of green, depending on the time of year and the point in the growing cycle. Coconut palms grow in dense groves, as do cashew and numerous varieties of fruit trees. The land is self-sufficient and has been for centuries.

It is in Tamil Nadu, in the late eighteenth-century principality of Raja Tulaja of Thanjavur (1763–1783), that we find mention in court records of Thanjavur Balasaraswati's family for the first time. The rule of Thanjavur principality by a family or its proxy has been recorded since the sixteenth century, when the palace was first constructed as a Nayak citadel. It was expanded during the eighteenth century by Maratha kings. (The huge sprawl is now owned by the Government of India and is leased and occupied, in part, by the Bobbili family, the historical royal Maratha household.) Numerous musicians, dancers, composers, dance teachers, poets, painters, and other artists populated the court, including seventeenth- and early eighteenth-century composers of the song form *padam*. Other compositional forms that were intended to be danced and that became a standard part of the bharata natyam repertoire, such as *swarajati, pada varnam*, and *tillana*, were introduced during the eighteenth and nineteenth centuries.

Traditional performers, poets, and other people of artistic and intellectual distinction entered the various royal courts when the artists' reputation in the general community came to the court's attention, resulting in an invitation. The artists usually did not live in the palace, but in homes they owned as esteemed members of the community. Artists who were patronized by a royal family were expected to bring honor and distinction to the court through the practice of their art. They were sometimes expected to undertake the artistic bidding of the royal family.

Raja Tulaja brought the famous *nattuvanar* (hereditary dance teacher, conductor, and choreographer) Mahadeva Annavi from his village to the Thanjavur court to systematize and teach the practice of dance already performed in the court. Annavi's efforts were a lesser-known precursor to the codification developed by his brother's grandchildren, Chinnayya, Ponniah,

Sivanandam, and Vadivelu, who became known as the Thanjavur Quartet. In the service of the court of Raja Tulaja's successor, Serfoji II, the four brothers organized existing dance practice into a single performance event for a solo dancer. The Quartet's codification is remembered now as the foundation of nineteenth- and twentieth-century bharata natyam.[6]

In bharata natyam, the dancer is accompanied by an ensemble directed by a dance master. The *nattuvanar* sings, reproduces the sounds of the dancer's feet with small cymbals (*talam*), and performs a practice of rhythmic vocalization (*nattuvangam*) that accompanies the movements of abstract dance. The use of cymbals to replicate the patterns of the dancer's feet is said to have been introduced by Sivanandam of the Thanjavur Quartet, but it seems likely that Sivanandam formalized that convention from an existing practice of dance.

Traditional artists performed two related but entirely distinct art forms, known as *periya melam* and *chinna melam. Melam* referred to the ensemble itself (among other meanings), and *periya* and *chinna*, meaning big and small, referred to the principal instrument in the two types of ensemble. The larger of the two instruments was the double-reed *nagaswaram*, which creates a bold sound that is still used in temple and processional music (*periya melam*). A smaller double-reed instrument, the *mukhavina*, was used in *chinna melam*, or bharata natyam, until it was replaced by the clarinet and flute as those instruments found their way to the concert stage in the first half of the twentieth century.

The words *periya* and *chinna* sometimes cause confusion, because "big" and "small" are occasionally understood inaccurately to refer to the sizes of the ensembles. In fact, the *chinna melam* dance ensemble is larger, consisting at a minimum of four members, whereas the *nagaswaram* ensemble consists of at least three members. Hand cymbals are used in both practices. In the *periya melam*, a performer using relatively large cymbals sounds the meter of the music while a deity is carried in procession, within the temple, and at weddings and other events demanding the auspiciousness of the sound and music of the *nagaswaram*.

Estimates of the size of the hereditary professional dance community in South India, the families who persisted in the practice of bharata natyam into the twentieth century, have varied from more than one hundred families to several hundred.[7] Social distinctions between "urban" and "rural" cannot be aptly applied to historical India. India's intellectual and artistic wealth sprang from villages as much as it did from cities, and more often than not was imported from the countryside to cities where palaces and major temples existed. The cultural and intellectual community was dispersed throughout the Thanjavur District and southern India. Some musicians and dancers became wealthy in land and possessions. Some were supported with food. Most families supported themselves as farmers, sometimes on land granted to their family by a temple or king. Arable land and jewelry were the currency of the traditional artist.

The Thanjavur court was a very competitive environment, alive with dance, music, and dance dramas from all over South India. Artists and intellectuals were pitted against one another in demonstrations of prowess designed to bring distinction to themselves and their patrons. But the allegiance of hereditary families was first to the art and their family practice, and second to their royal patron. In the court of Serfoji II, this eclecticism was reflected in other ways that were significant to the tradition of bharata natyam. The style derived from Maharashtran singing called *lavani* became very popular during the Maratha rule and affected styles of music performed in the court.[8] In the court records of around 1820, there is a complaint from a *nattuvanar* that he had prepared his dancers in a "northern" style of dance that had been requested by the king. The complaint stated that the dance teacher had complied with the king's wishes and that his dancers and musical ensemble were prepared but had not yet been called to perform.[9]

"A GARDEN OF GREAT SPLENDOR": THE FAMILY LEGACY
Balasaraswati's great-great-great-great grandmother, Thanjavur Papammal, was born around 1760. Papammal was a dancer and musician in the court in Thanjavur. She would have performed a form of dance that preceded and informed the work of the Thanjavur Quartet. Whether Papammal was the first generation in the family employed in the court is unknown. In any case, Papammal's daughter, Rupavati, also was recognized as both a musician and dancer in the Thanjavur court, and descendants of Papammal remained in the service of the court until the collapse of royal patronage almost a century later. They were professional artists, performing a repertoire that was intended for a secular audience, and which was not performed as ritual in the temple or during processionals.

Rupavati Ammal's daughter, Thanjavur Kamakshi Ammal, was born in 1810. Kamakshi Ammal's home was in a small lane off Elliamman Koil Street on the north side of the Great Temple dedicated to Brihadiswara. Perhaps this was also where Papammal lived with her family. Kamakshi Ammal was a musician and dancer in the court of Raja Serfoji II and is known to have taught the princesses of the court. She learned dance from a teacher named Bharatam Ganapati Sastri. She would have represented a family style of music handed down from her mother and grandmother and their antecedents. As a dancer she would have learned the musical repertoire of the then newly codified style of bharata natyam. She was sent outside of the family for training in music, something that has always been done within the family. She was later a music disciple of Subbaraya Sastri, son of composer Syama Sastri, and then of Subbaraya's son Annaswami Sastri. Subbaraya Sastri learned the musical style of his father, and also had the opportunity to learn under the saint-composer Tyagaraja, therefore representing a direct knowledge of both styles, as well as the influence of Maratha music popular in the Thanjavur court during the eighteenth and early nineteenth centuries. The Thanjavur Quartet and their family had learned the tradition of Mutthuswami Diksitar in the Thanjavur court, which they in turn taught to Kamakshi Ammal. Through these connections Balasaraswati's family came to represent direct links to the three most significant composers in the region in the late eighteenth and early nineteenth centuries.

For a period of about ten years, Kamakshi Ammal appears to have left the patronage of the Thanjavur court and moved to the court of Thiruvananta-puram (Trivandrum) in Kerala. The youngest of the Thanjavur Quartet, Va-divelu, left the Thanjavur court for Thiruvananthapuram in 1830. Balasaras-wati claimed—and there is evidence to confirm—that over the next several years Kamakshi Ammal became part of the musical entourage who accompanied Vadivelu. There is mention of a woman named Thanjavur Kamakshi Ammal in the court records of Thiruvananthapuram during the 1840s, and among other music teachers of Vadivelu we find that he learned from a court musician named Thanjavur Kamakshi.[10] The families later were known during Bala's lifetime to reinforce and contribute to each other's repertoire and musical concepts, as Balasaraswati's family did with several other sources. Balasaraswati's *guru*, K. Kandappa Pillai, was a great-grandson of one of Vadivelu's brothers, and he represented their family style of dance and music as a hereditary practice. The collaboration between these two families re-united an artistic relationship that had thrived for several generations in the Thanjavur and Thiruvananthapuram courts. Kamakshi Ammal moved back to Thanjavur at some point during the late 1840s.

Some ten or fifteen years later, around 1860, Kamakshi Ammal moved her family from Thanjavur to Madras, part of a general exodus of musicians and dancers following the annexation of Thanjavur by the British in 1858. She purchased a house on Nattu Pillayar Koil Street (Pillayar is the elephant-headed son of Siva, and *Koil* means temple) in the northern part of Madras, the busy, prosperous commercial center that was popular with artists who had moved to the city from the cultural centers in the south. After the move to Madras, Kamakshi Ammal supplemented her income as an artist by performing the role of *manikkatthar* (a woman entrusted to perform *pujas*, or prayer rituals, in the private shrines of patrons) in the home of Rangoon Krishnaswamy Mudaliar, a businessman. Tending to his family shrine, Kamakshi Ammal became known for her singing of poetic verses called *tiruppugazh* (medieval devotional verses composed during the sixteenth century and set to music during the nineteenth century). Perhaps unusually, she also had the capacity, flexibility, and willingness to perform *nattuvangam* for other dancers.[11]

A family story tells about a performance by Kamakshi Ammal when she was traveling through the French colonial capital, Pondicherry, in 1885. She was seventy-five years old. Someone who knew her reputation asked her to perform, in spite of her age. She agreed, although it is said that members of her entourage were surprised at her display of apparent audacity, and they tried to discourage her. Bala recalled what she had heard within the family: "She did not care. All she did to prepare herself was to drink a large glass of water and lie face down for a while. Remarkably, she gained a fresh look and dressed herself for the performance, and danced."[12]

Kamakshi Ammal had two surviving children, both born in Thanjavur. Her son, Appakkannu, was a violinist, whose teacher was Muthialpet Ponnuswami. Kamakshi's daughter was Sundarammal, Balasaraswati's great-grandmother.

Born in 1830, Sundarammal learned and taught the musical repertoire of bharata natyam, and was known to have a silvery voice. Unlike her mother, Kamakshi Ammal, and her grandmother and great-grandmother, Sundarammal did not perform dance in public.[13] However, we have reason to believe that Sundarammal did continue to dance within the home; both of her daughters learned dance, and one became recognized as a dancer. Sundarammal's granddaughter Jayammal, Balasaraswati's mother, was a highly accomplished musician who also danced, but only in the house.

Sundarammal, like her mother, performed domestic worship for a patron from the Mudaliar community, earning a salary of seven rupees per month. She gave birth to nine children, of whom three survived. She had a son named Narayanaswami who, like his uncle Appakkannu, was a violinist. He died, it is said, by drowning, sometime in the 1870s. She had two daughters, Rupavati and Dhanam, whom she routinely took with her to the Mudaliar's house as she performed her service, and there the two sisters sang together, as they did in other homes and temples. Both were trained in the family's music; Rupavati was to become a dancer, and Dhanam was to learn the stringed instrument called the *vina*. Sundarammal died in 1880, ten years before her mother's death.

Thanjavur Dhanam, Balasaraswati's grandmother, was born in 1867 in Kamakshi Ammal's house on Nattu Pillayar Koil Street in Madras. Eventually named Vina Dhanammal for the instrument with which she became famously associated, Dhanammal was one of the most revered South Indian musicians of the late nineteenth and early twentieth centuries.

Kamakshi Ammal died in 1890, the same year in which her great-grand-daughter, Balasaraswati's mother, Jayammal, was born. Jayammal was the third of four surviving daughters of Vina Dhanammal: Rajalakshmi, Lakshmiratnam, Jayammal, and Kamakshi. The eldest daughter, Rajalakshmi, raised her three younger siblings. Jayammal performed with her mother and with her sister Lakshmiratnam in both music concerts and concerts of

DESCENDANTS OF VINA DHANAMMAL

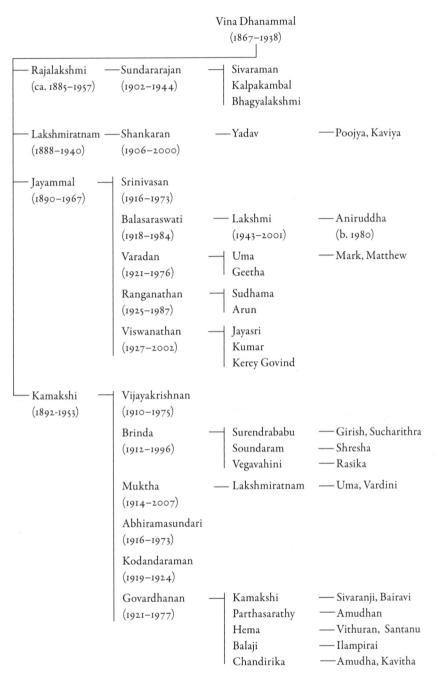

Vina Dhanammal
(1867–1938)

Rajalakshmi — Sundararajan — Sivaraman
(ca. 1885–1957) (1902–1944) Kalpakambal
                              Bhagyalakshmi

Lakshmiratnam — Shankaran — Yadav — Poojya, Kaviya
(1888–1940) (1906–2000)

Jayammal — Srinivasan
(1890–1967) (1916–1973)

Balasaraswati — Lakshmi — Aniruddha
(1918–1984) (1943–2001) (b. 1980)

Varadan — Uma — Mark, Matthew
(1921–1976) Geetha

Ranganathan — Sudhama
(1925–1987) Arun

Viswanathan — Jayasri
(1927–2002) Kumar
             Kerey Govind

Kamakshi — Vijayakrishnan
(1892-1953) (1910–1975)

Brinda — Surendrababu — Girish, Sucharithra
(1912–1996) Soundaram — Shresha
             Vegavahini — Rasika

Muktha — Lakshmiratnam — Uma, Vardini
(1914–2007)

Abhiramasundari
(1916–1973)

Kodandaraman
(1919–1924)

Govardhanan — Kamakshi — Sivaranji, Bairavi
(1921–1977) Parthasarathy — Amudhan
             Hema — Vithuran, Santanu
             Balaji — Ilampirai
             Chandirika — Amudha, Kavitha

dance. In time, Jayammal became the soul of the music of Balasaraswati's concerts.

During the 1870s, when Dhanam was a child, the family was obliged to auction the house on Nattu Pillayar Koil Street to pay creditors. They eventually moved to a rented portion of a house at 27 Ramakrishna Street, several streets away but still in crowded Georgetown, then known as the "Black Town" section of Madras. It is not certain if the family moved to that home before or after Dhanam's mother's death in 1880. The family lived together and in various combinations; they may not always have had a home. Sundarammal is said to have lived for some time, presumably with her daughters Dhanam and Rupavati, on the grounds of the Hindu Theological School on Mint Street in Georgetown.

The house on Ramakrishna Street was the first home that Balasaraswati lived in. According to the current owner the house remains essentially unchanged since the time Bala's family moved there. The family left the home in 1938, but even today the owner's family remembers that their tenant was a famous musician, and that the rent paid was seven rupees.[14] Vina Dhanammal was head of that househld.

Balasaraswati first revealed a passion for dance in what appeared to others in her family to be a child's fantasy. Many years later, in 1982, Bala commented to her daughter, Lakshmi, that those who wanted to understand her as a young child should observe her grandson, Aniruddha. Before he could speak or walk, raising one arm up from his crawling position, Ani would imitate the hands and facial expressions of his grandmother and mother while they sang.

AT THE START

It all began with play. As a child just old enough to walk to the door of Dhanammal's home, Bala was fascinated by a beggar who stopped regularly in front of the house on Ramakrishna Street, dancing wildly, chanting rhythmic syllables like those recited by a *nattuvanar* mirroring a dancer's footwork. T. Shankaran, Balasaraswati's cousin and the only son of Vina Dhanammal's daughter Lakshmiratnammal, recalled: "There used to be a beggar, a sort of maniac, who would jump up and dance like a monkey while singing '*tat tarigappa tei ta, tat tarigappa tei ta*.' Bala would imitate him, both dancing like monkeys. . . . All of us tried to snub him but the beggar could not be turned out. It meant a few coins for him; he made a regular visit to our house and the two used to dance. That was the real starting point for Bala's dancing mania."[1]

Years later Bala wondered, somewhat whimsically, whether the beggar had been an enlightened *yogi* with supernatural powers who could appear in disguises, as did Siva in the form of the mendicant Kankalamurthi. In fact, as the German Sanskrit scholar Max Müller reminds us, a form of madness was one of the possible outcomes of the practices of asceticism.[2] Certainly everyone in Balasaraswati's family recognized the wisdom of the beggar's choice of houses to seek a dance partner. "It may be true that I had dancing in my blood, as they say," Bala recalled. "I was a toddler when I danced deliriously with that street beggar. All called him a madman when he brought the house down with his frenetic dancing. Was he really mad? His unerring *jatis* [danced rhythmic patterns] reverberate in my mind. Who knows which *siddhapurusha* [literally, "a person with all accomplishments"] he was? I can still see the gleam in his eye. If I am dance-mad now, how could it be otherwise? . . . My first *guru* was a madman."[3]

Balasaraswati was born on May 13, 1918, to Vina Dhanammal's third daughter, T. Jayammal, in Christian Rainey Hospital in Madras. When Jayammal arrived with several other family members, the staff at the hospital was prepared. Many women in Jayammal's financial and social circumstances might not have been granted the extra consideration. But Jayammal's family was well known as distinguished artists. When Jayammal went into labor at home, word was sent ahead that she was on her way. The birth was expected to be difficult. Two years before, in 1916, Jayammal had entered the same hospital and spent three days in labor, eventually delivering Balasaraswati's older brother, Srinivasan, with the assistance of forceps, a procedure that threatened both Jayammal and her infant son. This time, shortly after the family's arrival at the hospital, while the staff was still busy preparing to deliver the baby, Jayammal gave birth to a girl.

After Balasaraswati and Srinivasan were born, Jayammal gave birth in turn to Varadan (1921), Ranganathan (1925), and Viswanathan (1927). A son born between Balasaraswati and Varadan died in infancy. At the time that Balasaraswati was born, Jayammal and Srinivasan, as well as Lakshmiratnammal and her son, Shankaran, and Kamakshiammal and her daughters, were living in the house on Ramakrishna Street with Bala's grandmother Dhanammal.

Madras: A Brief History

Dhanammal's home in Madras was in the area north of Fort St. George, the fortified seventeenth- and eighteenth-century bastion of British economic and political domination of southern India. From the mid-nineteenth century, Madras was the capital of the Madras Presidency, one of three administrative districts under the direct control of the British crown from 1858 to 1947. The region has been inhabited for more than two millennia, but the city as it is shaped today was settled, beginning in the sixteenth century, by successive waves of European colonialists who encroached on several adjoining villages and gradually incorporated them into a single municipal unit through a series of acquisitions of land by grant and purchase.

In the fifth century the region had been organized and ruled by the Pallava, a tribal kingdom of seafarers who are said to have traveled and traded as far away as Southeast Asia. They built in India the distinctive style of sculpture and temple construction evident in the town of Mamallapuram, south of Madras, a favorite place of Bala's. One of the oldest villages in the area, Mylapore (now in the heart of Chennai), was a Pallava settlement. During the mid-sixteenth century the first European traders, the Portuguese, built a trading settlement in Mylapore in spite of treacherous surf and the lack of a natural harbor. Their encroachment, an enclosing fortification that reached six hundred meters from north to south along the beach, forced the inhabitants of the ancient town of Mylapore back about four hundred meters from the shore. Portuguese domination of foreign trade with the region collapsed by the early seventeenth century, and the British, French, and Dutch began decades of competition for commercial, and then increasingly political, dominance. The British East India Company started trading in the early seventeenth century. By 1635 the land area occupied by the British settlement, several kilometers north of the Portuguese fortification, had doubled since its establishment five years before and included seven churches. By the middle of that century the British had become the dominant colonial commercial presence in India.

A British expatriate community grew around the fort that was built as a rudimentary bastion in 1640, protected by an outer wall. Beyond this wall was an open area, and beyond that was a section known by the colonists as "Out Town" or "Gentu Town," later called "Black Town." The Tamil name for this part of the city was Chennapatnam. It was first inhabited by weavers, dyers, and various merchants who supplied the English "factory" with goods for export. Eventually the area just north of the wall between the "White Town" and "Black Town" was inhabited by the "respectable" workmen; clerks, porters, peons, interpreters, and translators essential to the growing commercial operation. Other inhabitants were the administrative personnel, including headmen, accountants, watchmen, and merchants.[4] "Out Town" was renamed Georgetown in 1911 at the time of the coronation of King George V and his visit to India.

During the eighteenth century, until the Treaty of Paris in 1763, the British fought globally with the French, including battles for control throughout South India. From then on the only serious threat to British military domination of the region around Madras, including Thanjavur, came from Hyder Ali and his son Tipu Sultan. In 1780 British possessions in the region included the town of Madras and the several villages that surrounded it, as well as land north along the coast and farming land to the southwest. According to the colonial account of the history of Madras, following a defeat of British forces outside Madras in 1780 at the hands of Tipu Sultan, it was reported that "inhabitants of the country and villages fled . . . and out of the vast number who have houses and property in the black town, not above one half of them remained." As the British reassumed control after Tipu Sultan's soldiers left the region in 1782, villagers and the inhabitants of Indian Madras began to return.[5] Madras was the uninterrupted regional military and political center for the British from then on.

From its establishment to the mid-eighteenth century, the East India Company was dependent on the traditional merchant community, the Chettiars, to obtain goods for purchase. However, as the objective of the colonial presence in South India evolved from trade to political dominance and the

importance of Madras as a center of both commerce and colonial administration grew, the towns and cities that had been the homes and centers of
variously sized princely states, among them Thanjavur, diminished in importance. By the end of the eighteenth century, the princely states had lost any
vestige of authority. As far as the British were concerned, the royal family of
the Thanjavur court relinquished their right to rule in 1798, and the direct
patronage of artists by the court began to diminish, ending in 1858.

After the mid-eighteenth century, the prestige and influence derived from
a relationship to the colonial administrators moved from the Chettiar community to a group colloquially referred to by the newly-coined term *dubash*,
derived from a Sanskrit word meaning "two languages." Most *dubash* came
from the landholding farming community (*velalar*) who, after the dissolu-
tion of the royal courts, functioned as minor princes, *zamindars*. In this
capacity they owned and managed land cultivated by laborers from whom
taxes were collected on behalf of the colonial administrators — revenues
previously owed to the king. The *dubash* had learned to speak English and
to emulate to some degree the manners of the British, and they had moved
to Madras seeking employment with the colonial administration as mediators with the Indian community — as brokers, negotiators, translators, and
personal servants and assistants. Some of them amassed considerable wealth
and political influence and built what became known as "garden houses,"
which powered the expansion of Madras into its western suburbs. Many
dubash persisted in a role they, like the Chettiars, had filled in their villages
of origin: they patronized Madras's temples and the growing community of
transplanted musicians and dancers.

By the early nineteenth century, however, the British were beginning to
replace the *dubash* with civil servants recruited from the Brahmin community, many of whom settled in the ancient neighborhood of Mylapore.
The British established Madras High School in 1841 to train "a native elite,
mostly Brahmins, in the skills needed for filling civil service posts." The
Brahmin community, lacking the financial resources of merchants and land-
holders to fill the role of traditional patrons of the arts, developed a system
of private organizations, *sabhas*, which sponsored performances. Along with
the *sabha* came a new political body and sensibility that began to contest the
control of the performing arts and artist within the community.[6]

The professional artistic community moved from the cultural centers of
the south during the second half of the nineteenth century and resettled in
Madras. There was an established courtly tradition in the city, and patronage of the arts by the city's well-to-do, encouraging a highly technical and intellectually competitive practice of music performance called *pallavi*. There
also were numerous temples, some large, some very small, as there had been
for centuries. Patrons from the *dubash* and Chettiar communities provided

Mowbray's Road, Madras, ca. 1895. Courtesy of Vintage Vignettes, Chennai.

income and audience. There were temple musicians and dancers who were processional and ritual attendants, some of whom were connected by dedication to temples in the city, but who were famed as performing artists. The migration of musicians and dancers to Madras from temple centers in the south that included Thanjavur, Madurai, and Ramnad, and later Mysore, continued throughout the 1800s.[7]

Although the knowledgeable audience was small, during the last quarter of the nineteenth century it was fashionable for the privileged to present performances of music and dance not only at important family functions such as weddings and naming ceremonies, but also for evenings of performance in a salon environment. So for some musicians and dancers, a living was to be had in Madras. But for musicians who had the rigidity of standard and the devotional quality of the learning and practice of the arts found in Dhanammal's family, whatever fame might be found, the remuneration was modest. Having sold her home in Thanjavur when she left, Kamakshi Ammal appears to have arrived in Madras with some means; within a decade or two of moving to Madras, however, the family was impoverished.

In 1918, the year Balasaraswati was born, Madras was for some a city of opportunity and excitement. The British had built a capital to their liking. They had opened the first railway connection to the city in 1856 and had improved the Madras harbor several times, starting in 1861. They had developed a drainage system for the city and in 1872 had built a protected water supply. Tramway service began in 1895. The Madras Electric Supply Corporation began providing electricity in 1907. Two Indian newspapers, several colleges and high schools, museums, and libraries had been founded, as well as several large mills.[8] The city was beautiful as a colonial capital, with an abundance of stately buildings. A canal, built during the nineteenth century, traversed the city, and two rivers flowed from the west to the sea on the eastern side of the city. Madras was home to the nationalist movement and the Tamil intellectual movement, as well as to a dynamic press that exercised at every opportunity the freedoms allowed by the colonial authority. The adopted home of the Theosophists and eventually the philosopher Jiddu Krishnamurti, Madras also was at the center of international focus on India.

The city boasted numerous palaces. The royal family of Arcot alone built seventeen palaces of various sizes and descriptions within the city. Some inhabitants, including the merchants and *dubash*, built grand homes with pillars of rosewood, verandas, and parlor rooms with swings. Other citizens lived in more modest homes. Many from the community of hereditary professional musicians and dancers lived in the thriving community in north Madras, near the beach and its cooling breezes. A typical house was built around a central courtyard and had a door that opened directly onto the street that passed in front of it.

Vina Dhanammal's house was in a narrow lane two blocks long, wide enough for two carts to pass each other and for children to play in the street. The small home had two stories. The ground floor had a shallow enclosed porch, through which one entered a central room that was partially open to the sky; behind the central space were two rooms, one of which was the kitchen and the other used for storage. A very narrow staircase led to a room upstairs that was Dhanammal's alone. A shallow veranda overlooked the street below.

The menial tasks in the home were performed by a woman who worked in the house for many years, and who became Bala's first link to the place of veneration to which she eventually became deeply devoted. Vendors of everything, from vegetables and fruits to services like knife sharpening and rag collecting, would push their carts up and down the small lane, announcing their services and products in distinctive songlike calls. Laundering was done by a woman who would come to the house and take clothing for washing and ironing.

Georgetown, Madras, from the flag mast at Fort St. George, ca. 1900.
Courtesy of Vintage Vignettes, Chennai.

A Threatened Tradition

When Bala began dancing at her doorstep as a toddler, bharata natyam remained the purview of the traditional community; there were no performers who were *not* from the traditional artistic community. Some musicians who had known the repertoire for dance had shifted, when they could, to solo music concert practice, which was experiencing a parallel transformation of concert format, repertoire, and audience, but with less of the burden of the social stigma that had been attached to dance. Performances of bharata natyam still were held in private homes, although a movement to force performance out of homes that had begun three decades earlier had driven most opportunity away. Pressure to present popular entertainment sometimes meant resorting to dance pieces intended to please an unrefined audience. In one such performance, vegetables were tied to the dancer's dress and, as the dancer turned, were sliced with knives placed strategically on the periphery of the dance platform, and then cooked and served to the audience.

At the turn of the twentieth century, the variety of styles and types of performance included interpretations as diverse as those of the dance form as it is presented today. Some dancers were athletic and acrobatic. Some dancers relied heavily on reputations as beauties, and some had the celebrity of film stars. Some dancers developed a literal, artless approach to the interpretation of the love poetry of the tradition — it was what the audience had come to expect. There were dancers who maintained a standard of excellence that reflected the greatness the performance tradition had achieved. But lack of exposure to this level of artistry had eroded the critical edge from the audience, and many dancers were forced to compete by virtue of the speed of their feet, or the open coquetry of their *abhinaya* (expressive dance), or with their beguiling beauty.

By the early twentieth century, the performance of bharata natyam was increasingly at the heart of a public debate, positioned between reformers and abolitionists. As the critic and journalist R. Krishnamurthy recounted in 1933: "Twenty years ago [in 1913] dance concerts were very common in Tamil Nadu. No 'high society' wedding took place without a dance concert. As a young boy I once walked to the next village to attend such a wedding. During the dance program I saw two things that made a deep impression on me. The first was the heckling by toothless old men in the front row. The other was the gossip of youngsters assembled around the hall. They discussed the dandies who had at various times 'loved the broad' who was dancing and such similar juicy matters. The revulsion towards dance which I felt as a result stayed with me until just recently."[9] Krishnamurthy made that comment after seeing Balasaraswati for the first time. His earlier impression was not of the dancer or of the dance, but rather of the audience.

In 1918 scholar Ananda K. Coomaraswamy commented on the intellectual and artistic dilemma threatening the aesthetic and cultural traditions of India in the early twentieth century: "Pretty art which emphasizes passing feelings and personal emotion is neither beautiful nor true; it tells us of meeting again in heaven, it confuses time and eternity, loveliness and beauty, partiality and love."[10] And later: "Uncritical tolerance is content with prettiness or edification, and recoils from beauty that is 'difficult.'"[11] Coomaraswamy's words were prophetic of what happened to the performer of the traditional and esoteric arts of India. "The best," wrote Coomaraswamy as he discussed poetry from the perspective of Sanskrit treatises, "is where there is a deeper significance than that of the literal sense. . . . In inferior poetry, significantly described as 'variegated' or 'romantic,' the only artistic quality consists in the ornamentation of the literal sense, which conveys no suggestion beyond its face meaning."[12]

Balasaraswati came from a tradition in which the intent of the dance was the feeling it engendered in the observer. Traditional bharata natyam was not expressive dance in the manner it came to be reinterpreted. For the traditional artist, "technique is a garment which both disguises and reveals; disguises the person but reveals his art or, rather, his part . . . in his full panoply of technique and costume."[13]

Mylapore
Gauri Ammal,
1940s.

Balasaraswati, growing up in the midst of social controversy focused on dance, was drawn to the twin passions of dancing and devotion to God. When she was three, she lived for some time in a rented flat near Elephant Gate in Georgetown with her mother, Jayammal, and brother Srinivasan. The landlord, who lived below Jayammal's flat, had an image of Krishna painted on glass, a traditional style of painting from Thanjavur. Bala would dress and go downstairs each morning to sing and dance before the painting of Krishna, believing, as she said then, that she was awakening him. Making music and dance as acts of devotion were what the family did, and Bala was just doing what everyone else was doing.

Mylapore Gauri Ammal

Jayammal and her sister Lakshmiratnammal sang for a dancer from the traditional professional community, Mylapore Gauri Ammal, who influenced and inspired two generations of bharata natyam dancers, first teaching artists from the professional community and later mentoring many practitioners of various versions of the reconstructed style. Gauri Ammal was one of at least a dozen dancers who were well known when Bala was born. She represented a bridge between the practice of the early twentieth-century dancers and bharata natyam as Balasaraswati conceived and developed it throughout her career.

"The initial inspiration for me to take up dancing came from seeing performances of Gauri Ammal when I was very young. If this lady had not brought the dance to such a stage of development, the combination of music and dance that I have attempted to realize would not have been possible," Bala remembered. If anyone should be credited with the survival, rather than revival, of bharata natyam, it is Mylapore Gauri Ammal. "I had seen Gauri Ammal becoming the teacher of almost every budding dancer in Madras," claimed T. Shankaran, Bala's cousin and well-known music historian, referring to dancers of the late 1930s and 1940s.[14]

Mylapore Gauri Ammal and Jayammal, born in the same year, were close friends. When Balasaraswati was a small child, both Gauri Ammal and Kandappa Pillai, the dance teacher who became Balasaraswati's *guru*, were frequent visitors in Vina Dhanammal's home. Kandappa Pillai often attended Friday evening concerts at Dhanammal's house as well as the social gatherings that happened regularly on Sundays. Other times, when Gauri Ammal visited Dhanammal's home, she would sing *padams* (lyrical songs from the bharata natyam repertoire) with Jayammal and Jayammal's sister Lakshmiratnammal. Sometimes Bala would imitate Gauri Ammal's dancing, Shankaran recalled. "We tried to snub Bala to get her to not imitate Gauri *Totha* ['mother's sister'], but to no avail. The more we attempted to stop her, the more persistent and dogged she became. She used to sing the *padams* and followed the footsteps of Mylapore Gauri Ammal."[15] After concerts, Bala would help Gauri Ammal remove her bells, then would slip them on over her small ankles and begin to dance herself. Bala recalled: "I would dress up like Gauri Ammal . . . wear her jewelry and try to dance like her. There would be scolding by the family and some raps on the knuckles, but I couldn't be bothered by them."

T. Shankaran was in his teens during this time. "Yes, I have seen Mylapore Gauri Ammal perform. Those were days when bharata natyam was at a discount. I belonged to a bharata natyam family myself, and we were not encouraged to see bharata natyam or even attend music concerts. But in spite of it, it is in my blood and I can't escape it. I have seen any number of concerts by Mylapore Gauri Ammal because Jayammal and my mother, Lakshmiratnam, encouraged Mylapore Gauri Ammal by becoming her choristers. They used to sing *padams* for her and many of her contemporaries were jealous of this. They used to say, 'Should Dhanam's daughters stoop to this level to sing for bharata natyam?'"

It is startling how quickly the association between the family and dance was forgotten. This was only the first occasion that there was a public outcry in reaction to family members performing music for dance. Every generation did it, not just Dhanammal's daughters. A generation earlier Dhanammal herself was performing music for dance. A generation later Bala would be criticized for performing music for a dancer from the North, even though her own reputation for greatness stemmed in part from the fact that she sang as she danced.

During the eighteenth century the British had chosen to embrace, and in some cases emulate, the social customs and belief systems of the population of India on which their fortune rested. This approach included the encouragement and protection of the matrilineal family structure of the *devadasi* community and of their practices and service in the temple.

It was during the 1830s that the colonial missionary community first cast judgment on temple women. By the time of the British annexation of southern India in 1858, the worldview and social values and structures that supported the traditional professional community and their artistic practice had begun to collapse. As these changes occurred, temples were still permitted to provide support for women from the hereditary community; this did not ensure opportunities for performing artists, however, but merely allowed nominal payment of temple staff. Among women who had relied on a stipend in return for devotional service in temples, many fell into increasingly dire financial circumstances.

Families had historical roots to specific temples that were reaffirmed in a dedication ceremony; the dancer's ritual duty to the temple was inherited, as were other functions performed within the temple. In the traditional world, work was a fulfillment of one's duty. Girls who were born into the matrilineal hereditary community were usually dedicated to a family temple before their learning of an art or craft began. There was no single, defined universal method of dedicating a young girl from the dance community or from any other hereditary community; dedication varied from temple to temple, serving as the initiation of service to art or artisanship. Balasaraswati's dedication in 1922 or 1923 represented her initiation into the art of bharata natyam.

By 1922, however, dedication had become the focus of detractors of the hereditary community, and a small but highly vocal group was advocating against the dedication of girls to temple service, arguing that girls were being forced into sexual service. The concerns raised by antidedication advocates presumably were based on some actual occurrence, but I have found no reliable evidence of anything resembling a socially defined sexual role of the *devadasi*.

Nonetheless, it is now widely believed that in dedication a girl was ritually married to a deity and that in one way or another the implications of this ritual were sinister, even immoral. It is sometimes suggested that this "marriage" also made the young dedicated artist available sexually to patrons of the temple and that the temple artist somehow functioned as an enticement to increase temple patronage. The prejudice that threatened hereditary artistic practice was a result of the relentless critique by non-Indians — including the missionaries, administrators, and traders who peopled British

India—and by Indians who identified with the colonists' power and with social changes taking place within the British community in India and in the West. India was being reinvented.

For Balasaraswati a state of devotion and the practice of the arts were based in the same experience: *bhakti*. *Bhakti* refers to spiritual experience rooted in a personal relationship with the divine. And *bhakti* is at the heart of the intent of dedication. Late in her life, Bala commented publicly on the role of dance as it had been in her lifetime: "Bharata natyam is grounded in *bhakti*. In fact *bhakti* is at the center of all the arts of India. Our music and dance are two important offerings to God. There are many routes for experiencing the one great power. In India, for ages, we have realized that music and dance are the easiest and most dependable of all these paths. Music is worship through sound. A dancer, proficient in music, is able completely to melt and mould her body in submission to God. Dance has [always] been an important part of ritual. Like other modes of ritual, such as incense, flowers, camphor, and sweetmeats, the offering of music and dance has to be made in a spirit of worship, devotion, and surrender. There can be no room for error in this, or in other orthodox modes of ritual. Yoga, it has been said, is not easy to achieve for it is a state in which individual unites with universal. Yet, even for an ordinary being like myself, on some occasions and in some measure, dance and music have enabled a deep experience of the presence of God.[16] This experience may only occur once in a while but when it does, for that little duration, its grandeur enters the soul not transiently but with a sense of eternity. As one gets involved in the art, with greater and greater dedication, one can continuously experience throughout the few hours of the dance, the unending joy, this complete well-being, especially when music and dance mingle indistinguishably."[17]

For Jayammal, Balasaraswati's mother, the family's duty was to God and art. Other issues were not important. Jayammal was ambitious for the art. It was not the service to a particular temple that was important, but rather the dedication to a life of art. Jayammal and her sisters had been dedicated. Not to have dedicated Balasaraswati would have been exceptional, a change in a deeply embedded social and cultural convention. The family has an ancestral temple in Thanjavur, and Jayammal sought the sense of balance and purpose that would result from having Bala dedicated there. (Balasaraswati's cousins T. Muktha and T. Brinda were also dedicated, but to a temple in Georgetown in Madras.[18]) Although dedication was not illegal in the early 1920s, it is clear from the following account by Shankaran that there was a perceived need for secrecy.

Balasaraswati's family temple in Thanjavur is on Manuji Appa Street and is dedicated to Kamakshi, a form of the Goddess, Devi. Devi, or Shakti, is "Power" or "Energy," which is imaged in a female form. Devi is female because her power represents the creative principle. She embodies both Siva

The first known photo of Balasaraswati, taken when she was about four years old.

and Vishnu, and is the enablement of action — of destruction, creation, and protection — and of the power of Illusion, Maya. Out of the nothing that Shakti is emerges all creation. She is both existing and not-existing, beyond birth and death. Devi is the force, the power that emerges from opposites, the truth that exists between all paradoxes.[19] Understood in an infinite variety of ways, Shakti is the action of making dance. Existence itself implies action. It is the beauty of the universe that causes attachment of the individual soul to individual perception, or illusion. That illusion is Shakti. The basic action of music and dance is illusion. Balasaraswati came to understand herself as a vehicle through which Shakti acted, something she publicly referred to as "benediction." Many said that Balasaraswati created illusion through music and dance, but it may also be said that Illusion was using her.

Shankaran was with the group that traveled to Thanjavur in 1922 or 1923 for the dedication. "Though I was with the party in the temple I was neither interested nor mature enough to comprehend the implications of the dedication. . . . Jayammal's fortunes were at very low ebb. . . . My mother [Lakshmiratnammal] took Jayammal's family to Mannargudi . . . from there we proceeded to Thanjavur for Bala's dedication with help of a bold *devadasi* named Rajayee Ammal. It was all hush-hush because dedication of a minor, Bala, was in contravention of law. Luckily, the dedication was an informal *puja* [an act showing reverence to the divine] necessitated by the death of a priest and Jayammal's depleted purse."[20]

Shankaran's reference to "the death of a priest" places the event into a pattern of thinly veiled deceptions of temple authorities that were widespread during the 1920s and 1930s as the antidedication reformers' agitation increased in intensity. Dedications were performed under the guise of other ceremonies within a temple; items used in a dedication ceremony were hidden, for example in garlands of flowers or *tulasi* leaves (a basil-like plant associated with the Goddess, used in temple worship and for medicinal purposes), before they were placed at the feet of an image of God.

Another description of the ceremony sheds light on the nature of dedication, as it was understood from within the families involved. When Mylapore Gauri Ammal was asked about it, she said,[21] "Before the dancer is dedicated the priests will recite.... The coconut is given to the dancer. The five *pushpanjalis* [ritual offerings][22] will be recited and she gives the coconut to the dance-master and some money. The *pushpanjalis* are recited with the dance-master's cymbals, drummer and *mukhavina*."[23] Gauri Ammal finds meaning in the actual event, not its symbolism.

Balasaraswati was remarkable for having bridged a cultural gap emerging in India just before and during her lifespan. By the time of her dedication, more and more of the traditional community was being absorbed into a new social order that excluded and marginalized matrilineal families to such extremes that the families and their way of life became invisible and seemed to have disappeared. Balasaraswati's choice to live in a manner consistent with the family culture and social order that preceded her, and to remain in the public view, and the global public view at that, was an act of extraordinary courage. She was exemplary of the code of ethics that had for centuries given strength to the *devadasi* community.

The traditional dancer was a musician, and music was the medium through which the dance was learned and performed. Balasaraswati would explode into singing and expression of music through dance during her concerts, playing a role equal to the musicians who performed with her. It was customary for the traditional dancer to indicate when she was ready to move from one line of music to the next by standing in place and singing the line of song she was about to interpret in narrative dance.[24] (In modern practice this transition is rehearsed.) Traditional dancers would sometimes assume control of the music by singing themselves.

What was the traditional audience seeing when looking at dance? It was an old and canonized belief that the making of images, the practice of visualization, was the same in worship and in art. An image of the divine was not a static icon but rather a notation, a mnemonic aid for recalling a dynamic process, the releasing of the imagination as it focused on the attributes, the symbols of the process of imaging, the bringing to life of the divine. When a Hindu observes a form of the divine, the attributes that are represented create an associative process in the observer. A similar process is triggered by the associations with fable, the telling of events that characterize the divine in the same manner as physical attributes. When Balasaraswati performed, both she and some of her audience were able to see the associations in their

dynamic form. The image and revelations of God as the subject of dance
must be viewed with an understanding of the continuous state of query that
is the center of a Hindu's life. "It is important to enter this spirit of devotion,
almost of ecstasy, if one is to really understand what dancing and music still
mean to the people of India," Beryl de Zoete wrote in the late 1940s.[25]

The professional community was profoundly discouraged by the tide of
public misunderstanding rising against them. Some women from hereditary families turned to the performance of music for their profession; later
others would turn to film. As an indication of the level of discouragement
and outrage felt within the community, Govindaswamy Pillai, an esteemed
scholar and musician, did not want to see Balasaraswati trained as a dancer.
Shankaran reported that Govindaswamy Pillai "discouraged her from being
taught. The art was in the doldrums. 'I don't want to have this child exposed
to that kind of dislike by the people,'" he was reported to have said.[26]

In 1922, however, Mylapore Gauri Ammal and Jayammal shared the enthusiasm for having Bala trained; they settled on a young *nattuvanar* named
K. Kandappa Pillai to become her teacher. The opportunity to revitalize
the dance in the public view was before them. Bala's family knew the repertoire for dance, including the *padams* and *javalis* that Vina Dhanammal had
learned, supplemented by the *padams* and *javalis* her daughters had added to
the family repertoire. Jayammal had been learning dance from Kandappa's
father and surprised some family members by standing up to her mother,
Vina Dhanammal. Jayammal's sister Kamakshiammal also had rebelled by
asserting her own evolving musical sensibilities, and that process was to repeat itself in some form, one generation after another. Other family members, friends, and fellow musicians joined the debate about training young
Bala. Among the most influential voices was that of a musician from outside
the family, Ariyakkudi Ramanuja Iyengar, who firmly supported Jayammal
in her decision.

Balasaraswati acknowledged her mother as the one who made the greatest difference: "It was my mother, Jayammal, who had me trained as a dancer
despite strong family opposition. Not only were those days of the Devadasi
Bill but there was also strong family stress on the importance of music. . . .
It was Jayammal who selected Kandappa Pillai as *guru*, and after severe and
rigorous training in the morning, she would make me sit next to her in the
evening and train me in music. . . . But for Jayammal, I would never have
become a dancer. It was due to her untiring efforts and push that I learned
this art."[27]

Before there could be discussion of Bala being taught bharata natyam,
Vina Dhanammal would have to give her blessing. As members of the
younger generation exerted their influence over formidable elders, they each
discovered their own incentive for success. Jayammal became at first discon-
certed as she observed Bala's fascination with Mylapore Gauri Ammal, rec-

ognizing the implications; but she finally raised the question with Dhanam-mal. Bala recalled Vina Dhanammal's flat-footed resistance: "Grandmother, whose eyesight had weakened already, peered into space just for a moment and said 'No!' She didn't even budge when Gauri Ammal and Kandappa Pillai directly pressed the suggestion on her. But then she asked my mother one day [unexpectedly] whether her daughter (that's me) was squint-eyed. My mother answered in the negative. Next she asked if I had good, orderly rows of teeth. 'Yes,' said my mother. Next question: is she good looking? My mother said I was not a beauty but good-looking all right. Finally she asked if I sang well. I had to sing to prove it. The test was over. Grandmother finally gave permission for me to study dancing. Kandappa Pillai was then living just next door, and I started learning properly. I was about four then."[28]

So, at the age of four, Balasaraswati was placed by her mother and grand-mother under the tutelage of Kandappa Pillai, a strict perfectionist who became intent on Bala's becoming the greatest dancer of her day. Bala herself was unaware of the prejudices that gave rise to resistance to her training: "I was just a child. I could not begin to understand there was an issue. . . . Could I have understood the storm raging under me at that age?"[29] This marked the end of her childhood.

IN VINA DHANAMMAL'S HOME

The environment and home in which Balasaraswati grew up, in the constant presence of music and dance and the excitement that surrounded the rise of new art out of generations of artistic practice, left little room for anything else in Bala's life. She was eventually to be isolated from school and from any activity that might seem a frivolous use of her time. Her mother was an incessant driver behind the sixteen-hour days she endured for years. Her teacher, for whom Bala always maintained reverence, was also an increasing source of physical and emotional pain for the little girl.

The hereditary artist had a sense of purpose and cross-generational objec-tive, and implicitly accepted and trusted the forms of art that were learned. Although hereditary bharata natyam was not declared to be the exclusive domain of the traditional community, it was the domain of the traditional value system, from which the relationship of the artist to learning and per-forming the art emerged. The hereditary artist understood intuitively why what was done was done, how the traditional organization and structure led the artist toward a path of freedom and realization of the art; practice and discipline empowered the artist to invest each gesture with new life and fresh insight. Balasaraswati did not insist on performing the traditional concert format for its own sake but because the traditional format, just as with every other aspect of dance and music that constituted the traditional form, had an artistic intent and function. It was not because it had existed in antiquity. It was because it enabled the imagination.

Bala described her recollection of Vina Dhanammal: "She was the foundation of all the art in our family. I remember her only as a *guru* and an artist so perfect and complete. I still hear her music; it was so soft and mellow." Bala went on to describe Dhanammal's Friday night concerts in her home on Ramakrishna Street. "There would be *vidwans* [experts in musical performance], people who did not understand music, others who just stopped by. For two hours she would play to an absolutely still, rapt audience.... At those evenings, *ragas* with variations unheard of before would spill out. There was never a showy display of her virtuosity. No, no," noted Bala, "she played for herself with absolute involvement." With her unusually small *vina*, Dhanam created very soft tones of intense beauty. She sang as she played, and her voice, thin and clear, would merge into the delicacy of her *vina*'s sound.

"Every week, the fare was different. To her daughters, who occasionally sang with her, the suspense was great. Dhanam would spring surprises and render rare compositions not taught to them." About her *sangathis* (extemporaneously performed variations of a composed melody) Balasaraswati hastened to add: "They sounded so subtle and deft. But I have heard musicians mention that when they tried to incorporate some of her variations it was impossible. It just would not fit into their approach." It was sometimes said that Vina Dhanammal never improvised, but in fact she performed in a constant state of creation, never rendition.

Vina Dhanammal presented her Friday evening performances in her small room upstairs in the house on Ramakrishna Street. These performances have become legendary, and have in retrospect grown so in glory that they seem to have been attended by audiences of considerable size. In fact, only fifteen or twenty people could sit in the small room, jammed knee to back, and most of them were regular attendees. Bala recalled the events she attended as a small girl. "All that she created was on that *vina*. Not everybody could touch it. She handled it as if it were a child.... She would wear a striking *Kornad sari*, usually red or mustard.[30] Of course, jasmines were a must to be wound around her *vina*. Beginning at five in the evening, even fruit sellers would keep off our street on Fridays." The bustle of preparation would quiet down before five, and incense would be lit for that "just right" fragrance. Dhanammal would begin with fervid seriousness. The slightest noise or disturbance would dislodge her mood. In an interview with journalist Radha Sarma, Bala recalled a memory of an old beggar who would chant "*Om Hara Hara Sambasiva*" in Ramakrishna Street. "That man's singing was so loud that come Friday we would see that he [was] sent packing right past the street. We were nervous about that Sambasiva fellow."[31]

Vina Dhanammal

Dhanammal devoted all her attention to her music. Her home was an austere environment centered on discipline and the profession of the arts, populated by the great performers of the art. Early in her life Dhanammal had "her man," named Thirumalacharaya, who was well and reliably employed in the postal department. The best jobs were with the British administration. Lakshmi reported that it was said within the family that Vina Dhanammal and Thirumalacharaya (who had been one of Dhanammal's *vina* tutors) were very much in love, but that he had died at a young age, probably during the 1890s.[32]

Vina Dhanammal was one of the most influential musicians of her generation. She was fluent and capable of understanding the nuances of poetry in six languages: Tamil, Telugu, Sanskrit, Kannada, Marathi, and Hindi. She had a repertoire of well over one thousand compositions, mastered and unerringly and irrevocably committed to memory. She is today viewed by many as the bridge between twentieth-century *karnatic* music practice and the tradition of *karnatic* music as it emerged onto the concert stage at the end of the nineteenth century. She was a proud professional, an intuitive innovator with a repertoire extraordinary in character, volume, and majesty — pieces that were either handed down by the family, or entrusted to her by the composers and their disciples who sought her out to perpetuate their own compositions or individual interpretations of traditional works. It seems ironic, but in fact it was a measure of her reverence for making music that she preferred silence to music. It is said that in 1895 Vina Dhanammal was the first female musician to perform in a public concert hall in Madras.

Dhanammal taught all four of her daughters. As a mark of the detachment of the relationships between teacher and student, despite — or perhaps because of — being directly related, as soon as they themselves were earning as professional artists and teachers, Dhanammal's daughters were expected to pay their mother for each class. Insistence on the payment had several effects. One was that the student, in spite of the family relationship, never entered into a class unprepared. To do so would have been a waste of resources of several sorts, and certainly disrespectful. The payment also encouraged a completely unsentimental relationship to learning and the art, and this was essential to maintenance of the standard practiced within the family. It was a model of professionalism; teaching was a mainstay of reliable income.

Otherwise Dhanammal was uninterested in her children and, in fact, disconnected from any concerns that were not related to her art. Balasaraswati recalled this without sentimentality. "She was a great artist so naturally you would have to approach her with that attitude. Some people were in mortal fear of her because her criticism could be biting. She was a very gentle person, she loved children but no child or baby should cry in her house. Her ears were so sensitive. She said, 'When I am strumming the *vina*, the baby should keep quiet.' . . . An inherent aristocrat, there was a class about every thing that Dhanam did. *Sandal* paste for everyone who came home, offered in the right style [sandalwood paste was customarily offered to honored guests].

Betel nut powdered after a thorough soaking in coconut water. Malgouva mangoes, a special variety of *mittu* [*pan* leaf]; there was no compromise on quality for Dhanam the gourmet. Her perfumes [applied to her fingertips] were Tipu Swaga and a particular brand of *attar* [scented oil]. I don't think those *attar* shops even exist in Mysore these days."[33]

In the early 1920s Vina Dhanammal performed for the raja at the Vizianagaram Palace. While several *vina* maestros entertained the raja with their music during the day, Dhanammal was asked to lull the raja to sleep every night with her *Bhairavi raga*.[34] In return for her artistry, the raja offered to give Dhanammal anything she requested. She asked for a crafted shawl and a silver hookah made in the shape of a swan, with wings that would flap when the user drew on the pipe. The raja had the hookah fabricated to her specifications and presented to her.

Other celebrities from royal houses also were dazzled with her music: the Gaikwar of Baroda, the Maharajahs of Travancore and Mysore. Lords Carmichael and Ripon requested private performances. Almost all the musical giants of the early part of the century were completely overpowered by Dhanammal, including Maha Vaidyanatha Iyer, Patnam Subramania Iyer and Govindaswamy Pillai. "I still wonder how she wielded that influence over so many people," Bala once mused.

Vina Dhanammal's Teachers

Vina Dhanammal had first learned vocal music from her grandmother, Kamakshi Ammal, and later from Sathanur Panchananda (Panju) Iyer, from whom Dhanammal learned the compositions of Tyagaraja. Sathanur Panju Iyer was also a disciple of Suddamaddalam Tambiappa Pillai, a direct disciple of Mutthuswami Diksitar,[35] adding to the repertoire, interpretation, and tradition of music absorbed and transmitted by Kamakshi Ammal, her daughter, Sundarammal, and Dhanammal's uncle, Appakkannu.

The significance of who taught and influenced Dhanammal is that her style, the family's style, uniquely represents direct lineages of all three of what is known as the "Musical Trinity" of the *karnatic* tradition: the composers Tyagaraja, Mutthuswami Diksitar, and Syama Sastri. Other composers from the *karnatic* tradition and composers of the repertoire for bharata natyam further enriched the family style. When they were young, Dhanam and her sister, Rupavati, learned *javalis* from the Dharmapuri Subbarayar and *tana varnams* (compositions for music that are considered the models of *ragas*, or musical modes) from Muthialpet Tyaga Iyer. Dhanam and Rupavati sang together in performance until Dhanam began to learn *vina*, at about the age of ten.

The Mudaliar who employed Sundarammal was impressed by Dhanam's voice, and he thought it would blend beautifully with the *vina*. It was at his insistence, and at the suggestion of Sundarammal's brother Appakkannu, that the child who came to be regarded as the quintessence of the twentieth century's *karnatic* music tradition and the practice of *vina* began to learn this ancient instrument, which had not been played in the family previously. Dhanam had a *vina* teacher[36] who was employed as a clerk in the Mercantile Bank of India. She also learned music from Thirupambaram (a village east of Thanjavur) Nataraja Sundaram Pillai and an eminent violinist named Thirukodikaval Krishna Iyer (the maternal uncle of the distinguished musician Semmangudi Srinivasa Iyer). She was inspired by the *vina* technique of Kalyanakrishna Bhagavatar, a musician patronized by the court of Travancore. In these connections we can see the complex cross-generational links that bound the traditional community and its arts. T. N. Sundaram Pillai was the father of T. N. Swaminatha Pillai, who was to become the teacher of Bala's brother T. Viswanathan. Kalyanakrishna Bhagavatar's son taught at Wesleyan University in the 1960s, by which time Ranganathan and Viswanathan were also there.

Vina Dhanammal learned *padams* from a blind bard named Balakrishna Naidu, more popularly known as Padam Baldas. He had been patronized by the family of Dare House, from which Balasaraswati's father came. Baldas would refer to Vina Dhanammal as *Aggipetta*, meaning "Matchbox," because she learned music so quickly and voraciously. Dhanammal would remember Baldas's interpretation of the *Surati raga padam* and weep. She also learned *padams* from Padam Ponnuswami. Through Vina Dhanammal, the great tradition of *padam*, largely unknown to the Madras audience in 1930, would be preserved and transmitted, given further majesty and visibility by Jayammal's singing for Balasaraswati's dancing, and by the stirring performances of T. Brinda, T. Muktha, and T. Viswanathan.

An urgent quest for knowledge drove Dhanammal's art and life. She learned *thevaram* (a hymn form sung in Saivite temples)[37] from the minstrel Brahmanayakam Pillai when she was about sixty years old, and she learned from and taught the great musician Kanchipuram Naina Pillai.[38] Members of her family remembered an event that seems unlikely for Dhanammal but that reveals not only her spirit but the spirit of the entire art culture at that time. In 1936 a musician she had never met, Gottuvadyam Narayana Iyengar, arrived at her house at three in the morning on his way to catch the train for Mysore, asking for her blessings and instruction. Vina Dhanammal arose from bed, offered her blessings, and taught him a composition.

Dhanammal greatly admired *Hindustani* music. Her favorite musician was the singer Abdul Karim Khan. When she heard of his death, she is said to have lamented, "How could you part with your *tambura*?" It was Dhanammal's unassailable exactness in pitch that led to her first meeting with Abdul Karim Khan. The musicians of the North had a reputation for expressing the view that *karnatic* musicians were not particular about maintaining *suddh sruti*, or perfect pitch. On a visit to Madras, Abdul Karim

Khan heard Dhanammal render the *raga Attana*. Family lore says that, left
speechless by her performance, he handed to her the money he had earned
in a performance earlier that day—a very rare gesture for any traditional
artist. He had, in effect, entrusted her with his self-respect. After the event,
the two remained in close touch.

Viswanathan commented on his grandmother: "Before the turn of the
twentieth century there were many great *vina* players, mostly male, notable
for their various styles of virtuosity in quick tempos or flashy fingering. My
grandmother, Vina Dhanammal, concentrated on a lyrical style of playing
with the result that she specialized in song forms called *padas* and *javalis*
which are also part of the dance repertoire. We do not know how those were
sung and performed before her time in our family.[39] We only know how *she*
sang and played. . . . That style of musical quality must have been inherited
by Bala through her mother." It is said by several musicians in the family
that it is through *padams* that the family's style and knowledge of *raga* was
refined. "Every *prayoga* [characteristic phrase], every nuance of a *raga* would
be there in those songs. Not one phrase of a *raga* would be missing," said
Vegavahini Vijayaraghavan, one of Dhanammal's great-granddaughters.[40]
Viswanathan expressed the same idea, demonstrating how an aspect of the
family's art was so essentially encapsulated in these great compositions. "But
they are not performed this way today."

A key element of the Dhanammal family style is simplicity. Dhanammal was noted, among other things, for being able to express the essence
of a *raga* in a very short time, three or four minutes. It was that economy
of music that Balasaraswati expressed in movement. With a single gesture
of her hand or facial expression, she could represent an entire idea. "Bala's
approach to music was like my grandmother's, very subtle, neither too vig-
orous nor too fast. . . . It was the musical training which she inherited from
her grandmother through her mother which made it possible for her to
convey so much through her *abhinaya*. . . . Bala listened to a lot of music
in the family: my grandmother practicing and performing, my mother
practicing, her aunts practicing and performing. She slowly absorbed all
those musical subtleties of *padams* and *javalis* and compositions related to
dance."[41]

"It was the kind of silence when you felt you were breathing too loudly,"
said one of Vina Dhanammal's students, Savitri Rajan, of the atmosphere
that spread when her teacher would prepare to play. "She would never start
till she was absolutely satisfied with the *sruti* or tuning." Savitri remembered
Dhanammal saying, " 'Today my *vina* sounds like *Dhanyasi*,' or 'It seems to
want *Saveri*. I can hear the echoes of that *raga* by just plucking my strings.'
As she predicted, the *vina* would yield under mastery to the nuances of that
particular *raga*."[42]

Dhanammal was known to be passionate about teaching a particular mu-

Vina Dhanammal, sitting with box containing *pan* leaf and betel nut, ca. 1935.
Courtesy of *Ananda Vikatan*.

sician from outside of the family. "Dhanam . . . summoned her entire energies to teach one favorite pupil, Saravanam. With her she shared a very special bond. In the cool terrace of her home, Dhanam and Saravanam would
play together. Bala recalled her mother, Jayammal, describing listening to
Dhanammal and Saravanam as 'a profound experience.' Tragically for Vina
Dhanammal and the music world, Saravanam died during a child birth. Dhanammal refused to accept another student for a very long time. Once the music
sessions with Saravanam came to an end, Dhanam would brood by herself.
'She would lie down with her *pan* box [a box containing *pan* leaf, betel nut

shavings, lime, and other items used while chewing *pan*, a mild stimulant],

and keep humming very quietly.' "[43]

It was initially her uncle Appakkannu's suggestion that Dhanammal play *vina* instead of dancing professionally. However, consistent with the essential interrelationship between music and dance that is at the core of the family's art, Dhanammal was trained in the family tradition of dance, learning from her grandmother Kamakshi Ammal. She also sang for her sister Rupavati's dancing and is reported to have performed with Kamakshi Ammal. She is said to have most admired the dancing of Pudukottai Ammalu of Thanjavur, whose house was near Kamakshi Ammal's.

Vina Dhanammal never actually saw Balasaraswati dancing, having been blinded in 1926. Balasaraswati commented, "[Before she lost her sight] in fact, she is said to have stood before the mirror doing *abhinaya* for her own pleasure. The way she chose my songs, 'watched' my *abhinaya* [through the performance of the music] though blind, selected items for my dance, all prove her *abhinaya* connoisseurship! . . . As far as my dance style goes, although it derives from Kandappa Pillai and Mylapore Gauri Ammal — in my heart of hearts I feel that it would have been the *bani* [individual style] of Dhanammal had she chosen to dance. That is why my own heart could accept this style. You can see its perfect unison with our music." Bala recalled that Dhanammal was not particularly interested when she began to learn. "Well, she was not so interested really. Later, she sensed I was doing well but she never told me." It was Dhanammal, however, who maintained oversight of the content of what Bala was going to perform. She was particular that Bala not be expected to perform a piece whose subtlety or philosophical content exceeded what should be expected of a young person.[44]

Memories of two moments with Vina Dhanammal were particularly important to Balasaraswati. One was at a private residence in Sowarpet, where Bala was dancing *abhinaya*. From her seat in the audience, Dhanammal suddenly gestured toward her daughter Jayammal, who was singing, and began to sing herself. Another was a concert at Soundarya Mahal, when Dhanammal started singing from her seat. "Although she was blind by that time, she was the best critic of my dance. . . . If there is any way I [would] like to be known, I [would] like to be remembered as Dhanam's granddaughter," Balasaraswati recalled.[45]

Vina Dhanammal's Contemporaries

What sort of crowd spent time in Balasaraswati's childhood home? There are many stories that circulate within the family about the characters who had become part of the household. The common passion among the musicians who were frequent visitors was Vina Dhanammal's music. At her fabled Friday night performances they would sometimes sit together, an assemblage of young revolutionary musicians, most of them from Jayammal's generation, who were to shape the future of *karnatic* music.

The group included several musicians whose children later played a role in Bala's family's life and work. Pakkiria Pillai, mentor of Bala's teacher Kandappa Pillai, was at the heart of the group. Violinist, singer, and Tamil scholar Malaikottai Govindaswamy Pillai taught Pakkiria Pillai's son Vaidyalingam and Papa Venkataramiah Iyer, who taught Abhiramasundari, the youngest daughter of Jayammal's sister Kamakshiammal. Venkataramiah Iyer also taught violin to his son V. Tyagarajan (Tyagu), and encouraged his other son, V. Nagarajan (Nagu), to become a percussionist; Tyagu and Nagu went on to teach in the United States with Ranganathan and Viswanathan during the 1960s.

Kanchipuram Naina Pillai was a singer and composer and a student of Vina Dhanammal's. Highly regarded for his exacting standards and massive repertoire, Kanchipuram Naina Pillai was considered a great musician, even in the company of the extraordinary assemblage in Dhanammal's home. He was an expert in *ragam-tanam-pallavi* and was famed for his rhythmic intricacies in performance. (*Ragam-tanam-pallavi*, a singing practice of composed and highly structured improvised music that was prevalent before the modern contemporary concert format evolved in the first part of the twentieth century, is still performed as a specialty by some musicians.) He introduced the concept of integrating *korvai*, rhythmic compositions or structures borrowed from drumming practice, into improvised singing of music (*swara kalpana*). Balasaraswati's cousins Brinda and Muktha learned from Kanchipuram Naina Pillai—against Vina Dhanammal's stated wishes, because she considered his style of singing and rhythmic improvisation "masculine."

Maharajapuram Viswanatha Iyer learned *padams* and *javalis* from Dhanammal. When he was visiting the house in 1922, there was talk about discouraging Bala. He said, supporting her passion for dancing, "The child deserves it. Why not train her, because she has a tradition."[46] Viswanatha Iyer later received the President's Award, an honor offered by the Sangeet Natak Akademi (the national academy of music, dance, and drama) to the nation's artists. He and Balasaraswati both received the award at the same ceremony.

Ariyakkudi Ramanuja Iyengar, born in 1890, the same year as Jayammal and Mylapore Gauri Ammal, also died the same year as Jayammal, in 1967. He was like others in the group at Dhanammal's home—spirited, ambitious for the art and his career, and a revolutionary. He represented a direct disciplinary lineage to the composer Tyagaraja and also was a student of Vina Dhanammal's. He is credited by some (and discredited by others) for establishing the contemporary format for *karnatic* music concerts. Before Ariyakkudi's presentation of the revised concert format, the traditions of devotional music such as the *kritis* of Tyagaraja, and the *padams* of other composers for dance, were not mixed in concerts. *Padams* and *javalis* Ariyakkudi learned from Vina Dhanammal were added to his new conception of a two-part music concert, the second portion focusing on these compositions and others of similar mood. Ariyakkudi's new concert format appears to have been modeled after the nineteenth-century bharata natyam *margam* (path), the dance concert format codified by the Thanjavur Quartet.[47]

Flutist T. N. Swaminatha Pillai came from a family of *nagaswaram* players. He was brought to Bala by her aunt Kamakshiammal. Balasaraswati learned music from him, as did her cousins Muktha and Brinda;[48] he would later become Viswanathan's teacher. From Swaminatha Pillai the girls learned the concept of the development of *raga alapana*, melodic exposition without meter that precedes the performance of compositions. Muktha recalled to Shankaran that he would sit with them and explain, "This is how you should do it."[49] The performers of *nagaswaram* have the reputation as systematic developers of *raga alapana*, because in a religious procession the development of *raga* is slowly paced; a musician might expand on a single *raga* for an hour or more.

Some of the musicians among whom Bala grew up, including Kandappa Pillai, Ranganathan's *mridangam* teacher Palani Subramaniam Pillai, and "a few other like-minded musicians," were known to get together on the first of each lunar month, taking turns hosting a "high tea" at a restaurant in the city. "The mood was always relaxed, and the jokes pertained to ludicrous tidbits from concerts."[50] It was an irreverent and influential group. They enjoyed having a drink together.

Vina Dhanammal's Family

In 1930 there were about ten musicians in Dhanammal's extended family, including children who were to become musicians. Forty years earlier, the number had been about the same; and in 1950 the number was also about the same, although the family no longer lived together. In 1970 the number had dwindled to seven, in 1990 to six. Today the number is still smaller.

The musicians from this family were meticulous about their affairs as professional artists. Music was the principal activity of the home, and the management of the opportunities they had as musicians was their business. Family members performed with broken bones, serious illnesses, and emotional concerns that would distract most of us into incompetence. Art was a competitive business, but it was to be conducted with an artistic integrity born out of devotion and in a spirit of respect for generations of elders of distinction.

An ongoing process within the family was the adaptation of new musical material into the family style. Viswanathan described the constant flux and evolution of material as something he had observed for forty years, citing as an example the changes Balasaraswati made in a song that has since become

Vina Dhanammal with musicians and music patrons, 1911. The group members' various modes of dress identify their roles or professions. *Tavil* or *nagaswaram* artists appear without shirts as a gesture of respect when they are in the presence of images of the divine, or in formal assemblies like the one photographed. The men wearing shirts are concert musicians; those wearing turbans are nonmusician patrons and heads of *sabhas* (associations). From collection of B. M. Sundaram. Courtesy of Josepha Cormack Viswanathan.

Front row, from left: Unknown, Pazhamaneri Swaminatha Iyer, unknown, Budalur. *Middle row, seated on chairs, from left:* Munuswamy Naidu, Thiruppayanam Panchapakesa Sastri, Thanjavur Nagaraja Bhagavatar, Konerirajapuram Vaidyanatha Iyer, Thirukodikaval Krishna Iyer, Harikesanallur Muthiah Bhagavatar, Fiddle Govindaswamy Pillai, Tacchur Chinna Singaracharyulu. *Back row, standing, from left:* Unknown *tavil vidwan* (*tavil* master), unknown, Vina Dhanammal, Kumbakonam Azhaganambi Pillai.

an iconic part of the bharata natyam repertoire. "She changed the music according to her own imagination and creativity. As an example, in '*Krishna ni Begane Baro*' . . . it's hard to remember how we started — I vaguely remember how the opening phrase was taught to her by the musician from Andhra area."[51] This piece was recorded in the two documentary films on Balasaraswati[52] and performed by Viswanathan at the National Heritage Fellowship awards in Washington, D.C., in 1992.[53]

Our understanding of the concept of "traditional" is both challenged and defined by this process of change. Although Balasaraswati is often said to represent an artistic vision that is extreme in its maintenance of "traditional purity," that vision was simply humility in its truest form. For Bala, what she had learned, and what she was attempting to achieve, were greater than she and the gifts she brought to her task. Several of the most famous items in her repertoire, and eventually in the repertoire of bharata natyam, are compositions of the twentieth century and tunes from outside the repertoire inherited from her family, recast according to the rules of *raga* and the aesthetics of the family style.

Viswanathan commented on the tension between change and stasis that characterizes hereditary arts: "You cannot say, 'Don't change that.' That's obvious. . . . I agree that Bala has changed the music of Dhanammal. I feel that my mother changed it, and so did Brinda and Muktha. And so have I. Yesterday I played a piece. Is it the same as I learned from my mother? I doubt it; it must have changed. Yet they will say I belong to the Dhanammal School, and I do. The basics are there. The style is in the training. Once you have that, once it is solid, you can change; you'll know what to change. But before that point, you shouldn't change."[54] A musician reaches "that point" through a process of hearing innumerable variations of melody, and through the reinforcing of correct iterations from within a single system of music.

Vina Dhanammal, Jayammal, and then Bala had a great capacity for appreciating and learning from many sources and an innate desire to continue learning from anyone whose material they thought would enrich their own. Music was sung in the home constantly, and the repertoire and family style were transmitted through absorption and mentorship, rather than being taught in classes structured as they must be in an institutional setting. Transmitted in the same ways, and strictly monitored within the family, were the rules for change and development. Although the family style, recognized as the Vina Dhanammal style, is immediately discernible, different family members give it different interpretations. All of these interpretations are "correct." Members of a hereditary artistic family embrace the potential for diversity within the unity of their inherited style; that potential is the source of invention.

Balasaraswati herself commented on a lifetime of learning in an address to the Music Academy in 1973: "I have tried to keep myself open to learning from anyone of artistic integrity and to add to, and embellish, the thorough training I received from my family and my *guru*. From ladies traditionally trained in *devadasi* families I learned many things and received special help in languages, including Telugu, Sanskrit, and Tamil. One of them taught me to do an entire song with just my face — first with the music and then in silence. I would have to go through the entire emotional range of the *sahitya* [words], using only facial expression without the aid of hands or arms."

The single-mindedness of and adherence to a family style was most in evi-

Vina Dhanammal with her extended family, 1936. Photo by G. K. Vale & Co.
Front row, sitting on ground, left to right: T. Viswanathan, Bhagyalakshmi,
T. Ranganathan, Kalpakambal, T. S. Vasudevan. *Second row, seated in chairs,
left to right:* T. Brinda, Kamakshiammal, Lakshmiratnammal, Dhanammal,
Rajalakshmiammal, T. S. Dattadri (child standing), Jayammal, T. Muktha.
Third row, standing, left to right: T. Kodandaraman, Srinivasan, T. Sundararajan,
Meenakshiammal (Mrs. T. Sundararajan), Balasaraswati, Abhiramasundari,
T. Shankaran, T. Vijayakrishnan. *Back row, left to right:* T. Govardhanan,
T. S. Sivaraman, Varadan.

dence at the time of a concert, when there was a welling-up of energy, a common understanding of the job at hand. In the hours before the concert, there would be almost constant singing. Sometimes one person would sing while others were silent; sometimes several would sing at once. Sometimes one musician would prompt another with an idea; someone might sing variations of a particular line. Long periods might pass without conversation. Sometimes idle talk would accompany the music. Other family members who did not practice the art but were knowledgeable and protective of the family business would often be in the midst during this time of preparation.

When Bala was born, her grandmother Vina Dhanammal and her great-aunt Rupavati Ammal were the survivors of their generation. Three siblings had died, two of whom were musicians. But in 1918 all four of Dhanammal's

daughters were alive and in their professional prime. The eldest, Rajalakshmiammal, was thirty-three; the youngest, Kamakshiammal, twenty-six.
Each had a vision of the family style, a reflection of their interpretation of
their mother's art. Each had a vision of the family style as it was nurtured
in their children.

When Bala was a young girl, her grandmother, mother, and aunts traveled
often for performances. Bala, with her mother and brother, had moved back
into Dhanammal's house and was cared for by an *ayah*, an older woman
who lived across the street. "Then we all lived on Ramakrishna Street," said
Shankaran, who was living in the house with his mother, Lakshmiratnammal. "A Tamil family lived opposite us and Bala spent a lot of time there,
like a foster family for her, and where she learned to speak Tamil. Jayammal
and the boys spoke Telugu, their father's language. Their *ayah* was like a
real foster mother for the child when she was four or five years old. Later the
house [of those neighbors] was taken over by the Corporation [Madras city
administration] and turned into a school. Bala was registered there. They
also taught dance and music. Jayammal removed her from school because
the principal and teachers gave her chocolates so she would dance."[55] Jayammal was insulted by the casual enticement of her daughter and removed her
permanently from the school when Bala was about seven; from then on Bala
learned entirely at home.

There was no leisure in Vina Dhanammal's house. It was known that the
learning of language and music, and the shaping of limbs and muscles, happened most efficiently in young minds and bodies. It was not at all unusual
for children from the traditional community to perform professionally. The
arts provided income for the family, and the knowledge that was imparted
and absorbed was limitless in its scope and relentless in its intellectual
demands.

"Dhanammal would not allow us to sit around; one had to practice all
the time. It was not like having to face an examination once a year at the
university. Every single day you were tested and you had to pass the test every
day—this was the lesson she drove home. There was not the slightest scope
for lazing; one could never lie down during the day; her unbending maxim
was that all bodily comforts had to be sacrificed for advancement in the
art. Her eyesight had dimmed. Even so, if, in answering her, my voice came
from close to the ground, she would know that I was not sitting up but had
stretched myself [out]. What she used to say on such occasions still rings in
my ears. She would not chastise me directly but just exclaim: 'For students,
there can be no comfort or sleep' (*'Vidyadharanam na sukham na nidra'*).
This was as forceful as a whiplash."[56]

Fifty years later, during a residency at California Institute of the Arts,
Balasaraswati expressed her feelings about her early upbringing to dancer
Bella Lewitzki while they rested between classes. Lewitzki recalled, "What

I treasure more than my own personally gained insights were the times that she chose to sit with me and talk with me. We would do that on break. I learned something about what it is like to be a three-year-old child in a family of three or four. She told me she was of a family of musicians — this was the tradition, the heritage. . . . She said [that] for hours as a baby she would practice and she . . . wanted to play and was robbed of childhood. I had no notion that a child could be raised that way, especially somebody of the stellar quality, the artistry of this woman. So, for me, I thought back, how could she have come from this really barren lack of childhood, enriched by the family's artistry, but not enriched by the things one learns in play? She resented that still at this age, and she was along in years when I met her."[57]

One of the stories about Balasaraswati that had circulated for years within the family concerned a visitor who came to Dhanammal's house, sometime during the mid-1920s. The visitor stopped at the outside gate, where Bala greeted the stranger. The visitor asked who she was. As soon as Bala had responded that she was Vina Dhanammal's granddaughter, Vina Dhanammal called out from her room upstairs, above the street, asking who it was who dared to identify herself as Dhanammal's granddaughter without her permission. According to family legend, in her humiliation Bala promised herself — and astoundingly, her grandmother — that one day someone would come to the door and ask Dhanammal for Balasaraswati.

Dhanammal's family was bilingual. Jayammal's children spoke Telugu with their mother and grandmother, and Tamil amongst themselves. Dhanammal taught music to her four daughters, particularly *padams*, *javalis*, and rare songs. The eldest, Rajalakshmi, is believed to have started her lessons with the composer/musician Patnam Subramania Iyer. Lakshmiratnam, the second daughter, learned music from Kanchipuram Naina Pillai, North Indian music from Abdul Karim Khan, and something about Western music from a teacher named Miss Bantheman. Kamakshi, Dhanammal's fourth daughter, was taught violin; the aim was to build a concert team of vocalists and accompanists from within the family. Jayammal learned *tabla* for the same reason, with the guidance of Devarajulu Naidu, who was the *tabla* accompanist for all four sisters. *Tabla* was the customary drum accompaniment for female *karnatic* vocalists at the end of the nineteenth century. Jayammal also studied dancing for a short period of time with Nellaiappa Nattuvanar, Kandappa Pillai's father. Jayammal learned the music of *javalis* from Nellaiappa.

In the late nineteenth century *javalis* and *kolattam* were being performed by groups of dancers.[58] Nellaiappa had a troupe that performed the *javalis* of the Thanjavur Quartet; through him the *javalis* of the Thanjavur family came into Balasaraswati's family repertoire. *Javalis* were very popular in the late 1800s and were usually composed to be performed and danced in a rapid tempo. Several composers of *javalis*, however, preferred a slow tempo; three were regular visitors to Dhanammal's house.[59] "When my grandmother, Dhanammal, was alive, they came to our house, stayed with us and also taught music. It was interesting to hear about their teaching, their performances and the way they listened to music. Their talk, always humorous, was as good as their music," Bala remembered. Dhanammal's daughters learned the *javalis* of the Thanjavur Quartet, and then of the generation of composers who were inspired by the Quartet's compositions. When she was a child Rajalakshmi enjoyed playing in the street outside of Dhanammal's house, but was discouraged from doing so. One of the composers who would visit and teach in the house, Thiruppanandal (a village near the town of Kumbakonam) Pattabhiramaiyya, composed a *javali, "Poochi Vadu Nadu,"* (*poochi* means "bug"; *vadu* is "man") which he sang playfully to frighten Rajalakshmi and her playmates, including her younger sisters, out of the street.

Jayammal was interviewed in 1961 for a Census Report by her son Viswanathan. Viswa was a subcollector for the government of the Madras Presidency after graduating from the University of Madras with a degree in economics, the first in his family to graduate from college. In the interview Jayammal told a story that gives some idea of the currency of the professional community and explains how certain compositions came to be considered "family property."[60] Composer Dharmapuri Subbarayar had left Madras for his family village, promising to return. During the time that he was away, as Jayammal put it, "Our family had sunk [into] poverty. When Subbarayar heard this he gave us a big bag of money. That bag was nothing but a *javali*—no precious stone. The *javali* was 'Saki Prana' [in] *Jenjhuti* [*raga*]. . . . That was his last *javali*."[61] This piece became one of the mainstays of Bala's repertoire.

Vina Dhanammal stayed with one or another daughter after they had matured—often with Jayammal and her mate, Modarapu Govindarajulu, called Govind, of whom she was particularly fond. Govindarajulu was from a prominent *dubash* shipping family with land in Royapettah, where they lived in Dare House on Mowbray's Road, a large home surrounded by gardens. The family patronized leading *Hindustani* musicians. They were also devoted to Vina Dhanammal.

Part of the glue that held one generation to the next was students and families who were devotees of the Dhanammal tradition. Govind's maternal aunt taught several *javalis* to Jayammal when Jayammal was young. His elder sister studied music and presented musicians at house concerts. A capable musician himself, Govindarajulu eventually taught Bala several *javalis*. It was at first Jayammal's sweet voice, which "clung to the ears," that sparked the union between Jayammal and her mate. Govindarajulu was welcomed

Modarapu
Govindarajulu,
Balasaraswati's
father,
photographed
in the early
1920s.

by all of Vina Dhanammal's family. He was one of the privileged few allowed to touch Dhanammal's *vina*.[62]

Bala had cousins who were musicians: the three daughters of Jayammal's sister Kamakshiammal. The first two daughters, Brinda and Muktha, began learning music from their grandmother and mother, and then were sent to learn vocal music for several years with Kanchipuram Naina Pillai. Naina Pillai introduced them to the practice of rhythmic improvisation, crossing the line then accepted between male and female performance practices. Brinda learned *vina* from Dhanammal and earned great distinction during her career; for many, she is thought of with the same degree of reverence accorded Balasaraswati. Muktha, who lived a life and career somewhat in the shadow of her brilliant and severe older sister, was a wonderful singer and was widely recognized as a gentle and generous teacher. Kamakshiammal's youngest daughter, Abhiramasundari, known as Abhirami, was a violinist who often accompanied Jayammal and Bala's vocal concerts, as well as concerts by her two older sisters. Abhiramasundari died a well-recognized musician during the 1970s. It was said that the combination of these three sisters' music was an unforgettably cohesive sound — as was the music of Jayammal and her children Balasaraswati, Ranganathan, and Viswanathan.

Both Ranganathan and Viswanathan accompanied Bala at various times during their distinguished careers as performers and teachers. Ranganathan first learned *mridangam* for a short while from Bala's teacher Kandappa Pillai; then he studied with Palani Muthaiah Pillai and later with his son, Palani Subramaniam Pillai. Both were members of a famous *tavil* lineage (the *tavil* is a drum played in the temple music repertoire by the *isai velalar* community). Ranganathan's sensibility of drumming was shaped partly by

his combined experience in accompaniment of the solo *karnatic* repertoire
and performance style and partly by accompaniment of bharata natyam,
informed by masters of the traditional style of playing with dance. He held
the *mridangam* accompaniment of music to a standard established by Vina
Dhanammal, who would not use drum accompaniment for her own playing. It was a standard that demanded attention to the subtlety of music in
preference to virtuosity.

Viswanathan learned music from T. N. Swaminatha Pillai, the famous
flutist from the *nagaswaram* tradition. According to Viswanathan, he was
taught the fingering on the flute and exercises for six months, and from then
on, his entire training with his teacher was through singing. He developed
his style of playing through imitation on the flute of the vocal music he had
been taught, repeating his teacher's experience with learning.[63] Viswanathan's playing became distinctive among flutists for his inflection of the text.
Ranga and Viswa's teachers were regular attendees at Vina Dhanammal's
Friday night concerts, and regular guests in the house, as were the teachers
of Kamakshiammal's children. The continuity of music in the house extended beyond the bloodlines, and was connected through the compelling
greatness of Vina Dhanammal.

GURU KANDAPPA PILLAI

In the traditional hereditary community, children would first be taught
music by their elders, and then sent to teachers outside the family whose
style was compatible. Through this process, the family repertoire and musical interpretation was enriched from one generation to the next. However,
children who learned dance, although they learned music at home, were
sent by their families to dance masters from the beginning of their dance
training.

"Kandappa was my first and only *guru*," Bala recalled. "He conveyed to me
the legacy of the Thanjavur Quartet and he brought his own exquisite sense
of balance in standardizing the bharata natyam repertoire and recital program as we know it today."[64] Kandappa was a singer, as were many *nattuvanars*, and his music was influenced by Vina Dhanammal. He was familiar
with Bala's family repertoire and approach to singing the dance repertoire.
He sang *padams* during dance concerts he conducted until Jayammal began
to sing in his ensemble during the 1920s. He also played the *mridangam*
with several different musicians, notably including Balasaraswati's aunt
Lakshmiratnammal and Semmangudi S. Iyer. (Many accompanists refused
to perform with women. Some still do refuse.)[65] In addition, he had several
mridangam students,[66] including Balasaraswati's brother Ranganathan.

Shankaran recalled, "He had a *tambura* himself and had a peculiar way
of stringing it. He removed all the steel wires, replaced with brass, would lie
on the floor and play it. He used to tune them himself . . . lying down and

Balasaraswati's
guru,
K. Kandappa
Pillai, Almora,
ca. 1939.

singing, softly; he would never raise his voice. . . . I used to see him conduct Mylapore Gauri Ammal's *melam* [ensemble] because her teacher, Nellaiappa Nattuvanar, had died and Kandappa Pillai took over."[67]

Although Kandappa Pillai was a regular attendee at Vina Dhanammal's Friday night concerts, he would rarely speak directly with Dhanammal; he was more than thirty years younger than she. Viswanathan commented that he was the only *nattuvanar* who used to come and listen to her. "I don't know of anybody else in the dance field who came to listen to her."

It was customary for the *nattuvanar* in an ensemble to sing the *padams*, and *nattuvanars* were typically reluctant to relinquish this role. The singing of *padams* allowed the musician to demonstrate both his musical prowess and, more subtly, his relationship with the dancer. However, when Bala first performed, Kandappa insisted that Jayammal sing the *padams* and *javalis*. The combination of Jayammal and Balasaraswati became legendary. As far as Viswanathan could remember, there were no other women performing music for dance in the 1920s. It was a role reserved for men, and the men stood and followed the dancer as she moved while she danced. *Nattuvanars* were notably easily insulted, and to substitute another musician — let alone a female — in the most demanding musical role would place a *nattuvanar's* prowess in question.

"If today I am known somewhat in the world and honored by learned societies, it is because my most respected *guru*, Kandappa Pillai, taught me not only the art of dancing, he also taught me to fear praise and accept criticism,"

Bala said. "My *guru* would insist on my leaving the concert hall as soon as possible after the end of the concert lest the congratulations of friends backstage should go to my head. After reaching home, he would make sure that elders did not compliment me too much. The very next morning... I had to recall every single error I made in the previous evening's concert, replay the error, and demonstrate how it should have been correctly danced. In those days, I felt dejected and dispirited. Later, with the gradual maturing of my art, when my own soul gained satisfaction and when acclamation came from all around overflowing the barriers imposed by my *guru*, I began to realize how much his façade of strictness had helped me to develop. Yet, I hankered for a 'well done' from his lips."[68]

Kandappa Pillai married twice. His first wife died; his second wife was the granddaughter of Ponniah Pillai of the Thanjavur Quartet and the childhood playmate of Dhanammal's daughter Lakshmiratnam. Kandappa's ancestors had been in the service of the Thanjavur court during the seventeenth century, moved to Thiruneveli during the eighteenth century, and returned to Thanjavur around 1800.[69] Kandappa's father, Nellaiappa Nattuvanar, named for the family deity in Thiruneveli, trained dancers of an earlier generation. He taught music to Jayammal and Lakshmiratnam, as well as to Mylapore Gauri Ammal, but he did not teach music to his son Kandappa Pillai. Instead, Kandappa learned *nattuvangam* from his paternal grandfather, Kannuswami Nattuvanar of Baroda, and additionally music from his uncle K. Ponniah. However, his performance style was that of his father, Nellaiappa Nattuvanar. Accounts vary as to whether he learned *mridangam* from his father[70] or from other members of his family.[71]

Gurukula

The traditional system of teaching and learning is called *gurukula*. The *guru* was absolute master within the traditional professional community, and Kandappa Pillai exerted and maintained this authority strictly. Bala recognized both the horror and the necessity of the harshness of the relationship. "In this era of freedom, it is certainly not possible to follow the harsh practices of my *guru*."[72] Lakshmi commented that the family tolerated the abuse because this approach to teaching was the way of the traditional community. As students from families outside the professional community began to learn dance in the 1930s, those whose parents objected to the use of physical discipline were spared. But there are stories of corporal punishment by traditional teachers in South India, just as there are stories out of British public schools, and out of one-room schoolhouses in the United States. Attitudes have changed about teaching. Although Bala was physically hurt during the course of her learning, the injury was not so much the damage to the flesh of a young child; it was the violation of the spirit, of her trust. She would have done what she was being asked to do without physical pain and emotional deprivation.

In 1922 Kandappa Pillai was living near Dhanammal's house. Jayammal took four-year-old Bala to class at his home early every morning, after coffee and *idli* (a steamed, dumpling-like cake made of fermented rice and lentil flours).[73] There, Bala was trained in dance. In a class of eighteen students,[74] she learned the abstract dance movements called *adavus*. She was drilled for hours, sometimes carrying a bag of sand on her head to force her neck into correct position, and was struck with a switch when she made mistakes. Bala bore the scars on her calves and ankles throughout her life. Yet she accepted her teacher's role without question or reservation — an attitude of reverence that ironically prevented the formation of a more collaborative, more easily negotiated relationship between teacher and child-student. "My *guru* was my god and my duty was to obey his instructions faithfully. I danced to his *tala* and the constant sight of the cane compelled me to execute my lessons with greater caution," Balasaraswati said.[75] She commented to Narayana Menon, then director of the National Centre for the Performing Arts in Bombay, "He was a lion; the art was always greater than the artist."[76]

The critic B. V. K. Sastri commented on a story Balasaraswati had told him: "Once, when he asked her to perform a particular gesture, she faltered; he went into the kitchen and brought out a hot [coal], and branded her on her hand. She carried this scar. . . . Those teachers were always like that, in that generation. . . . That was a way of life at that time. For Bala particularly, [Kandappa] was a perfectionist. Unless the movements or gestures were perfect, he would not accept it."[77] According to Bala's account of this incident, both her mother and grandmother were there, in another room, but they "did not dare to intervene. As you must know," Bala commented, "amongst us, a *guru* is esteemed the sole guardian of his disciple." The *gurukula* system did not allow mother or grandmother to intervene; such an intervention would have ended the relationship.

Following a concert in Delhi in 1962, interviewer Maya Rao praised Bala for her dancing, and received a sudden, forceful reaction: "Do you know how many years of practice and hard study are necessary to earn that statement?" She showed Maya Rao the scars on her hand. "These will tell you the story of my career as a student of bharata natyam . . . I owe this to the great *guru* Kandappa Pillai who trained me. . . . He was an excellent teacher and never tolerated the slightest mistake in the rendering of *adavus* or *jatis*, not to mention major items." Bala described incidents when she was punished severely for a fault in her footwork or in delineating *mudras*. "At the time [it] was terrifying," Bala said. Then, Maya Rao reported, "She suddenly performed the *adavu* mentioned and asked, 'Have you ever seen an *adavu* performed with such dexterity and so much accent on grace?'"[78]

Bani Bai was a famous exponent of *harikatha*, a nineteenth- and twentieth-century tradition combining singing, *abhinaya* (performed seated), and philosophical discourse. She recalled Bala as a child: "My mother and Jayam-mal were great friends. . . . When Bala and I were young, we used to play together; Ranga and Viswa were not yet born. She was afraid of Kandappa because he was a strict teacher. She used to come and hide herself in my eldest sister's room. Jayammal would come and ask me why Bala had not attended her dance class. She would then come out of her hiding place and walk majestically to her master."[79]

Balasaraswati's daughter, Lakshmi, told another story: At this same time, when Bala was six or seven, she and her cousin Abhirami hid in the nearby Ganapati temple to escape Kandappa Pillai. Bala asked God, in innocent but audible prayer, to "take me soon." Kandappa Pillai, who had come into the temple looking for Bala, overheard this plea — obviously learned from an adult — and caught her. As a punishment he held her by her feet over smoking incense. "These punishments did not dampen her enthusiasm [but] gave Bala the zeal to work harder to win [his] rare smile of appreciation," Maya Rao reported.

Bala recalled that she enjoyed practicing the *adavus* at slow speed and never understood why the other girls in her class at Kandappa Pillai's house ridiculed her for this. She thought the slow speed was more beautiful than the quicker speeds. "Why did the other girls taunt me whenever I practiced *adavus* in slow motion? I could not understand them then, and I cannot understand it now." A review of a concert in New Delhi in 1955 echoes this recollection as a distinctive quality of Balasaraswati's art: "In the slow tempo, each gesture is unfolded in slow motion [so that] the immaculate accomplishment of the new gesture [becomes clear]."[80]

Kandappa's rhythmic compositions for dance reflect an adherence to principles of structure that set him apart among his relatives who also represented the Thanjavur Nattuvanar family tradition. Himself a *mridangam* player, he composed as if his ideas would be performed by a drummer. He was also influenced by Pakkiria Pillai, a revolutionary musician more than forty years his senior.

Pakkiria Pillai was born in 1857 into a family of *nattuvanars*. As a *nattuvanar*, he was skilled at the rhythmic recitation technique used in the accompaniment of composed pure dance and of the vocal repertoire of bharata natyam. He was also a recognized master of the drum, *tavil*. He became known as Konnakkol Pakkiria Pillai, because he developed unique expertise in the performance technique of rhythmic recitation known as *konnakkol*, an accompaniment and solo percussive practice in the performance of *karnatic* music. This practice appears to have been adapted from the performance of *jatis* (rhythmic syllables) during sections of abstract dance in bharata natyam, a practice introduced by the Thanjavur Quartet. Pakkiria Pillai also was a prolific composer of music for medieval lyrics called *tiruppugazh.*

A family story tells of the first time Pakkiria Pillai saw Bala. He had dropped by to visit Kandappa Pillai at his home and walked in on one of Bala's lessons. She was having difficulty with a section of pure dance she knew well, and was exhausted and hungry. Kandappa was insisting that she render the passage correctly before stopping to eat, and the situation was deteriorating rapidly; the more insistent Kandappa became, the more stubborn Bala became. "Who is this girl?" asked Pakkiria Pillai. Kandappa explained that she was the granddaughter of Vina Dhanammal. Pakkiria Pillai proposed a solution to the stalemate; he would compose on the spot a *tirmanam* (a section of pure dance) that Kandappa would choreograph immediately; Bala, as soon as she had danced it, could go home for the day. This broke the antagonistic spiral; Bala learned the composition quickly, and they all went off to lunch. The *tirmanam* remained part of Balasaraswati's repertoire.[81]

Ten years later, an event occurred that reveals more of the competitiveness of the hereditary community. K. Ponniah Pillai, grandson of the Thanjavur Quartet, had heard of the prowess of Kandappa's student, then in her teens, and he wanted to challenge both teacher and student. He composed a now very well known piece in *sankirna nadai,* a *swarajati,* a complex setting of melodic and rhythmic phrases in a meter of eight beats, each with nine subdivisions. The composer challenged Kandappa to choreograph it and teach Bala to dance it. "Kandappa Pillai was raving about Bala and so K. Ponniah Pillai challenged him," Viswanathan remembered. "It was a tricky piece but he did it. Bala was very sick at that time and Kandappa Pillai asked him to wait until she recovered from her illness. After she recovered, he did choreograph it. Kandappa's cousin, K. P. Kittappa Pillai, assisted in meeting the challenge, revealing something of the process through which material was shared and expanded. 'My father [K. Ponniah Pillai] taught Kandappa the *sankirna swarajati* and also instructed him to teach Bala the same. Kandappa and I devoted nearly fifteen days to get the *tirmanams.*' "[82]

Wealthy merchants who promoted Balasaraswati in her early career included Jalatarangam Ramanayya Chettiar and his family. The Chettiar family had been patrons of Vina Dhanammal and her family when times were hard. Their house on Arumugam Street in Georgetown was a gathering place for leading musicians from the north as well as from the south, and Vina Dhanammal's entire family were always welcome as guests there. Ramanayya Chettiar was a musician in his own right and gained recognition for playing the *jalatarangam,* a set of porcelain cups that are filled with precise amounts of water to resound with different pitches when stuck with small sticks. Ramanayya Chettiar was an influential man and commanded respect at major cultural functions presented by the Chettiar community. After Bala's career was launched, he would recommend her to prospective presenters, just as he did with other members of Bala's family. His wife often lent jewels and costumes, which Jayammal did not own, for Bala's concerts, and she remained a close family friend for her lifetime. Bala was always moved by this generosity, and she thought of Ramanayya Chettiar as her adopted father. He had two daughters who were both Bala's playmates; Padma was a close friend, a confidante until Bala died. Padma never developed an interest in Bala's art; she remained simply a friend.

Shankaran recalled an incident in Ramanayya Chettiar's house that occurred two years before Balasaraswati's ceremonial introduction as a performer, her *arangetram*. A group of musicians were gathered one morning during the Rama Navami (Rama's birthday) Festival in the spring of 1925, an event sponsored annually by Ramanayya Chettiar in his home. Included were Naina Pillai, Govindaswamy Pillai, Pakkiria Pillai, Gopalakrishna Iyer, Kandappa Pillai, and others. They were all gossiping and kidding around, and Bala, aged six, was in the house, dressed informally in a jacket and *paavadai* (skirt). She was "just jumping around," according to Shankaran. The subject of seeing Bala dance came up, and Ramanayya Chettiar encouraged the idea, saying, "It is only musicians, why don't you dance, Bala." Some of the group approved of the idea that Bala was learning to dance; others disapproved. But curiosity about how Dhanammal's granddaughter danced overcame any reluctance to encourage her. She was asked to give an informal performance. Her mother was there to sing.

Govindaswamy Pillai, who had discouraged Jayammal from having Bala taught dance for fear that she would face ridicule, made no comment, but watched in intense silence. Pakkiria Pillai leaned against the wall behind Bala instead of watching her from the front. When the others encouraged Pakkiria to join them, he said, "No, I am only interested in the sound of her footwork." After this performance the "regulars" at Ramanayya Chettiar's home began to debate the question of Bala's dance training and whether or not she should have an *arangetram*. Among those in favor was Ramanayya Chettiar, who supported Jayammal's decision to have an *arangetram* for Bala.

Arangetram

The *arangetram* was a rite of passage that involved the entire community. It was an occasion when the artistic ability of the young student could be reviewed and tested by elders. The young artist also was tested in her ability to withstand criticism and even ridicule. She performed first for the women of the community before facing the all-male audience that was typical of nighttime performances. "At one time the dancer was subjected to a severe appraisal of her knowledge and talent before she had her *arangetram*," Bala recalled. "A student had to dance first in the morning before a gathering of women — and usually the program lasted from nine-thirty to one. Then the next day she danced before a gathering of knowledgeable men directly interested in the art. This was in the evening hours. [Both groups contained] many persons with intimate knowledge of the tradition and the texts. Someone who had a barbed comment to make would very casually inquire, after the festive meal, why [a particular] movement was made to interpret a particular passage. Such criticism was loaded with sarcastic undertones and only if the performance was up to the standard did the dancer get her *gajjai* [bells] and have her *arangetram*. One could pass such tests only if one had deep devotion to the art, if the artist considered knowledge and talent as 'blessings from above.'"[83] For all hereditary students humility relative to the art itself was a requirement for progression in a career.

The *arangetram* was where the community's protection of the standard of performance of the arts began. The *devadasi*'s dedication to the divine meant she was answerable only to a vision that was granted divine status as a means of protection of the arts. In the *arangetram* it was first the women of the community who decided if a young student had the capacity to continue and to become a professional artist. That decision was in part a measure of the performance itself, but it was a measure of much more: of fortitude, the strength to persist with artistic values that are distinctly bred from the family's art.

A decade after Bala's *arangetram*, the *devadasi* community would lose control of that standard in the transfer of the performing arts from the professional to nonprofessional practitioner. It is difficult to argue with the original intent voiced by reformers in the 1930s, which was, in part, to make the performing arts available beyond the barriers of community. But the change raised a powerful dilemma. The issue was inclusion in or exclusion from a professional community and standard. The *devadasi* community was not a caste but a way of living. In the rejection of the professional practice and its practitioners in favor of a more inclusive standard of performance, the tenets of the traditional art form also were rejected. Among the changes that took place was a relaxation of the uncontestable, hierarchical relationship between student and teacher. In the traditional circumstance it was fundamental to the system of learning that the teacher would always know something that the student had yet to learn.

Bala's *arangetram* in 1925 was held at a small shrine to the Goddess, Devi, near but not attached to the great Kamakshi temple in Kanchipuram. The shrine, named Ammanakshi Amman temple, was enclosed by a small courtyard, overgrown with brush by the 1970s. To the side of the entrance to the sanctum sanctorum there was a platform where concerts were given by the famed musicians of the region around Kanchipuram. It was a great honor to perform at this shrine—and this was the platform on which seven-year-old Bala danced her first performance.

The Hindu calendar month *Aadi*, running from mid-July to mid-August, is associated with Shakti (Devi). Major temples used to hold festi-

Ammanakshi Amman Temple, location of Balasaraswati's *arangetram,*
Kanchipuram, 1990s.

vals in Shakti's honor during *Aadi* in hopes of forestalling acts of violence by
this temperamental form of the divine — such as the cholera epidemics that
historically plagued India as the waters rose during the ensuing monsoon
season. Each year's festival was headed by one of the leading musicians in
the district, with evening and all-night concerts. The festivals provided a
place for young musicians and dancers to be introduced to an audience that
included prominent artists from throughout the region. Many performers
got their start during the festival season.

In 1925 it was Kanchipuram Naina Pillai's festival. Originally Naina Pillai had objected to Bala's being presented at such an early age, but Jayammal insisted that he sit, listen, and watch, which he did, for more than three hours. Afterward, visibly moved, Naina Pillai presented Bala with a *sruti* box (a small harmonium with bellows that was used as a portable drone instrument, a substitute for the larger lutelike *tambura*) and an invitation to perform in his home soon after, an act that Bala never forgot.

"My debut at the age of seven is still fresh in my memory," Bala said years later. "It was my *arangetram* at Ammanakshi Amman temple.... I felt it was through divine grace. Each year during *Aadi Masam*, all the *nattuvanars* and singers came together to present a festival. By custom, each *nattuvanar* presented his disciple in turn. Being Kandappa Pillai's turn it was his wish to have my debut in the presence of the divine Goddess, and the eminent *vidwans* [musicians], and it was fulfilled."[84] Before the performance someone gave Bala some betel nut and *pan* leaves. This was her first taste of *pan*, and she continued to use it throughout her life, claiming her imagination came from its stimulating effects.

"I danced every day so there were no special rehearsals — each day's class was a kind of rehearsal. Though I did not rehearse with the musicians, I was not nervous. I did not think of it as an unusual happening. But when I heard the music, the *mridangam* and the flute, I felt a thrill and danced as one inspired. Which dancer can resist the reverberating sound of a good *mridangam*? I was so engrossed in the music. Hearing the music is what guided me. As soon as the *mridangam* player started tuning his instrument — my teacher sitting there with his *talam*, and the sound of the *tambura* — I felt a kind of excitement, my blood rising. All I wanted to do was dance." Throughout her life Bala believed it was one of her best concerts.[85] "It turned out to be a big event in my life; the atmosphere, the gathering of distinguished musicians and dancers, stay firmly put in my mind."[86]

Bala credited her successful career with having had her first formal performance in this temple, believing, in Lakshmi's words, that "the effect of performing at Devi's temple lasted her lifetime. She had not only the blessings of the august audience but the Goddess's blessing as well." Bala also said, "All my life my concerts have been enjoyed and blessed by such stalwarts. I consider this a benefaction."

On August 13, 1927, Viswanathan, named by Vina Dhanammal for Lord Viswanatha of Benares, was born. A month later, on September 13, Bala's formal public introduction in Madras took place at the home of Dr. Doraiswami Naidu, a homeopathic physician. In attendance again, as they were at her *arangetram*, were many of the leading musicians of the time, including Ariyakkudi Ramanuja Iyengar, Pakkiria Pillai, Tanjore Vaidyanatha Iyer, Marungapuri Gopalakrishna Iyer, and the *mridangam* players Palghat Mani Iyer and Azhakanampi Pillai. Bala danced a *trayasra alarippu*, the *Kaly-*

ani jatiswaram, and the *sabdam "Venyuda."* As she had at her *arangetram,* she danced *"Danike" varnam* in *Todi raga,* which she also sang, and several *padams.*[87]

During the 1920s the family of Bala's father, Govindarajulu, lost their property and wealth. It is said that ultimately Bala's father had begun to gamble compulsively and that he became unable to provide support for Jayammal and his children. He and Jayammal became estranged. Their separation was felt by all of the children in the house, who were fond of the affectionate Govindarajalu. Lakshmi's account reveals both Bala's sense of loss of her father and Jayammal's resentment of her mate's misfortune: "He loved his family, that's the basic thing.... But, once my grandmother [Jayammal] decided 'That is it,' no one could change her mind.... She never allowed Bala ... to support her father when she began earning.... When Grandfather died [in 1935], Seena [Bala's older brother, Srinivasan] did all the rites and everything was taken care of.... Balamma felt very badly because she was not allowed to attend the funeral. She fought with Jayammal and she ran to see him, or something. I'm not quite sure. She did see him, I think, after he died. But, what's the use? She wanted to take care of him. That broke her heart. Really broke it. This was something she could not get over."[88]

Within a few years after Balasaraswati's public dance debut, profound changes would come about in Indian dance, set in motion by social movements that had begun in the nineteenth and early twentieth centuries, both in India and in the West. These movements, unconcerned with the hereditary dance community at first, revealed themselves in the religious and social polemic discourse of England and the United States; they arose in response to the Industrial Revolution and the new sources of labor it required, including women and children from underprivileged families.

For Balasaraswati's family at the end of the nineteenth century, the concerns of the Protestant church and the suffragist and feminist movements in the West had been unknown. As these movements took hold in India, however, Balasaraswati's grandmother and aunts themselves became activists—but for another cause: their matrilinear family structure and values.

EVANGELISM IN INDIA

The British in India had contented themselves with being mercantile opportunists from the time of the establishment of the East India Company in the late seventeenth century until the early nineteenth century. The inclination and official policy of the colonists was to leave the social and cultural institutions of India alone; some British colonists settled with Indian partners, emulating Indian households of privilege.

But this pattern changed with the arrival of the Evangelical missionary. Evangelism had its start in eighteenth-century England and expanded into the United States during the following century; it spread to India through missions and churches established by the East India Company to serve the English community in diaspora. Evangelical missionaries began to arrive in India in the 1830s. Soon, not content with simply serving their own congregations, the new missionaries became determined to convert the religious practices and cultural and social conventions of India's Hindu and Muslim communities. Evangelical missionaries in India in the nineteenth century believed not only in the superiority of their religious beliefs, but also in the predestined virtue of their cause. Their own salvation rested on their success.

By the middle of the nineteenth century, Hindus and Muslims began to react fearfully and self-protectively to the oppression of the colonial presence and overbearing missionary message of the Evangelists. The Sepoy Rebellion of 1857 was one of several bloody protests in what some historians today refer to as India's First War of Independence. These uprisings precipitated a period of brutal repression and duplicity by the British. For their own intents and purposes, the British colonists had unified India through an infrastructure of transportation, communication, and civil administration that made the colonization of India extraordinarily profitable. But by this time India had been fragmented into six hundred princely states of various sizes and power that were easily turned against one another during the "independence" protests of the later nineteenth century; this diversity and decentralization was to the British advantage.

The Evangelist movement in the United States had lost its luster by 1870, but two movements, Transcendentalism and Spiritualism, followed in its wake. Spiritualism was raised by some to the status of a religion, valued and understood as a way for people to communicate with the "Beyond" for the purpose of learning and seeking guidance with a personal, nondenominational divinity. Having become acquainted at an occult meeting in Vermont, two Spiritualists, Helena Blavatsky, an adventuress of noble blood from Russia, and Henry Olcott, an American army engineer and lawyer, formed a lasting association based on their shared interest in the occult. In 1875 they established an organization in New York City that they named the Theosophical Society. One objective of the Society was to create a philosophical-religious bridge between ancient spiritual practices and then-modern scientific thought.[1]

In the late 1870s, shortly after the creation of the Theosophical Society, Olcott corresponded with Hindu and Buddhist reformers in India and explained that the objective of the Society was the reformation of American Spiritualism. This was to be accomplished through dissemination of Asian wisdom in the United States and, in turn, discrediting of Christianity and its assertions of superiority. Olcott had developed a perception of Buddhism before he visited Asia (admitting, for a brief period, that he knew very little about the faith). Olcott wrote several letters to Babu Perry Mittra in 1877 in which Olcott claimed the Society's mission would be "to promote the study of the esoteric religious philosophies of the East," and to expose the moral bankruptcy of Christianity. Olcott added that the objective would also be to publish "these grim facts [about Christianity] in non-Christian lands."

At the same time, invoking the spirit of liberal Protestantism, he asserted in a letter to India that "we should respect every man's faith, holding our own, nevertheless in chief affection." But in the end, Olcott reacted against Christian dogma, and declared his intention to form a league that resisted organized Christianity in India, where, he stated, it had set "itself up to be the one true religion [which] bears the curse of the eternal damnation against all who deny the supremacy, and by cunning and violence aims to subdue and corrupt the whole earth." Some historians claim that his rhetoric reflected the rancor of his mentor and Society co-founder, H. P. Blavatsky.

Initially, Olcott appeared to his Asian counterparts to be one of their own, and he was invited to form a branch of the Theosophical Society in Bombay. However, as Stephen Prothero states in his biography of the theosophist, "Olcott's ideology of the equality of all religions mirrored the missionary's ideology of religious differences in one crucial respect: It too refused to recognize the Buddhists and Hindus of India as full human subjects. Because of his refusal to accept the differences between himself and his Asian correspondents, Olcott came to understand these Oriental 'others' almost exclusively as reflections of his Occidental 'self.' Thus, Olcott's seemingly empathetic embrace of both Buddhism and Hinduism shared with missionary Christianity and British colonialism an imperial thrust. He was demanding that his Asian correspondents become 'anonymous theosophists'—adherents of a new ideology that was not self-consciously their own.... Long before his departure for India Olcott was mistaking his contribution to the sacred canopy for the sacred canopy itself."[2]

The Theosophical Society

The founders of the Theosophical Society traveled to India arriving early in 1879, and four years later were to establish a permanent base for the Society in Madras. As Olcott had explained in his letters to India in 1877, he and Helena Blavatsky had come to India expecting to return to the United States to continue their work there. But after establishing the Society in Bombay, the two traveled extensively in North India and, during 1880 and 1881, throughout India and Ceylon. Olcott was able to expand his interest in Buddhism as Blavatsky explored her interests in the Vedanta (the spiritual tradition at the core of Hinduism, concerned with self-realization).

It is not difficult to understand the appeal of Blavatsky and Olcott's message. They expounded a brand of universalism that embraced their interpretations of the beliefs and tenets of Hinduism, Buddhism, and Islam. They rejected the dogma of Evangelical Christianity and Christian orthodoxy that by 1880 had become offensive and threatening in India. Indeed, Olcott learned that unabashed criticism of the Evangelical missionary objectives in India assured him favor with his Indian supporters, sympathetic Anglo-Indians (British expatriates), and a pro-Asian constituency in England—the readership of a monthly journal he named *The Theosophist*, a publishing project he undertook initially to generate income.

In his first speech in India, Olcott expressed an attitude that was to become a banner of the Theosophists: "India will never revive her ancient glory until [the] Indian woman is rescued from ignorance and servitude."

His remark was not based on observation of Indian society, but rather on the issue of women's rights that had been adopted by the American Spiritualist reform movement as one of several social causes it supported.

Within months of his arrival in Ceylon in 1880, Olcott also declared the practice of the Sinhalese Buddhists to be false and modernized, and established himself as the diviner of a pure, ancient, nonsectarian practice. The tenets of Buddhism, he asserted, were delimited by Sanskrit and Pali sources, and the practice of Buddhism as he observed it was not as it had been textually defined.

In time, the leaders of the Theosophical Society were to become highly influential in the effort to redefine and glorify a "national" Indian history and culture, and they eventually found a source for this rediscovered history in the notion of a classical age that was declared a pan-Indian heritage.[3] Olcott's arguments were to contribute to the nascent Anti-Nautch movement in Madras and were echoed in the Society's support in the 1930s of a reconstruction of bharata natyam substantiated with Sanskrit textual and centuries-old visual references. Although the Society was—and remains—admired for its nonsectarian message, its membership represented primarily British expatriates and the Indian social elite; this was part of what gave the Society distinction and credibility.

Annie Besant

In 1889 Annie Besant, an English feminist and an activist in the establishment of labor laws protecting women and women's right to birth control in England, met and was deeply influenced by Helena Blavatsky, who had moved to England after her long tenure in India. Besant had been married to an Anglican minister but rebelled against her husband's conservative expectations and was divorced. She later declared herself an atheist, a response to a crisis of faith during the illness of one of her children. After meeting Blavatsky she "converted" to the universalism of Blavatsky's message of Theosophy. Besant subsequently wrote that through the principles of Theosophy she was able to imagine a new church, one that was focused on the love of man. In 1893 Besant moved to Benares. There, in 1898, she founded the Benares Hindu College and a corresponding secondary school. She brought George Arundale from England as a professor in history at the college in 1902. He was to become headmaster of the secondary school and then eventually principal of the college, which became Benares Hindu University in 1915.

Following Theosophical Society president Henry Olcott's death, Besant was elected president of the Society in 1907. Under her influence the Society assumed a more socially responsive and self-consciously philosophical and political personality, diverging from Blavatsky's legacy of concern with occult phenomena. The Society attracted into its membership some of the brilliant new young leaders of the agitation against the British Raj. Besant pursued personal research and writing about esoteric knowledge, but her social ethics and feminist politics provided the seeds of a definition of the repositioning of upper class Indian women.

Annie Besant's rise in Indian politics began about 1913, six years after her succession of Henry Olcott as the president of the Theosophical Society. It started with a series of lectures in 1913 (later published under the title "Wake Up India"), in which she addressed various aspects of India's "hoary ancient past" and laid the foundation for a five-year ascent as a leader in the establishment of a Home Rule movement. (Notably, before she moved to India, Besant—of Irish descent—was an energetic supporter of the Irish Home Rule movement.) In 1917 Besant was externed from Madras, along with George Arundale and freedom fighter Bahman Pestonji Wadia, to the hill station of Ootachamand in the Western Ghats. Her removal from Madras was a direct response by the British to the success of her opposition to British governance of India. Her dismissal to Ooty, however, only served to make her a martyr and to enhance her power as a leader in national politics.

Besant's strongest appeal was to a certain segment of the Brahmin community. Historically, there were several functions served by the Brahmin community. One was to act as legal advisors and administrators for feudal rulers. The traditional role as legal advisor and administrator—and the skills that role required—became the basis for the colonial preference for the Brahmin community as their administrators in the new urban environment of the nineteenth century.

It appears that Besant did not fully understand that her growing popularity within the Brahmin community, the likely inheritors of the administration of India if it achieved independent rule, was threatening to members of other, non-Brahmin communities. These other constituencies lacked the access, advocacy, and language skills enjoyed by Brahmins groomed by the British. Naïve about the political and communal realities of her assumed homeland, she voiced the rhetoric of the Theosophical Society, which understood India as one united nation and culture—not the case then, or today.[4]

Muthulakshmi Reddy

Dr. Muthulakshmi Reddy was one of many Indians whose lives were influenced by Annie Besant. Born of a *devadasi* mother into a middle-class family in the principality of Pudukottai in 1886, Reddy was attracted as a teenager to Besant's message of feminism. Reddy's education was exceptional for a woman in South India at this time. Encouraged by her socially progressive father, she became one of the first women in South India to enter the medical profession. She founded the Cancer Institute in Adyar, among other remarkable accomplishments. Dr. Reddy became an example of *devadasi* girls raised in modest and mainstream middle-class lifestyles at the end of the nineteenth century. She married a physician and raised a family in Madras.

In 1927 Muthulakshmi Reddy, by then a member of the Madras Legislature, introduced a bill favoring the prohibition of *devadasi* dedication in temples, which would amount essentially to the abolition of the *devadasi* community structure. In the service of this cause, Reddy made pronouncements about the *devadasi* that, especially given the prominence and credibility lent by her own heritage, were destructive to the traditional artistic community. In their sweeping generality and reference to immorality and the scourge of prostitution, Reddy's arguments reinforced in the public perception harmful stereotypes that abounded in the Madras of the 1920s.

The perception of *devadasi* women as prostitutes had been encouraged by the rhetoric of the Anti-Nautch movement that began in Madras in about 1880. Anti-Nautch advocates used the word "prostitution" for what they perceived as "social depravity and moral corruption in general,"[5] which certainly included the profession of dancing and the existence of matrilineal families headed by unmarried women.

In fact, prostitution was *becoming* a problem in the traditional matrilineal community, by then largely impoverished as a result of the loss of royal patronage and the decline of standards of practice and audience tastes. The increased incidence of prostitution in the *devadasi* community affected a relatively small number of women. However, no real effort to address the root cause through effective social action was ever attempted, and the entire community became the object of disdain, neglect, and disenfranchisement.

Reddy's eventual assertions of the equivalence of the family and social conventions of the *devadasi* community with prostitution, the basis for her most notable political action, rose not from inside the *devadasi* community, as has sometimes been implied. Rather, they reflected the new social consciousness of pre-Independence India to which she had attached her political advocacy.

In this context arose the question of who were the proper custodians for the artistic and philosophical heritage of South India. This discussion began and was sustained first at the expense of the traditional professional artistic community, and subsequently to the detriment of the traditional practice itself. The role and independent social status of the traditional dancer had been persistently attacked for several decades. Now branded as degenerate, many *devadasi* families sought to suppress their identity and establish new lives, hidden in the larger community.

When Muthulakshmi Reddy introduced the Prevention of Devadasi Dedication Bill in the Madras Legislature in 1927,[6] the *devadasi* community organized the Deputation of the Devadasis of the Madras Presidency, also called the Madras Devadasi Association. The Association's members included Vina Dhanammal; her daughters Rajalakshmiammal and Lak-shmiratnammal; Bangalore Nagaratnammal (who later founded the now-famous Tyagaraja Aradhana in Thiruvayaru); Salem Lakshmi Ammal; Salem Thyammal; Meenakshi Ammal; Doraikannammal; Mylapore Gauri Ammal; and the Association's president, Jeevaratnammal Kalyani. Seeking a way to oppose the powerful efforts of Muthulakshmi Reddy in the Madras Legislature, members of the deputation distributed handbills on the steps of the Legislature's Assembly building, expressing their dismay and anguish to the members of the Assembly. The Association also sent a letter to the Law Member, Sir C. P. Ramaswami Iyer, protesting against the legislation. At his request their letter was expanded into a full-fledged "Memorial of the Devadasis of Madras Presidency," a document of more than ten pages.

In the document the *devadasis* described themselves as "guardian angels of dance and music with a devotion that bears comparison with the ardor of the pundits reading Vedas in preference to modern pursuits." They asked for help in perpetuating the historical Hindu world view and their place in it: "Give us education — religious, literary, and artistic — so we will occupy once again the same rank which we held in the past. . . . You who boast of your tender love for small communities, we pray that you may allow us to live and work out our salvation and manifest ourselves in *gnanam* [knowledge] and *bhakti* [devotion] and keep alight the torch of India's religion amidst the fogs and storms of increasing materialism and interpret the message of India to the world."

After the meeting with C. P. Ramaswami Iyer, the Association expanded its membership and held meetings with *devadasi* groups in towns around the Madras Presidency, who wrote resolutions against the proposed anti-dedication legislation and sent them to the government. But the movement dissolved in 1928. Many men from the community (who stood to benefit from changes in inheritance laws) opposed dedication, and some *devadasi* women who were not artists (and who would benefit socially from dis-association from the stigma placed on their community) also supported the legislation.

Ironically, after all the agitation, the British Madras Presidency Government, consistent with its policy of noninterference with Hindu tradition, did not act on the proposed legislation.[7] The law initially proposed by Dr. Reddy, the Madras Prevention of Devadasi Dedication Act, was not to pass through the Madras Presidency Legislature until 1947. Meanwhile, however, in 1928 Dr. Reddy revived the matter in the form of an amendment to other legislation; in 1929 that amendment was passed, prohibiting performance of both dance and ritual movement in temples by *devadasis*. Dr. Reddy was still not content. In 1932, inflamed by two high-profile *devadasi* dance perfor-mances in homes during that year and a public performance the year before, she wrote a letter to *The Hindu*, an influential and popular Madras English language newspaper, insisting that dance be banished everywhere. Her letter ignited a public debate that was later said to have spawned a revival of interest in bharata natyam.

It is documented that there were still hundreds of hereditary dance families in Madras about 1915. However, the popularly accepted account of the circumstances surrounding the traditional community in the 1920s was that, in the words of the activist lawyer and supporter of traditional dance E. Krishna Iyer, "The dance art in India as a whole went into oblivion in the later part of the nineteenth century and the first quarter of the twentieth century, chiefly as a result of British rule in India."[8] American dance pioneer Doris Humphrey stated the same misconception from the perspective of a non-Indian modern artist: "The world-wide movement in the last twenty-five years [before 1958] to save the ethnic dance accounts for thousands more participants. In all parts of the Occident and the Orient, especially in India, the neglected and often decadent state of the native dance has been a subject of concern to all kinds of people: artists, anthropologists, government officials and cultural societies. As a consequence, not only were these dances rescued, but thousands of young people were and still are taught the dance heritage of their countries."[9]

Dancers popular in the early 1920s were recognized variously, but emphasis was on their virtuosity in "pure" dance. Swarna Saraswati was described as having expressive eyes and dancing *abhinaya* she learned from Mylapore Gauri Ammal. She danced to a wide repertoire, but her music was "awful," one critic said. Varalakshmi was slim and fleet-footed; Shankaran described her *tillana*, a lively composition that today concludes a traditionally formatted concert, as a "thrillana." The Kalyani Daughters, who performed duets, were among the most famous of the traditional dancers. Jeevaratnammal, the younger of the sisters, was highly regarded for her mime. Her sister, S. Kamalambal, a pupil of Baroda Kannuswami Pillai (Kandappa Pillai's *nattuvangam* teacher), had precise footwork, according to Dhanammal's daughter Lakshmiratnammal, from whom Kamalambal learned vocal music.

Vinabhashini and her daughter Raya danced duets in 1921. Vinabhashini was past sixty then but said to be rhythmically strong in her dancing. Vinabhashini's adopted daughter, Bala Ammal, also danced duets with her mother. Muthu Kanammal used to dance *"Viriboni"*[10] *varnam* in three different speeds. She was famous for her sure-footed movements; the walls were said to tremble when she practiced, causing the neighbors to complain whenever she danced at home. Mylapore Gauri Ammal complimented her footwork but commented that her *abhinaya* could be a little vulgar.[11]

There were other dancers, too, who competed for the modest rewards available to professional artists. Many were teachers; some left Madras for Delhi, Bombay, Hyderabad, and other parts of India to start schools and build followings of their own. Some remained in Madras to perform occasionally into the 1950s. Several of the generation preceding Bala recalled seeing her dance, including Pandanallur Sabharanjitam, Swarna Saraswati, and Hamsadamayanti.

CROSSCURRENTS

The recollections of dancer and musician K. Bhanumathi shed light on several aspects of South Indian dance in the 1920s and 1930s. Bhanumathi spoke with Bala's cousin Sulochana in 1990.[12] The famous dancer had begun lessons when she was seven and had her *arangetram* at the age of ten, under Papanasam Vadivelu Nattuvanar (from the village of Papanasam near the town of Kumbakonam). She then studied with Shanmukha Sundaram Nattuvanar.

Bhanumathi performed until she was twenty-seven. She recalled that in 1932 E. Krishna Iyer introduced her to an American woman who offered her a two-year contract to perform in the United States, promising great success. A "big story," said Bhanumathi. She also acted in films, including *Jaleja*. Acting and dancing in films were opportunities that opened up for the traditional community as the new technology matured into commercial entertainment. Bhanumathi was serious competition for Bala during the early 1930s; her mother had learned vocal music from Jayammal, and several of the pieces Bhanumathi danced were from Bala's repertoire. Bhanumathi could sing as she danced, which was the norm at that time.

She commented on the general standard of music: "There was a time when the music for dance was not too wonderful. The old *nattuvanars* did not sing properly. But Jayammal's music was very different. For all the others music was a black star. I sang for myself when the music was not up to par.... I saw Bala whenever I could. She had great *bhakti* and reverence. I feel no one else danced like her, either before or after her."[13]

Bala's early education was rigorous and, after the incident when she was enticed with chocolates to dance in the classroom, entirely under her mother's control. In the evenings, after her dance sessions, Bala worked on music with her mother, as she did sometimes with her grandmother. Her mother arranged for Tamil and Sanskrit teachers to come to the home and tutor her. A *mridangam* player taught her rhythmic skills and theory. Bala learned *padams* from Vina Dhanammal and from her aunt Lakshmiratnammal.

As part of the training to perform *abhinaya*, Jayammal always insisted that Bala observe everyone she met with great care — their facial expressions, their changes in mood, the strain and stress of emotions and their expression. This careful observation, when coupled with an understanding of the dramatic situation and complete absorption by the music, laid the ground-

work for Bala's sensitivity and greatness as an actress. It is sometimes said
that it is not possible to teach *abhinaya*, or expressive dance, but the masters did. "When I began my career I found dance teachers giving more importance to *nritta* [the rhythmic, abstract aspect of dance], neglecting *abhinaya* totally," Bala said. "As a result, the art of dancing tended to become a matter of mere mastery over technique; thereby, the real essence of dance, which is to give expression to life's moods in its variety, stood ignored. Seeing this I strove hard to give impetus to this forgotten art, or should I say, I wanted to give life to the art."[14]

Music from the North

Nayak records from the seventeenth century cite North Indian music as an influence on artistic practices in the Thanjavur court — an influence reflected in the use of *ragas* and *talas* of the north in compositions, and in the inclusion of instruments from the north in ensembles.[15] The music of the north was highly valued by families associated with the traditional practice, including Balasaraswati's family and her teacher's family.

The origin of the song form *tillana*, sometimes ascribed to a mid-eighteenth-century composer named Virabhadrayya, is a case in point. Bala said that her teacher claimed the *tillana* was North Indian in origin. Some agree, observing that the *tarana*, a North Indian song form that was popular in the Thanjavur court in the mid-eighteenth century, evolved into the *tillana*. There are, at the same time, eleventh-century Thanjavur temple inscriptions referring to *tillana*. Whether or not there is a musical or choreographic interconnection seems to remain unresolved, and perhaps most conclusively makes the point about the transparency of cultures and language barriers in historical India.

Balasaraswati's home in Georgetown was a meeting place for North Indian musicians, who would visit the house when they were in Madras for concerts. Often they would request that Dhanammal play for them, and in return, they would perform for Dhanammal. In that way Bala was exposed to numerous powerful and influential musicians from the north. In 1932 Jayammal took Bala to hear Abdul Karim Khan sing at the Kinema Central Theatre, and Bala fell in love with his music. Abdul Karim Khan had a large following in Madras, including many regulars at the Chettiar house where Bala played and gave her first informal recital, and he had taught Jayammal's sister Lakshmiratnammal. Throughout her life Bala heard and respected many other North Indian musicians, including Siddheswari Devi, Kesarbai Kerkar, Amir Khan, Ali Akbar Khan, Bismillah Khan, and Enayat Khan and his son Vilayat. Bala later learned music in the North Indian *khyal* style and seamlessly incorporated it into her performances. Her singing, with its sweeping phrasing, was clearly influenced by *Hindustani* music. She developed a profound understanding of the North Indian interpretation of certain *ragas*, earning the respect of the *Hindustani* musicians she admired most.

The opportunities for performance during the 1920s and early 1930s were scattered throughout the region, in villages such as Manargudi and Papanasam, in towns such as Kumbakonam and Chidambram, and in cities like Madras, Hyderabad, and Mysore. Artists performed in temples; at fairs; and, in spite of the campaigns against the presentation of dance in homes, at private functions such as weddings and family celebrations. There were those who were not swept up in the reformist movement. That audience was for the most part made up of connoisseurs, and the hereditary artist had demanding expectations of her audience. "The scope allowed for the imaginative faculty in bharata natyam makes it an art not to be passively appreciated and assimilated by the spectator, not even intellectually comprehended but, rather, to be perceived through artistic imagination bordering on intuition."[16] As time went on Bala longed for that audience; occasionally she found it.

However, in general the majority of the new urban audience knew very little about what they were to witness in Balasaraswati's dance, or to hear in the music that accompanied the dance. Some have argued that it was not until Balasaraswati's performance at the newly formed Madras Music Academy in 1933 that she was noticed by the socially prominent Madras audience. Others disagreed, saying that Bala was well known and performed frequently before then. Most of those performances were probably in private homes. In any case she was performing frequently enough that, at Kandappa Pillai's instigation, the concert presentation underwent important changes between Bala's *arangetram* in Kanchipuram in 1925 and her first performance sponsored by the Music Academy eight years later.

Kandappa Pillai as Revolutionary

Changes in South Indian performance venues and audiences necessitated changes in the performance presentation. Kandappa Pillai had been a great admirer of Vina Dhanammal, and it was her sense of refinement in music that was reflected in and distinguished his ensemble. The modifications introduced by Kandappa Pillai are significant for what they tell us about the processes of change within the traditional artistic community. Authenticity in bharata natyam became an issue for debate when the art form became detached from its creative source, but the controversies raised within artistic communities themselves are of a different sort. They are descriptors of the process of change of a traditional practice within the confines of its own integrity—within the aspects of the practice that seem to defy emulation and nonintuitive, self-conscious imitation.

Kandappa Pillai introduced a variety of changes, some of them imposed by the new social and performance environments, and some representing expansions of the traditional framework and material he inherited. His radical definition of the pure dance of bharata natyam was consistent with his family's legacy. This was the opportunity perceived and seized by Jayammal and Kandappa. The musical sensibilities defined by Dhanammal's family, the extraordinary musical repertoire of bharata natyam the family possessed and was expanding, and the remarkable cohesion of several artists from one family sharing a common musical core—drummers and dancers as well as melodic musicians—made possible a unique capability in performance. It may not be said that Jayammal and Kandappa intended to resurrect the practice as it had existed, although they may have had a strong instinct along those lines. They were simply acting out of an entirely contemporary urge to make new art. This was "tradition" at its most dynamic stage.

When Bala had performed her *arangetram* in 1925, the outdoor concert platform was illuminated with oil lamps. Each performance had a basic drone pitch that was made with a small bagpipe called *tutti*. In Bala's account, three or four male musicians in red or green turbans stood at the rear of the stage to her right, and the drummer stood behind her, drum slung on a sash around his neck and waist. As the dancer moved, the drummer would shadow the dancer's movements. In the traditional setting, this would mean not moving very far; dancers and their ensembles performed in confined or roughly defined open places. There was no concept of "using" a stage. In particular, the relationship of the dancer and the drummer was musically very close. At some times during a performance, the entire ensemble moved with the dancer. The musicians sang at a high pitch in order to be audible without amplification in large open spaces.

As concerts began to be performed in enclosed spaces, Kandappa lowered the pitch at which the drone was tuned, and therefore the pitch at which the ensemble performed, allowing himself and other male musicians in the ensemble to sing within a range better suited to the male register. This change also allowed Kandappa's performance of *nattuvangam* to be heard over the music of the ensemble without being too loud; customarily, the dance masters had to shout until they were hoarse as they performed *nattuvangam*. Kandappa also used a *tambura* for a drone instead of the raucous *tutti*, and having changed the pitch in the middle of the concert, he broke with convention and presented female singers in the second half of the performance.

During most of the 1920s Kandappa used several drummers on different occasions, including Munuswamy Mudaliar and Govindaswami. T. Kuppuswami Mudaliar became Balasaraswati's *mridangam* player during the early 1930s and was with her for the following fifty years. Kandappa Pillai replaced the *mukhuvina* with the flute and/or clarinet.[17] He had three fine clarinetists: early in Bala's career, on several occasions, the legendary accompanist Balaraman Naidu, who was from Mylapore Gauri Ammal's ensemble; later Kuppu Rao of All India Radio; and eventually Radhakrishna Naidu, who also had a distinguished solo career. The capacity to perform beautifully as both a soloist and a dance accompanist was rare, but Balasaraswati's musicians—including her brother Viswanathan, who began to perform with Bala in the 1940s—were also known for both. One of the vocalists in Kandappa's ensemble was Kanchipuram Ellappa Pillai, who would become Balasaraswati's *nattuvanar* following Kandappa's death in the early 1940s.

When Jayammal performed with the ensemble, Kandappa moved the musicians from a standing position behind the dancer to a seated position to the side of the dancer.[18] One of the reasons that he seated the musicians was out of respect for Jayammal and other women who joined her as accompanists, whom he would not permit to stand and sing on a performance platform. Kandappa refused to wear a turban, and no one else in the ensemble wore one. Turbans had traditionally been worn as a sign of deference to the royal family, but he objected to the extension of that deference to patrons who simply had the means to support performances. Kandappa also did away with the male musicians' upper-cloth, which had been appropriate dress in a temple in the presence of the image of divinity but was not appropriate for the performance platform. He replaced the upper-cloth with a shirt, the same garment concert musicians wore. There were critics who found these changes impertinent, but Kandappa would have expected that.

In traditional practice, at least into the 1920s, dance performances would begin with a composed section of drumming called *melaprapti*, sometimes accompanied by melodic instruments. It was short and called attention to the beginning of the performance. This announcement was necessary when the performance happened on the *mandapam* in a temple, where other activities could be expected to compete with the performance, but Kandappa felt it unsuitable for the concert stage. Another concert practice that has disappeared, and was disappearing when Bala started to perform, was the inclusion of a drum solo after the *varnam*. Kandappa choose not to follow the practice.[19] Instead, he added *raga alapana* (an improvised solo *raga* exposition) between the *varnam* and the *padams* to follow. This convention eventually gave way to an intermission, a concession to impatient and restless audiences.

For Balasaraswati, the performance of the pure dance element of bharata natyam, as with the narrative aspect, was an act of devotion. It was not the content of the dance, but rather its execution, that made it devotional. Bala claimed, "There is a purely rhythmic side to bharata natyam in which there is no portrayal of sentiments, scenes and events, but only the delicate and dexterous display of rhythmic patterns with no lyrical text. The rhythmic dance is devoid of sensual movements. It is a world of art all its own. Art as art is of the spirit and, therefore, itself divine without needing to describe

the divine. So here too the artist and the audience feel the spiritual orienta-
tion of dancing."[20]

Nattuvanars would compose to the capacity of each student; certainly no other student of Kandappa's performed the same material that he composed for Bala. She became the vehicle through which Kandappa could express the most demanding of his rhythmic ideas, a unique, powerfully formed and executed conception of the exactitude of rhythm and form. His rhythmic compositions were guided first by musical principles, and the dance was forced to conform. Bala often complained that Kandappa would have had to dance his compositions himself in order to understand the difficulties they posed, given the demands of the style itself and his distinctive musical imagination.

In the early twentieth century many musicians, including Kandappa Pillai and several others who were included in the audiences at Vina Dhanammal's Friday concerts, were changing their approach to the performance of rhythm. Kandappa established several conventions. The most outstanding was his approach to the compositions called *tirmanams*, which reflected the changing sensibilities of musical performance by his contemporaries, such as Naina Pillai and Kandappa's mentor Pakkiria Pillai. Another innovation was that while a *tirmanam* was performed, the music of the composition into which the *tirmanam* is set continued. (A convention had developed to stop the music during a *tirmanam*.) This continuation of the music was then and remains unique to Kandappa's style. In the style Kandappa shaped for Balasaraswati, the dance is subservient to, and becomes majestic because of, music.

There is some controversy within the families closest to Kandappa Pillai about the degree to which his approach to bharata natyam was revolutionary, and whether or not he altered the Thanjavur Nattuvanar family style. Within a hereditary style, diversity is the result of unity. An example of the difference in perspective this creates is the way Thanjavur K. P. Kittappa Pillai, Kandappa Pillai's cousin, responded when asked about the differences between the Pandanallur style and the Thanjavur style. Meenakshi Sundaram Pillai, Kittappa Pillai's grandfather, lived with his family in Pandanallur, and the Thanjavur style is named for the practice in the Thanjavur court codified by Meenakshi Sundaram Pillai's grandfather and great uncles. Kittappa Pillai's comment, and that of others within the professional community, was that they were all the same style. The traditional community did not consider differentiations among the various localities where the dance was taught to be stylistic differences. Kittappa Pillai's family represents both the Pandanalur and Thanjavur styles of bharata natyam and they do not distinguish between the two. The same is true of Balasaraswati and her family.

Balasaraswati stated that Kandappa Pillai did make radical changes, which she attributed to his musical sensitivity. She was referring in part to changes in the presentation of the dance and musicians and changes in the items that were and were not selected for performance. In addition, Bala's performances attracted drummers to the audience, and for Bala's brother Viswanathan this had to mean that Kandappa's ideas were revolutionary. Viswa declared, "Kandappa Pillai must have deviated from the old traditions. It was not like that [before] in the matter of *tirmanams*. If it excited all those musicians, he must have done something that was not done before. It was intellectual, and beautiful; that was the beauty of it; he did both, without ruining the movements, forms and patterns." The changes in musical content were seen as completely consistent within the family style, and were easily identified.

The traditional artists' recognition of a need to regenerate the dignity and artistic integrity of bharata natyam from within the professional community predated later efforts by the nontraditional community to "save" and advocate for music and the allied arts. Interestingly, the debate over the acceptability of bharata natyam to those outside of the professional community revolved more and more around the traditional performer, not around the art form itself. Within Bala's family, and for others within the traditional community, the real issues were the refinement of the art and its survival. It could only be from intimate knowledge of the art form that true improvement could be made.

The Anti-Nautch Movement

The initiative to discourage the traditional practice of dancing is often referred to as the Anti-Nautch movement. *Nautch* is thought to be a corruption of the Hindi word *nac* and the Sanskrit word *natya*. The term was probably first used by the British and initially applied to parlor dancing that became popular in Calcutta during the 1830s. But the word *nautch* became confused with a term for dancing in general, including the entertainment practices within the Mughal courts and the Mughal tradition of courtesanship.

The word *nautch* also came to be used interchangeably to describe the art practice descended from the Thanjavur court, perhaps because bharata natyam also was being presented in homes. Balasaraswati said that she always knew that the art was not to blame if some *devadasis* had misused it for entertainment and personal income; she emphasized that those dancers had incomplete knowledge and training.

Among the most potent ideas superimposed on Indians' self-concept by the British and European colonial and missionary presence were beliefs about the nature of female sexuality in nineteenth century Europe, where women who were forced to work to survive were unlikely to marry. They became factory workers, domestic servants and employees of work convents. A few, who had the talent, appearance, and capacity, became dancers. But like their unmarried counterparts in other occupations, dancers in the West were perceived as sexually untamed and available to young men of the bourgeoisie and aristocratic communities.[21] There is little doubt that by the mid-nineteenth century these imported beliefs powerfully influenced Indians' changing attitudes about traditional performers of dance and the need for reform of the laws that had previously protected the hereditary artistic community.

Before the end of the nineteenth century, leaders of the Anti-Nautch movement attempted through petition to mobilize opposition to the practice of secular dance, long before formal legislation prohibiting temple dedication was proposed and finally, in 1947, enacted. Some journals and newspapers in Madras supported the Anti-Nautch effort. These publications initially concentrated on building public opinion against attendance at nautch parties and against inviting *devadasis* to bless events in homes with their art. Even though the detractors' knowledge of history of the performing arts was questionable, the movement gained momentum in the early part of the twentieth century, largely stripping Tamil Nadu of a dance tradition.

In the early 1930s the Anti-Nautch movement came to loggerheads with the new, forward-looking perspective that characterized a provisional executive group who had formed the Madras Music Academy in the late 1920s. Concurrent with the continuing Anti-Nautch movement, there emerged a movement urging the "revival" of traditional dance, arguing that the art could and should be rehabilitated.

In April 1932 Bala had performed in a hall in the Triplicane section of Madras under the sponsorship of the Indian Cultural Bureau. A review in *Sound and Shadow*, a magazine focused on the performing arts in Madras, reveals the controversy of the time. A "direct result of the huge hubbub recently created by the iconoclastic [Anti-]Nautch social reformers has been a rise in the frequency of bharata natyam performances," the reviewer noted.[22] The traditional community was beginning to appear in the mainstream, after fifty years of defenseless ignominy.

In December 1932 the Anti-Nautch reformer-versus-revivalist controversy played out in the Madras press. The debate was precipitated by the public performance of dance at the felicitation ceremony of the incoming premier of the Madras Presidency's government. Having introduced a bill to prevent performances by traditional artists in temple environs in 1927, Dr. Muthulakshmi Reddy was enraged. E. Krishna Iyer (the activist lawyer who fought for the preservation of the traditional dance practice), who claimed much later to have been waiting for the opportunity, responded in the press that appropriate reform was demanded and that certainly dance should not be used by women to flaunt their wares for prostitution as was claimed by reformers. But, E. Krishna Iyer asserted, the dance itself must be saved. He pointed out that fifty years after the initiation of the Anti-Nautch movement, the dance practice had nearly been destroyed, but the social scourge of prostitution — the ostensible reason for the defamation of the traditional community — flourished, as it did everywhere and always had. The problem was not the *devadasi* community. It was the scourge of poverty.

In the debate between Muthulakshmi Reddy and E. Krishna Iyer that followed in the press, support favored E. Krishna Iyer. In sympathy with E. Krishna Iyer's perspective, *Swarajya*, an English-language daily newspaper, urged that the dance itself be practiced by girls of "respectable" families. In the end, E. Krishna Iyer wrote an open letter to the president of the Music Academy, in which he argued, "In view of the great interest created in the subject of Indian dancing by the recent controversy over the Anti-Nautch movement, and the precarious existence of the art, as evidenced by the difficulty of the Academy itself to find proper exponents of art at the present day, I request you to bring the matter to the notice of the music conference for the necessary lead in the matter and action thereon."[23]

According to E. Krishna Iyer, writing many years later, it was he who precipitated the public interest in bharata natyam through the debate carried out in the Madras press in December. His own description of the rise of the opportunity for the revival of bharata natyam is notable. He acknowledged the presence of families who still performed the hereditary art and who "preserved [the arts] tenaciously against odds.... The great opportunity ... culminated in December 1932 in a . . . controversy between [E. Krishna Iyer] on the one hand and an Anti-Nautch leader on the other [Muthulakshmi Reddy] over the nature of bharata natyam and the advisability of its revival.... That controversy greatly helped to open the eyes of the public all over India to the richness and greatness of the art and its importance in the scheme of national life as also to the need for its speedy revival and encouragement. In the result, a huge and unprecedented wave of popular enthusiasm spread over the country."[24]

There is no doubt about the significance of E. Krishna Iyer's efforts to promote bharata natyam, but from within the traditional community it was difficult to see his role from the same perspective. E. Krishna Iyer never claimed to be an advocate for the performers themselves. From inside the tradition this was at the very least completely perplexing. E. Krishna Iyer creates the impression that the performance of bharata natyam had collapsed. Yet the dance form had current hereditary performers. In the early 1930s there were more than a dozen dancers well enough established that they are remembered today; there would have been others whom we have forgotten. New opportunities did begin to open up for professionals who struggled to make a living. In addition to the staple performances at weddings and other family celebrations, there were benefit concerts, political gatherings, and an evolving network of *sabhas*, the cultural organizations that were emerging in Madras and that sponsored performances of music and dance.

Balasaraswati had developed a reputation for her music, and in 1932 the Indian Fine Arts Society in Madras honored her with the title *Gana Saraswati* for music. At the age of fourteen, Bala was shy about her performance of music, intimidated by the overwhelming presence of her mother and grandmother. "She was in such awe of Jayammal and Vina Dhanammal that though she was such a fine singer, she did not sing while dancing until [later] in her career. She had a very fine, but thin voice, and when asked why she did not accompany her mother, she would laugh and remark, 'If I did, it would be like a mouse squeaking beside the roar of a lion.' It took us [and others] years of gentle persuasion to goad her into singing alone sometimes, and once she [began] . . . she [truly] captivated the audience, [once] again with her superb musicianship. Organizers [began to arrange] a special hanging mike for her whenever she danced, so the public could hear her beautiful voice. Her admiration for Jayammal's music was so great that, while [she was] dancing [with] Jayammal singing, she would suddenly freeze and gape in wondrous delight at her mother's soaring, and divine, music. When she realized what [she had done] she would suddenly break into a hearty smile, shake her head with a satisfied, 'well done' [expression] at her mother, then continue dancing. To her, music was supreme and dance was subservient to [it]."[25]

Chinnayya Naidu

As Bala's career developed, Jayammal was the producer, manager, and accompanist of all performances. She set the programs, arranged concert dates, hired and dismissed musicians, and eventually cooked for the troupe on railway-station platforms as they traveled to and from concerts outside of Madras.

In 1932 Jayammal arranged for dance legend Chinnayya Naidu to teach Bala improvisation in *abhinaya*, in part to fulfill the challenge of reestablishing the place of *abhinaya* in the practice of bharata natyam. Because Chinnayya Naidu came from Andhra Pradesh, it is erroneously assumed that he performed and taught *kuchipudi*, a traditional practice from Andhra Pradesh with a predominant component of *abhinaya*.[26] *Kuchipudi*, in a revised form, became a popular inclusion in many modern bharata natyam and Dances of India programs, beginning in the 1950s. In the 1930s, however, the dance form was virtually unknown even in Madras. Bala credits Chinnayya Naidu with teaching her "to develop improvisation, by singing short phrases and with very few cues, [and asking] me to state which *nayika* [heroine] was appropriate."[27]

Viswanathan recalled, "I was very, very young, a little boy, and I remember Chinnayya Naidu came to our house. He was kind of darkish, a short man, balding with totally grey hair. He didn't shave every day, so his grey hair would stick out. He was very soft-spoken. . . . He was very kind to all of us—and very sweet. . . . I knew his wife and daughter. They used to come for a long time after Chinnayya Naidu died. They came to visit Jayammal and Bala."[28]

Around 1932, as part of her education Bala memorized the *Amarakosa*, the Sanskrit lexicon of all the names and attributes of the Hindu pantheon. She drew on this inner resource throughout her life, constantly surprising her audiences with her seemingly endless references to details of the lives of her heroes and heroines.

Madras Music Academy

The Indian National Congress, formed in 1887, was the first organized political body that opposed British occupation; it eventually grew into the Congress National Party at the time of Independence. During the rise of nationalism, beginning in the 1880s, and most actively in the 1920s and 1930s, Indians began to reach across regional and ethnic boundaries, seeking a common agenda for a unified government. To facilitate resistance to colonial power and the evolution of self-rule, the nationalists sought to reduce divisions caused by different languages, community structures, and social conventions.

In 1927 the Indian National Congress had held its annual session in Madras, a departure from the custom of holding it in the north of India. Performing arts enthusiasts from Madras had met the year before to voice their intention to establish an institution to promote "classical" music. That same group saw the opportunity to hold an All India Music Conference concurrent with the political meetings. The group established a reception committee; U. Rama Rao chaired the committee, and E. Krishna Iyer and P. Sambamoorthy were committee secretaries. Beginning on December 24, the committee ran an eight-day conference—the first of its kind in the south. At the end of the conference, the meeting passed a resolution urging the formation of a permanent institution to promote the performance of music. In this way the Madras Music Academy came into being. According to E. Krishna Iyer, funding for the new institution came from what was left of the budget to conduct the All India Music Conference.

Rama Rao, E. Krishna Iyer, and S. Rajagopalachari served as a provisional executive committee with a mandate to organize and initiate the work of an academy of music. Inaugurated in August 1928, the Madras Music Academy held an annual conference during Easter week for several years, later switching the date to the Christmas holidays. The mission of the Music Academy was to educate the Madras audience and to "help to inaugurate a period of ascendancy in the history of South Indian music and raising the art from its present oblivion." The mission statement went on to add that music had an important place in the national life, echoing sentiments of other leaders of rising nationalism, including Rabindranath Tagore.[29] It was not until three years later that the Academy added dance to its mission.

The Madras Music Academy first sponsored a concert of bharata natyam in 1931. A report of the performance appeared in that year's Academy *Journal*, in which the use of the term "bharata natyam" is notable. "An entirely new line was struck this year by the Academy commencing its season with a bharata natyam performance by [the] Kalyani Daughters of Thanjavur. It has almost become a fashion nowadays to condemn the Indian Nautch and look askance at it. In our view this condemnation is least deserved. Such of those as have feasted their eyes on the performance of Krishna Bhagavatar of Thanjavur of *Harikatha* fame, will testify to the grandeur of this art and expose the utter unworthiness of the criticism that is leveled against it. We are glad that the performance served as an eye-opener to those who came to witness it. We hope that in the days to come, public opinion will veer round and give unto *Abhinayam* its proper place."[30]

Setting out on a mission to codify the oral tradition of *karnatic* music, the Academy created an Experts Committee to review existing practice and compare the performances of traditional artists with the rules set down in historical theoretical descriptive texts. Based on this comparison, the Experts Committee propounded a consensus viewpoint on numerous *ragas*, deciding on the pitches of each scale and their hierarchy, the proper ornamentation, characteristic phrases, and other aspects of practice by the traditional performers.[31] In response to the committee's recommendations, and revealing an inevitable tension between practice and theory, a highly regarded musician commented years later to Viswanathan, "Let them say what they will, and then we will play what we want."

By the early 1930s the spirit of reformation pervaded both music and dance. A review of a concert given by Mylapore Gauri Ammal in April 1933 at the Mylapore Sangitha Sabha described the competitive environment for dancers and commented on the weaknesses in performance that some members of the community of traditional musicians themselves deplored. The reviewer, G. K. Seshagiri — who wrote under the pen name Bhava Raga Tala — characterized Gauri Ammal as "one of the few bharata natyam artists of this city. Unlike the Kalyani daughters of Thanjavur who have more of *attam* [dance], but are poor in *abhinaya* [mime], Miss Gowri [*sic*] is deficient in neither. . . . Another point is the very good accompaniment on clarinet [by] Mr. Balaram [*sic*]. In this respect, the Kalyani daughters who danced December 28, 1932 for the Madras Music Academy conference are very deficient, the accompanists being intolerable."[32] Gauri Ammal's singers were Jayammal and her sister Lakshmiratnammal, and the famed clarinetist Balaraman Naidu was also Balasaraswati's instrumental accompanist.

Early Performances

In July of 1933, at the age of fifteen, Bala was introduced to a larger audience in Madras when she performed at Sangitha Samajam under the sponsorship of the Music Academy. During his distinguished career the writer K. Chandrasekharan referred time and time again to Bala's performance that July. On that first occasion, he commented, as did critics after him, that Bala was not particularly beautiful, but that when she began to dance her eyes and pearl-white teeth dominated and transformed her face.[33] Chandra-sekharan found her costume, which consisted of a traditional full-length pajama and a half *sari* tucked in at her waist, unattractive. He also remarked on and commended Kandappa for singing only half of the concert, allowing Jayammal to sing the *padams* during the second half. He noted that the musicians were seated and described the *nattuvanar*'s deference to Jayammal.

Indicating a level of familiarity with hereditary bharata natyam unusual for a critic writing in 1933, Chandrasekharan commented: "Her uncompromising exposition of the *patakam* and *tripatakam mudras* [hand gestures], [was] totally different from the unaesthetic demonstration of latter-day dancers. The rigid stance with fully stretched arms for the *mudras* lent true flavor to the *nritta* tradition of Bala." Chandrashekaran went on to describe the musical accompaniment of the *abhinaya* portion of the performance. Years later, remembering that concert, he wrote: "[Bala] had rare good fortune to have her mother Jayammal who had a very powerful voice . . . with great grace and melody she could render songs which she had inherited from her mother, Vina Dhanam of great reputation. . . . That was the first occasion that I came to witness a performance by Balasaraswati. . . . That was a wonderful day for me. Before that performance I had no real idea what bharata natyam could be."[34]

In that "prerevival" period there were clearly performance practices that included "good" performers and "bad" performers of the traditional style of dance, just as there were both knowing and unknowing members of the audience. Following Bala's July 1933 performance, another review by Bhava Raga Tala appeared in the magazine *Sound and Shadow*. The critic seems again to intent on educating a growing audience for bharata natyam. The review refers to "imperfect artists" who do not understand what it is they sing or which emotional theme they are interpreting, and critiques such artists' inability to keep their attention on all four aspects of dance: melody, rhythm, object, and emotion. "The dancer must keep the song in her throat, show an object or concrete idea through symbol or gesture with her hand, keep the *tala* or rhythm with her feet and portray emotion through her eyes and brows, the most expressive parts of the face," the critic wrote, paraphrasing theoretical descriptions of dance. "The lay public cannot readily understand this part of the dance by merely watching. This is that area of the art called 'conventional' or 'a meaningless show of hands' by indifferent critics and reformers."

Not for the last time in Bala's career, however, the same reviewer also found fault with her dance. Interestingly, the reviewer praised Bala for her pure dance but criticized her *abhinaya* and her music, which suffered from her fear of singing in front of her mother. "As we began, the artist Bala is not gifted with beauty of form. Although she does show *bhavas* [intense emotion] for the eyes and *arthas* [purpose or intent] for gestures, this section of bharata natyam called *nritya* [expressive dancing] is not very good in this artist. For, in the best bharata natyam music and the dancer singing herself, keeping the *tala* with her feet, is essential to retaining the beauty of the art. Yet Bala sings quite low and very little. In her concert she rarely sang and when she did join her accompanist, her own mother, for one or two *padams* she could be heard by only a few people."

In the same review, Bhava Raga Tala comments on the music, the source of Bala's *abhinaya*. "Bala's mother sang a number of beautiful Telugu *padams*. These form a fine feature of Bala's dance. You can find them nowhere else. She [Bala] was taught and learned the *abhinaya* for many of the *padams* of which Vina Dhanammal is the greatest storehouse. This was the major part of the program and was very entertaining. Two Tamil items were included, and rendered through *abhinaya*. Her kite dance at the end was also very good. . . . On inquiry I learned that Bala knew the *abhinaya* for a few Sanskrit *slokas* [poetic verses in praise of God] but did not perform them, having danced until nine and [being] already weary." Bala had just turned fifteen. She was accustomed to being wakened very early in the morning; the day of and the day after a concert were no exception.

The review continues: "The artist's *nritta*, the dance with *tala*, was well done by Bala. She was given good training in this branch. Besides some well-known items in this branch, where *swaras* [musical notes] are set in a type of *sahitya* [words, meaning in this instance that the names of the notes were sung as solfège] to specific *talas*, an additional item was performed at the end.[35] A very limited section of this part of Bharata's art lives only with the *devadasis* and *nattuvanars*." The public mood is building, the review says; this is beautiful art, and there is much more of it to be unearthed.

The spirit of this review is suggestive of the new future that revivalists imagined for dance. "Special attention must be drawn to this branch [pure dance] by the public, for this is dance, pure and simple, involving no mysterious gestural symbolism, and could be well exploited by all those interested in physical education for young girls in our schools. These dances combine beauty and art with physical exercise."

The review concludes: "All is well with this art if every small source preserving it is diligently sought and each available bit is learnt, new reforms and small modifications, following the basic principles and technique of Bharata, can be created. All that is necessary is to take it up and issue it in modern get up. All we need do is create a modern edition of it. More dainty dress, softer *tala* and more delicate ankle bells are small things which will greatly increase the appeal of this art."[36] The suggestions for improvement of the practice and the call for the creation of a modern edition were an expression of a new public engagement with dance by the audience evolving in Madras.

This review dates from 1933, two and a half years before a revised version of bharata natyam was first presented in Madras. The review articulates no concern with vulgarity or lack of classicism. The major complaints that the writer raises about this fifteen-year-old dancer are that she does not sing when she dances and that she should improve her costume. At this time the dismissal of dance as being beneath the dignity of respectable people was widespread, and many who saw Bala for the first time expected that they would witness crude performance art. But the acceptance of bharata natyam slowly worked its way through the Madras audience. The tone of the Bhava Raga Tala review was echoed by others, the scholars and leaders of the community, as they discovered bharata natyam through Bala's performances. Through these tentative expressions of acceptance and endorsement by the intellectual elite, bharata natyam caught the attention of a burgeoning middle class.

"Krishna ni Begane Baro"

Bala commented toward the end of her career, at her Presidential Address at the Music Academy in 1973: "In my lifetime, I have seen the art of bharata natyam rescued from ignominy and restored to a position of respect and worldwide interest. Those who supported me in the past often had to justify and support the whole cause of dance. Tiruchi V. Kalyana Sundara Mudaliar, the great Tamil scholar, once arranged my concert at a wedding.[37] Among the invited guests were T. K. Chidambaranatha Mudaliar [known less formally as T. K. Chidambaram], and writer and critic R. Krishnamurthy; both had been opposed to bharata natyam and were surprised to see that it was being presented at a wedding. They were converted by the performance; they realized the sophistication and integrity of the art-form and that it could be performed tastefully at a high level, providing a legitimate artistic and even spiritual experience if approached in the proper way."[38]

The Tamil weekly *Ananda Vikatan* was the Tamil equivalent of the British magazine *Punch*. R. Krishnamurthy was the editor of *Ananda Vikatan* from the 1920s to the 1940s. He was a close friend of T. K. Chidambaram, and the two were among the leaders of the Tamil Isai (Tamil music) movement, which promoted the performance and teaching of Tamil songs. Also a distinguished novelist, journalist, and humanist, Krishnamurthy later started his own journal, *Kalki*, in 1940 with singer M. S. Subbulakshmi and her husband, Sadasivam. Known as Kalki, he also wrote about dance and music under the pseudonyms "Aadal Paadal" and "Karnatakam." Krishnamurthy became one of the people who would make their way through

the twisting streets of Georgetown on Fridays to hear Dhanammal's *vina*.
He became an ardent supporter of the family's music, and Dhanammal's
music was the subject of many of his articles. "The name 'Dhanam' means
'auspicious' and 'wealth,'" Kalki wrote of his first visit to Dhanammal's
house in Georgetown. "There are two different types of wealth: first, the
wealth of learning; second, material wealth. Dhanammal has none of the
second but all of the first. She is an aged blind lady, there's a quaver in her
voice. But true musicians still go to her house in Georgetown, not a proper
place for her."[39]

During the early 1930s a singer named Hayagreevachar from Dharwar in
Karnataka, whose style was closely aligned with Abdul Karim Khan's, visited Kanchipuram to see Naina Pillai. While there he met Jayammal's older
sister Lakshmiratnammal. She invited him to the family's home in Madras,
and he visited on more than one occasion. He taught Lakshmiratnammal
and Jayammal "*Krishna ni Begane Baro.*" In 1934, with Jayammal's singing,
Balasaraswati first performed "*Krishna ni*" during a concert at Rasika Ranjani Sabha in Mylapore.

"*Krishna ni Begane Baro,*" which is sometimes misunderstood to be a
padam, became legendary. In April 1984, writing two months after Balasaraswati's death, N. Pattabhi Raman published an article in the *Journal of
Sangeet Natak Akademi* in which he described a version of her first performance of the piece.[40] Presumably relating an account that had been given to
him, Pattabhi Raman wrote that Bala performed "*Krishna ni*" as a matter
of sudden inspiration, jumping onto the stage as her mother sang the piece
at a concert in Madras. In reality, as Bala told her daughter, Lakshmi, and as
Lakshmi told her son, Ani, the piece was very well rehearsed before the performance, and there was nothing sudden about its appearance on the program. Jayammal did not sing separately from the dance performance. From
an outsider's perspective the inaccuracy perpetuated by many retellings may
seem insignificant. But as seen within the family, Pattabhi Raman's description misled readers about how the family prepared performances, and about
how Bala's relationship to her mother affected her performances at the age of
sixteen. Balasaraswati would never have jumped up and appeared unexpectedly on stage while her mother was singing.

RENAISSANCE

T. K. Chidambaram is now regarded as one of the outstanding twentieth-
century scholars and critics of Tamil literature, music, and dance. After his
first exposure to Bala, Chidambaram launched an offensive of advocacy
for traditional bharata natyam and organized a "round table"[41] intellectual
forum at his home, where Bala performed *abhinaya* in an open courtyard in
1935. T. K. Chidambaram later claimed that that was the day when bharata
natyam was reborn. V. V. Srinivasa Iyengar, a retired High Court judge and

Studio portrait of Balasaraswati performing *adavu "Tha tei tam,"* 1934.

a guest of Chidambaram, was fascinated by the walk that accompanied Bala's expressive dance and is said to have exclaimed, "Leave the dance alone. What an unforgettable ambling gait!"[42]

One day in 1934 T. K. Chidambaram took several friends to meet Bala and her family. These friends included Mrs. Harijan Sastri of Madras, whose talented daughter Lakshmi later married Uday and Ravi Shankar's brother Rajendra. (Lakshmi became well known as a singer, under the name Lakshmi Shankar, and eventually moved to Los Angeles.) On request, Bala obligingly performed *abhinaya* for one or two *padams*. This was Mrs. Harijan Sastri's first introduction to the fine interpretation of bharata natyam honed by Kandappa Pillai, and the experience led her to enroll her daughter,

Studio portrait of Balasaraswati performing *adavu* "*Tei ha tei hee*," 1934.

Lakshmi, in the school formed in Almora by Uday Shankar several years later.

Toward the end of December 1934, Bala performed a concert of *abhinaya*. She was accompanied by her mother, who sang; her cousin Abhiramasundari on violin; and another woman, named Hamsadamayanti, who played the *mridangam*. From reviews it appears that the all-*abhinaya* program was seen as unusual, but within the traditional community it was not viewed so. It was the power of the family's great musical heritage that enabled the unusual concert format. Several years later, when Bala was diminished by ill health and had lost her *nattuvanar*, the all-*abhinaya* concert became her standard practice for some time.

Padam

The *padam* is a music genre that found perhaps its most powerful expression in the compositions of Kshetrayya, who was born in about 1595 in Muvva, in the Krishna District of Andhra Pradesh. Kshetrayya, as legend has it, was born into a pious Brahmin family, but in his adolescence he became a bohemian, a breaker of social conventions with a passion for music, poetry, and dance. Kshetrayya is said to have been initiated at some point into a *bhakti* [devotional] practice of Gopala Mantra, through which he experienced visions of Vishnu's incarnation as Krishna. In this ecstatic state he extemporaneously composed thousands of lyrics (documented by his devotees), embracing an exhaustive depiction and exploration of sacred and secular love.[43] Some accounts describe Kshetrayya as traveling with a devotee who accompanied his music with dance; others say that he was joined by dancers who lived in the communities where he stayed and composed during a twenty-year pilgrimage from temple to temple throughout Tamil Nadu in South India. In any case, the dance that accompanied Kshetrayya's music was *abhinaya*.

Kshetrayya, who lived in the century before we find Papammal in the Thanjavur court, was invited into the court of the Telugu king Vijayaraghava Nayaka (1633–1673) in Thanjavur. His artistic reach extended to the poets of the court of the seventeenth century, and the court poets embraced and emulated his *abhinaya pada* style of poetic writing in their work. Although Kshetrayya, in his composition of *padams*, reflected a time-honored tradition of devotional art, his compositions and their content and delivery were "modern."[44] Kshetrayya introduced into his poetry the ambiguity of imagery of God and king; both were addressed simultaneously in his poetry. This led to a controversy that surfaced in the definition of the reconstructed form of bharata natyam in the 1930s and 1940s.

In the music and imagination of Kshetrayya, we see why Balasaraswati used to refer to the precursors of the Thanjavur Quartet as "bards." As a measure of Kshetrayya's musical impact, Subbarama Diksitar, son of the great composer Mutthuswami Diksitar, complained in his mid-nineteenth-century commentaries on *karnatic* music about changes in *raga* and interpretation that had crept into the usage of Kshetrayya *padams*, one hundred and fifty years after their composition.[45]

It is not so important *that* Bala thinks of the forebears of bharata natyam as bards, but rather *why*. Consider the following paraphrased account: Around 1638, Kshetrayya was invited to a scholarly assembly consisting of both Saivites (Hindu followers of Siva and a school of philosophy) and Vaishnavites (Hindu devotees of Vishnu and a school of philosophy) that was being held in Chidambaram. On one side of the hall in Chidambaram, attending an image of Nataraja (a form of Siva), was a group of Saivite priests and scholars. Opposite them sat a retinue of priests and scholars attending to an image of Vishnu's form as Lord Govindaraja of Kanchi, whom this group served. In this hall, called Chitsabha, one may still find these two images of Siva and Vishnu. A challenge was made to Kshetrayya: He must "sing extempore a lyric in simple conversational style as addressed by a courtesan simultaneously invoking both Nataraja and Govindaraja, but the subtlety

of the lyric must bring out the most sublime truth of Vedic knowledge. The
challenge further stipulated that the superficial meaning and the esoteric
import must be brought out without word-splitting, pun, or any such verbal
jugglery. The lyric composed by Kshetrayya was sung extempore and when
it was being sung, his friend Mohanangi, or some close disciple danced then
and there interpreting the import of the song."[46]

The story of Kshetrayya at the Chidambaram assembly offers an insight
into the erudition, tenor, and competitiveness of the Thanjavur court —
into the depth of both the understanding of the nature of the creative process and the content of the tradition, as expressed by both challengers and
the challenged — that hints at why the bardic tradition meant so much to
Balasaraswati.

Modern Dance in the West

Among those who influenced the reconstruction of "classical" dance in
India were dancers from North America and Europe who were, ironically,
renegades from their own cultures — dancers who set out to redefine the
form and social place of dancing in their countries of origin. They shared
a fascination with "exotica" and invented expressions of "Oriental" dance
that had become popular with Western audiences by the late 1800s. Interest
in the Orient, at both the serious intellectual and popular levels, peaked at
the end of the nineteenth century. It was part of an anti-modern sentiment,
a rejection of the industrialized world in favor of the perceived transcendence of the ancient teaching of Asian traditions. "To try on the trappings
of different non-European cultures was itself seen as a way of breaking with
European art and forging a new distinctively American culture."[47]

The Chicago Columbian Exposition in 1890 was organized on the occasion of the 400th anniversary of Columbus's "discovery" of America.
The Exposition's primary purpose, unsettling in retrospect, "was to bring
together the fruits of man's material progress. Everything imaginable was
on exhibit — not only the achievements of Western civilization, but the better to show these off, life-size models of the more backward cultures of the
world."[48] The Exposition's midway was described as a "hurly-burly of exotic
attractions: mosques and pagodas, Viennese streets and Turkish bazaars,
South Sea Island huts, Irish and German castles, and Indian teepees." A
performer called Little Egypt, the prime attraction at the Persian Palace,
danced the "hootchy-kootchy," a "suggestively lascivious contorting of the
abdominal muscles" that was "almost shockingly disgusting" and hugely
popular.[49] The vaudeville circuit was the place to see the earliest of Western
impressions of "Oriental" dance.

By the beginning of the twentieth century several artists were performing impressionistic dance distinct from ballet that became the precursor of
modern dance. Performing both in garden parties of the well-to-do and in

art theaters in the United States and Europe, the pioneers included Loie Fuller, Maud Allen, Isadora Duncan, and Ruth St. Denis. St. Denis developed an impression of the dance of India, which she presented in 1906 in a solo dance named *Radha*. It was St. Denis's belief that "each gesture and pose should objectify an inner emotional state," and she conceived *Radha* as "an elaborate network of spatial and gestural symbols signifying emotional states, such as rapture, despair, or inspiration."[50] By 1914 St. Denis had partnered with the revolutionary male dancer Ted Shawn, and together they evolved what she called "aesthetic dance."

The connection between specific emotional states and the gestures and poses of dance allowed, in the Western conception, for dance that was not strictly defined by the rules and grammar of form, and by the constriction of the social concerns that bound ballet in the eighteenth and nineteenth centuries. The impression of narrative dancing from India was that it was driven more by whim and "feeling" than discipline and structure. Although that assessment of Indian dance was incorrect, the perception of an expressive dance based on emotion led to a revolution in dance in the United States.

As the twentieth century progressed, several Indians also contributed to the rise of new dance in the West. Uday Shankar began performing in Europe with Anna Pavlova in 1923; Ram Gopal first performed in the United States in 1938; Mrinalini Sarabhai first danced in the United States and Europe in the late 1940s; Indrani Rahman first danced in North America in the 1950s. A Western dancer named La Meri built a career in New York, showcasing versions of dance from all over the world. She introduced Ram Gopal, having seen him in India in 1936. Ram Gopal had learned something about different forms of traditional dance and was perhaps the first Indian to publicly perform several regional styles in one program. He toured extensively as a soloist and with his company of dancers before and after World War II, and he performed at Jacob's Pillow Dance Festival in 1954 and at the Edinburgh Festival in 1956.

In 1921, a young graduate of the University of Minnesota at St. Paul named Esther Sherman arrived in New York from Minneapolis. She had begun her performance career "at the Lake Harriet Canoe Carnival riding a canoe she had decorated with crepe paper to resemble a Dutch windmill."[51] She had performed in hometown theatrical productions of Russian folk dances and solo dances, variously costumed as a Greek nymph, a sultry Egyptian, and an Indian dancer, "Todi Ragini." Sherman had developed a passion for the dance of India, and after marrying a political refugee from India who had been a chemistry student at the university in Minneapolis, she moved east and began to find her way on the dance circuit in New York. Her performances of "Indian" dance were a success, and by 1926, having renamed herself Ragini Devi, her transformation was total. In one interview she told a reporter that she was a Kashmiri of high birth and had spent her childhood

sequestered in secret sanctuaries in India and Tibet, learning "dancing that
cannot be seen and music that cannot be heard by the untrained ear."[52]

The newly self-invented Ragini Devi traveled to India in 1930, where she sought out and learned dance from Mylapore Gauri Ammal and studied with a dancer in the court in Mysore. Having been invited by a charitable organization in Bangalore to participate in a performance of dance and music, she assembled a costume and performed the same routine she had presented in New York. She added a whimsical kite dance (a version was part of Balasaraswati's early repertoire) she had learned in Mysore, began each item with explanation and a demonstration, and charmed her Indian audience. Being broke but determined to dance, and encouraged by the audience response, Ragini Devi devised a presentation format for a reconstructed version of bharata natyam.

Dance "Reconstruction" in India

At the same time that Jayammal was beginning to realize her ambitions of bringing the hereditary performing arts of South India to new standards, others from outside the professional community began to conceive claims to the legitimacy of new interpretations of the traditional practice, based on iconographic and textual representations and descriptions.

Rabindranath Tagore had given prominence to the idea that the performing arts of India should be learned as a part of the establishment and perpetuation of a national identity. His belief was not that the traditions of India should be preserved as presumably they might have existed previously, but rather that a new art would grow under the influence of India's ancient heritage. This became a role central to Santiniketan, his family's institution in rural Bengal. Rabindranath Tagore's father, Devendranath Tagore, initially founded Santiniketan in the 1860s as an *ashram*, a place of contemplation, in the countryside about 175 kilometers north of Calcutta. Rabindranath Tagore opened a school there in 1901, and from this simple beginning Visva Bharata University, now internationally renowned, was established in 1921. By the 1930s Santiniketan had become a magnet for intellectuals and artists from all over India.

Tagore maintained close ties to the Theosophical Society, many of whose members expressed the same belief about the connection between India's heritage of tradition and the shape of its cultural future. During the twentieth century other organizations of various philosophies had participated in the attempt to create a less regionally defined performance art form. These organizations wished in part to advance contemporary Indian cultural expression and artistic traditions in anticipation of independence from a century of colonial occupation.

Annie Besant and the Theosophical Society offered a rallying place for a new intellectualism and a place to consolidate protest against British occupation. The British had proved that they were willing to use violence to subdue the Indian political movement resisting foreign control and cultural repression. This willingness, along with industrialized technology and commercial strength, was the root of British power throughout colonized Asia and Africa. But by the 1920s Annie Besant, along with tens of thousands of Indian and international members of the Society, had become a powerful lobby that helped bring global visibility to India's independence movement. The leader of the Theosophical Society since 1907, Besant also became, in 1917, the first woman president of the Indian National Congress. Besant's advancing political position enhanced the Society's national visibility.

There was a countermovement resistant to the rise of indiscriminate modernization, seeking instead to advocate for the dignity of the existing arts and intellectualism. One of its earliest voices was that of Max Müller, the German Sanskrit scholar; other voices would include the traditional performers and their advocates. The Justice Party, which supported a more regional focus on Tamil culture, was no less concerned with independence, but represented different values and concerns. But these efforts would not be successful.

Uday Shankar

The famous Russian-born ballerina Anna Pavlova embraced ballet with recast themes, costumes, and dramatis personae. Having toured globally, including several visits to India beginning in 1921, where she developed her own impressions of the dance techniques of the subcontinent, she settled eventually in London. There she met Uday Shankar, at that time an art student and later a legendary modern Indian dancer. In 1923 Anna Pavlova brought Uday Shankar into her troupe. She began to present elaborate dance productions with more "authentic" representations of Indian dance. When Anna Pavlova first presented her interpretations of Indian dance, she cast the role of the dancer as one would for ballet.

Uday Shankar was a Bengali Brahmin who grew up in the north of India. He was educated in Bombay and London and lived in Europe (primarily in England) from 1920 to 1930, becoming an expatriate, a Europeanized Indian. Early in Uday Shankar's life, at the turn of the nineteenth century, his father, Shyam Shankar Chaudhury, was a Sanskrit scholar living in Benares, and there Chaudhury became a follower of Annie Besant.[53] Uday Shankar, who was the older brother of sitarist Ravi Shankar, performed a version of dance fusion representing the various dances of India. He eventually performed with musicians playing Indian instruments, although he freely acknowledged that in his early performances his accompanists had no training, nor had he.

But Uday Shankar did little to dissuade his non-Indian audiences from considering him entirely authentic and classical in his rendition of dance.

He performed with Anna Pavlova in 1923 and 1924, then formed his own
company in Paris, becoming a sensation in France, Germany, England, and
the United States during the 1920s and 1930s. An aspect of his appeal was
that he represented the idea of "attempting to modify [traditional dance]
into a new, indigenous dance-theater . . . whose vocabulary and idiom were
modern." Part of Shankar's value to his manager, Arnold Meckel, who conducted several European tours with Shankar during the 1920s, was that he
had, Meckel believed, inherited an art form from which he was creating new
art.[54] The self-conscious transformation of traditional and vernacular-based
Indian art forms into rejuvenated, modernized, and urbanized art forms
appears to have taken hold on the stages of Europe and America as it did
in India.

Anna Pavlova toured Asia with her productions, and after her first visit
to India in 1921, toured in India in 1929 without Uday Shankar. She was
surprised at the response to her dance creations in India, and she claimed
thereafter that she believed she was destined to perform "Indian" dance.
Her performances must have caused some sensation, but she may have un-
derestimated how ingratiating an Indian audience and host might be when
a notable Caucasian artist representing the finest of European traditions
appeared entranced with India.

E. Krishna Iyer commented that when Pavlova visited India on tour in
1929, "she found the condition of its dance art as pitiable with few responsible or cultured people to take interest or enthuse over it." He declared
that a great cultural gap was looming in India.[55] The gap he described was
between "new" India and the traditions of historical India. It was eventually Uday Shankar who, in the early 1930s, set out to self-consciously bridge
that gap. The productions of Shankar's shows were highly regarded for their
technical perfection. In Europe he had worked with Pavlova's technicians on
staging. He would sit in the auditorium while she was rehearsing her company, considering it an extraordinary opportunity. He absorbed everything
he could — the lighting, the staging, and especially the costumes — and incorporated everything into his own programs. His work also reflected his
highly developed skills in painting and design. The concepts he absorbed
had a pervasive influence on the "dance renaissance" that was to begin soon
after Shankar's first visits to India in 1932. It was he who suggested that
bharata natyam should be presented outside South India, in other parts of
India and on tour worldwide. Balasaraswati's performances were among the
first to make hereditary dancers from different regions of India aware of
each other's artistic practices.

In 1933 Uday Shankar performed in Madras for the first time, giving
three concerts at the Elphinstone Theatre.[56] Uday Shankar's brother, Ravi,
was performing as a dancer in the troupe. The night before Uday Shankar
was to give his first performance in Madras, Balasaraswati was presented by

the Music Academy, having been sponsored by the Academy the previous month. Her first concert had not attracted a large audience but had elicited an enthusiastic critical response. Her second concert was very well attended. Uday Shankar, who had met Bala a year earlier in her grandmother's house, was there. His public endorsement after her performance was that Bala was "superb." He asked those present not to "expect any such grandeur from my performance tomorrow at the Museum Theatre [in Egmore]."[57] Bala's daughter, Lakshmi, recalled that Uday Shankar told Bala he was particularly "smitten" with her *adavu* "*tai dhi dhi tai.*"

This public acclaim from an international celebrity focused more attention on the fifteen-year-old dancer who had just caught the Madras public's eye for the first time several weeks before. It also provided an opportunity for audiences to see new dance recast from traditional forms that was achieving success in the West juxtaposed with new dance of from the heart of the traditional professional community. Among those who wrote about Bala's concert was Bhava Raga Tala, and the tone of his review had shifted from tentative to assertively enthusiastic. Suddenly bharata natyam had a history worth claiming, the reviewer suggested. "On Saturday, the 26th of August, Bala gave a performance of bharata natyam under the auspices of the Madras Music Academy at Gana Mandir. The hall was full, and a large number of people of both sexes witnessed the concert with admiration. It is a fortunate sign that our society has slowly begun to take a greater interest in bharata natyam. The tradition of bharata natyam goes far back into history, and I can say with authority that the dance, as it was done then and is now performed by our *devadasis*, is genuine and one hundred percent pure Indian classical dance.... Other forms of Bharata's system, such as dance and dance dramas, are available in Tamil land, yet this *sadir* is the national dance art of Tamil land, so to speak."[58]

In another review, R. Krishnamurthy (Kalki) wrote: "The performance was attended by Uday Shankar, known throughout the world as the famous Indian dancer, and his French partner. Afterwards he said it was a marvel, the best he had ever seen and that he had not seen such dancing anywhere else. Such is the opinion of Mr. Uday Shankar, whose own dance was shown thrice in Madras city, where high society paid exorbitant prices, who added that, compared to the bharata natyam he saw at the Madras Music Academy he personally knew very little.... Greater exponents of the art than Bala do exist. But who shall rouse the indifferent public? Who shall convince the ignorant, and those much more harmful spirits, the prejudiced?"[59]

PERFORMING IN THE NORTH

Immediately after Bala's August 1933 concert, Uday Shankar asked Jayammal if Bala could join him on his next world tour. Years later Lakshmi claimed that Bala wanted to go, but that both Dhanammal and Jayammal refused, Jayammal stating her concern that Bala would not be recognized on her own artistic terms in the midst of ensemble performances of deliberately more overstated dance, presumably more interesting for the "typical" Western audience. Ravi Shankar reported, however, that the issue was left open. In any case, Uday Shankar set out immediately to arrange for Bala to perform in Calcutta — partly in the hope, Ravi Shankar later recalled, that Bala might then accept the offer to tour with him. Ravi Shankar also reported that his brother arranged for Bala to dance in a private performance in Madras on the day following her concert, for which Uday Shankar paid her the generous fee of one hundred rupees. Bala performed a pair of *padams* at the hotel where Uday Shankar was staying. It was reported that a film was made at that private performance, but what it contained or where it went is a mystery. At the time it must have seemed insignificant. Uday Shankar soon after asked Haren Ghosh, his manager at the time, to set up Bala's first performances in North India.

During his brother Uday's tour of the south in 1933, Ravi Shankar first saw Bala perform. "I had met Bala even earlier, in 1932, when we went to Madras for the first time. This was at the house of her grandmother, Vina Dhanammal, who was almost blind at that time. We met the grand old lady a number of times, but one particular evening we all went to her very old and small house, and Vina Dhanammal played the *vina*. I still remember what she played. . . . I remember clearly that while listening to her, I had tears in my eyes, which goes to say that she had something very special, apart from technique. There was so much feeling, soul and emotion; that could bring tears to people's eyes. This is what Bala herself inherited."[60]

While in Madras, as part of the campaign to convince Jayammal to allow Bala to tour with him, Uday Shankar hosted a dinner for Bala and the troupe that had performed with her. An account of this event highlights the fact that in many ways the lives and lifestyles of many Indians had not integrated the mannerisms of the colonial population. This accommodation was the domain of an exclusive few who had had the opportunity to learn European languages, to travel abroad, and to be a part of the administration of British India. An essential component of becoming that community of people with whom the colonists were comfortable was to adapt to the colonial mindset and decorum. The aspects of life in which members of the traditional community did not understand how to conform to colonial behaviors — simple things like sitting at a table, drinking from teacups, and using tableware — became social liabilities that were leveraged against them.

T. Shankaran enjoyed repeating the story of Uday Shankar's dinner party. "After first seeing Bala's dance at Gana Mandir, Uday Shankar hosted a dinner for Bala, Kandappa, Jayammal, Ellappa, Kuppuswami, and myself at [the] Hotel Connemara [a well-known colonial hotel]. None of [his] guests were accustomed to the table manners for a fork-and-knife dinner. I tried

Uday Shankar, Balasaraswati, and T. Shankaran, Calcutta, 1934.

to wriggle out asking for only *idlis* [rice cakes] and coffee. Uday Shankar reminded us the dinner menu would never include *idlis* and the like. Meekly we stuck out our necks to be greeted with plates of boiled green peas and forks. I closely glued my eyes to Uday Shankar's strategy and the others followed my footsteps.

"The fork and the green peas proved slippery. My effort with bated breath to eat at least one by forking one pea to my anxious lips only resulted in many a slip between the fork and my lips. The servers watched us with dismay and soon removed the untasted food. All of us, except the host and his friend Haren Ghosh, were starved and frustrated. The dinner was a big joke of the day, with constant comments from Kandappa for a month. He never forgot to taunt Bala and his colleagues about the grand dinner which starved them. Life-long, Kandappa used to quip at invitations for lunch or dinner: 'with fork and knife?' "[61]

Bala, Jayammal, and everyone else in the family held in high regard Uday Shankar; his wife, Amala; his brother, Ravi; and all of his other family members. They did not judge Uday Shankar at all for his lack of artistic purity but instead admired him for his progressive artistry and his success. They respected him for his public humility as he encouraged Bala in the Madras press. They became close friends, and Uday would stay with Jayammal and her family whenever he visited Madras.

Following Uday Shankar's introduction to Balasaraswati in 1933, impresario Haren Ghosh began to make arrangements for her to dance outside of

Madras. Until then, Indian regional dance had remained regional. India was
still divided by language and cultural diversity, it was thought, and the performing arts could not become India's pride until they had migrated from one part of India to another.

It was arranged that Bala, along with several other distinguished artists, would perform at the All Bengal Music Conference in Calcutta in December 1934. Bala's concert took place in a building called Senate Hall. There Bala met Ali Akbar Khan who, as a twelve-year-old boy, was accompanying his father, Allaudin Khan. She also met Satyajit Ray, and again saw Ravi Shankar. She was particularly impressed with the *kathak* dancer Achchan Maharaj. She was surprised that a man was dancing a traditional form. Viswanathan remembered years later that she was astonished, and added a memory of his own. "I was very young, and here comes a man on the stage who is obese—a big tummy. Once he began to dance I couldn't [think of] him as a big, fat man. He was only divine and beautiful, dancing. His feet were like playing the *tabla*. His dance was simply incredible."[62]

Satyajit Ray saw Bala for the first time at that concert. "This was the first performance of bharata natyam in Calcutta and I happened to be present in the audience, as a schoolboy of about fourteen or fifteen. That was my first exposure to bharata natyam. Everybody was tremendously impressed with this very young girl who performed with such grace, charm and confidence. I was very struck by this completely new kind of dancing. I'd never seen anything like that before, the music and everything. It was already announced in the papers beforehand that this was a new kind of classical Indian dancing; and to be performed by one of its best exponents."[63]

Ravi Shankar recalled the concert: "It was something out of this world, even more so because Rabindranath Tagore, the great poet, was there, sitting in one corner of the stage on a special chair. I remember Bala was so excited.... Immediately she became like a star because it was the first time people saw pure bharata natyam performed, and by the best person. Actually my brother had asked her, and she was willing, to join my brother's troupe, and travel with us to Europe. To finalize this was another reason she came to Calcutta, but something happened (some people didn't want her to join the troupe) and she didn't. But during that period of several weeks she was in Calcutta, we became such good friends. We played and ran about; I saw that side of Bala which very few people have seen.... Since that time, our friendship has remained very strong, and I loved, admired and respected her very much. Later on when I left dancing and became a musician, I met her again after a long time."[64]

While the troupe was in Calcutta, they stayed with Venkataraman "Chinnanna" Sastri, whose nephew, Shambu, a musician and film actor, was a family friend. Shambu taught *"Jana Gana Mana Ati,"* a song of Tagore's, to Bala and Jayammal, and they began the process of recasting the tune in

T. Balasaraswati in concert at All-Bengal Music Conference, Calcutta, 1934, with T. Kuppuswami Mudaliar and K. Kandappa Pillai. Note that the musicians were standing at this point in the performance. Small tables support the two *tamburas* used to provide drone accompaniment, replacing the more portable but less melodic *tutti*. When Jayammal sang during the second half of the performance the musicians were seated to the side of the stage.

the family style, giving it their traditional shape of melodic phrasing and specific forms of ornamentation. Shankaran commented in a letter, "I don't remember if Shambu taught it the way in which Bala and my mother were singing." Viswanathan added in an interview, "I was very young when they were learning. They sounded totally different from when I heard it later on. [They] interpreted it into the South Indian style. The question is: the original tune. Was it closer to the way Jayammal was singing, in the Bengali style?" Later the tune would be performed by brass bands, and at Independence in 1947 it was to become the national anthem.

In 1934 Bala performed *"Jana Gana Mana Ati"* in Calcutta; two years later she would perform the song again in Benares at the All India Music Conference, and once more at the Indian National Congress Exhibition in Madras. These were the first, and likely the last, times that the song that became the Indian national anthem would be danced in *abhinaya*. Viswa commented on what would be, in retrospect, a historic event. "We didn't know [the song] would become the national anthem at that time, in the thirties. When they performed in Calcutta the audience liked it so much. They were thrilled to hear South Indians singing a Bengali song."

In the house next door to Venkataraman Sastri's house, a college principal named Ram Pai lived with his two teenage daughters, who were Bala's age. Pai's daughters were fascinated to meet Bala and spent as much time as they could with her in Sastri's small house. In their play, they taught Bala a *bhajan* in Hindi[65] attributed to the female saint Mirabai. (A *bhajan* is a type of devotional song, often with simple text and melody, and expressing love for the divine.) Pai's daughters also taught Jayammal and Bala, at their request, some folk songs in Bengali. Jayammal and Bala worked together to interpret these songs in the *karnatic* music style, identifying a *raga* that matched the feel of the melody of the songs. They explored the exposition of their choice of *raga*, emphasis on certain resting tones, and other considerations involved in the setting of music with text according to a vast, intuitively executed set of conventions and rules. Bala's ensemble would perform these pieces at the end of the concert. Audiences in the north loved the inclusion of the Bengali *bhajans*, and Bala's concerts were wonderfully received.

Many years later Viswanathan described the process of musical transformation and maturation: "In her early days, thirty or forty years ago, [Bala] worked on *padams* and *javalis* which had become obsolete. In fact, we worked together to revive those rare songs. I was impressed with her incredible sense of beauty and her aesthetic sense for music. As we worked I noticed that she would concentrate on a particular song for several weeks. We exchanged ideas concerning the ways in which a word or line might be interpreted. She thought constantly about that material without actually practicing the song or the *abhinaya* for the song. However, she would sing the song we were working on. I think she was trying to decide how variations should be interpreted in the music, what contour — shape — would best communicate the meaning of each particular word or line, through the music. After a long exploratory period, examining the possibilities of a song, it would appear in her concerts where we could, finally, see it performed. This process applied to lyric items only, not compositions with *nritta*.

"It was incredible how she communicated her ideas through *abhinaya* and music, blending [them] both so beautifully. This was the reason she was considered one of our greatest dancers, because of her ability to blend music and dance. We took a particular word or line and tried to see how we could interpret it musically to convey the meaning of the song; how many varieties could you have, how many ways you might express it through *abhinaya*; or, take the musical phrase and see how it influenced the dance musically and vice versa. Finally, we would decide certain things about contour, range, all sorts of things related to dance. We would then arrive at certain conclusions. Still, she thought of other possible variations. So many surprises would appear in a concert that were amazing."[66]

In subtle ways the ensemble's rhythmic practice was also being influenced by the tour in the north. The emergence of regional dance in a national context and the exposure to the broader wealth of India's performance traditions were exciting to Bala, Jayammal, and the rest of the ensemble, including Kandappa Pillai. Kandappa's *tirmanams* were rich with variation in the sound of the syllables he composed. According to Jayammal, Kandappa observed the *taranas* (a North Indian song form) and their accompanying *bols* (rhythmic syllables performed by *kathak* dancers), which included phrases such as "*Ganapati*" (the name of the benevolent form of Siva as the elephant god), rather than "*ki tha ta ka*," a typical South Indian rhythmic phrase. He incorporated some of these syllables in his own *nattuvangam* during concerts in the north.

Everyone in Balasaraswati's ensemble responded to the demands of the change in the audience as they first traveled outside of the south. The capacity for adaptation, and the comfort with inclusion and modification of material used for performance that is by some definitions "borrowed content," characterized Balasaraswati's family's artistic culture. And the capacity to understand another culture became a great strength for all of the members of Balasaraswati's family when they began teaching in the West three decades later.

By the 1930s a hybrid sensibility prevailed in popular Indian culture. Some performers catered to audiences' appetite for anything "English" or "foreign"—a taste that was a carryover from the previous century. (At the Thanjavur Palace a collection of Serafoji II's books, figurines, tableware, artwork, and many other objects from Europe remain on display.) Bala was very proud that when they adapted pieces from elsewhere in India, she and her mother did not alter their approach to music. Looking back at those years, Lakshmi drew a distinction between performing pieces in English and pieces in other Indian vernaculars. Her description reveals the rivalries common in Balasaraswati's extended family, sometimes expressed in caustic humor that must be understood in the context of the hereditary artistic family's effort to maintain the integrity of their practice and community. Lakshmi recounted, "Balamma told me she used to be very proud of her mother, because [Jayammal's sister Lakshmiratnammal] used to sing songs like 'It's a Long Way to Tipperary' and 'Twinkle Twinkle Little Star.' Bala would imitate how she sang these English songs." Lakshmi imitated her mother's shrill coloratura rendition of the songs as she told this story. "My Mommie used to get so carried away, in the middle of the night she'd be singing it for me." Lakshmi added that it was a different matter altogether when Bala would present a song of Tagore's like "*Jana Gana Mana Ati.*" "It's an Indian song, and the North Indian music [audience] already loved [it]. They had an association with hearing North Indian music like that. Going to North India [Bala and her ensemble] would put a North Indian *raga*."

In 1936, as a result of her appearance in Calcutta in 1934, Balasaraswati was invited to perform at the All India Music Conference at Benares Hindu University by Madanmohan Malavya, who was then vice-chancellor of the university. The audience in Calcutta had included several members of the Benares organization who arranged the conference. Tagore was there, and after the performance he presented a silk shawl to Bala's drummer, T. Kuppuswami Mudaliar—and asked Bala to present a private performance. In Benares, as it had been in Calcutta, this was the first occasion of the performance of bharata natyam. Bala danced with the same ensemble, but her older brother Srinivasan went as her chaperone rather than Shankaran. Tagore was reported to have been delighted.[67] Ragini Devi, the American who had been demonstrating and performing for several years, also made a presentation at the same conference in Benares.

In the *Indian Fine Arts Society Souvenir* magazine from 1948, E. Krishna Iyer refers to his having taken "Balasaraswati, a talented professional artiste in traditional Bharata Natyam to [Benares], where [my] discourses on the art and the dance by the lady artiste helped to bring home to the minds of North Indian connoisseurs also, the greatness, beauty and refinement of India's richest dance treasures."[68] Bala and Jayammal were stung by his claim that he was responsible for their appearance at the Benares conference, a claim that Balasaraswati categorically dismissed. I asked Bala's brother Viswanathan how it was that on several occasions this and other facts were changed or misrepresented, and he commented that it was a question, and had been for a long time, of who had access to and control of the press in India. There was no medium through which someone in Bala's family, or any traditional family, could refute the claims of E. Krishna Iyer and others of his public stature.

In 1936 Haren Ghosh arranged a concert for Bala at a music conference in Muzzafarpur.[69] "Though in a small and backward town in Bihar, this gave me immense satisfaction," Bala would later recall.[70] Bala considered this to be another of the five great concerts of her career. While traveling to Muzzafarpur, she was met in Surat by the distinguished North Indian musician Omkarnath Thakore. In that meeting he complimented her on her soulful music. South Indian music is thought by many to be a more cerebral, text-based tradition. To be met by Thakore and to receive this acknowledgment was an unusual and meaningful tribute to a young artist who had so much regard for the music of the north.

By 1935 bharata natyam performances by traditional artists were becoming accepted and encouraged. The credit for the change in public attitude was claimed by several individuals and organizations; but more significantly, the question was becoming who would now control the standard and teaching of both music and dance. In 1936 the *Journal of the Madras Music Academy* claimed, "The growing popularity of bharata natyam prompted the Music Academy . . . to take the initiative to call a meeting of representatives of various *sabhas* and associations in the city during the 1935 conference. The idea was to form a Council of Affiliated Institutions through which it could seek to ensure that the growing popularity of bharata natyam did not result in the seeping in of vulgarity." The meeting, however, failed to produce an agenda.

In addition to performing in northern India in 1934 and 1936, Balasaraswati also presented concerts in small cities and towns in southern India, especially throughout the Thanjavur District, where families who practiced the several dance and music traditions of the region still lived[1] and appreciated Balasaraswati's art. Although Balasaraswati's performances created acceptance in the north of dance and music from the south, they also contributed to the perpetuation of the performance of bharata natyam in the regions where it originated.

In the recitation and exposition of the Hindu epics and the philosophical, historical, and mythological content of ancient texts called *puranas*, popular expositors would not limit themselves to the words of the texts but would rather instruct and entertain the audience with commentary on a variety of subjects, including current local affairs. This was the material of traditional South Indian theater and of the *harikatha* minstrel tradition that became popular in the late nineteenth century. It was also the world of the traditional bharata natyam dancer in her performance of *abhinaya*.

In the hereditary practice of *abhinaya*, the dancer is a narrator, not an enactor, of a dramatic environment. The traditional dancer is fluent in evoking a roster of the types or categories of characters portrayed in the poetry—a heroine, a hero, and a go-between—which are appropriately cast for the mood and suggestion of the poetry and music. The dancer does not identify with the dramatic situations evoked or the attributes projected, but instead creates impressions of them. It is the discipline of a highly evolved concept of dramaturgy. Some have said that the dancer draws upon personal experience to create ideas in the performance of *abhinaya*. Although in some sense this may be true, it is not the dancer's actual experience that fuels the creative imagination of the traditional performer.

Balasaraswati commented: "The gestures used in bharata natyam must never be taken to be the gestures used in everyday life or in drama or in film acting. *Abhinaya* is as far removed from acting as poetry is from prose. No feeling, no emotion, no mood, no experience, no locale is portrayed in a self-conscious manner. They are all expressed in the suggestive language of imagination. Forceful contortions and violent movements are out of place in bharata natyam. Yet it does not simply portray the soft side of life. The deepest and weightiest of subjects are conveyed by suggestion more strikingly than in direct stage-acting. Dignified restraint is the hallmark of *abhinaya*. Even in the best of laughter there is a restraint on the mouth movement; even in the height of wonderment there is a limit to the opening of the eyes; even in the white heat of amorous sporting, the dancer has no use for movements of the torso but gestures only through the face and hands. It is this decency, decorum, and dignity that help to impart to bharata natyam its divine character. . . . The divine is divine only because of its suggestive, subtle quality. In *abhinaya*, though the artist and the audience have the direct inward experience of the divine, the outward expression which is responsible for creating that experience is only suggestively and subtly so."[2] The essence of the performing arts of India is suggestion. Lyricism is achieved through suggestion and the essential quality that suggestion brings to illusion.

During the 1930s, 1940s, and 1950s, Balasaraswati's art was at the center of a debate over the appropriateness of the narrative dance theme of human love, *Sringara*, on the modern stage. Had Bala stopped performing, the corrupted image of traditional bharata natyam as vulgar might have met no resistance. But she forcefully persisted. This aspect of the repertoire and *abhinaya* of bharata natyam was at the core of the art, she insisted. Bala believed that dancers were afraid to deal with *Sringara* because they did not understand or deliver it on the level for which it is was intended.

In Hindu culture the expression of the union of humankind with God is found throughout every aspect of the arts. There was no other reason for art-making. For a Hindu, mankind is female, and God is male. God is also understood to have a female principle, and the union of the male and female principles is an expression of the Infinite, the formless reality that remains when the innumerable forms of God made by man have been transcended. *Sringara* means literally "that which creates ecstasy." Mystical devotion and so-called "erotic" discourse are linked in the literature of all the world's religions. It is ultimately the universal recognition of isolation in union that the linkage seeks to reveal. We have no better means for understanding or experiencing the mystery of spiritual awareness and sense of isolation than by recognizing our own inexplicable complexities. These are most poignantly expressed through the directness and simplicity of human sexuality.

The theme of *Sringara* exists in Indian sculpture, painting, poetry, music, and dance, and pervasively in Hindu philosophy and cosmology. *Sringara* is an ancient concept that permeates the aesthetics of the Indian consciousness, and it is this generative theme and the rules that govern its treatment that may be described as classical. The poetry composed for bharata natyam was predominantly in *Sringara rasa*, the first of nine *rasas*, or "flavors," of aesthetics in the traditional arts of India.

From the perspective of the performer, dancing spiritually based *Sringara* compositions that refer to divinity as the object of adoration was the same as dancing secularly based *Sringara* compositions that make no reference to the divine and speak purely of human love. In the artistry of bharata natyam, human love and divine love are both expressive of devotion and surrender. In the *bhakti Sringara* tradition the soul yearns for union with the Absolute, represented (as they are in the lyrics and imagery of bharata natyam) by lovers, the *nayika* (heroine) and the *nayaka* (hero), guided by the help of the *sakhi* (friend, go-between, messenger) who Balasaraswati explained is the *guru* ("the one who removes the darkness").[3]

Balasaraswati was fully aware of a bawdy, irreverent quality to the repertoire of traditional bharata natyam. Although she was hardly prissy in her sense of humor in private, Bala was born into and raised in an environment of extreme refinement. It may be true that some performers of hereditary bharata natyam included the bawdy elements in their dancing, but Bala avoided them in concert, as did many other hereditary performers.

THE "REVIVAL"

Balasaraswati's refinement of the standard of the hereditary practice happened at the same time that there were calls from several directions for a new start. The resources — financial, political, and social — to achieve that start inevitably rested with families and organizations of privilege, who acted in the belief that the resurrection of the arts was their duty in a more inclusive national interest, transcending the regional characteristics of India and its people. They created institutions that were designed to replicate the role of the hereditary family, in effect becoming heads of new artistic "families." These new institutions became the mediators of standards and assumed the roles of repositories, purveyors, and perpetuators of the arts. An early example was the Royal School of Music founded in 1915 by the Wodeyar family in the royal court of Mysore. Throughout the 1920s most of the students there were from hereditary backgrounds, but the door was opened for nonhereditary students.[4] The Tagore family's establishment of Santiniketan in Bengal,

Uday Shankar's Performing Arts Centre in the mountain village of Almora in the north, and the Theosophical Society's foundation of Kalakshetra in Madras were other expressions of this revivalist spirit.

As some of the institutions built programs in the performing arts, including bharata natyam, they initially established connections to the tradition through hereditary teachers, whom they saw as providing a link to the traditional practice. Eventually, however, instruction in reconstructed bharata natyam was generally given by teachers who had learned the formal aspects of the dance within the institutional context. Out of the transition from family to institution arose a new concern for authenticity. The differences in Bala's dance were differences not in content, which is conventionally thought to be the definer of traditional versus nontraditional dance, but rather in the artistic process. It is *how* dancing is done that is a more suitable basis for distinction between hereditary and institutional dance than *what* the content is or *who* performs the dance.

Institutional learning was not intended to produce dissatisfaction with the "irrelevance" of the traditional form, but it did. A difference that characterized the reconstructed form of bharata natyam, in increasing measure, was the need and desire to alter the practice. An institutionally trained student may claim that he or she is maintaining a basic "traditional" structure, or that he or she is abandoning it, but the fact is that without the foundation of a family system of values, the student becomes focused on his or her personal perception of the art and its potential. This shift in the relationship between practitioner and the source of learning characterized the revived form of bharata natyam.

Rukmini Devi Arundale

Rukmini Devi, born Rukmini Shastri in the Thanjavur District in 1904, is regarded as one of the most influential of the developers, performers, and teachers of a reconstructed, modernized version of bharata natyam. Many see Rukmini Devi as the "rescuer" of the tradition of bharata natyam. She was introduced by Annie Besant to George Arundale, a colleague of Besant's, leader in the Theosophical Society, and political activist. Arundale and Rukmini Devi were married in 1920. He would eventually succeed Annie Besant as President of the Theosophical Society in 1934.

Rukmini Devi remembered seeing Bala for the first time at the Music Academy in 1933, after which she invited Bala to perform at the Theosophical Society in Adyar on the occasion of her birthday in 1934. "I invited her to my place, the Theosophical Society, to give one of the first performances, because I recognized she was talented," Rukmini Devi recalled.[5] At this concert Narayana Menon, who was to play a key role in Balasaraswati's acceptance in India, saw Bala dance for the first time.

The spirit that had characterized Theosophical Society cofounder Henry

Olcott's early revisionist work on Sinhalese Buddhism seemed to repeat itself fifty years later in Rukmini Devi's projection of a revised, pure, ancient, textually-based reconstruction of dance. Rukmini Devi made her debut in December 1935, when the public ferment over bharata natyam was an issue of several years' standing. The audience at the debut concert was invested in the principle being demonstrated by Rukmini Devi's performance; that is, whatever significance the performance assumed in later years, it was intended at the time to project the principles of Theosophy through what George Arundale called "The Fifth Interpretation." It would be simplistic to declare any single event or person involved in the reconstruction of bharata natyam to be causative. But the concept of the realization of a reconstructed, corrected, and revised "classical" dance style was consistent with the revisionary view of the Theosophical Society's founders — the founders' concept of the role of the arts in the resurrection of an "ancient," more essential, and "pure" Indian culture.

George Arundale wrote after Rukmini Devi's first performance: "And now to these four [the interpretations of previous Society presidents Blavatsky, Olcott, and Besant, and philosopher Jiddu Krishnamurti] would there seem to begin to be added a fifth, the interpretation of Theosophy in its aspect of Beauty, through the great Arts, through form and sound. We are at the beginning of a new era, both for Theosophy and for The Theosophical Society, during the course of which, while all other interpretations will surely grow in power and wisdom, the Beauty Aspect of Life will be much more definitely stressed. . . . We are hoping Theosophy as Beauty will incarnate in actual forms, so that we may no longer be confined to principles, but may perceive Theosophy through the dance, through music, through painting, through sculpture, through architecture, through ceremonial . . . showing the essential unity of life amidst a myriad divergencies of colours, sounds, gestures, postures: all in terms of Beauty. . . . And I venture to think that only those who are well acquainted with the science of Theosophy are in a position to perceive the nature of those essential principles of colour, of sound, and of form, which constitute the root-being of evolving life."

He went on, "I have reason to believe that Shrimati [Mrs.] Rukmini Devi will largely dedicate herself to this work, endeavouring to exemplify the great truths of Life especially through the medium of the dance. For many years she has been studying both in the West and in the East the fundamental principles of Art. She had the privilege of the friendship of one of the greatest of artists for all time — Madame Pavlova. In India she has for long been under the tuition of two of the greatest masters of dancing and music in Southern India."[6] By all accounts, Rukmini Devi had been studying with Meenakshi Sundaram Pillai for less than a year when she first performed and George Arundale published his remarks. Arundale's assertion appears

Oakland, California, 1972. Photo by Jan Steward. Courtesy of the photographer.

Oakland, California, 1972. Photo by Jan Steward. Courtesy of the photographer.

an overstatement projected to an audience whose concerns were other than the art form and its future.

In an interview late in her life, Rukmini Devi recalled Balasaraswati and her own early response to Bala's dancing. "I saw a large number of dancers. They were just beginning to come out, because, before that, hardly anyone knew of the existence of this dance, and I went to them. Some of my friends who knew I was keen took me. One [of these dancers] was Bala. . . . Of course, I knew [of] Vina Dhanam, a very great musician whose granddaughter was learning. So I was taken to her house so that I could see this little girl learning. It was Bala. She was just learning *'tei ya tei.'*[7] She looked very bright and very intelligent. Her *guru*, Kandappa, was there. There was also another well known person, Chinnayya Naidu, who taught her *abhinaya*.[8] So they were all there. So that's how I met her. Of course they were very pleased because very few people went to their house, or took an interest in dance. They were very happy and so I invited her. When she was able to dance, she came to the Theosophical Society and gave a demonstration there, for my birthday.

"When I first saw her dance on the stage . . . I thought she was very graceful, though she was very large and tall too. There was some charm about her, which a lot of people, at the beginning, didn't appreciate. But you know that a lot of people appreciate you after you become famous, not because you have the power to appreciate. She later on became famous due to people supporting her, and the dance itself became popular. She had a great tradition behind her. . . . She was very friendly to me. I was very sympathetic to all these professional dancers who were not popular at that time. I felt that my mission was to be not just a performer, but to help others too, to do certain things which are in better taste, and so on, like costumes (it was all a mixture in those days). In that way I tried to help many of them.

"I made many changes in costuming and staging and all that. She was very interested in all that.[9] Her mother Jayammal was particularly anxious that I should do something to improve the costume of Bala. [It is highly unlikely that Jayammal was interested in Bala's costume being modernized.] In those days the costumes were very untidy, the color schemes very poor. So I brought bundles of clothes, with proper color schemes, to try them on her. . . . Among the dancers I saw, she was the only one where the music and the dance were equally important. Because she was from a family of great musicians, her dance moves were deeply affected by this. She was able to convey not only the meaning of the dance, but also the emotion of the music. That's what I liked best."[10]

Embracing a New Order

Rukmini Devi had learned from a traditional source, but she challenged the hierarchical structure of the professional community by disregarding the guidance of Meenakshi Sundaram Pillai, patriarch of the Thanjavur Nattuvanar family and the man who was the most highly regarded teacher of bharata natyam of his day. Meenakshi Sundaram Pillai attempted to prevent Rukmini Devi from dancing in public after only a year of learning, but she insisted she would perform in spite of his effort to discourage her. She herself has acknowledged that he feared she would present a standard of performance that would fall short of the traditional expectation; he was acting in her interest as well as his own. Her experiment in being the first dancer from outside of the traditional community was also his experiment, and he had a great deal at stake within the traditional community where he was so highly respected. Their relationship ended with this event.

Once Rukmini Devi demonstrated that the emerging middle class was willing to accept her and her divining of an ancient form of the dance, the field was open. For this she is celebrated. The legitimacy that she claimed was based on her level of social acceptance, and that acceptance created the opportunity for other dancers of social mobility to make similar claims. The significance of the work of early performers of reconstructed bharata natyam was social.

Leaders of the reconstruction effort tried to project the idea that the knowledge and practice of the *nattuvanars* from traditional families were being absorbed into the pedagogy at institutions in Almora and Adyar, replacing the apparent monopoly hereditary families represented. But it was the *nattuvanars'* isolation and impoverishment that led them to accept teaching positions in institutions. Some of the most distinguished of these traditional artists, accused of demanding excessive compensation, were soon replaced by nontraditional instructors. In the traditional world, it was the artist who determined the terms of the engagement; in the modern world, it was the administrators of the institution.

In the traditional Hindu temple, the relationship between people was unbounded by community or caste; the balance and compatibility between people were grounded in function and purpose, not in hierarchy or social dominance. The Brahmin recited the *Vedas*, the oldest sacred texts of Hinduism, and performed other functions within the temple's sanctum sanctorum, a role that was certainly never questioned or resented. The music of the *nagaswaram* and *tavil*, which served an essential role during devotional events, was performed by members of the traditional community. In some temples cycles of song were offered directly to the deity by a singer (*oduvar*) from a non-Brahmin family-based tradition. These temple servants lived and worked together in close proximity. The respect given a dancer, and the respect temple servants had for one another, was based on *gnanam* (knowledge) and *dharma* (duty). The notion of hierarchical distinctions arose only when outside forces began politicizing religion; the traditional community did not politicize their duty.

On December 15, 1935, Vina Dhanammal performed in Madras and received this review: "Among the *sabhas* in Madras only one or two are really committed to furthering classical music. I think the recently created Triplicane Club Sabha will be counted among them. This *sabha* presented a performance by Dhanammal last Saturday. A *sabha* which presents Dhanammal needs no further proof of its commitment to classical music. . . . The performance ran for three hours and people stayed rooted to their seats like statues. All were afraid to breathe fearing it might disturb the flow of music. Someone with a sore throat was furious with himself: 'Why didn't I leave my throat behind?' A mother took her child out when it began to cry. This is the first time I have seen such a thing." It might seem that removing a crying child from a concert of music would be the norm, but as this reviewer suggests, it has not always been so. "The essence of music and its philosophy can be found in Dhanammal's performance," the review continues, but "it was not a success in terms of tickets sold."[11]

Another of the concerts that Balasaraswati considered her "five best" was a benefit held on February 1, 1936, at the Champaka Theatre in the town of Mannargudi in the Thanjavur District. The concert was presented in support of the newly installed *matam* (a center of teaching) for Saint Arunagirinathar, the composer of songs called *tiruppugarzh*, and was arranged by Konnakkol Pakkiria Pillai. Bala danced from ten at night until three in the morning; she performed *khanda alarippu* (an introductory piece in a meter of five), which she had danced at her *arangetram*, and a *pada varnam* in *Kamas raga*.[12] According to Lakshmi, some time later Pakkiria Pillai asked Bala to perform *khanda alarippu* for him, as he lay ill in bed shortly before his death.

Moving to Egmore

During the same period when the reconstruction of bharata natyam was taking shape, Jayammal aspired to leave the indignity of the family's poverty behind. After Bala's introduction in the north and the endorsement of Uday Shankar, Bala had begun to have success in the south. She was famous among her competitors, was performing more, and was becoming better able to demand satisfactory compensation for concerts. In April 1936 Jayammal purchased a small house on Dhanala Aravamudu Naidu Gardens Street in Egmore, an area of Madras to the southwest of Georgetown. Lakshmi described it: "At that time, Egmore was like a suburb, all along Poonamallee High Road. It was easier to raise children, quiet. Kandappa visited there. Bala was performing often." Ranganathan remembered the house: "Uday Shankar and his troupe stayed with us in that house. . . . Bala gave many, many recitals and she also danced for many of our friends. Some gentleman from Europe came there. That is the house where my grandmother died.

Balasaraswati on the rooftop terrace of her home in Egmore, Madras, ca. 1938.

The house is still there, behind the railroad track. The train shook the whole house."[13]

Poonamallee High Road was—and still is—a major artery connecting Georgetown, the historical center of the city, with its growing suburbs to the west. It led to the village of Poonamallee, twenty kilometers to the west. Lined with majestic trees, the road led to coconut and casuarina groves a few kilometers from Georgetown, passing the Madras High Court and the Central Railway Station, the hub of the Southern Railway system that services peninsular India, part of the system built in the first half of the nineteenth century. Another station, in Egmore, was the hub for the local rail network servicing the city and its environs and for trains running directly to the south, to towns such as Kumbakonam and Thanjavur. These were the railway tracks that passed by Jayammal's house. To the west, large garden homes lined Poonamallee High Road. Saint George's Anglo Indian Higher Secondary School, where the son of Raja Serfoji II of Thanjavur was educated, was along the road in an area called Kilpauk, near an old market bazaar called Anjiminkarai.

Musicians from Bala's family were in demand. T. Shankaran recalled with pride when "once, in June or July 1936, family members performed at four separate places: Dhanammal in solo *vina*; Rajalakshmiammal and

Lakshmiratnammal in a vocal duet; Brinda and Muktha in a vocal duet; and
Balasaraswati with Jayammal in bharata natyam. It was remembered that
the fee for the four concerts was about rupees three hundred total."[14] Three
hundred rupees was a considerable sum at that time.

Leela Shekar was a young student of Jayammal who would become a
lifelong friend and supporting musician. She described the scene at one of
Bala's concerts in 1936: "I first saw Bala when she was eighteen and I was
about twelve. My sister and I started learning music from her great mother,
Srimathi Jayammal, and both of us were so excited about seeing the already
well-known Bala dance. She was performing in a small hall in Triplicane,
a crowded locality in Madras. The hall was packed to capacity and people
were standing outside and trying to get at least a glimpse of Bala. My sister
and I had hardly enough room to sit. There were no chairs — all of us had
to sit on the floor."[15]

That year Bala was asked to perform at the Indian National Congress
Exhibition, which she did on several occasions afterward. A Congress Exhibition was a major event, which the Indian National Congress used to
expand its own agenda and attract an audience that was as diverse as possible, featuring the biggest names performing at the time. Bala's opportunity
to perform at the Congress Exhibition in 1936 may have been influenced by
the father of the Veggie Sisters, dancers from the previous generation who
had been trained by Kandappa's father. The Veggie Sisters' father managed
the production and distribution of the posters for the Exhibition. Other
traditional dancers at the event included Mylapore Gauri Ammal, Varalakshmi, Bhanumathi, and Jeevaratnam. Bala was considerably younger than
the others. Noted and popular musicians at the 1936 Exhibition included
nagaswaram innovator Rajaratnam Pillai and the singer M. S. Subbulakshmi, who had recently moved to Madras from Madurai.

Artists at the Exhibition were expected to promote the Indian National
Congress's political message. Bala danced a song about a spinning wheel,
"The Chakra." Bala was not politically concerned herself, but, as Lakshmi
commented when being asked why Bala would perform songs with political
meaning, "They were all professional artists, you know. They were asked to
perform in the Congress Exhibition. So she and Jayammal would find new
songs . . . apt for this situation. They sang that Gandhi song *'Indrakanam'*
and they had their own tune. That's the thing." The Exhibition audiences
were known to be coarse and disrespectful, but for the professional artist
these events were opportunities to be heard and seen, and to be paid for
performing.

On December 27, 1936, Bala performed under the auspices of the Music
Academy, sponsored by Lord Erskine, the governor of Madras. Vina Dhanam-

Studio portrait of Balasaraswati with M. S. Subbulakshmi, 1937. The two teenaged friends both became world-famous artists. From strictly disciplined households, the two asserted their independence by secretly arranging this photograph of themselves dressed outrageously in Western-style sleepwear and pretending to smoke cigarettes.

mal performed for the Academy, amplified for the first time, on December 30; Bala's cousins Brinda, Muktha, and Abhirami performed for the Academy on the 31st.

Hereditary bharata natyam was a family business, and family members would share with each other whatever they knew. The pride that drove the profession of the arts in the family was stronger than any disagreements or challenges within the family. Vegavahini Vijayaraghavan, T. Brinda's daughter, repeated a story about her mother, who had once learned but years later did not entirely recall a *padam* her aunt Lakshmiratnammal had taught her. Brinda asked Bala if she had learned the *padam*, and she had. Together they sat and pieced it back together, each contributing her individual recollections until it was complete and both of them had fully remembered the piece.

R. K. Shanmukham

Imagine for a moment the situation in which professional artists found themselves in the mid-1930s. They had lost their traditional place of employment, but they retained their profession. The transition from the practice of the arts as they had existed—embedded in the traditional social order and in a matrilineal family system—to alignment with evolving, very different cultural and social norms required the artists of the community to forsake their property, family structure, and culture. Most did, or seem to have done, without protest. Some women of Bala's generation married, but this was not an option for most hereditary professional artists. A woman from the *devadasi* community was still an object of derision and suspicion. The stigma that tainted her artistic heritage also tainted perceptions of her character and her family. For Balasaraswati's family, indomitable pride and an exceptional artistic legacy enabled their persistence.

It was against this social and cultural backdrop that Bala, aged eighteen, took a partner: R. K. Shanmukham. On January 1, 1934, Bala had performed in a pavilion set up in People's Park behind the Ripon Building, the headquarters of the Madras Corporation administration. The performance was sponsored by the Madras Music Academy. R. K. Shanmukham first saw Balasaraswati at this performance, and, impulsively, he asked a mutual friend to arrange an introduction. He had no gift to offer, but his friend was wearing a ring that Shanmukham admired. At R. K. Shanmukham's request, the friend removed the ring and presented it to Bala as a token of Shanmukham's regard. Bala's first reaction was annoyance at R. K. Shanmukham's use of an intermediary to present a gift.

But the attraction was mutual, based in part on their common concern for the traditional arts. Balasaraswati and R. K. Shanmukham also shared an interest in the pro-Tamil cause, which represented more than political identity. Although Bala was apolitical, she was passionate about Tamil cul-

R. K. Shanmukham, Balasaraswati's partner, ca. 1938.

ture. She was committed to the Tamil activist movement linguistically and emotionally, as was her mother. R. K. Shanmukham, twenty-six years older than Bala, piqued her intellect on this and other issues. He was unhesitatingly supportive of her dance and music, and protective of the rights of the *devadasi* community. R. K. Shanmukham gradually gained acceptance by the family, and by 1936 he was accepted by Jayammal, and Balasaraswati became his partner.

Sir Ramaswami Kannuswami Shanmukham Chetty was born in Madras on October 17, 1892. He was a statesman, industrialist, educator, and administrator. He was highly regarded for his genius in economics and finance, and he had a passion for literature and the fine arts. Shanmukham was active in the charged political environment of the day, which reflected the tumultuous politics set in motion by colonial reforms of the system of government in India during the 1890s and the increasingly cutthroat competition for favor with the British administration housed in Fort St. George. He was an early member of the Justice Party, formed in response to the struggle between the Brahmin-dominated Indian National Congress and a constituency that became characterized as "non-Brahmin."

The career that followed was brilliant. In addition to conducting his business activities in Coimbatore, where he built, owned, and managed considerable milling concerns, from 1923 to 1934 R. K. Shanmukham was a member of the Legislative Assembly in New Delhi. In the course of his career, he attended several international political conferences. He represented India at the Empire Parliamentary Conference in Australia and was a delegate at the International Conference on Labor in Geneva. In 1932 he was the League of Nations delegate at the Imperial Economic Conference in Ottawa. Knighted by the British in 1934, he was the divan of the state of Cochin[16] from 1934 to 1941 and was a participant in the Bretton Woods Conference in the White Mountains of New Hampshire in 1944. Shanmukham also served as India's first minister of finance, named by Jawarhalal Nehru in 1947.

Departures

The late 1930s brought a series of losses and changes to Bala's family, beginning with the departure from the family home of her youngest brother, Viswanathan. A musician who was close to Vina Dhanammal, and a regular attendee of her Friday performances and the Sunday "tea" sessions, was flutist T. N. Swaminatha Pillai. On January 2, 1936, Viswanathan, aged eight, heard the flutist at a performance sponsored by the Madras Music Academy. Within months after that event, Viswa decided to leave the house in Egmore to live in Thanjavur, to begin a traditional learning relationship with Swaminatha Pillai. Viswanathan's decision was very distressing to Jayammal, who wanted her son to learn from the great flutist but did not want him to leave home.

Vina Dhanammal gave her last public concert sponsored by the Madras Music Academy on December 28, 1937. Early in 1938 she visited an ailing Bala in Egmore. While she was there, a gentleman visitor from Bengal came to the house looking for Bala. He asked Vina Dhanammal who she was, and she was forced to introduce herself as Bala's grandmother. As other family members tell the story, Dhanammal recalled her granddaughter's taunt of years before and enjoyed the fulfillment of the prophesy. Later that year, however, Dhanammal fell ill in the house in Egmore, and she died there on October 15, 1938. Shankaran comments, "On her last . . . night of her earthly sojourn, Dhanammal slowly slipped into immortality murmuring, 'Kamakshi, Kamakshi.' Her youngest daughter, Kamakshi, bent over her face and asked, 'What is it, Amma?' Even in that state she said, disdainfully, 'Not you! It is Mother Kamakshi.' As she fondled her *vina* she said the only regret of her exit was parting with her *vina*. Calling, 'Gopala, Gopala' [Krishna], she expired in the early morning."[17]

That same year, 1938, brought a loss with profound artistic consequences for Bala and her ensemble. At the invitation of Uday Shankar, Kandappa Pillai left Madras and joined the faculty at the Uday Shankar Performing Arts Centre in the Almora District, four hundred kilometers north of Delhi, near the Nepalese border. Funding for the Centre came from benefactors with whom Uday Shankar had built relationships during his years in Europe and the United States, including patrons Beatrice Straight and the Elmhurst family from Dartington Hall in England. Shankar brought together extraordinary artists from disparate traditional communities to teach; this faculty provided expertise from various sources to enrich drama productions by Shankar, who had become an international celebrity in Europe. It is an irony that Uday Shankar's 1933 discovery and public embrace of the grandeur of the traditional performance practice resulted in one of the irretrievable losses in Bala's life. Kandappa had been lured to Almora with wages that Bala could not then possibly match. In the traditional system, the *nattuvanar* would receive a portion of fees, gifts, and other remuneration given to a dancer. Bala's income was modest, although it provided for her family.

The Almora Performing Arts Centre was to be short-lived, but it was briefly representative of the highest standard of teaching available from the traditional communities of Tamil Nadu, Kerala, and Manipur. The school trained more than a dozen celebrated dancers of various practices, several of whom remained with Shankar's dance company. But it did not become a resource for the perpetuation of these traditions; Uday Shankar wanted to create new interpretations of Indian dance.

Balasaraswati was furious with Uday Shankar, with whom she had developed a close friendship, for luring her *guru* and dance master away and leaving her stranded professionally, unable without her *nattuvanar* to perform full concerts of bharata natyam. For the Centre in Almora, however, the choice could not have been better. Mrs. Satyavati Gopalan, wife of one of the students at Almora, commented in an interview with Luise Scripps: "Guru Kandappa was exactly what Uday Shankar wanted because the *kathakali guru*, Shankaran Namboodiri, was very tough. If the elbow has to be here, then nothing can be other. You know what I mean. Uday Shankar used to say, 'Both these *gurus*, how they teach, it has to be exact.' Then comes the third *guru*, Amubi Singh for Manipuri. Ditto! It was the most perfect combination . . . the perfect trio. Uday Shankar could have said he has got the best of the *gurus* for these three subjects [the bharata natyam, *kathakali*, and *Manipuri* traditions]."

Mrs. Gopalan described Kandappa's teaching: "[He was] so particular about the students, that they have to do this much work today, even if it is one *adavu*, he went on, and on, and on, until the whole lot of them were doing that line. He won't switch off to the second *adavu*. . . . He wouldn't stop until he got the perfect line. He gave them only one or two *adavus* for the class in that hour. But he would go on and on and on until he got the heel, the toe, separate. He had to hear those three different sounds! They're not all the same, the heel, the toe, the flat. So all the three have got to be perfect. Then put them together and the line of the body. And the bend . . . and the feet, of course."[18]

Kandappa stayed at Almora for more than a year. Balasaraswati believed Kandappa was irreplaceable; she revered him as a teacher and musician. But her own career demanded that she persist without him. Without a *nattuva-*

nar, Bala was restricted to performing concerts of *abhinaya* with Jayammal

and an all-female ensemble.

The entire family joined together on the first anniversary of Vina Dhanammal's death, October 16, 1939, and performed a tribute concert for All India Radio broadcast from the studio on Marina Beach. The all-day concert included a vocal performance by Dhanammal's sister Rupavati Ammal; a vocal program by two of Dhanammal's daughters, Rajalakshmiammal and Lakshmiratnammal; a second vocal program by her other two daughters, Jayammal and Kamakshiammal; and another program by her granddaughters Brinda and Muktha, with granddaughter Abhiramasundari on violin and grandson Ranganathan on the *mridangam*.

Two months later Balasaraswati's partner, R. K. Shanmukham, opened the 1939 Music Academy Conference, where Bala performed on December 27 at the age of twenty-one. In Kandappa's absence, the discouragement felt by Bala and Jayammal was enormous. Jayammal was domineering in her command of Bala's career and her life. Bala was obstinate and fighting back. The tension between them sometimes became disruptive during concerts, where the two played out differences and struggles for power in the midst of performance.

Over the years that had followed Bala's successes and the purchase of the property in Egmore, Jayammal had begun occasionally to act belligerent. In spite of Bala's acknowledgment of Jayammal's great musical skill and unquestioning respect for her mother, Jayammal felt that Bala was receiving more than her share of the credit. This was not uncommon in professional families, in which successive generations of distinguished artists would vie with each other for acclaim as a younger generation matured and grew into their professional prime. As an expression of her discomfort, on several occasions Jayammal threatened not to sing for Bala, believing that this was the most compelling way of demonstrating her importance in her daughter's concerts. Bala was always grateful to Viswanathan for standing up to their mother, taking advantage of his position as Jayammal's favorite son and insisting to her that this was not the way it was done in their house. Jayammal always capitulated.[19]

Critic R. Krishnamurthy had written in October 1939: "I cannot say that Bala's performance has improved. What could improve when no detail has been found wanting before? She is unrivalled as an artist, yet regretfully, there are some unhealthy developments in minor aspects. Lately, a change for the better is noticeable in costumes and decor yet, while performing *abhinaya*, the rapport between mother and daughter is visibly deteriorating. *Abhinaya* is Bala's noteworthy feature with her incomparable expression.... Her inspiration arises from Jayammal's singing that was once the root of the unique understanding between them. Yet lately they betray a woeful lack of cooperation, visible when Bala glares at her mother on stage. Net result:

anger registers on her face when the context calls for pathos. . . . Bala's annoyance shows the change between mother and daughter on stage."[20]

Part of the problem was the microphone, newly added to the concert
stage. On-stage banter was not unusual among performers but it became
noticeable to the audience in the presence of an unfamiliar and intrusive
technology. Krishnamurthy deplored the arrival of the microphone in both
music and dance concerts. Though it might be useful to amplify vocal
music in large auditoriums, in Jayammal and Bala's case it would broadcast
their on-stage differences of opinion. This was particularly true in the time
shortly after Kandappa had left Madras.

Despite these difficulties, in 1939 Kalki Krishnamurthy referred to Balasaraswati as "unrivalled" in describing her first performance without her
nattuvanar. Ironically, however, he then praised Kandappa Pillai for conducting Lakshmi Sastri's program at the Madras Music Academy on December 26, 1939—Kandappa had traveled south from Almora to Madras
for the concert season. Lakshmi Sastri (later Lakshmi Shankar) was the
first student of Kandappa's from Almora to perform. "Miss R. V. Lakshmi's
dance was a special feast. She has blossomed into a star in just four years. . . .[21]
We should make hay while the sun shines, with such brilliant *nattuvanars*
like Kandappa and Meenakshi Sundaram Pillai still alive to carry on the
classical tradition. Kandappa is fortunate to train a talented pupil like Lakshmi. This teenager flitting across the stage has a great future."[22] Kalki's
comments suggest that interest in the hereditary dancers, whose personalities reflected the rigors and austerity of the traditional practice, was giving
way to enthusiasm for more glamorous performers that could be described
in terms such as "this teenager flitting across the stage."

Shortly after Lakshmi Sastri's concert, Kandappa conducted his last
performance with Bala during a concert series at Rasika Ranjani Sabha in
Mylapore. The event was notable, claimed Shankaran, because it was very
unusual to have featured female musicians or dancers in a program series
where men also were performing. The organizers of the concerts were trying to generate support for a temple in Thiruvarur and wanted to attract
as large an audience as possible—and in 1940 Bala was as big a draw as any
performing artist in the south.

Shankaran observed many years later that Kandappa "could brook no
compromise in his artistic visions. His concepts seemed all to the good in his
plan to save the endangered art form. . . . His alterations, though slight—in
presentation, content and staging—were positive and right-thinking. The
original genius of the dance was not diminished while its appeal for a wider
audience did not cater to an uneducated public. His strongest supporters,
master drummers, rhythm maestros, and musicians, understood and marveled at his genius."[23] There are no recordings of Kandappa Pillai leading
Bala's ensemble; the earliest recording of Bala's ensemble is from a 1955 pro-

K. P. Kandappa Pillai being received at Central Railway Station, Madras, after his return from Almora in 1940. Fourth from the left in the front row is Chittoor Subramania Pillai, and sixth from the left is T. N. Swaminatha Pillai. Kandappa Pillai is in the middle of the group wearing a dark *kurtha* and garland. To the right of the unknown man holding the umbrella is Alattoor Sivasubramania Iyer. Continuing to the right are Palani Subramaniam Pillai, then T. Balasaraswati, T. Jayammal, and K. Ellappa Pillai.

gram with Ellappa Mudaliar conducting, and with Kandappa's son, Ganesha, as backup, along with the rest of the fine ensemble. But Kandappa's *tirma-nams* and choreography were preserved and continue to distinguish the family style to this day.

A Changing Scene

Formed in 1928, the Madras Music Academy presented twenty-one performances of bharata natyam by the end of 1940. Between 1931 and 1937 thirteen bharata natyam programs were presented, all by traditional dancers. In 1938 the Music Academy presented a nonhereditary dancer for the first time. Of the eight concerts between 1938 and the end of 1940, two were performed by nonhereditary dancers with professional teachers, three were presentations by nonhereditary dancers of fusions of more than one regional style, and three were presented by traditional dancers; Balasaraswati performed in 1938 and 1939, and Bhanumathi in December 1940.

This change in the balance of hereditary and nonhereditary performers in concerts at the Music Academy between 1935 and 1940 signaled both the rising acceptance and popularity of dance and the shrinking audience for traditional bharata natyam. In 1935 several traditional artists were receiving acclaim never experienced before in their lifetime. But by 1940 these opportunities were all but gone. A modern version of bharata natyam was in the making, emerging seamlessly, or so it appeared, from a traditional antecedent. The public appetite seemed to favor the accessibility of the new styles of dance and dance drama, charmed by their costumes and glamour, and at the same time impressed by claims of authenticity and "classical" values.

During the 1940s it became increasingly apparent to Bala that her attempt to do justice to her art, her teacher, and her family was at risk of failing. Her health was poor. As a child she had had rheumatic fever, which left her with a damaged heart. A thyroid imbalance, undiagnosed and untreated, affected her energy levels during the 1940s and 1950s and caused her to gain weight unmanageably. Bala called these her "elephant days," and some critics made much of her size in the press.

Lakshmi commented: "There was a period when Bala was having a very hard time professionally, and it was at that time that she was a little fat and people were not asking her to perform. Yet when she performed, even if it was once a year or twice a year, even though she was fat, she had a full house and she was the reigning queen. No matter depression or hard times, she was recognized as the queen of dance."

As a reconstructed style of bharata natyam emerged, one area of experimentation was the use of musical compositions that were not from the repertoire composed for dance. The repertoire of music for bharata natyam consists of poetry set to music, sung by a musician, accompanied by instrumental musicians who emulate the words and inflection of the textual setting, the verbal characteristics of the music. Even the rhythmic patterns of the dancer's feet are accompanied by recitation of vocalized syllables. Ideally the song is sung by the dancer. "Yet it is not just dancing to the words in their superficial meaning alone. Nor is the music itself detached from the words and their full inner and outer meaning," declared Balasaraswati. Most practitioners and teachers from the traditional professional community agreed that pieces not composed for dance could not be suitably substituted for those that were.

The great *nattuvanar* Meenakshi Sundaram Pillai, in a speech reproduced in Kalakshetra Foundation's publication *Rukmini Devi Arundale Birth Centenary Volume*, remarked: "Departure from tradition, the inclusion of totally unsuitable pieces in the name of innovation only lowers the standard of this art. I am not against change. There is bound to be change and new ideas. But these can be called by a different name and not brought under the name of Bharatanatya. Such innovations make a sublime art ridiculous. . . . Bizarre costumes and inappropriate themes will only lead to destruction of this art."[24]

However, as traditional professional musicians were replaced as accompanists for dance in the 1940s, musicians with a different repertoire took their place, and these new musicians introduced the song form *kriti* (and the virtually identical *kirtana*) into bharata natyam concerts. Today, *kritis* have become standard features of bharata natyam performances. This development is significant; the poetry of *kritis* is in general more abstractly philosophical and the pacing of the text leaves relatively little room for narrative interpretation by a dancer. In contrast, in *padams*, the simplicity of the language and the pacing of the syllables in music leave more room for gesture in narrative dance.

As these changes occurred in what songs were performed with dance, Bala strongly resisted. She described the logic of the traditional concert format: "At first, mere meter; then, melody and meter; continuing with music, meaning, and meter; its expansion in the center-piece of the *varnam*; thereafter, music and meaning without meter; in variation of this, melody and meter; in contrast to the pure rhythmical beginning, a non-metrical song at the end. We see a most wonderful completeness and symmetry in this art. Surely the traditional votaries of music and dance would not wish us to take any liberties with this sequence."[25]

Commenting on the proliferation of young composers of dance music, Bala said: "We have a rich treasure of traditional compositions most suited for improvisation with excellently merged *raga bhava* [melodic and emotional qualities] for the *sahitya* [text]. For *abhinaya* the opening words of a lyric are most important for establishing the mood . . . and composers with no grounding in the intricacies of the art cannot be expected to do a good job here.

"For example, the word '*Chirunavvu*' in the well-known *tana varnam* [from the music concert repertoire] in *Bhairavi*[26] is so stretched out in the music as to risk the dancer herself being laughed at if she attempts to show 'laughter' at such inordinate length. In other parts of that *varnam*, the words and ideas come along too fast and furious for there to be time to cope adequately with them in terms of *abhinaya*. It is clear that the aspiring dancer must receive training in the art of music as fully as in the elements of dance if she is to understand these things and do justice to the great concept of the art as it has been developed by our ancestors.

"It is also essential that *raga* and *sahitya* be perfectly matched and in accordance with the necessities of expression in the dance. It is for this reason that I do not advocate the use of most *kirtanas* as vehicles for bharata natyam, although the idea is becoming fashionable in some circles at present. The scope of *sahitya* is often too limited and specific to allow for full development of *abhinaya* as is often the scope of the *raga-bhava*. Songs to be used for dance expression must be carefully chosen and one need only think of the almost unlimited scope of many of the *padas* and *pada varnams* to sense the great difference between them and most devotional songs or concert pieces."[27]

Often Bala's apparently conservative attitude about what repertoire was most suitable for dance was interpreted as an insistence on what was old or original. It was not. She was speaking of what music best suited the dance form the way she understood it. Bala's accompanist Leela Shekar recalled: "She was ever ready to learn, ever ready to absorb new things, new ways of music. When she liked something very much, she was the first one to go and try it. But she was a stickler, remaining very original, very classical; she would not go beyond the classical mold."[28]

Dark Times

Less than two years after Kandappa Pillai had left Madras in 1938, he returned from Almora. He fell ill, and died a few months later in February 1941. Kandappa had wanted to begin to work with Bala again, but after his concert with Bala in Mylapore his health failed, and there was no further opportunity. Speaking before the Indian Fine Arts Society in 1982, Bala recalled when Kandappa was near death and she had to read an article to him. "A chill ran up my spine as I read words of praise regarding me: 'the incomparable Bala is the great *guru*'s first and foremost disciple.' My tongue went dry and I stopped. With affection he said, 'Balanagamma [an endearment],[29] why did you stop? You are truly my dear disciple, first and last.' This was like a flood of nectar for me, having expected a shower of sparks from him! Suddenly I realized [that all those years] he had feasted on an inner joy, satisfaction much greater than mere words of praise, yet remained silent, keeping a strict reserve in my own interest, while risking a bad name. Only then did I fully realize how carefully he had masked that approval in order to truly help me advance in the art."[30]

Kandappa had a son named K. Ganesha. When Bala was learning dancing from Kandappa Pillai, she used to carry Ganesha on her hip, even as she was entrusted with the care of her younger brothers, Ranga and Viswa. She was Ganesha's constant babysitter (in Lakshmi's words), and as a result Ganesha was always present during Bala's dance classes. Through this connection Bala developed an attachment to Ganesha that was to survive the abuses of a relationship eventually racked with the scourge of his alcoholism. He absorbed his father's legacy of composed dance material and a technique with the cymbals that accompany the dancer's feet that no other *nattuvanar* emulated. "I learned the whole thing by watching. Similarly, Ganesha also absorbed the whole thing," said Lakshmi.

Kandappa Pillai died before he had a chance to teach his son. Bala took Ganesha into her care. He lived in Bala's home, where he was surrounded by music and dance. Bala was able to encourage him and taught him how to choreograph and teach *adavu* and pure dance sequences.

Without Kandappa Pillai Bala was lost; her dance master's temporary departure had become permanent. But her family was in no position to do without her income. As it was, they were to lose the home in Egmore that Jayammal and Bala had bought in the mid-1930s. It was not that other *nattuvanars* were not available for Bala's performances. But Balasaraswati did not want a different *nattuvanar*. A change in dance master would have resulted in fundamental changes in the style of concert presentation, and in the content. Issues like tempo and selection of items to perform were the domain of the dance master. For the traditional performer, the artistic relationship between the dancer and *nattuvanar* was inextricable.

There were very few interchangeable parts when it came to assembling an ensemble for bharata natyam. Vina Dhanammal's concern for Bala and her career aspirations, after she inquired whether Bala's teeth and eyes were straight and listened to her singing, was in part about her impending dependence on the musicians who would form her ensemble. Bala expressed the same concern about Lakshmi, suggesting that the problem of retaining a collaborative ensemble might also have challenged Bala's predecessors. Musicians had to be trained in the family style of music, and also trained in that style to perform music for dance. The discipline resulted in a dependency on specific musicians and would constantly test their loyalty. This was why Uday Shankar's offer to Kandappa Pillai was thoughtless and (certainly inadvertently) hurtful.

Later in 1941, Bala and Jayammal visited the village of Pandanallur, the home of Kandappa's uncle, the "grand old man" *nattuvanar* Meenakshi Sundaram Pillai, to discuss whether or not he might replace Kandappa Pillai as her *nattuvanar*. At the end of the meeting, however, all three were in agreement that their styles of both music and dance were different enough to prevent an easy transition. Bala would have to learn new *tirmanams*, and there were slight differences in technique. This was one of several challenges they would face if they were to work together; *nattuvanars* composed their own material and choreography.

But Bala was encouraged by supporters to continue to perform. As she had done since Kandappa Pillai left for Almora, she performed the interpretive pieces that allowed her to rely on her *abhinaya* and family repertoire of *padams*, and excluded pieces that would require a *nattuvanar* to perform; the all-*abhinaya* program was the same concert format that had surprised critics in 1934. The quality of Bala's *abhinaya* carried these concerts and continued to add to her distinction as a leading artist. *Abhinaya* had been the aspect of dance that was being ignored when Bala began to learn in the

Balasaraswati in an all-*abhinaya* concert at Rajaji Hall in Madras,
with T. Ranganathan (*mridangam*), T. Jayammal (vocal, with *tambura*),
and R. S. Gopala Krishnan (vocal). Early 1940s.

mid-1920s, and she now stood alone as the sole dancer who was capable of
performing a concert comprised entirely of *abhinaya* and its music. Eleven
of these all-*abhinaya* programs appear on the 1941 family tax report, mostly
in private homes.

R. Krishnamurthy had reviewed one of these concerts back in 1934: "It
is difficult for the uninitiated to understand the complicated patterns and
rhythms of the dance program's first half. The second half is mostly miming.
Balasaraswati managed to introduce this aspect as a full program, completely
eschewing *nritta* and doing away with the *nattuvanar* and drummer [her
usual drummer, Kuppuswami]. She was accompanied by her mother who
sang for her, her cousin Abhiramasundari on violin, and a lady named Hamsadamayanti on *mridangam* . . . an entirely female cast." Krishnamurthy
went on to say that the performance was astonishing, especially the way the
mimetic gestures were related to the song; he also mentioned that Bala sat
singing for part of the performance because she was unwell. His conclusion
was that the "*abhinaya* concert has come to stay."[31]

T. N. Swaminatha Pillai

In 1940 Jayammal convinced T. N. Swaminatha Pillai to move from
Thanjavur to a home she had found for him in Madras so that he could
teach her son Viswanathan nearby. Viswanathan had left home in 1936 to

begin learning with his chosen master, and Jayammal was determined that
Viswa continue learning, but in Madras. Jayammal used some of the income
from Bala's concerts to pay for the rented house and other expenses. Another cost of having Swaminatha Pillai teach Viswanathan was that sometimes Jayammal would offer to Swaminatha Pillai concert openings that had
initially been offered to Bala. This was particularly discouraging at a time
when opportunities to perform were becoming rare for hereditary dancers;
Bala was the last of the well-known professional dancers still performing.
It was a very high price to pay. Perhaps Jayammal's indifference to this loss
of opportunity for Bala reflected Jayammal's resentment of Bala's growing
reputation. Perhaps it reflected a desire on her part to have a male member of
the family, and a nondancer, evolve as a leading musician of his generation.

When a hereditary teacher passed on his or her art, the expectation generally was that the student would surrender allegiance to any other interpretation of style of music. But Viswanathan's teacher held Jayammal and the
Dhanammal family in such high regard that he was tolerant of a different
process, one that included Jayammal. Viswa reported that Swaminatha Pillai
would teach him a *kriti*, then say, "Go play it to your mother." Viswanathan
claimed that at the time he was too young to understand why his teacher
did that. There was no conflict between teacher and mother. "Whatever
my mother said was fine." Jayammal never interfered with Swaminatha Pillai's approach to improvised rhythmic music, a specialty. Swaminatha Pillai,
on the other hand, never resisted the changes made by Jayammal through
Viswa. "He never objected; he had a great respect for Dhanammal's interpretation of songs, and other things. That, I realized later on, much, much
later. [At that time] I said to myself, 'Well, he is teaching. Why do I have to
go and play to my mother?' You know, complaining and grumbling inside."
Jayammal would change the music, and then Swaminatha Pillai, having
asked Viswa about the modifications his mother had made, would encourage the changes. "She didn't even know that he did it. I played for her and
she would say, 'Well, this is how I sing.' I would change it. Things like that
happened. In other words, little subtle things, polishing it. He never corrected the changes."[32]

Bala and Jayammal were absorbed in a search for a new *nattuvanar*. After
two years of struggling without a *nattuvanar*, they agreed on a replacement:
Kandappa Pillai's cousin Kanchipuram Ellappa Pillai. Ellappa had been
Kandappa's assistant for several years and knew all of Kandappa's *tirmanams*. However, for Bala he was her *nattuvanar* but not her teacher, and
he never composed *tirmanams* that Bala performed. This was a continuing
source of irritation for Ellappa.[33] But the transition from Kandappa to Ellappa was musically excellent. Viswanathan recalled: "I remember one occasion when Bala was asked to dance at a wedding of the son of [the renowned
musician] *nagaswaram vidwan* Rajaratnam Pillai. I was in my teens and by

then I could understand what was going on. All the *tavil* and *nagaswaram* players and some dancers and singers who attended the wedding were all eager to see Bala's dance.... We were all concerned how the concert would go because we were among the cream of South Indian music, connoisseurs and experts in rhythm. They were thrilled, jumping up and down; some came to see if, without Kandappa, she would flunk. It was soon after Kandappa Pillai died and I realized, seeing this reaction, what he had achieved."[34]

Revived Dance

Medha Yodh was a woman from a Parsi family in Bombay. Medha's father was a physician; her mother, the daughter of a Sanskrit scholar, had had her formal education stopped at fifth grade and had been married at sixteen. In a moment of rebellion that was not uncharacteristic of young women of her generation in India (but still extraordinary), Medha's mother had left her family and studied in Spain with Maria Montessori. She later traveled on her own to China and Japan, then returned home and became a teacher and social worker in the slums of Bombay.[35]

Medha was one of the new dancers who were raised in families of privilege and social consciousness and who participated in the national cultural explosion and the discovery of India's wealth in culture, including dance. Like her siblings, Medha received an advanced education and was schooled in the arts, one of a generation from secure, educated, affluent backgrounds that openly favored and adopted Western aesthetic values. At the age of nineteen, having studied *Manipuri* and then bharata natyam, Medha left India to become a graduate student in biochemistry at Stanford University. Two decades later she would become a student of Bala's.

Medha, who eventually taught dance at UCLA, made the point that she took exception to some scholars who had described the trend toward the creation of a national dance among young pre-Independence Indians as a "reconstruction." As far as she was concerned that trend was not the result of a conscious "reconstruction" strategy but simply what was being lived. For the first time, India was offering the opportunity for educated, upper-class women, some with extensive exposure to the art forms and aesthetics of the West, to learn and perform dance from and in India. In an interview during the 1980s, Medha commented on what that time was like for her.

She credited first the fact that Rukmini Devi, a Theosophist, had studied dance from a traditional source—and the Theosophists' subsequent establishment of Kalakshetra as a teaching institution—as primary influences that helped make dancing "respectable." Medha also acknowledged the contributions of Sarojini Naidu and Kamaladevi Chattopadhyay, and the advocacy of Jawarhalal Nehru. Sarojini Naidu was a great orator, a nationalist, and a poet, and in 1925 she became the first Indian woman president of the

Indian National Congress. Naidu was a friend of Annie Besant, who was at that time head of the Theosophical Society. Kamaladevi Chattopadhyay was a social activist—a fighter for the causes of India's freedom, women's rights, and the causes of India's artisans and artists. She was the vice chairman of the Sangeet Natak Akademi in the 1950s and chairman from 1977 to 1982. Kamaladevi was a lifelong friend and admirer of Balasaraswati. She was perhaps the last nationally prominent public figure to visit Bala in the weeks before her death.

Medha observed that during the turbulent times leading up to Independence, there was no "This is right, that is wrong. The mood was of a growing sense of nationalism-based culture, a feeling that it was all India's and Indians' art. There was Rabindranath Tagore, and [Krishna Nehru] Hutheesing[36] studying at Santiniketan, as well as other dancers in Bombay." Previously, Medha commented, the only outlet women had for dancing was performing the *garba* (a popular group social dance performed within the Gujarati community) during the pan-Indian festival *Navaratri*. She recalled the excitement of Bombay and the growing enthusiasm and vitality of India during World War II, just before and at the time of Independence. "I recall what was happening in the city of Bombay. . . . What is amazing is that we lived it with the Tommies and the Aussies. And all the troops, flooding Bombay, flooding Calcutta. All we saw were soldiers. And the threat of Japan coming. . . . That is where the fight for freedom truly made Indians aware of the richness of our arts. Whether from the South or the northeast corner of Manipur, or folk and tribal dances—all of these were beginning. . . . All of them were suddenly becoming known. And, the existing performing artists—including Balamma—were just starting on their rise—like Ali Akbar Khan and Ravi Shankar—[contributing] further by letting the world know what it was all about."[37]

In 1942 the Japanese dropped a bomb just off Marina Beach in Madras. The entire country was gripped by a fear of invasion by the Japanese. There was a general evacuation of Madras, and Jayammal sold their house and moved the family to a small town near Chengulpet, the location of an ancient Saivite temple, about seventy-five kilometers south of Madras.[38] At the end of 1943, the year of Lakshmi's birth, Bala moved with her family back into Madras. Ranganathan claimed it was boredom, rather than a diminishing fear of the war, that drove them back into the city. In any case, the family settled again in Egmore, this time in a small rented house on Varada Naidu Road, near the Dasaprakash Hotel.

Roshen Alkazi (a student of Bala's from New Delhi) visited the house several years later. "Yes, the little house at the lane of Dasaprakash. [Bala] had become a legendary figure, so I was surprised when I went there to find her living in such dire circumstances, in this little house. There was just one room downstairs, a tiny sort of kitchen-like place with a little room near it, where they had a radio set. Then you went upstairs, there was a largish room, which was Bala's room, where she kept Vina Dhanammal's *vina* in a case. That was the only really magnificent thing in the house; extremely simple with a bit of veranda in the front."[39]

During 1943 Bala gave thirteen concerts, eleven of them prior to her daughter's birth in October. Seven were private performances; three were outside of Madras in Trivandrum, Kanchipuram, and Thiruvarur; and four were recitals of *abhinaya* alone. The last concert before Lakshmi's birth was on August 28. Named Dhanalakshmi Shanmukham, Bala's daughter was born during monsoon flooding in Madras on October 30, 1943. (Bala experienced several pregnancies, but Lakshmi was the only infant to survive.) Six weeks later, Bala performed at a music conference sponsored by the Asiatic Society in Calcutta, during which the Japanese bombed the harbor there. Ranga, who accompanied her on the trip, remembered: "During that concert the Japanese bombed. She was doing the *varnam*. . . . They turned off the lights so the Japanese could not see."[40] Back in Madras, on December 29, Bala performed at Sundareswarar Hall in Mylapore for the sixteenth season of the Madras Music Academy.

Bala gave ten concerts during 1944, including two full dance concerts in Madras early in the year. Making her first trip outside India, she performed in Ceylon (Sri Lanka) in April, taking baby Lakshmi with her. Bala's older brother Srinivasan, who took care of the family's business papers, recorded seven more concerts during the rest of that year. Two of those were *abhinaya* alone; four of the seven were in homes.

THE DEVADASI ACT

Bala's outspoken criticism of carnality in *Sringara rasa* as presented by some traditional dancers had been a matter of public record by the 1930s. During the 1940s she expressed parallel objections to puritanism and the shift away from the heart of the traditional practice. "If Balasaraswati objected to the carnality in *Sringara* of most *dasi* dancers, she was equally against puritanical and artistically impoverished Brahmanical dance. She could easily distinguish puritanism from purity, and poetic love from plebian lust," commented Ra Ganapati in an interview. And indeed, *Sringara padams* had the predominant share of her repertoire. Although many of Bala's most successful pieces—pieces that were identified with her during her career, such as *"Krishna ni Begane Baro," "Varugalamo," "Mukti Alikkum," "Ka Va Va,"* and several Tamil hymns—were non-*Sringara* pieces, their presence in her repertoire did not indicate a rejection of *Sringara rasa*. These pieces simply represented Bala's artistic scope and the breadth offered by bharata natyam as one of India's traditional dance and music forms.

A long-standing controversy between Balasaraswati and Rukmini Devi Arundale was to play out on a national stage in January 1945. Rukmini Devi did not avoid *Sringara rasa* pieces entirely, but her emphasis was on non-*Sringara* songs. These songs, their proponents argued, reflected a more philosophical voice that was more classical and dignified. But Bala's belief was that some musicians and dancers preferred non-*Sringara* pieces because they had small repertoires of *padams*. Bala would say, "There is nothing in the bank."

Rasa is at the center of a theory of aesthetics that permeates Indian poetry, painting, music, dance, drama, and other arts. The Sanskrit word *rasa* refers to the human emotional states, as theme and as an overarching aesthetic framework. The word has innumerable translations into English; "flavor" is one. The nine "permanent" *rasas* are love, valor, compassion, contempt, wonder, fear, disgust, anger, and — a later entry — serenity. At a performance each *rasa* is felt within the spectator through the experience of determinants, consequences, moods, and reactive involuntary emotive responses. Determinants, called *vibhavas*, include the plot, the background condition or theme, and the cast of players. The dancer might evoke images to describe the background, such as flowers opening in the warmth of morning sun, or sunlight in the late afternoon slanting through clouds of dust kicked up by cattle in the dry time before the monsoon. Consequences, *anubhavas*, are deliberate demonstrations of feeling, conveyed through gesture and facial expression. The myriad emotional states or moods that may be employed in a dramatic performance are called *bhavas*. *Bhavas* are understood to be further refined into transient emotions employed in a character, including various sorts of pleasure and pain, agitation and impatience. The involuntary responses, recognized by the spectator to have originated in the character's inner nature, include trembling, blushing, and sweating.[41]

Subsidiary feelings aroused by *bhavas* are called *sancharis*.[42] The heroine may feel disgusted with life, may hope for reunion, may be frustrated with her fate, or be angry with her lord who is slow to return from traveling. Accompanying these shades of feeling are the many effects of those feelings, *anubhavas*, which are essential to the bharata natyam dancer's projection in performance, gestures such as looking out of the window, fiddling idly with a finger, or pacing impatiently. There are various more generalized states — such as weeping, experiencing shock or surprise, and becoming numbed — that are called *satvika bhavas*. Theoretical abstractions about the dramatic arts apply these classifications to each of the eight (or nine) *rasas*. But the *rasa* that has always carried the burden of the artistic tradition is *Sringara*.

Audience members experience *rasa*, traditional aesthetics suggest, only through empathy with the performance. They must perceive it at the level of intuition, said Balasaraswati. S. V. Shesardri (a well-known music and dance critic in Madras who wrote detailed analyses under the pseudonym Aeolus, and a contemporary of R. Krishnamurthy) wrote about the mysterious quality of Bala's dance from the perspective of someone in the audience: "The characteristic feature of *abhinaya* in bharata natyam is that it does not build up feeling through isolated episodes. It would be truer to say that feeling is the transparent form of action in *abhinaya*. . . . Balasaraswati's distinction lies in the fact that she depicts action as the vesture of feeling. Her greatness lies in the fact that while identifying herself wholly with the feeling, she is yet apperceptive enough to explore it in terms of a rich variety of *mudras* [hand gestures]. . . . The magic of Balasaraswati's art alternately condenses and dissolves space into significant form and pervasive feeling."[43]

In a concert of *karnatic* music, as an introduction to most compositions, the musician reveals the *raga* (melodic mode) through the strategic performance of phrases called *prayogas* that identify the *raga*. In some of those pieces, a musician will further investigate the *raga*, demonstrating his or her own more penetrating and personal exploration of the musical mode. Balasaraswati's grandmother Dhanammal was famed for doing this on her *vina*. Bala did the same through *abhinaya*. Whenever she began a piece, she would identify the idea in its literal form first, then begin to dance what sprang intuitively from that, thus enabling the audience to follow her images.

Not only for Balasaraswati but for every traditional dancer, music was the vehicle for *abhinaya*. It was through the music that variations of interpretation of text arose. Balasaraswati was known for "improvisation" of *abhinaya*. In fact every traditional dancer "improvised." There was no concept of fixed or composed narrative dance; dance masters would teach the art of generating interpretive dance in numerous varieties. About Balasaraswati, Viswanathan commented, "Her timing in *abhinaya* was perfect. Where she should be very, very soft and quiet, sometimes completely silent without movement, she would convey everything with her eyes. Similarly she could reflect everything through her music. Sometimes there would be no ornamentation at all." Balasaraswati herself commented, "Bharata natyam, in its highest moments, is the embodiment of music in visual form, a ceremony, and an act of devotion. For more than a thousand years, the *Sastras* [ancient treatises] have confirmed that an individual dedicated to dance must be equally dedicated to music and must receive thorough training in both arts."[44]

Bala had the capacity to direct the viewer's attention in ways that resembled magic. She performed from a finely developed state of intuitive "self-forgetfulness," a complete lack of self- or external consciousness. Bala was an illusionist of the most refined sort. Her audiences throughout her career observed, and commented on the observation, that they had "seen" things.

As an analogy, in mime the artist creates the illusion of walking, moving
forward when he is standing still, or climbing a ladder when he has not left
the ground. What we "see" is the result of the illusionist's entering into the
process of movement so completely that our mind's eye invents what our
eyes do not actually take in. Bala was a master of mime, to which she added
the refinement and poignancy of great dramatic art, the skill of creating
emotion through gesture. These two skills were given movement and purpose in space and time through music.

Dance masters did not "choreograph" the hereditary form of bharata
natyam in the same sense that ballet or modern Western dance is composed.
In these, choreography concerns the organization of bodies and their movement in a defined space, the "stage." The Western concept of choreography
is conscious of filling the space, with balancing or unbalancing dancers as
objects of composition. Action itself is the object of the dance. Traditional
bharata natyam, in contrast, conveys the use of the space metaphorically.
The dancer depicting Krishna trying to reach a pot of curds suspended from
above does not leap or jump on the stage, but only employs a set of gestures
to convey the act of leaping. But it is not movement or narrative that creates
the illusion. Always a poet in her comments, Bala remarked to her friend
and translator S. Guhan, "It is the music that is deceiving you."[45]

Vikram Samvat 2000

The All India Dance Festival in Bombay in January 1945 was the scene
of another of the five great concerts in Balasaraswati's career—a concert
that also was emblematic of the *Sringara rasa* controversy between Bala
and Rukmini Devi Arundale. The festival, a program that twenty years
earlier would have been inconceivable, lasted from January 18 to January
24 in Bombay, presented on the alleged two-thousandth birthday of King
Vikramaditya, Vikram Samvat 2000. The event was held at the Excelsior
Theatre, sponsored by a committee eager to help revive dance, among other
indigenous arts.

The festival opened with a recital of bharata natyam by Rukmini Devi,
who was the predominant performer throughout. There were fourteen programs over six nights, each night of performance lasting five or six hours.
The festival included some of the major names in hereditary dance and
music, including Achchan Maharaj, whom Bala had admired in Calcutta
in 1934; Shambhu Maharaj, his brother, whom Bala had seen and admired
in Benaras in 1936; Ali Akbar Khan, a sarodist who was also in Calcutta;
and Vilayat Khan, who was a sitarist from a famous family lineage. Oddly,
with the exception of Balasaraswati, who was given a full program, each of
these hereditary artists (who would become internationally famous in time)
were granted short slots of time to perform, each sharing part of an evening
with as many as six other performers of lesser distinction.

There were several performers of *Manipuri*, including Nabakumar Sinha, the first traditional dance teacher who had been brought to Santiniketan in 1928 by Rabindranath Tagore. Other performers were students from institutions that taught the traditional arts, including Krishnan Kutty Nair from Kerala Kalamandalam and Mrinalini Sarabhai who had learned with Kandappa Pillai while at Uday Shankar's school at Almora. There were innovators of modern Indian dance, including Ram Gopal, who mixed several styles into one program, and Gopinath, who presented programs entitled "Palace Dancer." There were other nonhereditary performers of "classical" styles. In addition to her solo concert of bharata natyam, Rukmini Devi presented two dance dramas that she designed.

Rukmini Devi's presentation of bharata natyam and dance drama appeared inspired by her exposure to modern European ballet, including several performances of the Ballets Russes she had attended while she was in England with her husband, George Arundale during the 1920s. Under the direction of Serge Diaghilev, the Ballets Russes was powerfully influential in Britain, the United States, and Spain during the 1920s. Diaghilev's productions were conceived as complete works of art, presenting music, design, and drama in a balanced, unified format. Twentieth century bharata natyam dramas, invented by Rukmini Devi, introduced compositions from the music concert repertoire, redesigned costumes, stage props, lighting, and the understanding of *abhinaya* as narrative. The result was a performance idiom that reflected modern Western theatrical aesthetics and effectively distanced the new performer from the negative stereotypes by then attached to the traditional artist.

The juxtaposition of hereditary traditional dancers, nonhereditary traditional dancers, and nontraditional mixed and fusion dancers was a radical idea and seemed calculated to be provocative. The audience was being confronted with a new question of what dance form or forms, and which practitioners, were going to prevail as expressions and representatives of Indian national identity.

In the festival souvenir program, Rukmini Devi's prominent positioning is evident. She presented the inaugural performance, and her biographical profile appeared in the notes immediately after the descriptions of the various "classical" dance forms. "Srimati Rukmini Devi," the profile began, "has regenerated this art and rescued it from degradation and virtual extinction and restored it to its pristine beauty, by permeating it with religious and devotional spirit. She has succeeded in dramatizing it with appropriate music and costumes, and has rescued it from all monopolies, especially as regards teaching and conducting."[46] The notes go on to acknowledge Rukmini Devi's musicians by name. In contrast, the program notes included no profile or introduction of Balasaraswati, and mentioned none of the musicians in her ensemble.

Rukmini Devi's reference to "monopolies" was perhaps directed toward the *nattuvanar* teachers at Kalakshetra, from whom she had successfully wrested control of teaching and the conducting of concerts, which she then placed in the hands of nonhereditary teachers of music and dance, including herself. But whoever the intended target, the reference was an insult to anyone from the professional community, and Balasaraswati's family represented another "monopoly," the repertoire of bharata natyam.

In the inaugural performance on January 18, Rukmini Devi performed a traditionally formatted concert, and she included compositions whose poetry made reference to human love, *Sringara rasa* pieces from the traditional repertoire. I asked Medha Yodh, who was at the concert (and who provided me with the concert program), how Rukmini Devi's assertions about the unacceptability of *Sringara rasa* compositions for performance by respectable women could be reconciled with her inclusion of these pieces. Medha answered that Rukmini Devi's point was that if you were respectable, then *Sringara* would itself become respectable, and that if you were not, then the performance of *Sringara* was not.

The night of Balasaraswati's concert on January 21, the evening program began with a dance drama designed, directed, and performed by Rukmini Devi and students from Kalakshetra. The piece was a reconstruction of a *kuravanji*, an opera-like form that had evolved in the Thanjavur court. The program notes described the performance: "This *Kuravanji* is based by Rukmini Devi on the style found by her in a Temple festival. In discovering and presenting it, her object is not merely to give a pleasant evening but to reveal an object of patriotic, historical, and cultural value, for what you see is not the ingenuity merely of an artist, but the soul of a people of long ago."[47] Her sets were elaborate and beautifully executed. Mrs. A. R. Sundarajan, Balasaraswati's singer (a student of T. Brinda and a member of one of Madras's prominent families), recalled the event. "Just before Bala's program Rukmini Devi gave a dance drama—elaborate scenery, coconut palms—it looked just like Bali—gorgeous—we waited to give our nine-thirty concert."

It was well known that Bala's presentation of concerts was austere and that she used no stage props at all. She did not use statuary on stage, an avoidance that included the newly ubiquitous statue of Nataraja, an image of the dancing Siva encircled by a cosmic flame that was placed on the stage by dancers of the reconstructed style. To the uninformed eye Balasaraswati's staging would have appeared to be unsophisticated. New conventions such as brilliant and tailored costumes and elaborate staging and lighting[48] were becoming an expression of the modernized style.

Bala had expected that she would perform on the same set that Rukmini Devi was using, because removing it would be a disruptive event in front of an audience of hundreds of Bombay's wealthy and educated. And it was. At the conclusion of Rukmini Devi's *kuravanji*, after the curtain was closed but clearly audibly, stagehands struck the set. The detritus that was left — nails, wood splinters, and large amounts of dirt — covered the stage. While the curtain was still closed, Jayammal insisted on being the one to sweep the floor.

When the curtain opened, Bala danced on an empty stage. She remembered the concert as one of great vigor and triumph, as do others who were there. As Mrs. Sundarajan told it, "We thought they would leave some decor, but, within ten or fifteen minutes they removed everything! The stage was totally empty — not even a backdrop. I think this so upset Bala that she danced wonderfully — *abhinaya*, *tirmanams* — [everything] had such enormous energy. It was as if she decided to say, 'I want to show art is not just stage trappings.' And she proved her point. The audience was thrilled. Even with her typical, old-fashioned costume."

Balasaraswati's musical ensemble consisted of Jayammal; Mrs. A. R. Sundarajan as supporting vocalist; Ellappa Pillai as *nattuvanar*; Kuppuswami Mudaliar on the *mridangam*; and Viswanathan playing the flute. Ranganathan, who played the harmonium,[49] was there as chaperone.

While Bala was in Bombay, she and Ranganathan stayed with R. K. Shanmukham at his home in the Malabar Hills, an elegant residential section in the hills above the Bombay coastline. While there Bala learned music from a student of Abdul Karim Khan's named Kapileswari Bhuwa, a Maharashtran Hindu who had a school in Bombay. R. K. Shanmukham had contacted someone at the school, and Kapileswari had responded by saying, "Oh, I know Balasaraswati. My *guru* spoke highly of that family. I would be honored to teach her." He came every morning to work with her.[50]

During the rest of 1945 Bala was invited to give two more concerts, both private and in Madras. One took place in February and one in March; in one she performed only *abhinaya*. Twenty-one months later, at the end of 1946, Bala gave her single concert of the year at the fourth Tamil Isai Festival at St. Mary's Hall in Madras. This was to be the last performance she was invited to give for almost three years, and her only concert in a period of almost five years.

On January 26, 1947, India celebrated its first Republic Day. Four months later, the Devadasi Act, originally introduced by Dr. Muthulakshmi Reddy in 1928, was passed in the Madras Legislative Council. The act declared unlawful "the performing of any dance by any woman in the precincts of any temple or religious institution or in any procession of a Hindu deity." Bala later commented proudly and with respect that even after the passage of the legislation, Mylapore Gauri Ammal continued to dance in the sanctum sanctorum of Kapaaliswara Temple in Madras. Nevertheless, the hereditary art Bala had attempted to raise up in the eyes of the nation and of which she was so intensely proud had been overwhelmed. By the end of 1947, the defamation of the *devadasi* had been legislated, and it appeared that both the art and the artist had been banished and replaced.

As a result of the long-postponed passage of the Devadasi Act, Balasaraswati lost much of her audience and her income. She was anxious for her daughter's future. And at twenty-eight she found herself in a dark emotional hole.

Bala had been sick for several years. Her relationship with R. K. Shanmukham was often a source of frustration and contention. They spent much time together, but their relationship suffered from the conflict of two towering personalities, one eager to be viewed as an authority on Balasaraswati's art, the other determined to maintain her independence. Among other disappointments and tensions, R. K. Shanmukham and Balasaraswati disagreed about the extent of his involvement with and support of his four-year-old daughter, Lakshmi.

Devi Karumari Amman

Several issues raised in this book are so complex or so ancient or so intensely personal that they would not be raised at all if it were not for the place of importance that these things held for Bala. One of these issues is the way in which Balasaraswati became a devotee of a personal form of the divine. With most people, Balasaraswati did not speak of her spiritual experience. She deplored public exploitation of devotion. Lakshmi and a few of Bala's closest friends made up an inner circle with whom she would be expressive.

In general, Bala was skeptical of people who assumed the mask of God, but there were some who had her full respect and trust, including Sri Chandrashekarendra Saraswati Swamigal, the Paramacharya of the Shankaracharaya *math* of Kanchipuram,[51] and certain *sanyasis* (religious ascetics). One who held her entire regard for years was a *yogi* (practitioner of spiritual discipline) named Padakacheri Swamigal. His *samadhi* (place of burial, tomb) is in Thiruvotriyur, which is the site of an eighteenth-century shrine to Siva and the Goddess, now located on the outskirts of the city of Chennai. Lakshmi reported that it seemed that the Swami would appear at the house whenever Jayammal was very sick with asthma, a chronic problem that plagued her. Over the years, Padakacheri Swamigal reassured Bala repeatedly that things would go well in her life after she had visited a form of Shakti, the Goddess, called Devi Karumari Amman.

A woman who cleaned and did menial work in Dhanammal's home during Bala's childhood was a devotee of Devi Karumari Amman. Once a year, at the full moon of the Hindu month beginning in May, the woman visited at a small shrine dedicated to Devi Karumari Amman in the village of Thiruverkadu, to the west of Madras. The servant had a speech impediment. The significance of this detail, remembered through four generations, was that the temple at Thiruverkadu, known by devotees to be a source of comfort and wisdom, was a place of refuge for the disenfranchised: people lost to addiction, financial ruin, illness, widowhood, deformity, abuse, and spiritual despair. In spite of the remoteness of the shrine, the sweeper returned there year after year. Each year she left the temple with *sambal* (sacred ash), which she was instructed to give to the girl in the household who was a dancer.

By 1947 Bala had been hearing the name of the shrine for years, and she recognized its connection to the *sambal* that had been sent through the sweeper when she was a teenager living in her grandmother's house. Late that year, for reasons not known with any certainty other than that it was a period of profound discouragement, Bala visited the shrine dedicated to Devi Karumari Amman for the first time. Her health had been very poor, and her way of life and system of beliefs had been legislated as immoral and illegal. Years before, Padakacheri Swamigal had told her that she should not be deceived by the simple appearance of the place, and that she would find there the presence of the divine, and relief. "All you will be given to eat is rice and *dhal*. But that is where you will find Shakti," he is said to have told her.

In 1977 I first visited the shrine at Thiruverkadu with Balasaraswati and her daughter. Lakshmi had been going there with Bala since she was four years old. I never asked questions of Balasaraswati about the shrine or what it meant to her. I have come to my understanding of the place both through repeated visits of my own and through being in the presence of Balasaraswati and Lakshmi's devotion.

The unpaved road that led to the village of Thiruverkadu would be dusty or puddle-pocked, depending on when we went. Bala would be sometimes be thoughtful and quiet, sometimes singing, at times excited like a child. I did not understand fully the shifts in her demeanor, but I understood from the first time I went with her that this was a place that Bala entered as would a child into the home of someone completely familiar, a trusted figure of authority. The families who tend to the shrine and a few of the people who came, for various reasons, to live there have become acquaintances and friends of mine. Within the family for whom the shrine to Devi Karumari Amman is a hereditary responsibility, one male in each generation emerges as a medium through which at times the presence of the divine is conveyed. That person is the headman of the family shrine, and he is treated with deference and reverence. For devotees such as Balasaraswati, through the medium the presence and words of Shakti, Devi Karumari Amman, are manifest.

The legend that describes the origin of a temple is called the *sthala purana*.[52] It is a legend held to embody the truth. A challenge involved in understanding such a legend, however, is to realize that there are events, objects, moments of wonder that exist in reality, making the "legend" real.

There is no value to a belief that does not, in some manner, acknowledge the believer. A *sthala purana* is not a retelling of an allegory that has a moral or historical significance but rather is at the heart of a passionate presence. It does not require that all believe, but it provides safety and meaning for those who do. This is the *sthala purana* of Devi Karumari Amman in Thiruverkadu:

> At the end of *Kali Yuga*,[53] Shakti assumes the form Devi Karumari Amman. In order to advise and comfort people on the human level, she makes herself manifest in human form.
>
> The challenge, Shakti says, is that her appearance through a human medium will be a cause of suspicion and mistrust. Therefore, Devi Karumari Amman first takes the form of a black cobra. As a way of interceding into the material and human realm, she bites a woman who is a sweeper from a Harijan family in Thiruverkadu. The old woman dies almost immediately, and the grief-stricken family takes the body to the house. By committing this harm, Devi creates for herself a debt to the family.
>
> The body lies in the house as the family waits for relatives to arrive from a distance. Finally the mourners take the body to the cremation ground, but as the corpse is placed on the pyre, the old woman seems to come to life. The villagers, out of fear, begin to beat her with sticks. She speaks to them, saying humans do not have the capacity to differentiate between good and evil. "Seeing the horror of my form, you assume I am evil. You do not recognize who I am." She explains that she is Devi Karumari Amman and that it was she who took the form of a snake and bit the woman.
>
> She declares that she will become the breadwinner of the family for the next twenty-one generations. In order to protect and provide, she explains, she will become manifest through one of the male members of each successive generation. "Your entire family will never lack for food or shelter; but nor will they ever be wealthy." And to this day the family has had only what they needed to live, no matter how they were employed or what wealth was given to them.

After Devi's first appearance, the first family member who became Devi's medium, sometime in the early 1900s, was a man named Paalyam, who earned a living as a laborer in the fields that surrounded the village. Paalyam became known, as did his descendants, as a *yogi*, and through him the Goddess would appear each Sunday. At first the Goddess would appear only in the home of the woman she had bitten, and that family alone became devotees of this unknown form of Shakti. Gradually, however, word spread within the village and others, overcoming their trepidation, came to experience the appearance of the Goddess.

Devi Karumari Amman is worshipped without *margam*; that is, without a particular mode or way of worshipping. She is constantly in motion. She says, "I am a *paraari.*" The word *paraari* has various meanings, including "nothing" or "other," "servant," "unattainable and superior," and "supreme spirit." Devi Karumari Amman is the protector of the poor and disconsolate. There was no permanent image of the Goddess; instead, devotees would paint her image on the side of an earthen pot filled with turmeric water and branches of the *neem* tree at the time that they anticipated that the Goddess would appear. Turmeric and *neem* are traditional and very effective antiseptics, and therefore are considered to be agents of the divine. Shrine attendants sprinkle these purifying agents over those assembled when the Goddess appears.

In the third generation, Devi Karumari Amman appeared again through a male family member, and insisted this time that the medium wear female decoration: nose and toe rings and copper bangles (copper because they were affordable by the family). The suggestion of the blurred distinction between male and female is deliberate; devotee and the medium are confronted by the ambiguity of *maya* (illusion; or, as a deity, Maya), who creates, perpetuates, and governs the dream of duality in the phenomenal universe. During this generation, through the medium's (or vehicle's) instruction, devotees gave a physical form to the Goddess as Devi Karumari Amman and created a small image in stone.

The first time Bala visited Thiruverkadu, the vehicle was in its third generation. Bala was to witness the transition to two more generations before she died in 1984. As Lakshmi recalled, on that first trip in 1947, no one in Bala's small entourage had any real idea of the sort of place they were visiting, but the sage who told Bala she would visit Thiruverkadu had described it to her: Where Devi is, the land would be parched and covered in low brush and thorns; hence the name Thiruverkadu. (*Thiru* means "holy," *ver* means "thorn," and *kadu* means "forest.")

In late 1947 Balasaraswati was penniless. Resolved, she removed a ring from her hand and borrowed a small amount of cash in order to pay for bus tickets for herself, her mother, her daughter, one of her aunts, and an old friend, C. P. Srinivasan.

After the fifteen-kilometer bus ride, the group got down and proceeded to a place where local villagers moved between the farmland and their homes by arranging to ride on lorries carrying sand across a small river that separated the road and village. Having made their way across the river, the group found that they had to walk through a coconut and mango grove to the village and the small temple. C. P. carried Lakshmi on his shoulders. They had been told to expect that some form of the Goddess would appear to them. Lakshmi's account of this story was that Bala and Jayammal giggled as the unfamiliarly rustic drumming that precedes the appearance of the Goddess began. They were nervous in their uncertain anticipation,

Lakshmi recalled. Devi did not appear. The group made their way back to
Madras disappointed.

The following day, mysteriously, Bala made the same trip again with everyone except her aunt. On this occasion Devi did appear. The medium, named Thambu Swamigal, was blind and needed to lean on someone's arm to move around. He was a very quiet man with long white hair. According to Lakshmi, when Devi Karumari Amman appeared Thambu Swamigal resembled exactly a frail aged woman, particularly when his hair was tied into a bun. During the visitations from Shakti, he was able see and needed no assistance to walk.

First there was an explanation from Devi Karumari Amman as to why she had not appeared the day before: The aunt who had come with them would have gossiped about Bala's problems, which would have been revealed. The aunt would have benefited by spreading that gossip. The Goddess continued:

You pawned your ring to come see me. You have come here because you have nowhere else to go. No matter that you have a husband, or brothers at home, you are alone. Like all these who have come to me for protection and help, I will also help you. Like rain falling to the ground, and slowly rising to become the sweetness of the milk of a coconut, I will meet your needs drop by drop. You will not need to worry.

Balasaraswati was not alone in her discouragement. Traditional family practices were disappearing in other parts of India. Institutions were replacing traditional ways of teaching and learning many kinds of knowledge. The passage of the Devadasi Act of 1947 did not just affect the matrilineal community; it resounded throughout the hereditary arts. Like bharata natyam and other traditional dance forms in India, a style of dance-theater called *kuchipudi*, from Andhra Pradesh (until Independence a part of the Madras Presidency), experienced a reconstruction in the 1940s and 1950s. One of the sources of the renaissance in interest in the style of *kuchipudi* was a dancer named Vedantam Lakshminarayana Sastri.

VEDANTAM LAKSHMINARAYANA SASTRI

Vedantam Lakshminarayana Sastri had come to Madras in 1948 and arrived at Bala's home, offering to teach her. An orthodox Brahmin, he moved from his village in Andhra Pradesh to Madras, and through her work with him Balasaraswati expanded her already legendary capacity for *abhinaya*. Vedantam Lakshminarayana Sastri would eventually be recognized as a great master of *abhinaya*, attracting many of the leading dancers in Madras, including Mylapore Gauri Ammal, who came to study with him. But when he first arrived in Madras, he sought out Bala.

Viswanathan remembered the first time Vedantam Lakshminarayana Sastri visited Balasaraswati's house in Egmore. He arrived without announcement. Explaining at the door why he was looking for Bala, Vedantam Lakshminarayana Sastri complained that no one seemed to be interested in his art. He later said that he had heard of Bala's fame as an *abhinaya* artist, and he wanted her to be a repository of his art, which he knew would otherwise be lost. Bala was reluctant to work with him, because meeting his fees would be difficult, but family friend C. P. Srinivasan offered to pay them. Srinivasan was a connoisseur of the family's music, as well as of Abdul Karim Khan's singing.

At first Vedantam Lakshminarayana Sastri would come each day from Mylapore by hand-pulled rickshaw; Bala paid the rickshaw charges. Despite arriving in a sweat after the long ride in the sun, Vedantam Lakshmina-

Balasaraswati with her mentor Vedantam Lakshminarayana Sastri, Madras, ca. 1948. Courtesy of Sangeet Natak Akademi Archives, Delhi.

rayana Sastri, in his orthodoxy, would not touch water in Bala's house during the entire day he was there. Soon after he began teaching Bala, however, Jayammal found him a place to live nearby in Egmore that met his modest needs and where he stayed for about two years.

Vedantam Lakshminarayana Sastri taught Bala almost daily at her home. Lakshmi described what she remembered of his astounding physical control. "He could sweat on command, weep at will, make his hair stand out, change the color of his skin. Yet his true genius lay in his enormous variety of improvisational techniques."[1] Bala said, "In my thirties, Vedantam Lakshminarayana Sastri opened great new vistas for me, especially in *varnam* improvisation. He shared his immense knowledge and, in a very real sense, gave me the confidence to attempt those things I do today.... I would pierce him and he poured forth."[2] Bala was like a sponge. The master's admiration for the young student equaled her respect for him. Bala, never rude, chose only those aspects suitable to her style, technique, and aesthetic. Following his morning lesson with Bala, Vedantam Lakshminarayana Sastri learned songs from Jayammal, adding to his already rich repertoire. Bala said he once told her, "If I had a singer like your mother, with her music I could have taken my art throughout the world."[3] According to Viswanathan he hesitated and then added, "I didn't have a singer like your mother," and he laughed at his own joke.[4] It was an unusual exchange across the cultural differences that existed between geographical regions of India.

Viswa asked if he could watch Bala's lessons, and he was invited to observe the classes. "He would take one line, and say, 'these are the ways you can improvise,'" Viswa remembered. "He was preparing her systematically, so that she could learn to do her own things. . . . Some things were a little obscene. Bala said, 'I won't do it.' He said, 'I want to teach you this sand dance [an old folk style from Andhra Pradesh],' but Bala said, 'I don't want all those things, Guruji. I want to do *abhinaya*; all these things, I am not interested.'"[5] During that time Bala arranged for a series of photographs to be taken of the *mudras* he had taught her, so that she would not forget the esoteric lexicon of gestures. Bala absorbed the *mudras* into her intuitive language, and they remained with her for her lifetime.

It is sobering to consider Bala being taught to improvise, an art for which she was already receiving widespread accolades. "The *mudras*, or hand gestures, may be said to be the alphabet of the suggestive language of bharata natyam," Balasaraswati said in her keynote address at the Congress on Research on Dance in Hawaii in August 1979. "Many of the *mudras* are common to both the *Tantra Sastra* [very loosely defined, the scripture of spiritual knowledge, or in this case the hand gestures of Tantric Yoga] and bharata natyam." Bala demonstrated the concept of connotative hand gestures employed in dance as she continued: "I would like to point out a single example of how *mudras* acquire new meanings in bharata natyam. The *mudra* of joining the tips of the thumb and the forefinger is called *chin mudra* in the religious scriptures, meaning 'the sign of wisdom.' It is the symbol of realizing the oneness of the individual soul, signified by the forefinger, with the one Over-soul, signified by the thumb. The *chin mudra* is accepted in this spiritual sense in dancing also, but see what new meaning it acquires in addition. It is the sign of wisdom only when the palm is held up in a graceful slant. The same *mudra*, when the palm is held stiffly upright, depicts the valor of a bowman who holds the arrow between his two fingertips. When, with the palm back to [away from] the audience's view, the dancer touches the mid-point of her eyebrow with this *mudra*, it conveys her putting on the mark of beauty, the *tilak*. So the same *mudra* serves for three entirely different concepts: spiritual wisdom, valor, and preparation for beautifying the lover.

"The gestures of bharata natyam eliminate all inessentials and strikingly depict concepts and objects by creating minimal semblance to the original mainly by virtue of the *mudras*. For example, in other dance systems, including Indian dance systems other than bharata natyam, an elephant is depicted with a fund of details like its high and bulky size, pillar-like legs, winnow-like ears, resilient trunk with its different movements, majestic gait, and so on. But see how, with the simple *mudra* of the four fingers, the stiffly bent first and forefingers signifying the tusks and the dropping middle fingers denoting the trunk, the elephant is unmistakably suggested in bharata natyam.... Similarly, in bharata natyam those same two fingers which stood for the elephant's tusks become the horns of the cow when tilted up perpendicularly and the other three fingertips joined together picture the face of the cow. And, with a wave of the right hand the dancer also represents the cowherd who drives it."[6]

In 1948, Bala was invited to star in a film based on R. Krishnamurthy's historical novel *Sivakaamiyin Sabadam* (*Sivakaami's Vow*), in which Bala was the model for the heroine. She declined. She was proud of having achieved a reputation on the stage without resorting to films to aid her career. She had prevailed in her art alone when nearly every leading actor and vocalist, and some dancers, had already jumped at the opportunity to perform in film, a sure path to popularity and success. In spite of her impoverishment and neglect by the public, she was steadfast in her principles.

A NEW START

In the family tax records for 1941, Bala had listed eleven engagements. In 1942 none were listed; Bala had been ill with heart problems resulting from rheumatic fever. In 1943, however, she gave thirteen concerts; in 1944, eleven; in 1945, three; in 1946, one; in 1947, none; 1948, none; 1949, one. After the passage of the Devadasi Act in 1947, Bala was not asked to perform again until the last months of the decade.

Late in 1949, after thirty months without opportunity to perform, Bala was asked to dance a small private recital. The event renewed her spirit and artistic drive; emerging from her involuntary reclusion, during the early 1950s Bala became a fixture in the performance seasons of Madras, Delhi, and Bombay, and in smaller cities throughout the country. She received two sorts of acclaim: for her supremacy as a musician and dancer of unparalleled capacity and soul; and for her perseverance in her heritage, the traditions of music and dance that she embodied.

Balasaraswati was always grateful to the Sanskrit scholar Dr. V. Raghavan, who in 1949 was the secretary of the Music Academy and one of Balasaraswati's staunchest supporters. Bala expressed her appreciation and acknowledgment of his contribution on numerous public and private occasions. At a time when the traditional community and its artistic practice had received withering public rebuke, Dr. Raghavan stood firm in the midst of the tide of social resistance and offered Balasaraswati both an opportunity to teach and the respect afforded by the advocacy of the Music Academy.

Dr. Raghavan directed several Western visitors and scholars to Balasaraswati's home. Among them was the anthropologist from the University of Chicago, Milton Singer; his book, *When a Great Tradition Modernizes*, which includes a chapter on Balasaraswati's family, informed many in the

West of the changing culture of Madras. Another visitor, musicologist Harold Powers, went on to become a distinguished scholar of Indian music and professor at the University of Pennsylvania and later at Princeton.

Beryl de Zoete was a London-born dance ethnologist of Dutch descent; along with the German artist and photographer Walter Spies, she published a book in 1937 called *Dance and Drama in Bali*. In 1949, when de Zoete was in India working on another book and was being guided around Madras by the dancer Ram Gopal, Raghavan asked Ram Gopal to take her to see Bala. De Zoete's wonderful descriptive book on dance in South India, *The Other Mind*, resulted from that 1949 visit. In it she comments that she would like to think that it was partly because of her enthusiasm that, soon after their encounter, Bala danced in a public concert in New Delhi.[7] Years later, more than crediting de Zoete for that performance, Bala attributed the renewal of her career to Beryl de Zoete.[8]

Viswa was there and remembered: "Raghavan sent [de Zoete]. . . . She said, 'I would like to see you dance.' Bala said, 'No, I have stopped dancing. I don't want to dance anymore.' But de Zoete said, 'I just want to see [you].' Ram Gopal was with her. He said, 'Bala, please dance for her. . . . We aren't expecting you to give a full concert, just dance whatever you can.'" De Zoete and Ram Gopal then left for Kanchipuram, and returned a few days later. They contacted Bala again, and she had decided to agree to dance.

Ram Gopal made the arrangements and rented a small hall called the Rasika Ranjani Sabha for the performance. Bala performed with Jayammal, Viswa, Kuppuswami, Ganesha, and Ellappa. Viswa continued in his recollection. "We all went at ten o'clock in the morning. There was Ram Gopal, Beryl de Zoete, and a few others — about five or six people. Bala started dancing, and de Zoete said, 'I'm very happy. This is just what I wanted to see.' Bala danced beautifully. De Zoete was very impressed, and wrote down a few notes. She said she would like some photographs." Jayammal refused, very likely because she was conscious of the weight gain Bala suffered because of her thyroid dysfunction. The absence of photographs in *The Other Mind* is notable.[9] It is also notable that this ensemble could reassemble to perform, without rehearsal, after a considerable period of inactivity.

The section of de Zoete's book on bharata natyam focuses on two dancers, Shanta Rao and Balasaraswati. De Zoete is disarming in her innocence of the politics of the Madras performance environment. She found offensive the affectation of Western stage presentation that she saw in Shanta Rao's performance and that was becoming increasingly common in Madras, and said so. Her complaint is reminiscent of A. K. Coomaraswamy's remarks in *The Dance of Shiva*, written thirty-five years earlier, about Indians' misapprehension of Western aesthetics and the danger that misunderstanding posed to Indian performing arts.

The writer K. Chandrasekharan was among the leading figures of Tamil Nadu who had supported Rukmini Devi's aim of promoting decency in the art of dance. However, unlike some other critics, Chandrasekharan remained capable of depersonalizing his criticism and avoided championing any single artist on the basis of preference. His standard for beauty was recognized and was consistently influential. On October 23, 1949, K. Chandrasekharan reviewed Balasaraswati's return to the public stage in a concert at the Museum Theatre. In the review he notes a "deplorable dearth" of bharata natyam concerts conforming to the dance art's strict requirements and commented that Balasaraswati's program was a rarity. Chandrasekharan chastises "so-called artists" for their "divergence" from the dance's inherent beauty and their "craze for showing off the be-jeweled body [and] frequent costume changes and stage effects. Bala's austerity was striking, by contrast to the usual gaudiness." Despite her "none too fragile frame," he comments, her *kalapramana* (literally "time promise," or sense of rhythm) and mastery of the *rasas* "drew heaven's drops to parched hearts."

Chandrasekharan includes praise for both Jayammal and Ellappa for "satisfying the audience in *padams* and *javalis*." Their treatment of Kshetrayya's *padams*, he says, united the entire audience into "one heart hopeful that this rarest of arts might live again." He speculates whether anyone will be capable of replacing Bala's "entrancing fountain of ideas" and commends the sponsoring organization for "rescuing this precious possession of the Dhanam family" at a time when "physical attributes had become popular."[10]

Ram Gopal had brought de Zoete to Bala's rehearsal of a dramatic production, *Sarabendra Bhoopala Kuravanji*. Historically performed primarily in temples, these operatic dance dramas generally concern the affection of a heroine for the deity of the temple or the local ruler. The heroine praises the deity (or lord), asking that her maidservants bring her lover to her. A character common to most *kuravanjis* is a gypsy who appears and describes the prosperity of the region. She reads the palm of the heroine and predicts the fulfillment of her desires.

Drama has had a long history in India. Royalty often authored new works, and some dramas, including *kuravanjis*, were popular as long as the royal courts existed. *Kuravanji* became popular in the Thanjavur court in the late eighteenth century. Much of the musical repertoire for the form was the family legacy of the Thanjavur Quartet. The words of Bala's production, *Sarabendra Bhoopala Kuravanji*, were written in praise of Raja Serfoji II, who was a devotee of Siva in the manifestation of Brihadiswara, as he is found in the "Big" Temple in Thanjavur. The king especially favored that temple and added shrines to the temple's vast complex. Brihadiswara Temple saw annual performances of this particular *kuravanji* until 1950.

Although the beginning of Balasaraswati's teaching career is often associated with the school that she established in 1953 at the Music Academy, she had actually begun teaching years earlier: As she worked on the production of the *kuravanji* during 1949, Bala had prepared a half dozen students to dance roles in the opera.

The first presentation of Bala's production of the *Sarabendra Bhoopala Kuravanji* was on December 27, 1949, at the eighth Tamil Isai Festival at St. Mary's Hall. The Tamil Isai Sangam was directly competitive with the Music Academy in those days. Bala's partner, R. K. Shanmukham, who had cofounded the Tamil Isai Sangam, had wanted Bala to premier the production at its annual program during December and January; according to T. Shankaran, it is most likely that R. K. Shanmukham prepared the scenario for the drama. Jayammal was the leading vocalist, using lyrics set to music composed by the Thanjavur Quartet.[11]

Sarojini Kumaraswami, a student of Jayammal's, was one of the musicians Bala asked to sing for the *kuravanji*; Sarojini assisted Jayammal as a singer from this time until the late 1950s, when she moved to the United Kingdom. In 1963 she would perform in Bala's concerts at the Edinburgh Festival. Remembering the *kuravanji* many years later,[12] Sarojini described the experience: "[Bala] asked if I would sing and I said yes, of course. She had six girls as *sakhis* [women friends] and Bala was the *kurathi* [a gypsy, an itinerant fortune-teller]. It was wonderful to watch her put the whole thing together. We were with her from the word go. We got together every evening at least for an hour, when she would go through one *tirmanam*, one song. . . . To see it, to see [how] the dance shape changed, was watching the master at work. Viswa and Ranga were also there, and sometimes Kittappa Pillai joined because this *kuravanji* used to be [performed] by the Pandanallur family . . . at the Great Temple in Thanjavur; Kittappa knew the music. Weekday rehearsals went for an hour, not longer, for the girls had their schoolwork to do. A van picked all of us up, and returned us afterwards. Sunday was different. We gathered much earlier and Bala would see that plenty of food was brought in, like a picnic every Sunday. It was during those rehearsal times when we were so close to her, that we could see the mother in Bala. She was not just a teacher, but was full of love for all the girls. Not once did she lose her temper. . . . Whatever she wanted to correct or have done differently was said as though she spoke to her own child. No harshness and that is remembered even now. . . the kind of person she was. . . warmth, tenderness and love, qualities that were seen and experienced."[13] Creating these presentations buoyed Bala's spirits and was a reassuring and reinvigorating experience for her.

At the end of 1951 she presented the second performance of her *kuravanji* for the ninth Tamil Isai Festival at the Museum Theatre in Madras. Positive reviews of the *kuravanji* by a critic calling himself "Rasikan" appeared

Ensemble for Balasaraswati's production of the *kuravanji Sarabendra Bhoopala*, photographed on the entrance steps of Saint Mary's Anglo Indian Higher Secondary School, Madras, December 1949. Photo by G. K. Vale & Co.
Front row (from left): Lakshmi Shanmukham (Balasaraswati's daughter), unknown, Nirmala Ramachandran, Uma Sastri, Geeta. *Second row (from left):* Ranganayaki, Shanti Radha, Hemamalini Vijayaraghavan, T. Balasaraswati, unknown, T. Jayammal. *Third row (from left):* Unknown, T. Ranganathan, unknown, K. P. Kittappa Pillai, uncertain (perhaps Radhakrishna Naidu), T. Viswanathan. *Fourth row:* both unknown.

in Tamil and English on January 12, 1951. "The public of Madras were regaled [by] Srimathi Bala Saraswathi [*sic*] and her [talented] troupe. . . . [This drama] was cast entirely in the style and technique [of] Bala's, inimitable and unsurpassable. . . . Modeled on the fundamental principles of operatic exposition every movement, gesture and pose were perfectly harmonized and synchronized . . . the effect was scintillating. . . . Contrasted with other [such productions] now sprouting up, Sri Bala's interpretation placed the accent on the divine Kurathi."[14] The choreographic vision and concentrated energy required to mount a major theatrical production expanded Bala's creative repertoire. However, she did not attempt another dramatic production until 1974, when she worked in the United States and with mostly non-Indian students.

Beginning with a concert at the Madras Music Academy on January 2, 1950, Bala began her solo career again. Gradually other opportunities to perform emerged. She presented a second concert for the Music Academy at the 26th Annual Conference on December 29, 1952 at Sundareswarar Hall in Mylapore.[15]

The Balasaraswati School

On May 5, 1953, Balasaraswati's partner, R. K. Shanmukham, died at the age of sixty-one. Despite the volatility of their relationship, Bala was despondent, and she vowed to give up performing entirely. Close friends, notably Dr. Raghavan, M. S. Subbulakshmi, and M. A. Rajagopalan, supported her during this time. M. A. Rajagopalan was like an older brother with whom Bala would speak with about her private feelings. His cousin was Mrs. A. R. Sundarajan, who had sung with Bala's ensemble in Bombay in 1945. Her family had been close to Bala's family since Dhanammal's generation; her father and her father's father were devotees of Vina Dhanammal. Bala had taught her music, and eventually she sang with Lakshmi's ensemble in India. Bala would drop in to visit her, one of very few people with whom Bala felt comfortable doing that.

Within weeks after R. K. Shanmukham's death, at the urging of Dr. V. Raghavan, the Madras Music Academy opened the Balasaraswati School of Indian Music and Dance in a small outbuilding on the Academy's grounds. Dr. Raghavan's eldest daughter, Priyamvada, who had been learning privately with Balasaraswati since 1950, was the school's first enrolled student. The Sangeet Natak Akademi provided a generous yearly grant of ten thousand rupees.[16] At this time there was little doubt in the public view about who was responsible for the continuation of the traditional practice of bharata natyam in its most contemporary form. Justice T. L. Venkatarama Iyer represented this view in his short address at the opening of the school: "I had held the mistaken notion that bharata natyam was an indecent art — in poor taste, undignified — and that one should turn a deaf ear to the very mention of it. Now, having seen Balasaraswati perform, I can appreciate its stature and glory, the rich beauty of the art."[17]

In commemoration of the opening of the school, Kalki wrote: "The all-time great exponent and performer of this art is Balasaraswati. There need be no second opinion or contradiction to this remark: it is accomplished fact. About fifteen years ago there was a revival of this art in Tamil Nadu. The credit goes to Balasaraswati who made it possible and helped it to happen. Last week the Balasaraswati School of Music and Dance was declared open to train young artists in this great tradition."[18] Tamil scholar T. K. Chidambaram wrote Bala a note: "Your school is begun. Only you gave new life to bharata natyam. Still, you must give more — fresh life to preserve, foster, and save it for posterity. I am truly delighted to see the school established with you and your dear mother as its teachers."[19]

After taking Kandappa Pillai's son, Ganesha, into her care in 1941, Bala had taught him his father's wonderfully musical style of *nattuvangam*. Jayammal had taught him music, although Jayammal complained that Ganesha never became capable of singing in concerts as his father had. So Bala nurtured two singers, Kanchipuram Gnanasundaram and S. Narasimhulu, to accompany her in the first half of her dance concerts.

At the school Ganesha taught the rhythmic aspect of the dancing, including the musical aspects of the types of compositions his father had revolutionized, and choreography. Bala had encouraged Ganesha to have his own students even before her school was established; Bala would help Ganesha with teaching *abhinaya* and certain pieces, but they were Ganesha's students. Bala had taught Ganesha how to compose, and he eventually created *tirmanams* that were extensions of his father's vision. Ellappa, who was conducting Bala's ensemble, had his own students at the school.

Despite the public support she received at the time of the opening of the school, and in particular the support of friends, Balasaraswati had bouts of discouragement. She was physically unwell. A rheumatic condition that had first been diagnosed in the 1940s was causing unsightly and painful swelling in her hands and joints. And Bala's return to the public stage was not a resounding reunion with her audience. She was rarely invited to perform. For many, the Devadasi Act of 1947 had put an end to that era in India's history. Bala had become a legend and, for many, had simply disappeared. As Bala's opportunities to perform diminished, her teaching became an important artistic outlet as well as a source of income.

Some misinterpreted the traditional artists' instinct to be protective of their family repertoires as possessiveness, a wish to monopolize the arts. Certainly, in an orally transmitted practice, a family's treasure lay in its proprietary repertoire. Hereditary families were in the business of knowledge. The gift of a song[20] represented distinction and distinctiveness, and therefore prestige — and income. Teaching was as much a part of the continuing

K. Ganesha Pillai, K. Kandappa Pillai's son, 1962. Photo by Gary Margolis.

health of the hereditary form as were learning and performing, and teachers from the professional artistic community would freely share knowledge, including musical compositions, if the objective of the student was genuinely the pursuit of knowledge.

There have been from time to time grudging remarks about the difficulty of learning with Bala and suggestions that she was unwilling to teach. Some have suggested that she was impatient and aloof. I have never met a serious student of hers who was not, to the contrary, in awe of her capacity to teach and of her enthusiasm and commitment.

One dancer who studied with Bala during the 1950s was Roshen Alkazi. She was born to and grew up in a privileged family in Bombay, and studied costume design for theater and the history of medieval Indian costume at the Victoria and Albert Museum in London before she married Ebrahim Alkazi, an eminent theater director. By the end of her career she had designed costumes for more than seventy of her husband's productions at the Theatre Group and Theatre Unit in Bombay, and then at the National School of Drama in Delhi, which Ebrahim Alkazi founded. She was a student of Indian and Western dance, a poet, and was for many years the director of the Art Heritage Gallery, a contemporary art gallery in New Delhi. Her husband, also born in Bombay, moved with his family to New Delhi in the early 1960s. The Alkazis were exemplary among India's modern intellectual elite.

Roshen Alkazi described the magic of her experience encountering Bala first in 1952 and eventually learning with her: "As a young girl, I had studied forms of Western dance and started studying Indian dance at age sixteen. I studied with various teachers in Bombay but wasn't really satisfied with any one. There was . . . an institution called Noopur which organized classical Indian music and dance programs. Going there one day for a dance rehearsal, I saw this plump woman and several musicians arriving in a taxi. They seemed confused so I asked if I could help. They explained they had come for a performance and didn't know where the stage was. I escorted them there and left them there at this little stage, which is on the terrace. She didn't speak to me at all; we communicated through her musicians who spoke Tamil to her. At the end of my rehearsal, I noticed the music starting up and thought I would just pop into this performance for just a few minutes, standing in the back. At the end of the three-hour performance, I found myself in the front row, practically standing on the stage, so enthralled by this performance, I didn't even know how I got there. Then I asked who this dancer was and was told by the organization that she was this famous dancer Balasaraswati, who I thought was a legend and no longer existed. This memory lingered in my subconscious as I went on in my dance studies.

"Suddenly, four years later, I told my husband I was going to Madras. I had a baby [boy] of two and a girl of nine. He asked me what for and I answered I had to go now, seeing what for when I got there. He was quite against the idea of my going alone with the children, but he agreed because I was adamant. The only person I knew there was Dr. Narayana Menon, who was station director of All India Radio in Madras at the time. My husband phoned him, asking him to keep an eye on me while I was there. [After I arrived in Madras] Narayana contacted me inquiring what he could do; embarrassed, I stumbled, 'Oh, I want to learn dance.' He asked if I wanted to learn with Rukmini Devi and I said yes.

"I went [to Rukmini Devi's school, Kalakshetra] on several occasions but declined when she asked me if I wanted to join the class. Then [Narayana Menon] said, 'Look, this evening I am going to see Balasaraswati's class at the Music Academy, where she teaches children five or six years old.' Then the name rang a bell; I didn't even know that Bala was staying in Madras. So I went with him there. Narayana, jokingly, speaking to her in Tamil [which he subsequently translated], said, 'Bala, this young lady has come from Delhi and I have taken her to Rukmini Devi Arundale, but she hasn't signed up; why don't you teach her?' She looked at me and said to Narayana, 'Yes, I'll teach her.' She asked [through Narayana] if I had studied dance. 'Yes,' I said, 'for many years.' 'Tell her,' she told him, 'if she comes to me, she must come as if she is a small child who knows nothing, and starts from *tei ya tei*. I am not going to teach her any item of dance. If she wants to learn, she must learn from the beginning.' So, immediately, I said yes, and started the next day. I found a house in Madras, put the children in school, and told my husband I was starting to study dance. I studied with her for a year and a half.

"Six months after starting, she said, 'You know, you only get one hour, three or four times a week. What do you do with the rest of your time?' 'Nothing', I answered, 'I'm only studying dance; I have my children, and all.' She said, 'Would you like to come home and study at my place?' I said, 'Bala, I can't afford private tuition. I have the expense of a second home.' 'Don't talk about money. I'm not asking you for any money. Would you want to come study at home, then I can give you some attention?' I said, 'I'd love to come; I'm just at home in the mornings.' She said, 'You come from tomorrow to the house.' So that's how I started going to her house to study."[21]

Bala and Roshen would push Bala's bed out of the way, and Roshen would practice there. Bala would teach, sometimes for several hours in a day, and then she would retire downstairs for a coffee. When she felt the spirit, she would dance *abhinaya* for Roshen, as she did sometimes for other students. She would have an idea—something would cross her mind—and she would begin to sing and dance. The spell was delicate, and easily broken by a rustling paper or closing door. Bala enjoyed speaking of her ideas if she felt the listener's interest was genuine. She was fastidious about her use of language, and it made her very shy to speak English. But she had grown up around English and understood it. When she relaxed, her spoken English, heavily and beautifully accented, was eloquent, though not perfectly grammatical.

Roshen Alkazi continued: "She revealed the greatness of India to me, who thought myself an educated person, who knew through books, but I knew what I was looking for was to understand India through its art form. For art, to me, is the start of it. And she revealed that to me. I learned everything about aesthetics just looking at her. And it's not as if I did not know things before. I had been in the theatre; my husband is quite a fine exponent of theatre and comes from a very literate family. I feel a lot, I've been abroad. So uniquely encapsulated in her form was the whole history and tradition of our country. When you look at our bronzes, you can understand the grace of the movement of the bronze in Bala's dance. If you listen to our music, it

was through her dance and music that I understood *karnatic* music. Everything that I had been searching for in aesthetics I came to know through
her. There's a purity in her which has to be there in a practicing person at
that level of interpretation.

"So that humility she had in regard to things like music was what that
whole family had; and that was their secret. When you know a drop, and
you know there's an ocean, you're humble and you learn all the time. You
never close your mind to that form. . . . It's so enormous, and unless you understand that, how can you possibly even start to interpret? What the other
dancers do (I'm not criticizing them) is dip a little, take out something and
think they've got the whole. And that limits them. And that's why whenever
she performed, or sang, she was so frightened, because she knew she was
attempting the impossible. Because it was so true, she revealed to us the possibilities and extent of that form, because she would do something (maybe
she called it a drop) that was a drop of truth. Then you began to realize the
enormity of what it was and how great it was. That is our culture.

"And it's what we are all searching for when we look at India or try to
understand India. We are all looking for that mysterious thing which is
India; and she suddenly revealed it, in a flash or for fifteen minutes or an
hour, when she was in that mood. Suddenly you felt you had seen some
truth, a glimpse of something. She had encapsulated all those times and
civilizations in that flash, which is very difficult to understand from books,
or knowledge, which is on just one level. . . . The very fact that she did a line
of *abhinaya* in so many ways shows that the truth is so mysterious, that it reflects so many things. The fact that she could capture those things and show
them to you was so astonishing. . . . It was difficult to say what it was, you can
only feel it. And only to those who are receptive. But for everyone who knew
anything of dance and had met or seen her, it seems to have left an indelible
impression on their mind. It was as if they could relive that moment."[22]

An interview with Balasaraswati appeared in *Women's World* on October
25, 1953. Bala was a purist, the article stated, and deplored the democratiza-
tion of the art and the inevitable deterioration in standards. Real art, Bala
insisted, should be able to stand without props, excessive costumes, or other
distractions on the stage. Commenting on the wave of innovation and mixing of styles that had become dominant during the 1940s, Bala stated she
believed that a dancer's basic concerns should first be to uphold the high
standard of the art and then, through thorough knowledge and practice,
to pursue adaptation and innovation. The accompanying music required a
singer who had an understanding of the poetry as it might fire the imagination of the dancer; Bala's dancing incorporated moments where melody and
movement would mimic each other. "Only strenuous practice and absolute
concentration will impart precision to movements which mark a true artist,"
declared Bala.[23]

Dr. Charles Fabri, a Hungarian émigré who was the art and dance critic for the Delhi *Statesman*, expressed a poignant perspective after a performance in New Delhi in 1954. "Of Bala one writes almost with bated breath . . . to whom can one compare the moon? What standard yardstick have we for Bala, for she is the standard of all that is finest in bharata natyam. Her last visit to New Delhi amazed her awe-struck audience, [a] most tiring program, of superbly delivered dances . . . [that] represents an age already passed. Nothing can recapture the spirit of this type of dancing. Our minds have changed, our aims and ideals are different, ergo our dancing will be different too."[24] Was this perhaps a clue to the reason that Bala had been shunned from public performance during the 1940s? Did she represent something incomparable—even threatening in its mysteriousness—and therefore, from the perspective of the new practitioner and audience, less "relevant" to the expectations of the democratized art that had begun emerging during the 1930s?

Thiruthani

At Bala's *arangetram* in Kanchipuram in 1925, Pakkiria Pillai had told Kandappa Pillai that he must take Bala to dance before the *prabhu* (Lord) in Thiruthani. This temple, which sits on the crown of a massive monolithic rock, is one of the six major sites of worship of Lord Murugan, son of Siva, in Tamil Nadu. As a seven-year-old child, Bala recalled, she thought that Murugan would not be made of stone there, and that He would be living there. She recalled wondering how He would like her dance, but she never told anyone about her desire. Kandappa Pillai did not take the urging seriously, but Bala remembered Pakkiria Pillai's words and carried an unspoken vow for many years. Lakshmi recalled the day in 1954 when Bala felt she had to make the trip to see Murugan.

Bala knew there would be no unusual event at the temple on that day, and therefore it would not be crowded. She gathered up her bells, and with Lakshmi, Jayammal, and her friend C. P. Srinivasan, off they went to Thiruthani by train, planning to arrive in the late morning, after the regular daily *puja* was completed and the usual small gathering of worshippers would have dispersed. On the train to Thiruthani Bala fell asleep and dreamed of Murugan, who asked her, "You are not coming to see me? Come see me. Then you will understand." In the dream Bala rode on a peacock's back to strange places, as Murugan does in Hindu mythology—and reminiscent of the way she would dance the flight of Murugan's vehicle.

At that time dancing in or near temples was outlawed under the Devadasi Act, and in order to get past the priest, who they judged could not be convinced with a bribe, Bala created a small dramatic tale. She claimed she had rushed all the way from Madras intending to buy the necessary offerings—such as coconut, flowers, and sandal paste—after she arrived;

but, having arrived too late, she would not be able to have the *archana* (a ceremony requiring specific objects for the offering) performed. The priest was touched and he volunteered to purchase what was necessary from shops along the bottom of the hill, and then return to do the ritual. Bala knew his errand would take half an hour. She felt the watchman was bribable and gave him a small amount; she asked him to close the doors to the sanctum sanctorum, leaving Bala and her small entourage in the privacy of this intimate space until the afternoon rites.

Bala put on her ankle bells and danced while her mother sang. She danced *khanda alarippu*, performed with a *tiruppugazh* (a medieval poem set to music),[25] "*Koorvel Parritta*," dedicated to the Murugan at Thiruthani; and set in *Madyamavati raga*; and "*Nila Mayilvahanano*," a song in *Nilambari raga*. She was there uninterrupted for more than half an hour. Bala's expectation, she told Lakshmi later, had not been to dance in the sanctum sanctorum; she had expected she would "dance in some corner." After years of quiet yearning, Bala had fulfilled her vow. "Did I really dance?" Bala wondered later in an interview. "I only remember the joy I felt at that moment of fulfillment—years of yearning had finally come to an end. After that what dancing He manipulated through me, He alone knows."[26]

Lakshmi was eleven at the time. "I was very young, but I did go with her to Thiruthani. It was quite an experience. I still remember how she took her bells with her and she started dancing at the sanctum sanctorum, right inside, and nobody said a word there. . . . There she danced, my grandmother sang. She danced in front of the deity. It was as though nobody could see that somebody was dancing there." The temple workers went about their business as if nothing were happening.

Bala had been ill for some time. She began to recover shortly after the visit to Thiruthani.

A PASSIONATE REALITY

In a period of six years Bala had gone from being a retired legend, subsisting on fees from teaching, to being recognized as India's great dancer. Increasingly it was the public's perception that Bala was becoming a transcendental devotional artist; the worldview that informed Bala's dance was a passionate reality. Her close friend S. Guhan recalled, "In Bala's experience, the mythological characters portrayed in bharata natyam were not distant; they lived 'side by side' with her. Often, in conversation, Bala would tell a *puranic* story with such immediacy and relish that one would have to remind oneself that she was not narrating an incident that took place that day in her home or neighborhood."[27] (The *puranas* are a group of religious texts narrating the history of the universe, usually stories related by one person to another.) When she was on the stage, she could intuitively make references to the images derived from that reality. She did not consciously imagine different ways of interpreting a text; these things came to her as she danced. And that was her art in *abhinaya*.

Balasaraswati described the simplicity of her reality. "Mythological characters, especially the divinities, are not obsolete to us, but are more living than those who are living side by side with us. Many of us recite with devotion portions from the *puranas* during our daily religious observances. We never tire of hearing discourse on the *puranas* by erudite scholars. We have holy days to worship the various divinities. Our magnificent temple sculpture was inspired primarily by the *puranas*. The divine characters are the sublime simplified to our level so as to sublimate us. Rooted in the *puranas*, the dancer considers it her unique privilege to portray through *abhinaya* not only the devotee, but the deity itself. A very rich harvest of inspiration and material for improvisation is reaped by the artist from the fertile field of the *puranas*."[28]

Lakshmi agreed that it was probably true that Bala didn't realize when she was transported and "became that thing." Whether or not she realized it, Lakshmi said, "Bala loathed being quoted in a review or article to be saying, 'I become the baby Krishna. I become Yasoda.' . . . Whenever she was doing Krishna or Murugan or Siva, she never *becomes* Krishna or Murugan. But she becomes engrossed in the experience of dealing with these powers." In this interview, Lakshmi initially intended to defend the statement that Bala would not *become* a character. "She didn't become that character. She became a description of that character. She was a describer." But as Lakshmi spoke, within several sentences she ended up describing the process of making dance, which is apparently at odds with the idea of an objective relationship to character. "If she does become the mother, Yasoda, it is very easy to approach Krishna. . . . There were times she became Yasoda! She actually became that. Even though she says she didn't." But then Lakshmi explained the paradox: "She remained herself because she was that already. She knew how to contain herself, or restrain herself. When we talk of her being Yasoda, she becomes the mother easily. She also becomes Radha, the lover of Krishna. That is how she was able to portray *Sringara rasa* in all those things."

What is the significance of offering objects to images of God? They are described often: flowers, milk, sandalwood paste, rice flour, incense, fruit, coconuts, *pan* leaves, *tulasi* leaves, and other things. These are offered every day in every shrine. They are all emblems of human life as it passes, and their offering is about surrender, the offering of lives over to the feet and head of God. As Balasaraswati created the illusion of doing *puja*, she created the illusion of the elements of the *puja*. It is not the *action* of doing *puja* that creates the illusion, but rather *being* all of the components of the ritual of the *puja*—the fire, the water, the grinding of sandalwood paste, and the milking of a cow—that are joined into the act of devotion expressed

Recipients of President's Award, Sangeet Natak Akademi, Delhi, March 27, 1955.
Balasaraswati is at far right. Photo by Govind Vidyarthi.

through *abhinaya*. Bala prepared herself for this as she prepared herself for a
performance. An observer could see it because she was passionate about it in
reality. That is the way in which Balasaraswati would create magic. She was
not *imagining* she was laying flowers at the Lord's feet; she *was* laying them
at his feet. Balasaraswati understood the objects' meaning as she perceived
them from her own interior, and from her absorption in the gesture.

Sangeet Natak Akademi

Birju Maharaj, a younger colleague of Balasaraswati's, was born into a hereditary artistic family with ancestral roots in the northern city of Lucknow.
He was the son of the *kathak* master Pandit Achchan Maharaj, whom Bala
had seen in Calcutta in 1934, and the nephew of Shambhu Maharaj, whom
Bala had seen in Benares in 1936. "We had boxes of jewels but no jewels in
them. The only gem we retained was our family art — the wealth of *kathak*,
our mythology and our lores. With this little wealth we traveled to Kanpur,
Gorakhpur, Bombay, Calcutta, Dehradun. . . ." Birju remembered Delhi
in the early 1950s: "In the Delhi of the early post-Independence days, there
was little art.[29] To get different talents together from various parts of the
country under one roof was a great task." That "one roof" finally came into
being with the establishment of the Sangeet Natak Akademi in New Delhi
on January 1, 1953.

Bala began 1955 with a concert for the Music Academy,[30] but the high point of the year came in March, when she received the President's Award from the Sangeet Natak Akademi. The Akademi was founded with a mission to honor artists and to encourage them in "maintaining the highest standards in music, dance and drama." Two years after its inauguration, dancers were among its awardees for the first time. On March 27, 1955, at the National Physical Laboratory, the Sangeet Natak Akademi presented awards to the *nagaswaram* player Rajaratnam Pillai;[31] singer Viswanatha Iyer; Balasaraswati; and several North Indian musicians and dancers, including Shambhu Maharaj.

Dance critic Subbudu (P. V. Subramaniam) exclaimed: "Gone are the days of monarchy and crowned kings. Now the dance of democracy is everywhere. Yet there remain uncrowned kings and queens who rule our hearts. . . . Her brilliant performance suggested that our treasured bharata natyam will remain an unmatched, leading art everywhere for many thousand years to come. '*Krishna ni Begane Baro*' is a very refined and pleasing *padam*,[32] but as performed in Bala's style all were left in utter wonderment. Is one to speak of Jayammal's music first or of the enthralling notes of Viswanathan's flute? Or Radhakrishna's fine clarinet? Or Ellappa's sweet strains of song? Or the fervent appeal in Balasaraswati's call to Krishna to come quickly? Watching her dance movements, her immaculate gestures and facial expressions, all joined to evoke magical wonder in the wizardry of Krishna, Lord of Mathura; the audience was stunned, astonished. In brief, we might say that for half an hour we wandered in Brindavan watching Krishna's many *lilas* [pranks]."[33]

A staff reporter from *The Statesman* described the demonstration Bala presented: "Within a few minutes she held the audience spellbound, and before she finished many people were deeply moved. . . . It is impossible to escape the magic of her great art: the dancer disappears, and what remains is bharata natyam at its most perfect, in its purest and almost divine form."[34]

Critic Faubion Bowers had recently written a review of Bala stating the impression that she gave expressive mime a predominant position in her performances. Bowers was commenting, without realizing it, on the continuing tendency for bharata natyam dancers to focus on pure dance and poses; he was unaccustomed to the breadth and balanced role that the expressive aspect of dance held in Balasaraswati's style. This change in emphasis had resulted from the shift away from music and *Sringara rasa*, the center of the tradition of *abhinaya*. The *Statesman* reviewer continued that in her performance Bala had refuted Bowers's implied opinion that "Bala has turned to expressive mime because pure dancing is too tiring for her at this age; the performance on Sunday night proves that she can infuse pure dancing with wonderful beauty, with movements of flowing grace quite unimaginable until you see her. . . . There could be no doubt of the audience's gratitude for such a rare display of artistry."[35]

Balasaraswati in Delhi, April 1957. Photo by Fumio Koizumi.

Shambhu Maharaj

For Balasaraswati, the idea of finding herself in Delhi receiving an award from the central government would have seemed inconceivable a few years earlier—and being there in the company of North Indian *kathak* dancer Shambhu Maharaj would have seemed even more remarkable. But Bala's perception of what it meant to be a dancer had changed. Years later she recalled responding to Uday Shankar's invitation to attend the 1936 Music Conference at Benares where she first saw Shambhu Maharaj dance. "The tradition of *kathak* was new to me. . . . I was too young to really appreciate the artistic beauty of the style then. The dancing had no *nattuvanar* and, strangely, no singer. [In 1936] I had not seen male dancers perform before [except for Achchan Maharaj, briefly, in Calcutta]. Of course, I had seen Uday Shankar but his style and settings were singularly different. It was ten years later before I saw [Shambhu Maharaj] dance [again] at the Vikram Festival in Bombay [in 1945]. His half-hour dance was too meager to get a full taste of it. I had to wait another ten years to see him again. Last month [in 1955] I met him in Delhi at the Presidential Awards celebration.

"Shambhu Maharaj is about fifty years of age, yet his legs seemed as young and energetic as those of a boy of sixteen. Those with eyes to see should have seen him perform his *adavus*.[36] One must see them to experience them; otherwise it is mere words. His movements were so rapid it seemed as if he had an express train tied to his feet. The accompanists played *sarangi* [a bowed stringed instrument] and *tabla*. His footwork began with "*ta dhin dhin na, ta dhin dhin na*" with rhythmic ring and sweetness beyond compare. There was no *nattuvanar* to keep *tala* [sounding of the meter with cymbals], yet the *sarangi* player and *tabla* artist kept time very clearly. The *tala* danced that day was similar to our *adi tala*. . . . *Rasikas* [connoisseurs] who long for a full measure of *laya* [rhythm] in instrumental music would find contentment here. Too, the affinities and distinct differences between South Indian and North Indian music traditions were very clear.

"Shambhu Maharaj's *abhinaya* was replete with *bhavas*. His performance was [on] the day of the Holi Festival in Delhi [during which celebrants shower one another with brightly colored powders or colored water]. Appropriately, he danced the theme of Krishna splashing colored water on the *gopis* and brought before us the scene of Krishna's 'playful gaiety' with great delicacy. Maharaj, at fifty, was no longer attractive, yet he was, without doubt, a grand personality. He never tried to hide behind makeup. He wore the usual white pajamas [pants] and *jubha* [shirt], ear-studs, a mark on his forehead, and tinkling bells from his knees to his ankles, bells as big as those worn by bullocks on village roads. His bells moved with perfectly controlled rhythmic beats. One moment all the bells jingled, the next moment only two rows rang, and in another only a single bell. The bells were completely under his control, a truly incredible feat!"[37]

Birju Maharaj

Shambhu Maharaj's nephew, Birju Maharaj, credited Bala with helping him and North Indian dance gain audience in Madras.[38] The friendship and artistic sharing between these two families has lasted several decades. Ranganathan, who had first learned drumming from Kandappa Pillai and who was Bala's *mridangam* accompanist when Kuppuswami did not play with her, recalled with admiration what he had learned from Birju Maharaj about playing *tabla* and about how a drum could be used to accompany dance. The *kathak* dancer was a drummer, Ranganathan emphasized. "Even now," Birju Maharaj mused in a 1985 interview, "When I think of Bala, of her talent and virtue, I am reminded of the times I spent with her in Madras. I had the good fortune to stay at her house, where I spent many hours practicing songs and dances with her brother Ranga. We had long sessions playing duets together. I tried to match his renditions on *mridangam* on my *tabla*."

He continued, describing a remarkable event, "One day I was scheduled to dance in a program and to my great surprise Balaji [*ji* is a Hindi term of respect added to a person's name] offered to sing for me, and she did. My *kathak* dance and her *karnatic* music made a great combination, I thought, but some people in Madras criticized her for serving as my accompanist. She replied that she did not differentiate between artists of North and South, and felt all artists should support each other, especially those with talent. Taking place in the evening, the program of my *kathak* dancing and her *tillana* created an unprecedented atmosphere that I can remember even to this day." Bala loved seeing her *tillana* danced so exquisitely. She recalled later the words of Kandappa Pillai, who said that she would appreciate the subtle beauty of *tillana* only after seeing it in the hands of an ace interpreter from the North. Bala had learned from her teacher that the *tillana*, with brisk movements and footwork, was a glorious example of the contribution of *Hindustani* music to the enrichment of the South Indian musical tradition and bharata natyam.[39]

"She set a trend of widespread travel for many artists throughout India. For example, my grandfather would only travel within a radius of fifty miles due to the inconvenience of train travel [at that time]. When facilities improved, artists began traveling much further — so Balaji could then visit Bombay, Calcutta, and Delhi, where she gave many performances. We gave many performances throughout the South. Likewise, whenever Balaji came north people were extremely impressed with her artistry.

"Both Balaji and Shambhu Maharaj showed me that all great artists think alike, whether from the South or the North. We helped open the path for artists between the North and the South. Balaji came to the North often and I visited the South quite often. In my performances there, I found people of understanding responded spontaneously to — and appreciated — my art."[40]

Birju Maharaj remembered visiting Bala's house for the first time when he was eighteen or twenty years old. "I stayed with her about twenty-five days and I remember the excellent array of food, including *idli* and *dosa* [a thin pancake made from rice and lentil batter; like *idli*, a South Indian favorite]. Whenever I returned to her house after my performance her mother would perform certain rituals to protect me from the 'evil eye' [*drishti*]."[41]

Sapru House

On March 28, 1955, the day after the afternoon awards ceremony and short performance at Sangeet Natak Akademi, Bala gave a full concert at Sapru House in New Delhi. The performance was arranged by Kapila Vatsyayan and sponsored by Shanmukhananda Sangeetha Sabha (a Delhi music association). Sapru House was the favored gathering place for students, journalists, intellectuals, and scholars. It is located near Triveni, the Sriram Cultural Centre, Rabindra Bhavan, and Lalit Kala Akademi, which comprise Delhi's cultural hub.

The performance that night drew a packed house. The audience received Bala with warmth and respect, and her dancing evoked more than a dozen reviews. As revealed the day before, despite rumors that she could no longer present a concert that included pure dance, the "two and one-half hour recital belied any gossip."[42] The audience included the Vice President of India, several diplomats, and numerous Indian and non-Indian scholars. *The Statesman* heralded her as the "very first flower of the dance renaissance.

She cast a spell over the Sapru House audience . . . an unforgettable display of the highest artistry.

"It is difficult to explain the reason for the enchantment, but when Balasaraswati dances the dancer disappears, and her entire personality merges into the dance. . . . One does not see the performer going through her paces, but the whole, undiluted beauty of the dance itself. The humility and self-effacement of this greatest of all Indian ballerinas is so complete that the spectator forgets her, taken up by the sheer beauty and expressiveness of the dance. The dance is what matters, not the dancer . . . [an effect] achieved by superb mastery of the technique. It is a joy to watch the transition from one pose to another, the evolution of every *mudra*, the complete extension of every finger. . . . On the expressiveness of her face, observe the simple means [by] which she achieves this extraordinary *abhinaya* . . . by living behind that mask; every expression seems to spring from inner conviction. . . . All magic, not a single moment without some delight."[43]

"Balasaraswati is neither the master nor the slave of technique. It is part of herself. More than a dancer [she is] an artist with the highest dramatic power. When she dances she ceases to be a dancer and becomes one with the character she portrays. This is great art. But it is greater still when she retreats from herself and identifies with her heroine taking us, too, out of ourselves into her strange world."[44]

While the ensemble was in Delhi, Jayammal and Bala sang a concert that was broadcast throughout India by the Delhi station of All India Radio. Viswanathan accompanied them on the flute and Ranganathan on *mridangam*. A review in the *Hindustan Times* commented that the performance was a "consummate exposition of *karnatic* vocal music." Noted particularly was the way the entire ensemble performed as one, "impressing me with something North Indian musicians are not quite conversant [with]. . . . Some beautiful bits of *sargam* [music sung in solfège] [seemed] exactly as they ought to be; that is, the consistent notes appeared not as static, mutually exclusive entities but as partakers in a common flow of musicality."[45]

Returning to Delhi again later that year, on November 3 Bala performed the opening concert at the National Dance Festival at the Industrial Fair Theatre in New Delhi, with Ellappa as *nattuvanar*. Again the reviews were outstanding. "A better exposition of bharata natyam I have yet to see."[46] "She showed unison with music, *laya* and the emotional content of a song to a degree that was never before presented in the Capital. It seemed as if her *abhinaya* was determining the mode of music, her steps the notes of music, her [stances] the code of the *karanas* [sculptural representations of dance found in some temples]. Bharata natyam at its best."[47] "[Despite] her informal manner on stage, her artless make-up and simple costume, she compels one to accept her supremacy as an artist, seeming indifference to showmanship. She has, by all standards, no equal in the very difficult and highly personal art of *abhinayam*. . . . Balasaraswati is undoubtedly the greatest bharata natyam dancer today and possesses the most complete gambit of dramatic expression. . . . This attribute has led to a misconception that her abstract dance and footwork are on the wane, lacking in precision and grace. This impression is erroneous and is the result of the spectator's obsession with her heaviness. . . she has a faultless sense of rhythm and can manage effortlessly the most difficult *jati*."[48]

Beginning in the 1940s, Bala's thyroid condition had caused her to retain fluid and gain weight, for reasons she did not understand. She was in no manner an indulgent person, certainly not an overeater. She was not insensitive to how she was seen. Reviewers commented upon her simple makeup and dress, but these were hallmarks of her time, of the modesty of the traditional artist, not the casualness of a woman who did not care. A nonperforming observer might have imagined that Bala effortlessly performed one sublime, flawless concert after another. But each concert demanded tremendous concentration and focus; sometimes she became nauseous before performances. Her ability to rise above self-consciousness, knowing how the public viewed her form as she danced, is one more mark of Bala's remarkable strength as a person. She taught this strength to her daughter, who was eventually to face performing with a progressive condition that robbed her skin of pigment, and then with the effects of a medical treatment that robbed her of her hair. Part of the greatness of both Bala and Lakshmi was their ability to transcend a level of superficiality, leaving the observer unaware of the body and dress of the dancer.

Martha Graham

There was new interest in Indian dance among dance communities in Europe and North America in the mid-1950s. In 1956 the U.S. State Department arranged for and produced a tour of Asia by the American modern dancer Martha Graham. Included in the tour was a private performance for Graham and her troupe by Balasaraswati, an event remembered vividly decades later by protégées of Martha Graham who were in the audience. Although several of Bala's contemporaries had already performed in the West, Bala did not leave India, except for a short trip to Ceylon, until 1961. But she was known around the globe by those who were familiar with dance in India.

Among several early twentieth century dance movements in the West, two intersected in different ways with the emergence of bharata natyam. One movement, during the 1920s, was led by Anna Pavlova, whose vision of an Indian-influenced ballet incorporated the setting and choreographic elements of dance pieces that included a narrative element. Another experiment was "expressive" dance, a movement born in the United States and Germany that rebelled against ballet and centered on the emotive quality of how the dancer moved—on dance as an expression of emotion. This movement became associated with Ruth St. Denis and Ted Shawn and their dance company, Denishawn.

Many of the key figures in modern dance have acknowledged a debt to Asia's classical dance, including Martha Graham, Antony Tudor, Erick Hawkins, Merce Cunningham, Jerome Robbins, Doris Humphrey, Charles Weidman, and Lincoln Kirstein. Three of the second-generation pioneers of American modern dance, Martha Graham, Doris Humphrey, and Charles Weidman, toured with Denishawn in Asia, performing impressions of Indian dance. It was clear that these performances were just that—impressions—and were not intended to represent the traditions of India authentically. Those impressions became the foundation for the revolution that followed when these dance innovators broke away not only from ballet but also from Denishawn and started their own dance forms. An underlying quality that characterized the offshoots of Denishawn was that each artist started his or her own style of dancing. Each identified himself or herself as an originator rather than a descendant; they all had outgrown Ruth St. Denis's interpretations of Egyptian and Indian dancing.[49]

In January of 1956 Martha Graham and her company toured India as part of a global tour. The troupe had been in Calcutta and headed from Madras to Colombo, Delhi, and Bombay before continuing westward. Bala attended Graham's Madras concert, and Lakshmi recalled that although Bala had never seen Western modern dance before, she was excited by the performance; as Lakshmi put it, she "understood its power." Bala and Graham became lifelong friends.

The U.S. consulate arranged a concert by Bala for Graham's troupe while they were in Madras. Donya Feuer was one of the fourteen dancers touring with Graham.[50] She was also a choreographer and made a prize-winning Swedish film, *The Dancer*. Feuer described in conversation with Luise Scripps her first encounter with Bala. The troupe had visited the Shore Temple at Mamallapuram, which stands on a rocky promontory that in 1956 was cut off from the shore at high tide. After lighting candles, the group "had to escape quickly before the rising tide could make it impossible to reach shore." From the small, ancient, cavelike sanctum of this seventh century Pallava temple to Siva the troupe went to a theater to see Balasaraswati dance. "I recall Balasaraswati and a small band of musicians came onto the stage. She seemed overweight and wore simple costuming. The musicians began playing and at that moment she began to dance. Her size was no longer visible and I was completely mesmerized. It was very beautiful. I think she must have danced about an hour. Even though we could not understand the words to her songs I did not mind because her message seemed clear. It was an extraordinary experience. I was so intensely involved that I think I was on another plane. I recall it still and can see her before me."[51]

Donald McKayle, another dancer on the tour, also remembered the event:

"It was in Madras, and it was a concert given, I think, especially for us. The Graham Company was traveling under the State Department and it was the first cultural exchange in dance. I do remember Bala very, very clearly. . . . There was dinner prepared for us. We sat at a very low table in a little room with plantain leaves. . . . They brought the food and we ate with our fingers. It was really quite wonderful. There was a cleansing of the hands. It was a beautiful time and after that we were taken to Bala's performance. It was a small theater and she was on stage with her musicians around her. She did a whole performance for us with the pure dance and then the expressive dance. It was really quite, quite beautiful. . . . I didn't see Bala again until CalArts [in 1972]."[52]

The intersection of modern dance and hereditary bharata natyam revealed an attraction and affinity between the innovators of experimental performance art and the traditional practitioners from all over the world. It was the way that people made art, and why, that became the center of that attraction. It is remarkable that these two artists from the West, and others connected with Martha Graham, remembered Bala's dancing so vividly. Of course the details of who the gods were that she depicted, or which of the many pranks of Krishna she portrayed, or how the lovelorn maiden was suffering, were not at all a part of their recollections. What they were identifying with was Balasaraswati's relationship *in that moment* to her dancing and the manner in which the music was produced. Bala became famous for this immediacy.

The scholar Kapila Vatsyayan commented on Bala's continuing ascent toward greatness: "As she grew, one began to see that her dance was not just a matter of technique, or a rich repertoire, or her capacity for innumerable improvisations. What you saw, in essence, was this content of life (or beyond life) as interpreted by Bala. When she began to dance, Bala was the whole inner beauty of her Self, which was not herself because she was no longer ego-based in those moments, and that was a great experience. Because there are very few dancers in the traditional scheme of things who can be called creative at that level, because one repeats so much, renders so much, interprets so much; in Bala's case you could not make that mistake at all. . . . In that thin line between creativity and repetition, Bala was a truly creative person; no two performances were the same. Of this generation she was a genius in her art."[53]

During 1955, 1956, and 1957, Bala danced at concerts sponsored by the Music Academy. She began presenting compositions in her repertoire that posed the greatest demands on her strength. She wanted to prove that she had the stamina to perform the strenuous aspects of pure dance, and she was feeling the maturity to select pieces that were particularly challenging for her. On December 25, 1955,[54] she gave the debut performance of *Sab-*

dam Karpagambal, composed by V. Raghavan, venerating the deity at the Mylapore Temple. She also presented one of the masterpieces of the Thanjavur family, a *swarajati* in *Huseni raga*, performing it for the first time since Kandappa's death in 1941.

Bala's performances for the Music Academy were being referred to as "annual." One reviewer in the *Indian Express* suggested that her single performance per year was the "only public performance she accepts nowadays." But Bala was developing a reputation she did not deserve. She was performing whenever she was asked, and she rued the fact that she was asked to perform so rarely.

After her concert at the Madras Music Academy in December 1956,[55] a reviewer wrote: "It is a wonder if there is anything in Indian art that gives as complete a sense of satisfaction to both the aesthete and the grammarian as the dancing of Bala. . . . Her performance left the audience in speechless wonder at the perennial freshness of her art. . . . The music of Jayammal (and party) and Bala's dancing were a mutual inspiration. They merged so completely that the audience was completely thrilled throughout the concert."[56] Another writer commented, "Her performance of *Purvikalyani jatiswaram* in *adi tala* at the Madras Music Academy was the pièce de rèsistance. . . . This particular piece was specially composed for Bala's tutor Kandappa Pillai by Ponniah Pillai, grandson of the late Aadi[57] Ponniah Pillai. It was almost a challenge to the *nattuvanar* Kandappa Pillai who successfully met it by having Bala, then in her teens, dance [it] without a single lapse in the rhythm. Bala never danced that *jatiswaram* again until this year at the Academy."[58]

Thanjavur Jayammal

In April 1957 Bala and Jayammal performed a vocal concert of *padams* and *javalis* with *abhinaya* at the Sangeet Natak Akademi in Delhi. While they were in New Delhi, Meenakshi Puri interviewed Jayammal and Bala for the *Sunday Statesman*. "The sole South Indian vocal concert was by Jayammal and Balasaraswati singing *padams* and *javalis* rendered in chaste style devoid of frills with emphasis on lyrical content and the mood inherent in the *raga*. . . . How did Balasaraswati manage the upper octave with such ease? Jayammal's tonal colorings in the lower octave while her daughter reveled in the upper, [gave] fullness to the whole, and [were] extremely pleasing."[59]

Jayammal comments in the interview that Bala's preeminence in the performance of both music and dance was rare. "Living memory records few cases of an artist combining mastery over both music and dance," she said to the interviewer. "It is unusual even in our family [having] devoted itself to music and dance for seven generations." Jayammal commented that she thought it was tragic that "bad dancing and indifferent musical accompani-

T. Jayammal accompanying Balasaraswati in concert, Delhi, 1960. Photo by Marilyn Silverstone. Courtesy of Magnum Studios, New York.

ment should be . . . tolerated in . . . bharata natyam." Bala's mother added at this point in the exchange, "The *nattuvanar* beats the stick and the dancer beats the floor." When asked why she thought there was deterioration in the standards and the expectations of the art, Balasaraswati suggested it was the result of the fuss generated around young dancers, the pressures to perform an early debut, and the indiscriminate acclaim given to young dancers before they had found their feet.

Jayammal was acerbic in this rare opportunity to be publicly expressive, a role usually left to her much more circumspect daughter. It was ironic, said Jayammal, that the government would exclude traditional artists as representatives abroad of India's traditions. This was a subject to which Bala tended to avoid direct reference, speaking usually about the arts themselves, rather than the artists. Jayammal commented that it was not possible for an artist to flower with a tradition of less than three generations. "Without that tradition we have only performing horses or mules." Bala and other family members would cringe at this stinging indictment, uncharacteristic of the family public style, but Jayammal had virtually no other opportunity to express her resentment of what had been lost during her lifetime.

On April 23 Bala once again drew a full house in Noopur at her "truly superb performance," as the *Times of India* recorded. The concert was arranged by Dharma Kumar, who was an enthusiastic supporter of Balasaraswati. "Few artists of her caliber now people the world. She stands unique, peerless, unrivalled in bharata natyam. To watch her dance is to feel a rare emotional ablution, which cleanses the mind of all dross and impurity. She raises the art to a higher, nobler, more aesthetic plane, [and] manages to attune the mind of the audience to [that] loftier tone. Balasaraswati is our *prima ballerina assoluta*, our national pride, our repository of a great art in its purest form, a veritable institution, and we are fortunate to have lived in the same age, and seen her dance. . . . She must now be the only bharata natyam artiste who can hold the stage for an hour or more [elaborating on] a single line. Gifted with an extremely fecund imagination, she has the power to evoke rich and vivid images. . . . The curve of [her] arm in *tirmanams*, her flawless *nritta*, is beautiful beyond description. So too her expressive hands: supple, gifted, with the power to convey a world of meaning within the ten fingers."[60]

Padma Bhushan

On December 20, 1956, the education secretary of the Government of India had written a letter to Balasaraswati, proposing that she be awarded the *Padma Bhushan* for 1957. On January 26, Republic Day, 1957, *The Hindu* in Madras carried the announcement of the awards of *Padma Bhushan*, which included Balasaraswati. *Padma Bhushan* was introduced by the central government in January 1954 to recognize service of continuing distinction to the nation, the second class of a four-part award. Bala would receive *Padma Vibhushan*, the third class, in 1976.

On October 14, 1957, Balasaraswati received a letter from the office of the president of India formally announcing her investiture as *Padma Bhushan*. She attended the investiture ceremony at Rashtrapati Bhavan in New Delhi on October 28. While she was in Delhi, she recorded a program arranged by All India Radio. T. T. Krishnamachari, secretary of the Music Academy in Madras, an industrialist and later India's finance minister (the position first held by Balasaraswati's partner, R. K. Shanmukham), arranged an automobile tour for Bala and Lakshmi of the area around Delhi before their return to Madras. They drove to Akbar's palace, Fatehpur Sikri, built during the second half of the sixteenth century as one of the capitals of Akbar's Mughal Empire. Bala danced there and, according to Lakshmi, "was carried away."

Sometime in late 1957, an opportunity to have a film of Bala made arose unexpectedly. The Films Division of the Government of India was making a series of documentaries, one of which was about the Meenakshi Temple in

Balasaraswati receiving the *Padma Bhushan*, October 28, 1957. Courtesy of Sangeet Natak Akademi Archives, Delhi.

Madurai. Narayana Menon, K. P. Sivanandam (a descendant of the Thanjavur Quartet), and Bala's cousin Shankaran were asked to consult on the Meenakshi Temple film, and the three of them saw it. The original soundtrack of the movie contained no music, however, and Shankaran complained that the film would be useless without it.

The filmmaker was Vishnudas Shirali, the original conductor of Uday Shankar's music ensemble, and he had been at Bala's performance in Calcutta in 1934. Shankaran, who had accompanied Bala on the Calcutta trip, recognized Shirali and introduced himself. Meeting Shankaran was enough to fire Shirali's imagination, and he insisted that they send for Bala and film her.

The All India Radio studios on Beach Road in Madras were still under construction. When Bala arrived, she found nails and rubbish under foot, and no fans to move the air in the windowless studio. The space for her to dance and for the musicians to sit was very small. Infuriated, Bala still performed the sequences they suggested, knowing they were intended for the documentary film. Sadly, however, the film was never finished, and later efforts to find the footage of Bala's performance failed.[61] At the end of Bala's life it was apparent that her dancing was never adequately captured on film. Only today can we fully appreciate the significance of the failure to complete this project.

THE QUEEN OF DANCE

In the midst of the rising public acclaim of Balasaraswati as a performer, she had been nurturing a group of students, assisted by Kandappa Pillai's son, K. Ganesha. Bala had been teaching several of the students before her school was opened in 1953, and they joined her classes at the Music Academy. The first to have an *arangetram* was Kumari Indira Reddy, in January 1956, at Museum Theatre in Egmore, Madras. Reddy presented eleven items, conforming entirely to a traditionally formatted program. Other *arangetrams* followed. Priyamvada Raghavan, V. Raghavan's daughter and the first student enrolled in Bala's school at the Music Academy, had her *arangetram* later in 1956. In September 1959, "Baby" Chandrakala had her *arangetram* at Children's Theatre in Madras. But she became a star of Telugu film and gave up dancing at her father's insistence—a disappointment to Balasaraswati. A few months after Chandrakala's debut, in December, Sasikala performed at the Museum Theatre in Egmore. In June 1960 Vijayanthi performed at the Museum Theatre with K. Chandrasekharan presiding; Chandrasekharan had been a noted intellectual and an advocate of bharata natyam since the 1930s. On October 4, 1960 Uma and Rama Prasad performed together at S.I.E.T. College Hall, Teynampet. Nandini Raghavan, Priyamvada's sister and also a student at the Academy, presented an *arangetram* later in the decade. Bala's last student *arangetram* would be two decades later.

Balasaraswati and her daughter, Lakshmi Shanmukham, 1956.

At Home

Things were changing within the house and within the family. The role of head of family, and the financial responsibility, fell to the matriarch. That is not to say that male offspring of a traditional professional family did not contribute financially — they did. But when a male family member married, he and his new wife left the hereditary home and had responsibility for a new home. In 1958 Bala's younger brother Varadan married a woman named Eunice from a Christian family in Mangalore, and he moved out of Jayammal's house.

In 1955 Balasaraswati had performed in Madras in the rented house of an American Fulbright scholar, Robert Brown, who had recently completed doctoral studies at UCLA and had come to Madras to conduct dissertation research on Indian music. After arriving in Madras Brown had heard that Balasaraswati's brother Ranganathan was at that time employed as a bookkeeper in an orphanage in Madras called Bala Mandir. (The mother of Bala's musician Leela Shekar founded this remarkable institution.) Ranganathan, who would go on to a brilliant career performing, recording, and teaching in the United States, commented on several occasions later in his life that working with children at the orphanage meant as much to him as anything else he had done subsequently. Afflicted by polio at a young age, Ranganathan learned the hard way about being a disadvantaged child, and he was ridiculed by some of his young classmates in school. He left school after the eighth grade.[62] Brown set his sights on convincing Ranganathan to teach him, at which he succeeded. Ranga, as he was known to his hundreds of admirers and students, became Brown's teacher and Brown would come to have a significant impact on the careers of several members of Bala's family. The next was to be Viswanathan.

During the winter of 1957–58, Mantle Hood, head of the Department of Ethnomusicology at UCLA and Robert Brown's mentor there, met Balasaraswati while visiting Madras for the first time. He was also introduced to Viswanathan, who Hood and Brown suggested come to UCLA as a student. A year later Viswanathan again left home, this time on a trip by boat from India to the United States, via the Suez Canal and a stop in Turkey. Viswa entered the master's degree program in ethnomusicology at UCLA as a Fulbright scholar. Jayammal could feel the unity of the family breaking up and was distressed. Perhaps she sensed a loss of control; more so, Viswanathan was her youngest child, and she hated to see him go after so many efforts to keep him in the house.

Times had also changed for Bala. She had become an artist of national significance and had received the Indian government's recognition. She no longer needed to fight prejudice against her community. Ironically, as she became her community's sole representative, the resistance to performance by traditional artists had largely disappeared. There were persistent detractors who continued to decry traditional bharata natyam for a lack of classicism and inherent vulgarity, but those voices were enfeebled by the power of Bala's art. Her performances and teaching transcended cultural, social, and national barriers, in part because she would so reluctantly engage with the arguments and controversy that swirled around her.

"Ninnu Joochi"

Still at the heart of the continuing debate about the definition of bharata natyam was the inclusion of *Sringara rasa*, the narrative theme often misunderstood now, and certainly then, as the "erotic" element of the art. The traditional artist did not shy away from the twin aspects of love in the poetry of bharata natyam — love of the divine and human attraction — which were understood as universally felt experiences. *Sringara* was not the subject of the dance; it was the vehicle for the subject of the dance and the artistic imagination. Using the imagery of love, the poetry expressed both man's relationship to God and love between man and woman an ambiguity introduced by Kshetrayya.

The Tamil poetry of the *Sangam* Period is an art depicting human love; it is not suggestive of spiritual relationships. (*Sangams* were historical or legendary assemblies of Tamil scholars and poets, the oldest recorded *Sangam* poems are dated to about the fourth century BCE.) The relationship between young man and young woman was itself sublime; and its delicacy, immediacy, and poignancy were the soul of a great literary tradition.

Bhakti, contrasted with *Sringara*, is devotional fervor generated by a

sensed personal relationship with the Infinite, rather than an emotion. *Bhakti*, in the context of modernized bharata natyam, was not used in a dramaturgical manner as *Sringara* was, but instead became the subject of dance. *Bhakti*, as it is sometimes danced, depicts images of devotional ritual and intensity. The poetry of the *kriti* evokes God and the interaction between man and God as symbolic and philosophical, rather than evoking the intimate view of man and God that was projected through *Sringara*.

Lakshmi made a subtle point about Bala dancing *Sringara*. The example Lakshmi had in mind was the Kshetrayya *padam* "*Ninnu Joochi*." The piece describes the heroine longing for her Lord, Krishna. "It was a love song wherein the lady [Radha] is pining for Krishna. . . . There is no *bhakti* in it, no union of the *paramatma* and *jeevatma*. It is only the poetry and the music. But when she presented it and she projected the line '*Ninnu Joochi*,' all Bala, being Bala, wanted was to see Krishna. That was her only aim. Bala's soul was always seeking Krishna." Lakshmi posed a rhetorical question: Could Bala have performed this piece as a love song about a woman missing a man, as an ordinary mortal? Of course not, was her answer. "It's because it is Krishna and she is Radha—that is why that came out. We say it isn't *bhakti* because it isn't *bhakti* as one of the emotions. She [creates real] *bhakti* because Krishna is there, she is longing for Him. But she transforms this love song into *bhakti* when she does it. . . . It doesn't mean when she is explaining about the dreams she would show Krishna coming and kissing her, touching her, embracing her and all the naughty things he would do. Those aspects are all there. But the audience would leave the theater with their heads full of her singing."

From this point forward in this interview, Lakshmi alternated between singing "*Ninnu Joochi*" and commenting on the piece. She began to sing:

Ninnu Joochi . . .
I haven't seen you, Krishna, for so many days.

"This is human longing," said Lakshmi, interrupting herself. "There is no devotional aspect here. This is not *bhakti*." Lakshmi then continued to sing, translated as:

It has been so long since I last saw you.
My sari is soaked with tears; in my sleep I am weeping.
After dreaming of you, it seems you are here.
I wake seeing the curtains move and think it is you.
Feeling your presence, I thought I saw you in the shadow.
When I felt a breeze on my cheek I thought it was your breath.
A fragrance was only a flower.
And I arise, sensing your presence. . .
I haven't seen you, Krishna, for so many days. . . .[63]

Balasaraswati after a concert in Bombay, ca. 1958. Photo by Subodh Chandra.

"That was Bala! When she was dancing or when she was in her room talking to me about this, she'd just forget herself. This is not devotion, not yearning for *bhakti*. But when she performed this, as a song, as an item, you would never think of it as a love song. The audience would not think that way. They would think we are all longing for the Great One to come and see her. That is how she projected such material. . . . She transformed it into an altogether different subject." This was where Bala emerged completely uncontested. It was not the object of the art that was compelling; it was the action of making art. She would invest her dance with the same delicacy seen in other transcendental expressions of art whose object is the world of human love.

Bala was unequivocal: "*Sringara* stands supreme in the range of emotions. No other emotion is capable of better reflecting the mystical union of the human with the divine. I say this with deep personal experience of dancing to many great devotional songs which have had no element of *Sringara* in them. Devotional songs are, of course, necessary. However, *Sringara* is the cardinal emotion which gives the fullest scope for artistic improvisation, branching off continually, as it does, into the portrayal of innumerable moods full of newness and nuances. Some seek to 'purify' bharata natyam by replacing the traditional lyrics which express *Sringara* with devotional songs. I respectfully submit to such protagonists that there is nothing in bharata natyam which needs to be purified afresh; it is divine as it is and innately so. The *Sringara* we experience in bharata natyam is never carnal; never, never. For those who have yielded themselves to its discipline with total dedication, dance, like music, is the practice of the Presence; it cannot be merely the body's rapture. . . . Yet the spiritual quality of bharata natyam is not achieved through the elimination of the sensual but through the seemingly sensual itself, thereby sublimating it."[64]

Bala's student Roshen Alkazi spoke of her perception of the experience of *Sringara*. "I'll tell you what it brought to life in me. In Hindu philosophy, there is one aspect of *sadhana* [a means of accomplishing something spiritual] which is through the physical union of a man and a woman. It is very difficult for people to understand and accept how this can be, except on a very namby-pamby level, once you see the sculpture of [the temples of] Khajuraho with their very specific details of men and women in union together or other forms of art. I think, personally, what Bala made me realize was that I began to see the truth of this kind of *sadhana*. It was possible in the union of the male and female to reach these sublime truths of self-realization. . . . I don't think that most people give credence to this particular *sadhana* as being a realization; but I think Bala in her innermost being, realized when you say union with God, it can [be in] so many [different] ways. And this is one of the ways of union with God, the joining of the male and female. When she expresses those *padams* of Kshetrayya, she doesn't

Balasaraswati at Sangeet Natak Akademi dance seminar, Delhi, April 1958. Photo by R. P. Dhamija. Balasaraswati's musicians are (*left to right*): T. Kuppuswami Mudaliar, N. Radhakrishna Naidu, K. Ellappa Pillai, S. Narasimhulu, T. Jayammal.

deny the physical union. She accepts the physical union, but takes it into the cosmic union. She is able to make that transition which makes you understand this particular aspect of Hindu philosophy. . . . I don't think any other dancer has tried. If they tried to do it, it comes out awkwardly."[65]

Seminar on Dance Arts

Bala had been sick for several months at the beginning of 1958. Rumors were, again, that she would not be able to perform when she attended the First Annual Seminar on Dance Arts, presented at the Sangeet Naṭak Akademi in New Delhi from March 30 through April 7. But on April 1 Bala presented a demonstration of *adavu* danced by her student Priyamvada, daughter of V. Raghavan, with Ganesha as *nattuvanar* and Viswanathan and Bala accompanying her musically. During the same presentation, Balasaraswati demonstrated *abhinaya*.

As part of the seminar, on April 2, Rukmini Devi presented a demonstration and a paper, "My Experiments with Dance." Rukmini Devi emphasized the need for students to be trained according to the *sastric* traditions. Several debates underlay the rationalizations for the reformation of bharata natyam. One argument was that bharata natyam, as practiced by the traditional community, and as configured by the Thanjavur Quartet, did not wholly conform to *sastric* canon. In support of this idea, reformers pointed to the *Natya Sastra*, a two-thousand-year-old, orally transmitted, elaborate theory of dramaturgy, thought to describe a lost practice of the dramatic arts.

The *Natya Sastra* was first produced in print in Sanskrit in 1894, and was first translated into English in 1950. Many of those who advocated the classicism defined in the *Natya Sastra* had not read the treatise — including, by her own statement, Rukmini Devi. However, in the effort to set the revised style of bharata natyam above the existing professional practice, new dancers needed to be convinced that there was a basis for their convictions as artists, a system of belief. Thus, the reformers raised the *Natya Sastra* to a "classical" level, positioning it as a "fifth" Veda, and favored the restoration of the dance practice to this newly adopted standard of classicism.

Rukmini Devi began her paper at the Seminar on Dance Arts with a description of her understanding of the historical context in which she had begun to dance. "At that time [the mid-1930s] Bharata Natyam was called *Sadir* and there were many bad associations connected with that *Sadir*. It had acquired a very bad reputation because of the lives of the dancers themselves who were not all they should have been. But I felt that there was something marvelous in the art which should not be lost." Rukmini Devi read this statement, reminiscent of the program notes for the 1945 All India Dance Festival, while Balasaraswati sat at the front of a distinguished audience. Bala had resisted the uninformed modification in the performance practice since it began in the 1930s, but Rukmini Devi went on to present her rationalization for making the sweeping changes to the concept of the art that became the backbone of the reformed style of bharata natyam.

"I am a great believer in the *Sastras* and in tradition. I also feel that the traditional dancers had something very wonderful. In fact, they had more dedication than many of us have today. . . . I also believe we should follow tradition but we must remember not to accept everything just because it is in the tradition. Though I learned the art in the traditional way, I felt then that there were many things that had to be changed. This is a very important point that I want to stress. If you wish to follow tradition — even as I did — there is no need literally to copy everything."[66] In fact, no traditional artist would argue against the notion of change. Change was and is in the fundamental nature of a traditional practice — but not as deliberate, self-conscious alteration.

Maya Rao, the Delhi-based *kathak* dancer, published her account of the event in the *Illustrated Weekly of India* in June 1962. "The question had come up about the eroticism in Kshetrayya's *padams* and if they should be removed from the repertoire of bharata natyam because bharata natyam was supposed to be something sublime and not contain these erotic elements in it. This angered Bala tremendously. Rukmini Devi gave an account of her pioneering efforts to popularize bharata natyam and remarked that she excluded *Sringara rasa* from her repertoire as it seemed too erotic for a respectable woman to present. Bala could not brook this statement. She raised such a hot discussion in favor of *Sringara rasa*, quoting chapter and verse from Kshetrayya, Jayadev, and many other poets, that the other had to give in. Bala would not stop there."[67]

Another account of the event published in July, however, contradicted Maya Rao's version. "Rukmini Devi observed [that] 'Bala was not present [when] I made the alleged statement. . . . Presumably prompted by [Viswanathan] she appeared on the stage to refute what I had never said. I am not against *Sringara*. One of the most successful pieces in Kalakshetra's repertoire is Jayadeva's "*Gita Govinda*" [a twelfth-century epic poem describing the myth of Krishna that Rukmini Devi cast as a dance drama]. How can any artist be against *Sringara*? I am against vulgarity.' "[68]

According to Roshen Alkazi in a later interview, in Bala's rebuttal at the seminar, she "gave definite ideas about the *padams* and how she felt this very sensuality and eroticism, if done coarsely could mean something else, but if done rightly, it was something which would enrich the repertoire. She challenged a group of critics and scholars that if they would come the next day to a reception given at Kamaladevi Chattopadhyay's house, she would do these *padams* and show them how she felt they should be done and how rich they were for any really worthwhile interpretive dancer."[69] Reporting four years after the event, Maya Rao wrote that at the reception at Kamaladevi's, Bala "took each line of poetry and elaborated on the meaning with sensitivity and nuance, carefully, as always, keeping her gesturing hands above her waist as it is considered lewd to drop them below, and showing beyond all doubt that these texts could not be reduced to a tawdry eroticism."[70]

Maya Rao also reported knowing that Bala had recently recovered from a long illness — and that she intended to present to the group of experts at Sangeet Natak Akademi on April 3 both the elaborate *sankirna jatiswaram* and the demanding *swarajati* in *Huseni raga* she had danced recently at the Music Academy. Maya, as well as others, tried to persuade Bala to replace the two pieces with less taxing compositions, but Bala was adamant. "She sat on the floor, chewing *pan*, unsmiling, a mysterious glint in her eyes. Once the curtain rose Bala almost ran on to the stage and began with a brisk *alarippu* [and] *sankirna jatiswaram* to an entranced audience, for forty-five minutes, marveling at the clarity and fluency of her style. She immediately took up *Huseni swarajati* and gave a beautiful rendering, punctuating each passage with the most intricate *tirmanams*. . . . She was greeted with a thunderous ovation." Moved by this overwhelming response to her *nritta* items, Bala exclaimed, "So, I have won the battle," referring to the criticism that she no

Balasaraswati in studio performance, August 1958. Photo by K. Khanna.

longer had the physical capacity to perform the demanding abstract component of bharata natyam. She later remarked, "I wanted to retrieve my reputation for *nritta*; otherwise it would be unjust to Guru Kandappa."[71]

The characteristics of Balasaraswati's style include strictness of form and
the musical challenges of her composed pure dance. As Bala learned to perform *tirmanams* and other components of pure dance, it was the exactitude
with which her *guru* insisted that she execute them, and the unrelenting
submission to the rules of consistency and form, that characterized Kandappa's compositions. For her entire career, whenever Bala made a mistake in
performing her *tirmanams*, she would repeat them, even though her errors
were rarely perceived by anyone in the audience.

Bala had been ill almost all the time since the early 1940s. She was finally
treated by a doctor named A. Srinivasan, who prescribed a diet with no salt
or sugar and recommended lots of rice and fruit to control her weight gain
and improve her general health. Bala cooperated with good humor, although
she complained that she had been deprived of her favorite foods. Reducing
food to what was necessary to sustain her was discouraging. Bala was an extraordinary cook and a lover of fine things. Bala's mother and grandmother
also were excellent cooks. Bala once casually commented to me that she
didn't know if she was a great dancer, but she knew she was a great cook.

Later in 1958 Bala was invited by the Government of India to tour Russia. Travel was new to the traditional community, and it took persistent ef-

fort by Bala, who had been overlooked when previous missions had been arranged, to persuade her troupe to make the trip. She proceeded to have warm clothing made for her musicians at considerable personal expense. But Jawaharlal Nehru, who was directly involved in making decisions about the impressions that India would project abroad, was convinced by advisors that so soon after Independence it was important that India should convey a particular, modernized image—and that the Russian audience would not adequately appreciate Balasaraswati. One week before the troupe was scheduled to leave, the government canceled Bala's tour and replaced her with another dancer. By way of explanation, a government spokesman told Bala that the decision to prevent her from making the trip was a way of "saving her the humiliation" of not being well received. The lack of regard shown for her situation, the financial difficulties the episode caused her, and the strain it created in her relationship with the members of her ensemble made Bala very angry and mistrustful of the central government.

Chidambaram

Humility is easily confused with lack of self-knowledge, or with self-effacement. Bala's humility was the aspect of her relationship to her art that allowed her to continue to perform in spite of both the insults she experienced and the acclaim that was laid at her feet. Although like any artist Bala experienced her share of criticism, her burden was the praise. Her teacher had taught her to leave immediately after a concert and to ignore all remarks. This was not to protect her from negative response but rather to preserve her relationship to her art in the face of praise. Many claim humility; few have had their humility tested so severely. Bala understood the challenge her artistry presented. She recognized herself as a slave of a discipline and a great art form. Her achievement in art was always relative to her discipline and the art itself. It was about knowledge and devotion, not the exhibition of knowledge and devotion. Praise, although she always received it gratefully, was never what motivated Bala. Bala's motivation lay in the pursuit of an ideal, and that was what she shared with her audience.

In January 1959 Bala performed an *abhinaya* demonstration at the publication of a book written in Tamil entitled *Bharata Natyam* she had co-authored with V. Raghavan. At the end of 1959, Bala performed at the Music Academy in the winter season without her brother Viswanathan, who was in school in Los Angeles. During 1960 Uday Shankar and his wife, Amala, settled in Madras, but they lived five years in the same city without contact; they only encountered each other again at a concert of Bala's in New York in 1965. It was also in these years that Bala met the philosopher, writer, and teacher Ra Ganapati, who would remain a very close friend and confidant and was an important contributor to this historical account.

In 1960 Viswanathan returned from his two years in the United States,

Balasaraswati in studio performance, August 1958. The musicians are (*left to right*): T. Ranganathan, T. Janaki, T. Viswanathan. Photo by K. Khanna.

and on Christmas Eve he performed with Bala at the Music Academy. Bala's unique interpretation of the *kuchipudi* style of dancing was included in the program, as well as *sankirna jaathi jatiswaram* in *Purvi Kalyani raga* and the *sabdam "Devadevanam."*

A few days after the 1960 concert at the Music Academy, Bala announced to Lakshmi, without warning, that she wanted to attend the chief festival for Siva in the form of Nataraja held in the temple in Chidambaram,[72] about two hundred kilometers south of Madras. The ceremony is held at night. "I recall an incident deeply etched in my memory," Lakshmi remembered. "It was two or three days after the performance. . . . Bala developed an unusual frenzy to attend the festival and got me also infected."[73] Bala asked a friend to lend them a car and driver, and she and Lakshmi set off. It was nearly eleven o'clock at night when they reached Chidambaram. After resting for about two hours in a lodge in town, they rose, bathed, and set off for the temple, expecting to be early enough to find a good vantage point for witnessing the *abhishekam*, or sacramental bathing, of Nataraja.

The two were in high spirits. Bala's state of devotion had intensified during the six-hour drive with its streams of conversation punctuated by long silences, broken by Bala's singing. When mother and daughter arrived at

In concert at Madras Music Academy, 1958. *Left to right:* T. Jayammal, Sarojini Kumarsawami, K. Ellappa Pillai, and N. Radhakrishna Naidu.

the temple, they were struck by the cold — it was late December — and as they made their way into the center of the massive courtyard of the temple, they found themselves among thousands of worshippers, being jostled and pushed by the chaotic throng. The two women realized they had made a mistake rushing out of Madras unaccompanied. They were helpless and felt threatened by the great crowd. "Both of us were weaklings," Lakshmi said ruefully.

In spite of the cold and the overwhelming situation, Bala cheerfully began singing *"Vazhi Maraittirukkude"* ("The Way Is Obstructed"), the song of an outcast, Nandan, who after long travel finds the bull Nandi (Siva's mount, or vehicle) obstructing his view of the Lord, and asks it to move "just a little." As Bala continued to sing, in the midst of the throng of people, she reached a line she sang with sudden deepening feeling, *"Inda urinil vandum en papam tireno?"* ("Will my sins not be absolved though I have come to your holy place?"). Perhaps alerted by her singing from the midst of the mass of people, a police officer who was there to help regulate the crowd spotted Bala. He and his constables elbowed their way through the worshippers, and the officer introduced himself as the relative of a well-known musician. The officers cleared a path, and Bala and Lakshmi were seated in the front row to witness the *abhishekam.*

Before leaving, they greeted a temple headman, who was from the hereditary community of Brahmins known as Diksitar. As Bala and Lakshmi headed back to the car, another Diksitar rushed toward them, holding a Tamil newspaper in his hand. He exclaimed that the reviewer of her concert a few days earlier hailed Bala as Natarani, the Queen of Dance, and added the almost obvious remark that the Natarani had come to take *darsan* of Nataraja (King of Dance). Bala turned grave and without exchanging a word got into the car. As she and Lakshmi left, Bala (who usually didn't bother with such things) said with uncharacteristic rancor, "It is one thing for some newspaperman to indulge in such hyperbole as 'Natarani.' But should it come out of a Diksitan's[74] mouth to equate me as the Natarani with the Nataraja?"

From the temple compound they drove to Vaitheeswaran Koil near Chidambaram, an abode of Murugan. As Bala stood before the image of Murugan, tears trickled down her cheeks, and she murmured, shaking her head, "Did you not punish me because I deserved it?" Lakshmi had no idea what was troubling Bala. On leaving the temple, at Lakshmi's insistence Bala confessed that her distress was over her rendering of the *sabdam* at the Music Academy a few days before. The third item in a dance program, *sabdam*, has four lines of poetic text separated by short sections of abstract dance, usually in praise of a deity or king, with language laden with images and philosophical content. The *sabdam* Bala performed at the Music Academy was "*Devadevanam*," in praise of Lord Murugan, son of Siva.

Oh, Beautiful Son of the God of Gods,[75]
Famous dweller of Thiruthani,[76]
Nephew of Vishnu, bearer of the conch and disc,
Oh Murugan, who rides the peacock,
Great teacher of your Almighty Father,
You who whispered the meaning of "*Om Pranava.*"
The *devas*, demons, and *rishis* were in ecstasy with your triumph
    over evil.
Husband of Deivayanai,[77] my salutations to you.

Whenever Bala performed this item, she—and her audience—had grown accustomed to an exposition of a myriad of interpretations. "How beautifully she could bring the *devas*, *rishis*, gods before them in thrilling variations on familiar stories. She, along with her audience, seemed transported to some heavenly plane. Her audience felt they were present in the lives of their gods.... We had seen Bala do *Devadevanam*; the description of Murugan when she says *Devadevanam*," Lakshmi recalled. "She brings down Lord Subramaniam [Murugan] as a small child playing with his spear in his hand; sitting on his mother's lap, sitting on his father's lap, and the incident where he becomes angry because he was not given the fruit. The parents [Siva and Parvati] and their children are sitting together, enjoying themselves, when Narayana [Vishnu] comes and gives them the fruit, a mango. Both children ask for the mango. At that moment Siva says, 'Whoever goes round the world and returns first will get the fruit.' The basic concept in Hindu thought is that the mother and father are the world to their children, so Ganesha takes the fruit and goes round his parents three times and comes to them and says, 'Give me the fruit. I am here. You are the world for me.'" His parents have no choice but to give him the fruit.

As soon as the challenge is made to the two children, Murugan mounts his vehicle, the peacock, and sets off to circle the world. "Murugan got on the peacock; and [this is] the way she would show him on the peacock, flying." Lakshmi showed from her seated position how Bala's hand might have moved. "And he flies around the world. When he arrives back, he says, 'Where is my fruit?' His parents know their son and how hurt he will be. They show that they have given it to [his brother] Ganapati. He says, 'It's not fair. I flew around the world, just for this fruit.' He feels he was cheated, gets very angry and leaves for the Palani Hills [in the Western Ghats, now in Kerala]. At that moment when he leaves, he renounces the world. He removes all his finery and adornments and takes only his peacock and his staff. Like a mendicant, wearing only a loincloth. Very, very powerful. Even a shaved head, because nothing can affect him. It was that kind [of depiction] I have seen Bala enact. How she would be Parvati, begging the child to return. 'Don't get angry with me, my darling.' Then, she [Bala] would become so powerful, like Murugan reacted, because he had decided to renounce the world."

So often, we do not know what is happening until it does not happen, and we miss it. Lakshmi went on: "Ordinarily, when she danced *Devadevanam*, she would become the mother, and Murugan was there. On that day, she turned and he was not there. On so many occasions it was done so powerfully. Sometimes, in the next line, he recites the *pranam* [a verse] to Siva, where he is the teacher and his father is the disciple. Murugan is the sixth sense. Siva is made of five elements. Murugan is the deity who comes out of Siva's third eye as the sixth spark. . . . *Gnanam* is that salvation when you have reached that stage where the full lotus with one thousand petals has opened up. This experience is the key to the life force in Bala's art; one must allow for her functioning at that level of the sublime. It was her direct relationship inside of her. And what came out was her relationship to that unknown sphere. It was a very personal connection. That personal connection was not there that day. And she felt that she was deprived. Somehow he [Murugan] punished her ego that day."

Lakshmi described the situation after the concert: "She was disappointed and heartbroken. . . . [Critic] K. Chandrasekharan and Saama [*Kalki* cartoonist C. Swaminathan] really reacted. Chandrasekharan went straight to his home instead of going backstage to see Bala. I could see Saama's tears. That night the two of them discussed it on the phone. The following day Chandrasekharan came to see us. You know, when you go to someone's house for condolence? It was with that tone that he said to Bala, 'What happened, Bala? *Enna aacchu?*' Apart from those two, [it seemed] no one else understood. It had nothing to do with the audience. . . . It had nothing to do with anyone else present. She took it very personally. I was there. I saw it. I went through it [with her] the whole night. She felt very personally that He [Murugan] just corrected her ego. That's what it was. And she cried. I can tell you, I couldn't control her. That was what she was conveying in her presence. That is why she was great. Because she was totally connected, personally connected. And that she was able to send out, that radiated in the audience. And that radiation was not being given out that day."[78]

Udipi

In the summer of 1960, Bala's student Chandrakala, whose family was from Bangalore, arranged a performance at the Udipi temple dedicated to Krishna. A problem Bala sometimes experienced with students raised in families of privilege was that they and their families did not understand or strictly observe the expected protocol between a student and the student's family, and a teacher and the teacher's family. A generation earlier, no parent of a student would have expressed expectations of a professional dance teacher. But the parents of Bala's students sometimes misunderstood the nature of the relationship. As a result, Bala had not planned to go to Udipi, anticipating a problem and choosing to avoid any potential conflict with her student's father over whether or not Bala would sing for Chandrakala. But the father insisted that Bala accompany them on the trip, and she did. In the end, Bala was very excited that her student was to dance before the great image.[79]

It apparently had not crossed Bala's mind that she should dance there also. Her older brother Srinivasan was with them, however, and after the group arrived in Udipi, he encouraged Bala to dance, even calling her foolish for coming all the way and not dancing. Lakshmi remembered that Bala seemed frightened at the very talk of her dancing before Udipi Krishna. Her brother took matters into his own hands and arranged the opportunity. Bala, perhaps emboldened by her experience dancing at Thiruthani, agreed.

Lakshmi recalled that Bala arrived in great excitement, dressed in a white *sari* with green borders, her face radiant. She danced "*Krishna ni Begane Baro*" and on the line "*Jagadoddharana*" mimed a tale from Draupadi's tenure in the clutches of the villainous Dussasana. Dussasana plays dice, and at stake are Draupadi and her honor. With each winning roll Dussasana unwraps Draupadi's *sari* once. As the *sari* gets thin, Draupadi cries out for Gopala (Krishna). In the legend Krishna comes to her aid with a *sari* of infinite length. When Bala mimed that cry, which is of course only suggested in the dance, those who were there reacted as if they heard an actual cry. Bala did not continue with her performance of the piece, a freedom she sometimes longed for on the concert stage.

Those in charge of the temple ignored the orthodoxy that would not allow Bala's performance before the image of the deity in the sanctum sanctorum. The top *acharyas* (teachers, leaders) of the temple heard that a dancer was performing before the image. They rushed to the spot, perhaps to prevent her from dancing; seeing her dance they instead presented her with *prasadam* (food offered to an image of the Divine and distributed to worshippers after a religious ceremony) when she had finished. Bala's reaction was a childlike delight that Udipi Krishna, whom she had awakened so often as a child, had finally seen her dance.

Balasaraswati's family moved from a national onto a global stage at the beginning of the 1960s. The fortunes of the family were cast in part by achievements in the United States and elsewhere outside of India that began for Balasaraswati in 1961. Yet although her circumstances changed, her audience changed, and her sources of income and professional support changed, Balasaraswati remained deeply rooted in the world of South Indian tradition. The depth and scope of that world — the images, personalities, and histories that many of us might describe as the abstractions and mythology of a Hindu devotional life — were real for Balasaraswati. That landscape for her was constant, and her dedication and purpose were constant, an extension of what she had been taught: to be unperturbed by the comments and circumstances that swirled around her. Bala was fascinated by the wider world, ever curious and respectful. But she was not a part of it, and it was not a part of her.

ONTO A WIDER STAGE

In 1961 Bala was invited to a festival in Tokyo called the East-West Encounter, facilitated by the Congress for Cultural Freedom and the City of Tokyo. The Festival was held from April 16 to May 6. There, Bala was in the midst of some of the best traditional artists from other parts of India and various regions of Asia as well as prominent dancers, musicians, and scholars from the West. Bharata natyam had attained international stature not only because it had attracted a Western audience but because it was accepted and admired by artists from all over Asia who were also receiving international exposure for the first time.

During the early 1960s Balasaraswati would perform throughout the United Kingdom, Europe, and North America. She first performed in North America at Jacob's Pillow in 1962, and went on to tour throughout the United States. Over the next twenty years she performed several hundred concerts in North America, some of which have become legendary. She performed at the Edinburgh Festival in Scotland in 1963, where again she and her musicians, some of them family, were in the company of distinguished artists from India and the West.

Balasaraswati began to teach in the United States at this time. In a dozen different programs on both coasts, she eventually nurtured hundreds of students in the United States, some of whom remain devoted practitioners of her style today. These students represented a new challenge for Bala: She found it necessary to teach more than the rudiments of dance, accommodating her students' different cultural and social backgrounds and their unfamiliarity with the gestural vernacular that Indians know instinctively.

The United States was being transformed by dramatic cultural changes. A rebellion from within its urban African American community found its expression in dozens of civil uprisings; the time had come for America to begin to be accountable for its history and to become inclusive of all its people and differences. Ironically, the United States was at the same time prosecuting a controversial war in Southeast Asia that was sensitizing many of its youth to the tyranny of ethnocentrism. That war was being fought disproportionately by the poor and disadvantaged. These cultural shifts in the 1960s opened the door for an enthusiasm for anything Asian and non-Western, echoing cultural shifts at the end of the nineteenth century, and sparked an appetite for discovery of other ways of looking at and experiencing the world. Stories circulated about travel across West Asia to the Indian subcontinent, which had become one focus of discovery. Ravi Shankar followed his brother Uday's path to the West, and created huge mystique. The process of discovery was bidirectional, and it was part of what Bala loved about her experience in the West. Everyone was learning. It was acceptable to be mystified and unsure.

The emerging field of ethnomusicology and the inclusion of non-Western forms of dance and music in college curricula grew out of this expanding awareness and concern, reflecting changes in American college faculties and student bodies. Viswanathan had come to UCLA as a Fulbright Scholar in 1958 and joined what was to become a trailblazing group of academics participating in a graduate program directed by Mantle Hood, a protégé of Charles Seeger. Students were learning the performance arts they were talking and writing about. Advocates of the new perspective abandoned dependence on Western notation and transposition of scale and meter into Western-conceived structures in favor of insights gained through their immersion in global cultures and practices.

Bala was ideally suited to this new environment. She was both entirely accessible and recognizably unaffected by Western expectations of Indian dance. Kapila Vatsyayan commented on why she thought Bala found a following in the West: "Anyone who is sensitive to movement and the perfection of movement would be moved, even outside a cultural context.... There was too the personality that Bala brought and communicated. Apart from her being a very successful performer, in limited groups or audiences, she was a stupendous teacher; that was what gave her the students and admirers that

she has [in the United States]. She's in a class by herself. People abroad were
also attracted by the fact that she, almost by volition, was not glamorous; there was a certain type of austerity, a straightness about her. These can be endearing qualities, especially for artists who rise to such heights where you expect there would be a public and private image. But [instead] you get a simple person like Bala. She was very complex at other levels, but in life and great performance, this was no doubt a very unique experience for people; therefore they were committed to it."[1]

Tokyo

The dream about flying to strange places that Bala had during her train ride to Thiruthani in 1955 had been a mystery; but, as Murugan had promised in her dream, it gradually started to make sense to her. Kapila Vatsyayan, who was then at the Sangeet Natak Akademi, contacted Bala to suggest that she be India's representative to the East-West Encounter in Tokyo, a celebration of Asian and European traditions of the arts. Japan, like the rest of the world, was being transformed by economic and cultural shifts that were reflected in events like the East-West Encounter. The Encounter was just a beginning.

Bala was hesitant at the first suggestion of this new opportunity, having been disappointed several years earlier when she was invited to represent India in a government-sponsored tour of Russia but at the last moment was replaced. Bala mistrusted the government, and Kapila Vatsyayan had to convince her to accept the invitation to the East-West Encounter, even though she knew that in fact there was again resistance to having Bala represent India. The conference director, Nicolas Nabokov, had been told that Bala would be a disappointment to an audience expecting a more exotic image of Indian classical dance. Nabokov, a cousin of the novelist Vladimir Nabokov, had planned and organized several significant international conferences and performing events that took place during the 1950s and 1960s, while he was secretary general of the Congress for Cultural Freedom.

This time Dr. Vatsyayan successfully fought to keep Bala on the roster. "When I did decide to take Bala, to get government approval for her participation, eyebrows were raised and attempts were made to prevent her going. In fact, I was told (perhaps, in hindsight, this is mentionable) that the decision should be reversed and she should not go. At that time it required a certain amount of fight and courage to speak up for Bala's art. All I can say for myself is that I did offer to resign if she was a failure in Japan."[2] Other artists from India on the roster were North Indian instrumental musician Ali Akbar Khan, who went on to the United States in his career; *drupad* singers the Dagar Brothers; and the troupe from the Kathakali Kerela Kalamandalam, the leading performance and teaching institution in Kerala.

At home in Egmore before departure for Tokyo, 1961. *Left to right:* V. Nagarajan, T. Shankaran, T. Viswanathan, T. Balasaraswati, T. Ranganathan, Lakshmi Shanmukham.

This was Bala's first trip outside of South Asia. She was accompanied by Viswa and Ranga, as well as Lakshmi and Ganesha. Bala had wanted to leave Lakshmi in Madras, as Lakshmi was in her first year of college, an opportunity Bala had worked hard to create. But the principal of Lakshmi's college was an admirer of Balasaraswati's family art, and she insisted that Lakshmi would learn much more about the world from traveling to Japan with her mother than she would by staying behind in school in Madras.

In Tokyo Bala's troupe performed at the Metropolitan Hall. The building, named Tokyo Bunka Kaikan, was designed by the architect Kunio Maekawa, who was considered by many to be the father of contemporary Japanese architecture. The Bunka Kaikan was constructed by the Tokyo Metropolitan Government to commemorate the 500th anniversary of the city, and to provide an international place of pride for a nation and city devastated by war. The East-West Encounter was the first major event to be held in the hall.

In the mornings Bala and her ensemble presented a series of lecture-demonstrations in the Recital Hall before a distinguished audience of artists and scholars. These morning sessions were part of the immense success the ensemble enjoyed.[3] In the evening Bala performed in the Main Hall for an audience of more than two thousand people. Among them were several Western dancers, including Dame Margot Fonteyn, as well as performers from India, Japan, Thailand, and China.[4] Among the American participants in the Encounter were ethnomusicologist Robert Garfias and experimental music composer Lou Harrison.

Many challenges faced performing artists as they began to work outside of their cultures. The most obvious were the problems inherent in performing for an audience that knew nothing about the relevant cultural tradition, including the norms of relationship between artist and audience. Artists from Asia encountered unexpected exuberance in the West; Western artists encountered what seemed like audience indifference in the East. The effects of these colliding expectations ultimately fell on the performers.[5]

Following the first morning seminar, Bala's ensemble performed in the evening. Viswanathan, the only one in the ensemble with experience performing outside of India, brought his impressions of the highly expressive audiences in the United States — but those impressions could only mislead them now. Viswa reported that before their presentation the entire ensemble was concerned how they would be received. During the concert there was none of the audience participation and encouragement that would be expected in India. No one had prepared Bala and her ensemble for the austerity of the Japanese audience. "They just clapped at the end of it," marveled Viswanathan. "They looked very, very expressionless. The hall was packed. No reaction or expression. Nothing. When we went offstage, Bala said, 'I think they didn't like it. It's going to be hard. And we have more concerts in different areas. I don't know.'" For all of them, the awareness that there had again been an attempt, with its attendant insults, to have them removed from the program placed tremendous added pressure on the ensemble.

But at the end of the performance the first night, Encounter organizer Nabokov approached Bala backstage, fell on one knee, kissed Bala's hands, and in a voice audible to everyone backstage apologized to her for having almost been swayed by the attempt to have her replaced on the program. Dame Margot Fonteyn, too, embraced Bala, then said to Kapila Vatsyayan, "And all through, I thought *I* was a dancer."[6] And, according to Lord George Harewood, after the curtain had come down at the end of the performance, the audience had risen to its feet as if on cue, and had thunderously applauded the concert. In spite of these overt signs of appreciation, Bala and her ensemble remained unable to judge the reaction to their performance that first night and went to bed dejected. Bala particularly felt that she had disappointed her advocates.

The following morning they learned through a translation of Tokyo newspapers that reviewers declared the concert a tremendous success.[7] Balasaraswati went on to present three more concerts in Tokyo, and then performances in Osaka and Yokohama.

Lord Harewood, who was then artistic director of the Edinburgh International Festival, described the performance from the perspective of the audience: "She had an extraordinary authority, an extraordinary mastery; and of course she was immensely communicative. There she was in a very large, dull hall, on a Western-style concert stage, so to speak, with no atmosphere,

Performers at East-West Encounter, on the stage of Metropolitan Hall, Tokyo, 1961.

nothing special about it. But the moment she appeared, she produced the atmosphere; she took [hold of] the audience, and the audience was immediately involved in what she did.... You would have to be blind to miss the fact that you were in the presence of a great dancer."[8] The person Bala considered the best critic of her narrative dance, her grandmother, in fact *was* blind.

The performance at Tokyo was a turning point for Balasaraswati and her troupe, as she was recognized by these first-rate international performers. And it was a turning point for the world of dance; Balasaraswati was to leave an indelible impression on those who saw her perform. In her usual way, Bala believed that her great success in Japan was the consequence of her recent offering of dance for her Krishna at Udipi.

The Asia Society

Following the concert in Tokyo, Balasaraswati accepted an offer from the Asia Society in New York for a tour — a decision that some people in India regarded as a sellout on her part. Money was a consideration, of course. Bala's family was dependent on her income. The family continued to live in the three-room rented house in Egmore; Bala had not managed to save money, and the prospects of earning enough to save were dim. Now approaching her middle years, Bala was unsure, given her constant bouts with bad health, how long her dancing career would continue. She was concerned that she had nothing to leave for her daughter. Lakshmi's father, who had amassed wealth during his dynamic career as a statesman and businessman, had left both Bala and Lakshmi without an inheritance.

Despite any initial doubts, however, in hindsight the Asia Society tour represented the beginning of the international acceptance of the great distinction of the performing arts of India and renewed opportunity for Bala and her family. The Asia Society, with the support of the John D. Rockefeller III Fund, had put Isadora Bennett in charge of developing a touring program of artists. In 1961 Charles Reinhart, then a young member of Bennett's staff who went on to have a distinguished career in the dance world, traveled to India and visited Bombay, Delhi, Calcutta, and Madras to finalize the arrangements for several performers. In 1962 Bala left India for her first U.S. tour. With this acknowledgment, Balasaraswati's place in her own culture was brilliantly established.

Audiences in the United States were not prepared for the unified vision of dance and music performed by Balasaraswati's family ensemble or for the power of the unrehearsed narrative portions of her dance. Many who had seen other interpretations of bharata natyam expected choreographed narrative dance with prearranged and rehearsed music, rather than simultaneously improvised performance by musicians and dancer. Part of the magic was the impact created by the character of hereditary performing arts; the performance was clearly conceived in the moment, but all members of the ensemble were performing with a profound understanding of one another and of their shared relationship to the dancing.

"Modern dance didn't come full sprung into the world," declared Charles Reinhart in an interview with videographer Smita Shah. "There was this great antecedent. We owe a great deal of debt to the classical art forms of Asia, and of course, Bala was the queen of her classical art form. . . . She was a very important part to show the quality of what existed in Asia. . . . Bala did a tour across the country. Little towns and cities across the country. She was a big hit." Reinhart did not travel with the troupe on the Asia Society tour he had helped organize but followed their progress through reports that came to him. Most Americans in the audience had no context from which to understand what Bala was doing. Reinhart reflected that probably "not more than one percent understood what Bala was doing, but I know that ninety percent appreciated what she was doing and recognized her greatness. That you could not help but see. So isn't that what's most important?

"I think the American public reacted to Bala with awe. They didn't un-

derstand what she was dancing and the fine interpretations of her movement, but they were in awe of this great artist and many of them understood
they were in the presence of one of the greatest artists of the world.... And
that what she did, in a sense, while being very important, to them was not
even [as] important as Bala [was] herself, because they could understand
Bala's genius without her interpretation, and that has to do with the excitement of that handful of great performers who could deliver anything and
make it an experience of a lifetime.

"I also was one of those who did not understand the intricacies of the
eye movement or the hand movement or the stories and my heart stopped.
You watch Bala in the beginning and you wonder, 'What's happening?'...
Slowly, she begins to warm up. She stands a little back, and she slowly
begins to build and all of a sudden, something happens in you and you
realize — your eyes widen and your mouth opens a bit and you realize — this
is as good as it's ever going to be, and the enjoyment of watching dance and
the appreciation of dance and 'I am in the presence of one of the half a
dozen greatest performing artists in the world....' That to me was the
message.

"You don't deal with this intellectually; this is an emotional response
that you're getting. This isn't something like one and one is two. This is
something which just invades your body and you just feel it and it's like
something that moves up and down your body and you don't even try to
explain it, you just enjoy it and appreciate it. So, that's Bala.... If you want
to understand any culture, you'd better understand their arts."[9]

Jacob's Pillow

Balasaraswati's tour in 1962 began in August with a week at the Jacob's
Pillow Dance Festival outside of the small town of Becket, in the Berkshire
Hills of western Massachusetts. Jacob's Pillow was originally a farm settled
in the late eighteenth century by a family named Carter; the site was at
the crest of a hill on the stagecoach road between Boston and Albany. Lo-
cally, the road, with its repeated switchbacks, became known as "Jacob's
Ladder." As was true all over New England, the rough pastures were strewn
with boulders, among them one with a curious shape resembling a pillow, in
front of which the Carter family built their home, naming the farm "Jacob's
Pillow."[10]

Ted Shawn had started his work at Jacob's Pillow in the early 1930s, building the studio that became the original performance and teaching space on
the old farm; the facility eventually expanded into several farmhouses and
other outbuildings. The land is secluded and partially wooded, with views
of a valley below. Built as a refuge and venue for alternative dance during the
formative years of Denishawn, the Pillow was one of several seasonal festivals
that started during the 1930s, including Tanglewood and the Bennington

Festival, which attracted the patronage of the wealthy summer community that had begun to frequent the Berkshires in the late 1800s.

The Jacob's Pillow Dance Festival and School brought audiences from New York and Boston together with some of the best- and least-known of modern dancers, as well as newly emerging dancers and performers of dance from other cultures and parts of the world. Several representatives of Indian dance had performed there before Bala, including Shanta Rao, Indrani Rahman, Rita Devi, Ram Gopal, and a group of Ceylonese dancers.

Lakshmi recounted the troupe's ride from New York to Jacob's Pillow in 1962. Met by a limousine at their midtown hotel in New York, Bala and her ensemble were dazzled by the drive up the heavily wooded Taconic Parkway on the eastern ridge of the Hudson River valley and the scenic beauty of the Berkshire Hills. When the group arrived at Jacob's Pillow, Ted Shawn opened the door of the limo and immediately assumed the pose of Nataraja, exclaiming, "I am Nataraja." Bala was embarrassed, though in no way offended. The Indian flag was flying in Bala's honor.

On opening night at Jacob's Pillow, Ted Shawn told the assembled audience, "Tonight you are in the presence of greatness." During the week that followed Bala shared seven programs with an experimental dance ensemble called The First Chamber Dance Quartet, founded the year before by choreographer Charles Bennett, and with Maria Tallchief, a Native American ballerina, who danced with Scott Douglas. The First Chamber Dance Quartet performed Bennett's choreography to a Japanese folk song; a world premiere of a piece called *Summer Pergola*, choreographed to a composition by the eighteenth-century Italian composer Luigi Boccerini; and a parody of modern choreography that would become a signature piece of the quartet, set to Edgar Varese's edgy *Pi R Squared*.

The ballet danced by Tallchief and Douglas was George Balanchine's choreography of the pas de deux from Igor Stravinski's *The Firebird*, and Russian composer Alexander Glazounov's ballet *Raymonda*. The eclectic nature of the program was consistent with the programming objectives at Jacob's Pillow in the early 1960s.[11] The day after Balasaraswati's last concert on August 25, ethnic dancer La Meri presented a demonstration with her students entitled "The Enrichment of Contemporary Dance through the Use of Ethnic Source Materials."

After Bala's first performance, Ted Shawn had told guests that presenting Balasaraswati at Jacob's Pillow was one of his "greatest accomplishments. Her art has been an international force for peace and amity among peoples."[12] Kapila Vatsyayan commented in an interview: "Ted Shawn has spoken of Bala as the messenger of peace and amity. When one great artist says that about another great artist, one should consider that a great compliment. And [coming from] a person like Ted Shawn, with his experience and exposure and having been a bridge between or among dance cultures

After Balasaraswati's first performance in the United States, at Jacob's Pillow Dance Festival, August 1962. Dance Festival founder Ted Shawn garlands Balasaraswati. Photo by John Van Lund. Courtesy of Jacob's Pillow Dance Festival Archives.

both in terms of what he did and what he promoted, this remark on Bala can have many meanings. One, naturally, was that a person so beautifully and richly rooted in her own tradition carried that message as easily to the United States, where she worked for many years. Not for a moment was Bala affected by the U.S. or [did she lose] her own security in herself, and this is what peace is all about. That you recognize the otherness of the other, be yourself and yet be able to make your dialogue. For a person of Bala's caliber to be able to do this showed both the strength of the tradition and her own strength, because a lesser artist could have been blown off their feet as many others have been."[13]

New York-based critic Walter Terry wrote of Bala's first performance at the Pillow, "The most articulate forefinger in the world of dance made its American debut last evening at the Jacob's Pillow Dance Festival. A forefinger which could summon or dismiss, invite or caution, assure or tease, make an airy comment or project an indisputable command . . . [characterizing] her special approach to her art, not based on physical virtuosity but on nuances, shading subtleties. . . . She has been called the Muse of India and truly she is a great actress whose purpose is to reveal, not merely to startle the beholder."[14]

After the week at Jacob's Pillow, the ensemble went on to Wesleyan University in Middletown, Connecticut, for a two-month residency. In the years that followed, Bala and other artists would find at university and college campuses not only audiences but environments capable of sustaining long-term relationships among artists, their audiences, and those who came to learn from them.

Thanks to a fortuitous sale of an educational publishing business Wesleyan had owned,[15] the small liberal arts school located halfway between New York and Boston was in a position to consider academic programs most colleges its size could not, including an expansive music program in the new field of ethnomusicology, the study of "ethnic music." Composer Richard Winslow and a friend, composer John Cage, were influential in the establishment of an avant-garde music program at Wesleyan; Winslow was on the music faculty, and Cage had visited the campus in 1955 and then had been in residence in 1960–61. Another faculty member, David McAllester, was an anthropologist who had focused his work primarily on Native American music and ceremonies. McAllester, one of the four founders of the Society for Ethnomusicology (eventually the overarching academic organization for ethnomusicology), had established Wesleyan's first courses on non-European music in 1956. Sometime during 1960 Winslow, as he described it, had a dream in which musicians from all over the world were performing together. He described this dream to McAllester, and the two presented the idea to Wesleyan's president, Victor Butterfield.

The concept was appealing to the progressive president,[16] and in 1961 the school hired ethnomusicologist Robert Brown, whose doctoral work in India had been guided by Ranganathan. In his notes to the music faculty at the time of Brown's appointment, Winslow commented: "The year [1960–61] has been a disturbing one — overall, I think, for healthy reasons. The world is in a state of attempted adjustment, the college is in a state of attempted adjustment, and the arts are not immune. At one obvious level, for instance, musical styles have changed very rapidly; the phonograph record has made obvious many things which only five years ago were mysterious and has made available in great quantities the work of an incredible avant-garde and the music of the Orient. The very nature of what we teach is thus called into question and the attitude of students . . . toward traditional materials is unpredictable. . . . We should move into the area of Oriental music as part of our offering. As of this writing, Mr. Robert Brown . . . will come into the Department. . . . Mr. Brown is a specialist in the Music of India and is conversant with the Orient generally."[17] Brown was in his second year at Wesleyan in 1962 when Bala first came to the college.

A friend and collaborator of John Cage's was dance pioneer Merce Cun-

A lasting friendship: Lakshmi Knight, Luise Scripps, and Merce Cunningham after Lakshmi's concert at the Asia Society, New York, 1994.

ningham, who had earlier seen bharata natyam dancer Mrinalini Sarabhai in New York.[18] He had heard that Bala was at Wesleyan. "Friends from India had spoken of Balasaraswati. I heard she was to perform at Wesleyan and drove up. She came out on the small, makeshift stage, stood for a moment or two, looked about, moved her feet slightly causing the ankle bells to tinkle. She went over to the side where the musicians were. Looking quite like a mother, she leaned over to talk to one of them who was her daughter. Shortly the musicians started to play and she began. The transformation into dance was instantaneous and vivid. It was as though illumination came on from all angles at once. Here was bharata natyam done in full splendor and magnificence, and here was a dancer such as one rarely had opportunity to see."[19]

Bala taught dance classes while she was in residence at Wesleyan, to Wesleyan students as well as to others who moved to Middletown to learn from her. She had already shown a great capacity for guiding and mentoring Indians who made themselves available for learning on her terms. Bala embodied a different vision of the performance traditions of South Asia than had been seen previously in the West. For some, including much of the American professional dance community, a renewed search for understanding of the traditions of India was informed by Bala's quiet and entirely self-assured presence. In meeting or seeing her, one was left with no doubt about her certainty of purpose or her clarity about her art. The institutions that sponsored Bala's teaching, while recognizing that students would in all likelihood not continue learning the art beyond a period of some weeks or months of intensive study, made it possible for the students to pursue almost without distraction the magic of Balasaraswati's instruction.

Bala and Lakshmi lived in an apartment close to the Wesleyan campus and the building in which they were teaching. The wife of a faculty member lent them a television, which was new to both of them. Bala developed a fascination with the half-hour daytime serial dramas known as "soap operas" (a term originally applied to radio serials sponsored by manufacturers of laundry products presumed to appeal to the majority of their audience — housewives). Bala began to insist on watching each day. She enjoyed Indian film, provided that the dancing was respectful and musical, and was an admirer of several Indian dancers, most from the traditional community, who made their living performing in movies with a lot of popular music and dancing — and with melodramatic plots similar to those of American soap operas. Under most circumstances Bala would not be particular about when she might be available to teach. She loved teaching, and she enjoyed and was responsive to the serious interest of her students. But Bala would quietly tell Lakshmi that she needed to get back to the apartment by the time *As the World Turns* began. She would speak in Tamil, which almost no one understood. Or, if necessary, she would invent excuses to get back to the apartment — perhaps housework or a letter that needed to be written — when someone would delay them after classes.

Following the residency at Wesleyan, Balasaraswati went on tour in October 1962. Their initial concert was in Washington, D.C., and First Lady Jacqueline Kennedy, who had a fascination with India, asked to meet Bala. From Washington the troupe moved on to the University of Pennsylvania in Philadelphia, and then to Princeton University. Following were presentations in New York at the Martha Graham School, Columbia University, and the Juilliard School. After Bala's performance at Juilliard, Allen Hughes wrote in the Sunday edition of the *New York Times* that "such events would scarcely seem noteworthy, for bharata natyam has been seen [performed] by many Indian and some American practitioners in varied interpretations of the art, but Bala makes all the difference."[20]

From New York they flew half way across the country for a program at the University of Chicago, and then on to Los Angeles for a concert at UCLA. They drove north from there for concerts in San Francisco and Berkeley. Bala's performances were reviewed in major newspapers and dance magazines, and these reviews were in turn enthusiastically reported in the Indian press.

In San Francisco Bala performed at the studio of Welland Lathrop (who had danced with Martha Graham during the 1940s) for an invited audience of seventy-five people, and the next evening she danced at the Palace of Fine Arts before an audience of hundreds. Coincidentally, both Lathrop's house and the Palace of Fine Arts had been designed by the renowned Berkeley architect Bernard Maybeck — and a friend and mentee of Maybeck's, Julia Morgan, designed the beautiful wooden church that became the home of the Center for World Music, where Balasaraswati was to teach in 1974.

It seemed not to matter to Bala whether the audience was large or small. Renee Renouf wrote in *Thought* magazine, a Delhi-based periodical: "Those who attended both evenings [in San Francisco] did not expect her to surpass herself, yet she outshone herself. . . . She bestowed on us such a manifestation of spirit that we rose, some blinded by tears, to give her a standing ovation. Those who followed her tour traveled through fog and rain to her programs. A band of devotees stood weeping as she boarded the plane for Hawaii."[21] Bala and her ensemble flew on to Honolulu for an appearance at the East-West Center.

Following the tour, as the rest of the ensemble went back to India from Hawaii, Ranganathan returned to Connecticut to become Wesleyan University's first Artist in Residence. Ranga blazed a trail for dozens of musicians and dancers representing more than ten performance cultures from around the world who joined and succeeded him, and who have populated Wesleyan's prestigious World Music program over the years since 1963.

The Edinburgh Festival

One of the attendees at the East-West Encounter in Tokyo had been George Henry Hubert Lascelles, the Earl of Harewood, a cousin of Queen Elizabeth II. Lord Harewood was an advocate and connoisseur of the performing arts and in 1961 had been appointed artistic director of the Edinburgh International Festival in Scotland. Founded in 1947 to present opera, music, theater, and dance of "the highest possible standard, representing the best artists in the world," the festival was known for its conservative programming; but the program in August 1963 was unconventional. Inspired by what he had experienced in Tokyo, Lord Harewood arranged to bring some of the leading Indian artists to Edinburgh. There they met up with Western artists that included violinist and conductor Yehudi Menuhin, lutenist and guitarist Julian Bream and composer Benjamin Britten. Bala had eight scheduled performances at the festival.[22]

In an interview Lord Harewood described how the 1963 Festival was born. "I had planned a big kind of Indian invasion of the Edinburgh Festival, which worked. It was spearheaded by Ravi Shankar and Ali Akbar

Edinburgh Festival, 1963. T. Balasaraswati with (from left): Ali Akbar Khan, Narayana Menon, Yehudi Menuhin, and T. Viswanathan.

Khan as instrumentalists, the northern musicians, while the *karnatic* musicians were Balasaraswati and Subbulakshmi. So I had very good generals, so to speak, for the invasion. It was a tremendous success. I knew immediately [after Tokyo] that Bala had come and I think we arranged a week of performances. It was quite difficult to do because Bala made all the stipulations that anyone does for a performance, and she insisted on exactly what a Western dancer would have refused. She said, 'I want a hard floor, a stone floor; I don't like these springy floors; I must have something to stamp on, something which totally resists me, stone if possible.' I don't think we had a stone floor, but we certainly had a floor that nobody could dance on and that's what Bala wanted, an absolutely firm one. We found this in quite a small hall . . . not smaller than the one in Tokyo, but anonymous, and we decorated it very slightly. . . . It was completely sold out from the start. If there was a seat left, it went after the first night."

After her first performance and the response the following morning, it was clear that eight performances would not be adequate to meet the demand to see her. Lord Harewood continued, "I asked Bala if she could stay on, and she said, 'Yes, why not, that's what I like to do, to dance.' So we arranged another week, and I think in the end, she did double the number of performances. That was the only time I remember doing that while I was at Edinburgh, simply doubling the number of appearances by a single artist. It was very remarkable; it was tremendously successful. She became then a sort of new goddess in people's lives, and people talked and wrote about her, and in England she became famous."[23]

Scottish critic Clive Barnes, reviewing the festival for the *New York Times*, wrote: "She makes no concessions to Western taste and demands relentless concentration, inducing an almost hypnotic effect. Her style and integrity are such that they transcend the usual barriers that restrict lesser artists to their own cultural backgrounds. Such talent and artistry as Miss Balasaraswati's are truly universal."[24]

Narayana Menon described his introduction of Bala to the audience in Edinburgh: "And at the Edinburgh Festival, [in] the very first program . . . we discussed what the Indian participation was going to do. Ali Akbar Khan was there, Viswa and all his people were there. Yehudi Menuhin and I talked in front of a very large audience. Suddenly I noticed Balasaraswati was there and we had not said anything. 'Bala,' I whispered, 'please come up.' She was very unwilling to come up. She had not done her hair, and her *sari* was rumpled. 'Come on, come on. Will you please do, in *abhinaya*, what I ask you to do?' She was almost unwilling, as she stood there. And then I said to the public, 'I want to introduce to you now the great dancer Balasaraswati.' And everybody looked. 'She wants to tell you how happy, how excited she is to be in this beautiful city of Edinburgh.' Then she described the beautiful city with such *abhinaya*. . . . The audience stood up. In less than a minute's time, she had conquered an audience. She had got the audience, cameras clicking, film and television people. From that moment, Bala was the star of that festival. And she had a fantastic success.

"From the first note of music there, from that first moment, it was total enchantment," Narayana Menon went on. "She hardly spoke to anybody, though people tried to speak to her. Whether she was in the festival restaurant, coming to watch a performance, going out somewhere, people said, there goes Bala."[25] Informal late evening gatherings in Edinburgh brought together an extraordinary assemblage of musicians from the West and from two entirely distinct Indian musical cultures, represented by artists who had known and respected each other for years. It was a very unusual situation. The group included Ali Akbar Khan, Ravi Shankar's *tabla* player Allah Rakha, and harmonica virtuoso Larry Adler, as well as Julian Bream, Ranga, Viswa, and Narasimhulu. They made music together for hours, crossing and re-crossing the barriers that were presumed to separate the cultures, east from west and north from south.[26]

The successes of her early tours to the United States and England enabled Bala to purchase some land in a part of Madras called Kilpauk, a few kilometers to the west of Egmore. Still partially agricultural, Kilpauk was originally a colonial section of the city that the British had settled during the early eighteenth century. The land Bala purchased had been part of a coconut grove attached to a large garden house that faced Poonamallee High Road. Bala had a vision of the sort of house she wanted, with cantilevered balconies and a veranda overlooking a terraced garden. Over time, that was the house she built; and it was there that, in 1965, Lakshmi began formal study with her mother.

Kilpauk

The veranda at the back of the house in Kilpauk was wide and deep. A wall of doors opened from the living room onto the veranda and the garden. At the rear of the garden Bala had terraced steps created, places to sit during performances on the veranda. The house included four large bedrooms with separate bathrooms; there were a living room, dining area, and kitchen both upstairs and down. Bala wanted the space to accommodate her extended family and finally to afford some privacy for Lakshmi and herself. At last there was a stable home for Bala, Lakshmi, Jayammal, and Bala's brothers Srinivasan and Viswanathan. Ranganathan joined them after he returned from the United States in 1965. Varadan, although a frequent visitor, lived with his wife and daughters in their own home.

One of Lakshmi's pleasurable recollections of Jayammal in the new house was Jayammal's arrangement for finding relief from the heat of the summer. There was a small storage area behind the downstairs kitchen that was connected to the rest of the house by a thatch-covered veranda. Jayammal and the entire family loved to throw dice and play cards, in particular gin rummy, which they would play for whatever change they had in their pockets. Jayammal would order a block of ice to be placed on a table with a fan behind it in the storage room. Those gathered for a game would sit in comfort with Jayammal's improvised air cooler. Lakshmi claimed that Jayammal, whenever she had the opportunity, would cheat without remorse.

Teaching Lakshmi

Perhaps the most pernicious effect of the movement against women of the hereditary families was the erosion of the art from within the families themselves. The late beginning of Lakshmi's career in dancing resulted from Bala's fear of the social stigma that crippled the traditional practice. Lost was the heritage of South Indian families who, generation after generation, practiced music and dance, having absorbed their families' art from infancy.

On the veranda of Bala's new house in Kilpauk, 1965. From left: Viswanathan,
Lakshmi, Balasaraswati, Srinivasan, unknown, Ranganathan.

When Lakshmi was born in 1943, Bala had every reason to believe that dancing, the profession of dancing or being a musician, and even the great artistic legacy of the family were dangerous associations for her daughter. Bala had faced down the stigma herself; she had no desire that her daughter battle the same challenges. But in the course of Balasaraswati's life the world changed.

New factors now shaped Lakshmi's engagement with the career of dance, namely, the family's experience in the United States together with the change in India in the perception of the hereditary arts. During the 1950s and 1960s dancing was becoming socially acceptable and encouraged as a form of refinement for young women. It was Lakshmi's observation of this development in the United States that emboldened her to suggest to her mother, in a manner that convinced Bala, that she begin to learn openly — that she become known as one of Balasaraswati's students.

Each of Bala's students had a particular claim about what they had learned. Some continue to describe having had a special intimacy with Bala or having learned something unique from her. As commented previously, this was one of the marks of Balasaraswati's genius; each student *did* have a particular and distinct intimacy with Bala; each student did learn something unique about the art. Bala never discouraged any student, and she always maintained that all of her students were the same for her; she had no favorite, nor did she state in public that any student better represented her style or approach to dancing than any other.

Since childhood Lakshmi had been an informal student of her mother's and the family's art, just as other family members had been; she had observed and absorbed everything. When Beryl de Zoete wrote about Bala in 1949, she wrote about "little Lakshmi" in the midst of the group performing the *kuravanji*. When Bala and Ganesha started to teach at Balasaraswati's school at the Music Academy in 1953, nine-year-old Lakshmi was at the back of the group. And in fact, although on several occasions Bala had stated that she did not want her daughter Lakshmi to learn to dance, Lakshmi started to have classes privately with Ganesha, who lived in her home, in the early 1950s. But his correction took the form of pinching Lakshmi's ankles, and Bala ended the classes. Ganesha's physical contact with Lakshmi was not brutal in its intent, but for Bala it brought back memories of physical abuse that were unbearable.

Accounts differ as to how Bala and Lakshmi decided that Lakshmi should begin more formal study with her mother. Viswanathan says he knew nothing about Lakshmi's desire to learn from her mother until Shirley Hood, wife of Mantle Hood, the head of UCLA's program in ethnomusicology, asked Viswa, "What the hell is going on, why won't you let Lakshmi learn?" Lakshmi certainly wanted to dance, but she would not have complained to Shirley Hood. Knowing Viswa well, however, Mrs. Hood would have felt free to ask him about what she could observe happening. Lakshmi's version was that she approached her mother after the first American Society for Eastern Arts session in 1965, where she saw students who were her own age and older learning from Bala. She realized she too could, and should, dance. After they had returned to India, Lakshmi suggested the advantage of being able to assist her mother when she was teaching. Bala had also observed the social changes taking place around her.

The classes Lakshmi began to take with Bala in 1965 were an extension of the relationship they had always had. Lakshmi had already absorbed Bala's ideas and aesthetics and the fundamentals of dance, and had begun to sing for her mother's concerts. Lakshmi and Bala now entered into a process of teaching and learning that lasted for almost twenty years. It was a slow process in traditional families, and neither Bala nor Lakshmi had any reason to speed it up. Bala would sit down with Lakshmi and teach a piece of music — "having a dance class," as Lakshmi once casually described it to me.

Lakshmi was a conservative, deliberate learner, as her mother claimed she herself had been. Until one hand gesture or detail in music had settled in her mind she would refuse to move on to another. Lakshmi learned both dance and the musical repertoire for bharata natyam, as well as significant portions of the family repertoire of *karnatic* music compositions.

Part of Bala's skill as a teacher was her ability to teach Lakshmi to overcome the fear about singing that had built up in Lakshmi over the first two decades of her life. As Lakshmi described herself, "Yeah, then I would get frightened and wouldn't know. . . . With my mother, I was so dumb there were times I couldn't understand one line, one *swara*, one passage. Sometimes she would cry with me because I couldn't get it." There was, of course, a reward for the slow learning. Looking back, Lakshmi said, "I have absorbed it. . . . I have merged with her. That is why I believe what she said before she died, 'Lakshmi, I will never leave you. When my *atma* goes it will go right into your heart. I won't go anywhere.'"

Touring in the West

Bala began to show subtle signs of deterioration in her health, and the limitations these problems imposed on her dancing were made especially difficult by the expectations set by her new worldwide fame. She must have been the first to recognize the limitations; progressively they also became a challenge for Lakshmi, and then for Bala's student and supporter Luise Scripps, who managed a series of tours and teaching residencies during the 1960s.

Luise Scripps was one of the people whose lives were changed by Bala's residency at Wesleyan in 1962. Mrs. Scripps, in turn, would eventually have a major impact on Bala's career. She and another woman from the San Fran-

cisco Bay area, Livia Frank, had been students in classes taught by Kapila
Vatsyayan in Berkeley in 1960. Mrs. Scripps was among those present at the
airport when Bala and Lakshmi left for Hawaii at the end of Bala's first tour
of the United States in 1962. Someone asked Bala if she would return to the
United States, and she replied, "If you ask I shall come." Out of this brief
exchange grew the idea for an organization named the American Society
for Eastern Arts—and Luise Scripps and her husband, Samuel H. Scripps,
whose grandfather had founded a publishing and news empire, were in a
position to act on the idea. In early 1964 Luise and Sam Scripps moved to
Madras, and Luise learned with Bala, performing at the Kilpauk house at
the end of her year's study. The Scrippses returned to California, arriving in
February 1965 in San Francisco, where they began to finalize plans for the
first summer program of the American Society for Eastern Arts.

During the spring of 1965, Bala embarked on a thirteen-concert tour of
Europe.[27] Beate Sirota Gordon and Luise Scripps arranged the tour, and
Luise traveled with Bala and her ensemble. Her first performance was at
the Musée Guimet in Paris, where Bala met the Japanese-American sculptor Isamu Noguchi. Noguchi had collaborated with Martha Graham on
her revolutionary set designs, using three-dimensional abstract objects and
sculpture rather than backdrops and other conventional scenery.

The group traveled from Paris by car through Basel and on to Geneva,
where Bala performed. They drove back to Paris by way of Dijon. From Paris
the group flew to London. The first concert in England was on June 6, 1965,
at the Victoria and Albert Museum, arranged by the Tagore Indian Centre.
Again the troupe traveled by car to a concert in Manchester and then on to
Dartington Hall in south Devon, a medieval estate connected to a progressive secondary school. Uday Shankar and Ragini Devi had appeared there
before. The owners of the estate had helped to fund the establishment of
Uday Shankar's school in Almora.

Bala gave a demonstration the first night and a concert the second, both
in the school dining hall. The young actress Sheila Ballantine then took
Bala's group to visit Stratford-upon-Avon on their way to Yorkshire, where
they performed at the Georgian Theatre in Richmond. The following night
they performed in Aldeburgh, and then returned to London for six concerts
at the London Commonwealth Institute.[28] The tour ended on July 7 with a
performance in Cumberland. Viswa left for India, where he was teaching at
the University of Madras, and the rest of the group left for a residency and
tour in the United States.

The U.S. residency was part of the first program of the American Society
for Eastern Arts, conducted at Mills College in Oakland, California, beginning on July 10, 1965, directed by Clifford and Betty Jones. ASEA functioned
for more than a decade and brought outstanding musicians, dancers, and
other artists to the United States, primarily from India and Indonesia. In

the summer of 1965 Bala, Lakshmi, Ali Akbar Khan, and their ensembles lived in a new home the Scrippses owned in Lafayette, in the hills east of the San Francisco Bay area. Bala taught with her ensemble, and Ali Akbar Khan and Shankar Ghosh (a well-known *tabla* player) taught North Indian music. The programs at ASEA marked a transfer of authority to Asian artists who presented themselves without interpretation or intervention by Westerners. Balasaraswati and Ali Akbar Khan represented an expertise and professional conviction that would permanently shape Americans' view of Indian performing arts.

For the opening night of the ASEA program[29] on July 10, 1965, the Mills campus was a fitting setting. Mills was the birthplace of California's electronic and experimental music scene. A movement in music parallel to the transformation of dance in America had begun at the beginning of the century, and in the 1960s non-Western music was at the forefront of the contemporary American performing arts scene. The world of traditional arts offered new visions for artists, and musicians found expressive freedom in the exploration of those traditions.

What some audience members at Bala's concerts in the United States discovered was that how Bala performed was clearly distinguishable from how other dancers who had preceded her in the West had presented bharata natyam. It was this difference in artistic process that cut across cultural barriers — as it had done thirty years before, when Bala first performed for a skeptical audience in Madras and then for audiences throughout the rest of India. Among those who saw that how she made her art was distinct were composers of experimental music.[30]

A month after the opening of the program, on August 15, Bala gave a demonstration of *padams* and *javalis* at Mills, and another concert. At the end of August she performed at the beautiful Mediterranean-style Villa Montalvo Performing Arts Center in the Santa Cruz Mountains in Saratoga, south of San Francisco; back at Mills College for the end of the ASEA program, she danced again on September 10.

Leela Shekar, a student of Jayammal's, traveled from India to join the tour. She had been living in Calcutta for many years, but she had stayed in touch, and her friendship with Bala was current and strong. She had begun performing with Bala after she resettled with her family in Madras several years before. When their family relocated to Madras, Leela thought of Bala as her older sister. Leela Shekar's husband was a friend of the family; a very conservative person, he was reluctant to let his wife travel alone to the United States. Bala approached him and asked if Leela could accompany her on tour. Shekar knew it was important for Bala, and he agreed. Bala was always grateful, as she was to all of her musicians.

Continuing a tour that had begun in Paris in May, after her teaching residency at Mills College Balasaraswati set off on a two-month nationwide

Balasarawati teaching at Mills College, Oakland, California, 1965. Photo by P. Peters.

tour involving more than thirty concerts. The endurance she and her ensemble demonstrated as they performed in their extemporaneously presented, physically demanding, and rhythmically exacting style is remarkable, especially in light of the fact that they toured from one coast of the United States to the other and back again. They covered more than ten thousand miles in two months, half of that distance by automobile — an unfamiliar experience for residents of India at that time.

The troupe first headed south from the Bay Area, traveling down the spectacular central California coastal road to perform at the Esalen Institute in Big Sur. The institute had been established three years earlier, and was associated with some of the diverse personalities at the forefront of an emergent counterculture in the United States, including Alan Watts, Aldous Huxley, Gary Snyder, and Joan Baez. Farther down the coast, in Los Angeles, there were two performances at UCLA, hosted by Mantle Hood. Bala met photographer/artist Jan Steward, who would later photograph her in concert. The ensemble then drove north to Eugene for a concert on October 4 at the University of Oregon, and then on to the University of Washington in Seattle on the 6th, where Robert Garfias, like Viswanathan and Robert Brown a student of Mantle Hood's, was building a program in ethnomusicology. Garfias had seen Bala perform in Tokyo in 1961.

On October 7 the ensemble flew to Washington, D.C., where they presented four programs at George Washington University, the State Department, and Howard University. At a reception at the Indian Embassy, Bala and Lakshmi met B. K. Nehru and his Hungarian wife. Nehru was the Indian Ambassador to the United States and a cousin of Jawarhalal Nehru. The Nehrus became lifelong friends of both Bala and Lakshmi. On the 11th, after one of two programs at the State Department auditorium, Jean Battey commented in a review in the *Washington Post* that "Bala can communicate even to an audience unfamiliar with her country; we can sense the complexity of her art form and that she has achieved the mastery that allows her complete freedom in it. It has been a privilege to have her here."[31]

The group traveled north to Philadelphia for a concert at the University of Pennsylvania on October 13, and two nights later they performed at Swarthmore College to the west of Philadelphia. They drove several hours the following day for a program on October 16 at Bennington College in the hills of southwestern Vermont, where with other dance pioneers Martha Graham had begun teaching in 1934. On October 17 they drove to Middletown, Connecticut, for demonstrations and a concert at Wesleyan.

On October 21 the troupe traveled the one hundred miles to New York, where they performed at Theresa L. Kaufmann Auditorium at the 92nd Street Y, the pioneering New York modern dance venue and school where Martha Graham, Doris Humphrey, Charles Weidman, Hanya Holm, and Anna Sokolow had all taught at some point in time. The concert was sponsored by the Society for Asian Music. At the performance Bala met Uday Shankar for the first time since he had left Madras with Bala's teacher, Kandappa Pillai, in 1938. Lakshmi later described the meeting: "When he saw her perform that night he wept profusely. Bala thought his reaction was partly remorse for having taken Kandappa Pillai to Almora, depriving Bala of her *guru*. Although he helped give her career a boost, he also caused her many difficulties. She was delighted to see him nevertheless."

Dance critic Clive Barnes wrote in the *New York Times* the next day. "A dancer such as Bala makes nonsense of ethnic boundaries. Faced with an artist of the stature of this great bharata natyam dancer, one looks and wonders, and salutes a great dancer when one sees her." Walter Terry wrote in the *New York Herald Tribune*: "One did not have to be a bharata natyam student to savor its beauties — it was sheer heaven, first to watch the dancer make mercurial but exact sculptures in space with her delicate fingers, and to observe her mobile face as she commented with a smile, with the lift of an eyebrow, a frown, or a glance of invitation upon her gestural sentences." Walter Sorrell wrote in the *Providence Sunday Journal*: "One of the most amazing experiences when seeing a great master is the almost mesmerizing effect she has on her audience, nullifying cultural barriers or the strangeness in her dance. What one sees is her spinning of gossamer subtleties, gestures full of poetic statements. . . . The hands begin to flutter, suddenly the slightest movement [has] meaning. She tells her stories with her head, arms and hands as if they could be heard." From New York the troupe drove west for concerts at the University of Michigan in Ann Arbor on October 23 and at Flint Junior College the next day. They doubled back, again by car, to Hamilton, New York, where they presented a program at Colgate University.

Luise Scripps had been managing Ali Akbar Khan's tour of the United States, which had been happening concurrently with Bala's tour, but she now joined Bala. Arriving in Rochester, New York on October 31, the troupe performed several programs at the University of Rochester, then drove from there to Chicago for a concert at the University of Chicago on November 6. Two nights later they appeared at Michigan State University; they returned to the University of Chicago for a lecture-demonstration and concert on the 9th. From the beginning of the East Coast tour on October 7 to the flight to Colorado on November 10, the group had presented more than twenty concerts and lecture-demonstrations, and had traveled more than three thousand miles by automobile.

In Colorado Bala was severely affected by the high altitude, and on November 11 Lakshmi took her mother's place in a performance at the University of Colorado in Boulder. Neither Bala nor Lakshmi considered this Lakshmi's *arangetram*; her formal introductory concert would not happen until eight years later. That she was able to perform in Balasaraswati's place was both an indication of how much Lakshmi had absorbed and a display of courage by Lakshmi — which went largely unnoticed. The need for the substitution was the first public sign of Bala's illness, which until then the family had kept carefully hidden out of a combined desire to protect Bala's privacy and to avoid public notice of her poor health.[32]

From Colorado the troupe traveled to Albuquerque, where Balasaraswati presented a demonstration of hand gesture at the National Meeting of the Society for Ethnomusicology. On November 14 Bala performed at the University of New Mexico. From there the group flew back to San Francisco, and on the 18th they presented a performance at the intimate Little Theater on the campus of the University of California at Berkeley. On the return trip to India, six months after they had left home, they stopped in Hawaii and performed on the 22nd at the University of Hawaii.

Back in India

As her fame spread outside of India Bala gained new respect at home. It had been out of Indians' attraction to a Westernized aesthetic that a revised style of dance had been born, but it was the hereditary form that caught the Western eye. Inevitably, some people saw Balasaraswati's dancing as anachronistic and inaccessible. Offers of engagements in Madras came infrequently, as dozens of dancers found their way to the concert stage in an increasingly politicized performance environment. But beyond Madras, in other parts of India, Balasaraswati's reception was warmer. Narayana Menon, when he was secretary[33] of Sangeet Natak Akademi, captured the irony of Bala's relationship to the Madras audience: "Her artistry and integrity have helped bridge more than mere oceans. At home she has swept across the chasm of indifference and neglect, linking this day with a magnificent part of its heritage. It is the spirit which she has preserved, her greatest contribution to a so-called dance revival, ersatz in content and dictated by whims of fashion and phonies. Because the spirit cannot be 'adapted' Bala is incapable of compromise."[34]

Bala brought forward in her art aspects of the traditional practice of dance that lay hidden from other practitioners. Reticence and economy characterized Bala's *abhinaya*. She limited her interpretation to the highlights of the symbolic narration; her *abhinaya* was suggestive of emotion rather than descriptive of action; her ideas were briefly stated; and she never lingered on one image but passed on to the next, "never allowing the *abhinaya* to sag by over-indulging any single symbol, but presenting a kaleidoscopic variation from one to another that showed the richness of her imagination," in the words of one tribute.[35]

The subtle element of gestural language, *satvika*, conveys the inner knowledge of the dancer: the sense of isolation, faith, and joy that she has to communicate. If we use common discourse between two people as the analogy, words are the medium of semantic communication. But there is much more to communication — the subtleties of tone, facial expression, and body language. "When all that is expressible through language is stated," one critic wrote, "there is still a residue of meaning which can be communicated only through direct rapport of feelings. All great art has sought this elusive residue of experience and tried to express it in non-verbal use of language. In literature it has been attempted through the breaking up of the syntax; in painting it has been attempted through the breaking up of the line and mass into color and texture; in sculpture this has been attempted through the breaking up of volume into plane and surface. Thus there has been always a sacrifice of the perfection of the language for the expression of the perfection of experience. This sacrifice lies at the heart of all creation. . . . And it is only an artist that has the perfection of the language at his or her command that can afford to break it up for conveying the perfection of experience. In Balasaraswati, her *satvika abhinaya* takes over complete command from the beginning. . . . In the white heat of her feelings, Bala has no need for the external trappings of movement and *mudras* to convey those feelings. She becomes the vehicle of these feelings completely."[36] At times, Balasaraswati danced *abhinaya* without the language of hand and body gesture, using simply her face and the music.

A complexity of Bala's art was that she did not sing only when the text fit the gestures she performed, the poetry of her *abhinaya*. She would sing the text while she performed gestures with a meaning unrelated to the literal meaning of the text. "The artist must gesturally bring out not only the outer meaning of the words of the song, but also interpret all their implications and inner meanings, sometimes building episodes around a single repeated line of text. But through all this she must not change the actual words of the song that she is vocally rendering. Even while she is gesturally enacting monologues and dialogues that are far removed from the actual words of the song, she must not utter the words fit for those situations, but only keep repeating the actual words of the song's text. That is, whereas she is gesturing myriad changing moods and environments, she is vocally adhering to the same unchanging phrases in the text. Another interesting feature is that, though the words are the same, she may make appropriate gestural variations called *sanchari* comparable to melody variations called *sangathis*, variations which help to bring out the many shades of the inner meaning of the text. Only if the artist is a true musician and enters into the spirit of the song through the music, can she interpret the song to perfection by simply keeping the movement of her hands and eyes in consonance with the ups and downs, curves and glides, pauses and frills in the melody, irrespective of the actual words of the song but in keeping with the dialogue that she has gesturally woven around them."[37]

On New Year's Eve in 1965, Bala performed at the 39th Music Conference at the Music Academy.[38] By this time Bala's imaginative mastery was legendary in India. However, relatively few in the audience actually understood Bala's ideas; she was always grateful for those that did. Among those whose opinion she still valued were *Kalki* cartoonist Saama and long-time admirer K. Chandrasekharan. The two would meet at Bala's infrequent concerts.

"She remembered everything, and would ask me what I noticed. 'Did you see? Did you notice? What else did you see?'" recalled Chandrasekharan. He remembered in particular an occasion when Bala danced the *pada varnam* "*Mohamana.*" In the last section of the composition, there is the phrase "the birds are chattering." Bala danced this line using one hand to show the bird chattering near her ear. Casually, as the bird nattered on, she quietly closed its beak with a simple gesture of her fingers of the other hand. As soon as she closed the beak, its wings began to flutter. "Right after that *'Moha-mana,'* Saama and I rushed to the greenroom. He said, 'Bala! The bird! The way you tormented that bird! It was so unusual.' [She] smiled and said, 'You noticed that? Good.' Then she would join in with us. 'Look at the way that bird fell into my hands so I could play with it.' "[39] Bala was speaking of the process of making images into dance. The bird fell into her hand. It came to her. She created the illusion, and then she watched it, and played with it.

Bala's Musicians

Balasaraswati attracted powerful musicians, and her ensembles were fabled. Over her career they had included her mother as a singer; her students Gnanasundaram and Narasimhulu as vocalists; her cousin Muktha (and on one occasion her cousin Brinda) as well as Sarojini Narayanaswami and Mrs. A. R. Sundarajan as vocal assistants to Jayammal; three distinguished clarinetists on different occasions; Viswanathan as singer and flutist; and during almost her entire career either Kuppuswami or Ranganathan as drummer. There were other highly skilled musicians. One of the reasons her ensembles were so successful was that there was a place in the course of the performance for each musician to be in command. It was a quality of her performances, and of her style, that was unique. That quality hung on the issue of the mutual respect of masters.

The role of the *nattuvanar* was reinterpreted in bharata natyam's revised modern style as being subservient to the dancer, and the rhythmic compositions performed were subservient to the dance choreography. This relationship changed when the *nattuvanar* was no longer the authority in the ensemble, a change that occurred during the early 1940s.

Balasaraswati's chief vocalist for much of her career was her mother, and it was she who set the musical standard of Balasaraswati's ensemble. The parts of the performance that involved *abhinaya* were never rehearsed. So all of the collaboration of music and dance in *javalis* and *padams*, the lyrically interpreted portions of the *varnam*, *sloka,* and *viruttam* would emerge, sometimes in unexpected ways, during performance. The dancer could determine the shape and direction the melody would follow, and the singer could contribute to the direction of the dance — both the actual nature of the movement and the line of poetry being performed. The dancer knew the music intimately, and the singer understood the dance. The singer used several improvisational forms or processes, including *raga alapana* and *niraval.* These structures allowed the improvised thrust of melody that was characteristic of the music in Bala's concerts. It was not the setting of the text that determined the shape of the dance but rather the melody that carried the text.

Improvised dance is incompatible with rehearsed, fixed music. In the development of an idea in bharata natyam, a line of text is repeated, but the melody evolves. Musical variety grows out of the singers and instrumentalists' imaginations as they — often one after another — create melodic variations enabled by the grammar of *raga* and *tala*. This allows the dancer to explore a line of text during numerous iterations of the poetry as a line is repeated in performance. If a musical ensemble does not have the skill to continue to generate melodic variations that match the character or quality of the dance, the concept of improvisation fails. Similarly, if a musician begins to develop a phrase of music, that development needs to be understood and encouraged by the dancer. If not, the result is a distraction of the balance of the ensemble and discontinuity in the performance. The instrumental accompanist provides support for the singer without distracting the music; this is accomplished through parity rather than in hierarchically defined positions in the ensemble. Bala's accompanying instrumental (flute and clarinet) musicians would each become soloists at some point in the performance. The instrumentalists would sometimes trade melodic phrases with the vocalists, requiring a compatible understanding of the improvisational characteristics of the music.

For most of her career, Balasaraswati's drummer was Kuppuswami Mudaliar. It was he who established the style of accompaniment that she came to expect, in which there were certain sections of dance where the drumming became supreme. In the instances of her "walks" that followed sections of composed pure dance — for example, as she "walked" backwards in the *varnam* — Kuppuswami would provide a carpet of rhythm that freely investigated the spaces between Balasaraswati's steps, which she placed with assurance and delight. Senior drummers sitting in the front row anticipated these wonderful, confounding moments in the performance. Kuppuswami was the only dance drummer to receive the President's Award from the Government of India, and he was certainly the only dance drummer to receive — in 1936 — the high honor of being draped with a silk shawl by Rabindranath Tagore.[40]

When Bala toured outside of India, her brother Ranganathan provided drum accompaniment. Ranga had the distinction of being trained by masters in accompaniment of both dance and the *karnatic* concert repertoire. His accompaniment of *padams* was unparalleled, and his combined experience in both traditions was virtually unique.

AMERICA 1966

The second American Society for Eastern Arts residency was held in 1966, again at Mills College. Bala and Lakshmi came without either of Bala's brothers. Ranga was in India, having returned from the United States in November 1965; and Viswa was completing his tenure as head of the Department of Music at the University of Madras, a post he had held since 1961.

Bala's health presented increasing difficulties. "We did not realize at the time that Bala's heart was out of sync and most likely the diabetic problems which flared later on had already begun to affect her," Luise Scripps remembered. Mrs. Scripps found and introduced to Bala a distinguished cardiologist in San Francisco named Francis L. Chamberlain. Bala would later say that it was Dr. Chamberlain's care that allowed her to dance the remaining years of her career. Yet, Mrs. Scripps remembered, "each year the complicated preparations needed to help Bala perform, travel, teach, and basically stay well enough to continue, demanded more and more of Lakshmi's subtle management and my own energies whenever I could help. . . . Her illnesses began to take a toll on her nature. Lakshmi and I slowly learned to recognize the signals of imbalances in her system. The more recalcitrant she became, the most likely her system was the cause. Still, she managed to perform under increasingly difficult, and dangerous, conditions. I marveled at Bala's ingenious ways of trimming and somehow managing to adjust herself, her program, her energies, so that she could present fine concerts despite her physical problems."

Returning home to Madras after the summer of teaching, Bala was diagnosed with tuberculosis, then common in Madras. In spite of this illness, Bala performed in early December at Krishna Gana Sabha,[41] and on December 20 she performed for the 40th Annual Music Conference at the Music Academy.[42]

Viswanathan traveled to the United States in the fall of 1966 to begin work toward his doctorate at Wesleyan. Several months later, on February 2, 1967, Jayammal died at the age of seventy-six. Viswanathan was told that his mother called for him as she was dying; some family members held it against him that he was not there to attend her death. But the forces of opportunity were pulling the family apart.

Balasaraswati had spent her entire life in her mother's company. Now abruptly released from Jayammal's control, she was temporarily at a loss. But in due course a transition within the family occurred, as it had before and has again since. Bala was now the matriarch, and her daughter lived with the matriarch's benevolent expectation of devoted support and deference. The relationship that emerged between Lakshmi and Bala, like Bala's relationship with her mother, was driven by mechanisms that facilitate hereditary practice. The difference was in the temperaments of the three individuals and the spirit of the two mother-daughter relationships. Bala was threatened by Lakshmi's independence, as Jayammal had been by Bala's, but Bala's gentleness and her desire for opportunity and change for her daughter were things that Jayammal could not have imagined.

S. Krishnan, a journalist who wrote about Bala on several occasions, was a close family friend and knew the family from an inside perspective. "Lakshmi was truly Bala's constant companion and advisor until her mother

passed away.[43] Her innate instincts and clear logical mind served to save
Bala, as well as herself, many a close call. Much like her grandmother, her
practical, far-sighted sense helped protect Bala as Jayammal protected her
brood. Jayammal had controlled Bala's life, both private and professional,
and remained in command until her last breath. Her daughter was known
to [chafe] under her mother's powerful reins."[44] After Jayammal had died, it
was partly Lakshmi's humor that enabled her fundamentally independent
spirit to coexist with and endure without resentment expectations of deference and dependence.

Brothers

The bharata natyam community expected male members of professional
families to forge their own futures. This expectation posed a conflict of
identity as the hereditary families were marginalized in the early and mid-
twentieth century: The message to the men was to abandon their family cultures and to repudiate their family heritage. Musicologist B. M. Sundaram
recalled episodes that illustrated the stresses of those transitional years. Sundaram, who himself was born into a *devadasi* family, described visiting the
household of a renowned dancer from the traditional community in a village
in the Thanjavur district, hoping to interview her, but being chased away by
the men of the family. On another occasion he visited the house of a dancer
in Madras. He recognized the elderly woman who answered the door as the
artist he was looking for. Despite his repeated efforts, however, she refused
to acknowledge who she was and asked him to leave her in peace.

In response to these stresses, professional artists and families who continued to perform had to develop the skill to do business with the full breadth
of society, dealing with the wealthy and the pious, the learned, the pompous,
and the political. Bala and her brothers had the advantage of this adaptabil-
ity as they found their way outside of South India. Viswa and Ranga both
were successful as soon as they began to live and work in America. They
recognized the opportunity to be heard and to teach without the stigma
placed on their community burdening their spirits.

In traditional families, there are those who do not become professional
artists. But even if family members do not follow professional careers, they
often absorb elements of the hereditary practice and may receive some training. Bala's cousin Shankaran learned music, as did her cousin Vijayakrishnan, but they did not sing professionally. Bala's brother Varadan worked in
the airline industry; for some time he was a regional manager for Swissair.

Varadan was skilled at mimicry and gesture, however, as a story related
by his daughter Caroline illustrates. A visitor from Scandanavia called at
Bala's home, directed there by someone in Europe who knew her. Bala and
Lakshmi were away in New Delhi. Varadan was alone in the house, as he
explained to the visitors. When asked if he also was a performing artist, he

Viswanathan, accompanied by Ranganathan, Los Angeles, early 1970s.
Photo by Jan Steward. Courtesy of the photographer.

said that yes, he performed *kathakali*, the dance theater form from Kerala.
Varadan had been schooled for a year in Kerala, spoke Malayalam, and was familiar with the movements and mannerisms of *kathakali*. He proceeded to entertain his guests for some time with an extemporaneous rendition full of highly stylized facial expressions and body postures. Several days later Bala returned to Madras and met her visitors, who explained that they had met her brother, "the *kathakali* expert." Bala was helpless except to give an ironic smile and nod familiar to those who knew her well.

The success of Ranganathan and Viswanathan's careers in the United States hinged on their ability to find and maintain secure teaching positions with institutions that supported them and the art they represented. Wesleyan University was among the pioneers in programs teaching non-Western performing arts, and the musical activity on campus produced a "scene" that provided audience, advocacy, and patronage — as had also developed over the previous five years at the American Society for Eastern Arts, UCLA, and the University of Washington. Ranganathan had taught at Wesleyan from 1963 to 1965. In 1968 he returned to the United States with Bala and Lakshmi to participate in a residency at UCLA from July 1 to September 6, and from there he went on to resume his post as Artist in Residence at Wesleyan. Viswanathan was still there at that time, completing his Ph.D. course work. This was when I met Ranga and Viswa.

At Bala's concert at Jacob's Pillow in 1962, one of the attendees was an American named Jon Higgins. He had just graduated from Wesleyan and had entered the university's fledgling graduate program in ethnomusicology, unsure of an area of specialization. After hearing and seeing the concerts at Jacob's Pillow, Higgins decided to focus his attention on South Indian music; he studied first with Robert Brown, then with Ranganathan. A year later, in 1964, he traveled to India as a Fulbright Scholar and began to study with Viswanathan. By 1966 Higgins had astonished audiences in India, and it seemed that Viswanathan had discovered a way of teaching *karnatic* music that circumvented the years of practice and apprenticeship assumed to be required. In 1969, after completing doctoral studies at Wesleyan, Higgins traveled to India again and began an apprenticeship with Balasaraswati, at the end of which he wrote a dissertation that was later published as a book, *The Music of Bharata Natyam*.

After returning to India in December 1968 from the residency in Los Angeles, Bala found an opportunity to express her respect and gratitude to a friend. To those that she trusted, she was unhesitatingly generous. One of those was Lord Harewood, who had invited Bala to the Edinburgh Festival in 1963. Lord Harewood remembered, "I was in India once with my wife, who had never been before, in 1968. Towards the end of the trip we were in Madras. Unfortunately, we intended to see Balasaraswati and Subbulakshmi, but I'd been bitten by a mosquito and got Dengue Fever. Bala had a recital which I couldn't go to but my wife went. She said Bala sent her wishes and wished she could come to see me.

"After four days the fever was over. I got a message that someone had come to see me. My wife knew about this. In came Bala, with Lakshmi, and we talked about my getting Dengue Fever and missing her recital. And then she asked: 'Would you like me to do some *padams* for you?' Then the musicians came in (it was a very large bedroom) and she performed, for about forty minutes I think. She mimed, and sang; it was a wonderful experience. To have one of the greatest dancers in the world come and dance in your hotel bedroom for you has a certain old-fashioned ring about it. It certainly hadn't happened to me before, or since."[45]

"A Radiant Aesthetic Force"

The focus of Bala's life had changed. She was now turning inward to the task of transmitting her art, not through an institution, but through her family. In 1971 the *Indian Express* published a long interview with Bala in which she exposed a more philosophical attitude about her life's work: "I think all artists have difficult times. When I was just beginning they said, 'She is too young.' In my teens I was too thin, later the complaint changed to 'too fat'—and now they say I am 'too old.'" Although she had been dancing for forty years, she felt her days were not yet over. "Even now I am dancing as boldly as before, not for fame or anyone, but because I still like to dance." She shrugged off reviews and categorizations of all varieties, asking, "Why can't they try to appreciate what it all means? Still I will dance if even one person wishes to see me"—and merely smiling when reminded by the interviewer of the thousands worldwide who came to see her.

During the interview Bala did admit that as a stage artist she was conscious of and concerned about the response to her dancing. But she expressed increasing detachment and, at the same time, engagement with her own response to the demands of her métier. Bala described her approach to dancing as developing "every moment, to depict each nuance," yet remaining detached from the characters and moods she created. She retained the duality of the creator and the creation, she said. Her cryptic explanation: "What is the point when the sugar cane becomes another sugar cane? It should be just *like* a sugar cane. It should taste sweet—but it should be more than that. I tell you about a thing, what it is, but do not become that thing. I remain myself."[46]

Shortly after Bala performed at the Music Academy on December 29, 1970, she gave a performance at Tejpal Auditorium in Bombay,[47] where she was honored by a "Bala Felicitations Committee." Narayana Menon, A. S. Raman, and S. M. Y. Sastry led off with an address of welcome.

Well in advance of the event, Bala had written to the Felicitations Committee that she was a professional artist and performed for set fees, rather than for collections made on her behalf as the committee had suggested. The committee felt that she would be paid more if a collection, a "purse," was offered, and in spite of her protests, they arranged for a substantial purse — sixty thousand rupees — to be offered along with a silver plaque at the conclusion of the concert. The singer Kesarbai Kerkar, who Bala admired, made the presentation there on the stage.

Bala had no alternative but to refuse the purse, suffering a considerable loss of income (she was paid nothing) and the embarrassment of a gaffe made public. The Felicitations Committee, among many others, had not understood the pride Bala felt as a professional; the event, although very well intentioned, once more exhibited insensitivity to the values and protocol of the professional community. That Bala appeared to some to be ungrateful was humiliating to her. Yet her public refusal of the purse had been entirely foreseeable, since she had stated her position repeatedly and unequivocally.

Despite this awkward moment, Bala's concert that night was admired in the press. "A face so soft and mobile that it can mirror each quiver of the soul. . . . Bala [is] the most perfect medium for *abhinaya* yet to be seen in our times. A great artiste, greatest of all living bharata natyam dancers, Bala has the added advantage that she is not a revivalist of the dance-form, but one of the few last surviving representatives of the authentic tradition in which dance is a deep-felt spiritual experience!"[48]

On New Year's Day 1971, Bala performed for the 44th Music Conference at the Music Academy.[49] A few weeks later, on January 21, 1971, Mylapore Gauri Ammal died, and Bala had lost the last of the three persons she credited for her career: first Kandappa Pillai, years before; more recently Jayammal; and now Gauri Ammal. This latest loss left her profoundly discouraged. Nevertheless, in April 1971 Bala performed again at Sapru House in New Delhi, sponsored by the Indian Cultural Society.[50]

Beginning in July ASEA held its third summer program, this time in Bali; about twenty American students traveled to Indonesia to learn Balinese performing arts and to participate in the first Pan-Pacific Ramayana Festival. As a way of lifting Bala's spirits, Samuel Scripps suggested that Bala and Lakshmi join them in Bali to observe the festival. Bala was cheered by the trip and what she saw. She was fascinated with the differences in the dance imagery used to suggest the familiar characters drawn from the great Hindu epic about Rama. She was inspired by being again in the midst of performing artists from other parts of Asia, connected in imagery and myth in the same way that the performing arts in India are connected by the shared epic mythology. Bala seized every opportunity to take time away with Lakshmi to teach her.

After returning to India Bala performed for the Bharatiya Music and Arts

Society Festival at Shanmukhananda Hall in Bombay on October 30, 1971, with an ensemble that included Ganesha, Muktha, and Lakshmi, who was singing more and more regularly for her mother. "A superb performance," declared a review the next day in the *Indian Express*. "All that is noble and grand in the art of *abhinaya* stands revealed through the subtle vibrations emanating from Bala.... Bala does not demand attention. She enthralls the audience. Even the conventional *alarippu* seemed to pulse with a serene, persuasive quality that welled up in an exalted strain in the *varnam*.... Bala overwhelmed her audience with the quintessence of her art. If one marveled at the incredible range of the engrossing imagery, one was amazed by the vigor of her *nritta*, the precise execution of the *tirmanams* superbly [performed] by *nattuvanar* Ganesha, the chiseled purity of her *hastas* and the eloquence of her *mudras*."[51]

On New Year's Day 1972, Bala performed at the 45th Music Conference of the Music Academy[52] and once again received glowing notices. A reviewer wrote, "It was music that moved the soul, [and] achieved communication with each *rasika* as though she was performing exclusively for him, an intimacy of artistic relationship which Balasaraswati alone can achieve."[53] In the early spring of that year, Bala performed at the National Centre for Performing Arts at Homi Baba Auditorium in Bombay. "[For] those present at the Homi Baba Auditorium, Bala's recital came as a glorious spiritual ablution.... Throughout one was only conscious of a radiant aesthetic force."[54]

"Taught by a Living Person"

Later that spring, the California Institute of the Arts School of Theater and Dance invited Balasaraswati for a residency from April 3 to June 16. In 1970 Robert Brown, Ranganathan, Viswanathan, and a group of students of Indian and Indonesian music from Wesleyan had moved to the high desert north of Los Angeles to join the first year of operation of CalArts. The school was the realization of the vision of Walt Disney and his family. The concept, which was revolutionary at the time, was to establish a professional school in all the performing and visual arts, and to create an environment in which professionals from different disciplines would be forced into and enabled in interaction. The school also recognized in its programming that the arts were a global phenomenon. In the School of Music, North Indian music was being taught by Ravi Shankar and his entourage; Ghanaian music and dance, and Javanese music and shadow puppetry were taught by other well-known performers.

CalArts is in Valencia, California, located in a single, vast, multi-level building enclosing an area of eleven acres. To the north the school overlooks the expanse of high desert of the Antelope Valley with the San Bernardino Mountains beyond it; out of view, down the concrete strip of Interstate 5, is the San Fernando Valley. When the school opened in 1971 it was a visually incongruous presence situated two miles from the nearby town of Newhall. Newhall was high desert cowboy country, a daunting contrast to the new community of artists and student artists. The planned opening of the facility was delayed, and the first year of operation began in 1970 on the leased grounds of an old convent named Villa Cabrini, set amidst olive and orange groves in Burbank. But a large and destructive earthquake centered in the mountains south of Newhall, the Sylmar Quake, occurred in the morning of February 9, 1971, forcing the condemnation of several buildings on the grounds of the convent, and the campus in Valencia opened before its construction was completed.

The faculty was distinguished, and put Ranga and Viswa on a very different footing as musicians in the United States. Being at CalArts was an opportunity for Ranga and Viswa to be acknowledged as professionals. The music faculty included percussionist John Bergamo, bassist Buell Neidlinger, clarinetist Richard Stoltzman, composers James Tenney and Morton Subotnick, and numerous other artists who represented the best of a generation. The dance faculty included Donald McKayle, who had seen Bala perform in Madras when he was touring with Martha Graham's troupe in 1956; and the associate dean of the School of Theater and Dance and director of Dance, Bella Lewitzki, who had not seen Bala dance previously but knew of her through her connections with UCLA.

In an interview years later, Lewitzki recalled where the idea to have Bala come to CalArts started: "Bala was part of a dream that I had dreamed, which was . . . that history should be taught by a living person so that it was a totally encapsulated story one got. Instead of anecdotes, reading about, or dry pages and facts, one would live, as it were, with the individual that was deserving of being recorded in history. And, certainly, Bala was that. . . . At California Institute of the Arts, fortunately, we had the right to shape our program with very little interference so we did just that. We shaped it as we thought fit.

"It was decided that those students in the School of [Theater and] Dance who wanted to learn from Bala, and were accepted by Bala, were excused from the rest of their program, except for the academic programs to meet accreditation requirements. . . . They were able to focus almost all of their attention on learning from Bala. . . . I think she must have taught something like three hours in the morning and three hours in the afternoon. Our object was not to exhaust her, nor to deprive her of all her information in one fell swoop, but was to expose our students to her. . . . In my own mind, I think I reconfirmed something I already knew — that within the art form itself, lies something so beautiful that if you devote yourself to it fully, out of it comes the flowering that looks like a Bala. All those years, all of that input, resulted in Bala. And it was, for me, very confirming. I don't think it needs to be done with quite the severity that this woman had to undergo, because she apparently has not practiced that with her daughter. She wanted to see a little more freedom with her daughter, she told me."[55]

Donald McKayle had very specific recollections, partly because he had already brought the aesthetics of Indian dance into his own work—and because he had seen Bala previously: "I remember being tremendously impressed with the expressive dance. I just thought it immediately opened a whole picture of life that she was trying to get across. I was completely carried away by it. I had studied Indian dance prior to this so that maybe I had some inkling of gestures that the other people didn't have. But, I don't think that was necessary in order to get a real feeling of what she was trying to express.

"But a lot of the things I learned from her became incorporated in my work, like the sound of the feet on the floor. I would do things where I would lift the toes and get a certain sound and let them slap onto another.... It is just the whole use of the back, the arms, the head, the neck.... I robbed her warm-up [*alarippu*] for my class because I felt that it extended the energy all the way out to the extremities. Also, it gave them a very different use of their bodies, so they didn't have a face that was observing the rest of their body, which was dancing. It became a much more total look.

"I've found over the years, that those people that have worked with me a long time have a very different way of performing than those who come to me at the beginning and don't have it. So I feel that that was one of the things I got from working in this art form and Bala was a very important force of that.... And there is belief behind it. There is actual performer belief behind it. That conviction cannot be imitated. It is very strange. Even if they don't feel it after the moment is gone. It doesn't matter, it is in the dance."[56]

The summer of 1972, after Bala's residency at CalArts, ASEA held its fourth program from June 18 to August 11, returning to Mills College. Bala brought from India K. Ramiah Pillai, whom she had been training in the practice of *nattuvangam* and music since 1956. Ganesha, tragically, was becoming increasingly unreliable from the progressive effects of alcoholism. She also brought vocalist Ramadas, who—unusually—knew the bharata natyam musical repertoire. Lakshmi continued to perform regularly as a singer, and Ranga and Viswa were now musical leaders of the ensemble. The family provided their students, Indian and non-Indian, with opportunities to perform. At a concert at the 25th Anniversary of Indian Independence at the Palace of Fine Arts in San Francisco, the ensemble was joined by violinist Gordon Swift (an American student of Viswanathan and of lifelong friend and musical collaborator V. Tyagarajan). He had coincidentally attended Bala's first performance at Wesleyan in 1962. The summer ended with a concert at Veterans Auditorium in San Francisco, with an ensemble of Ramiah, Ramadas, Lakshmi, Ranga, Viswa, and violinist L. Shankar.

Shankar soon went on to join jazz guitarist John McLaughlin in his ensemble, Shakti, which was a fusion music phenomenon in the mid-1970s and remains popular with a modified ensemble today in India.

For several years Bala had suffered from dry lips, which she attributed to nervousness. In September 1972, immediately following the conclusion of the Veterans Auditorium program, Bala was hospitalized after an examination in which she was diagnosed with severely elevated blood sugar, confirming diabetes. The mystery of what had been causing the problems that had affected her work and her heart was solved. Bala began a regimen of insulin she followed for the rest of her life. While she was in the hospital, she learned of the death of her oldest brother, Srinivasan, from complications related to alcoholism. Srinivasan had managed the family financial and logistical affairs for many years, and his progressive illness and the losses it resulted in were a sadness to everyone. Even though his problems had caused difficulties for the family, Bala was stunned by the news.

Her physician in San Francisco, Dr. Chamberlain, would not release her from the hospital immediately following her diagnosis, and Bala was forced to cancel a concert at Colgate University, something she had never done before. But Luise Scripps did manage to get her released in time to meet three obligations on the East Coast, where the rest of her ensemble was already waiting.

The first was a performance at the Asia Society in New York on September 18. It was Bala's first appearance since her hospitalization, and the first time she had performed with the benefit of insulin. Her dosage had not yet been stabilized, however. Lakshmi, Luise, and Bala's brothers were quietly very nervous during the performance; they had been warned that Bala might experience neuropathy and lose control of her limbs unexpectedly if the insulin level was too high. This had been the reason for her doctor's reluctance to let her leave. No one in the audience recognized the distress of the ensemble members. But several people recall the severity of Bala's mood; it was as if the austerity of her dance expressed her recognition of her condition, and of the initiation of a potentially very serious alteration of her blood chemistry.

On September 22 Bala performed at Alice Tully Hall at Lincoln Center to a sold-out audience. Anna Kisselgoff, who had reviewed Bala for the *New York Times* during her Asia Society tour in 1962, and Charles Reinhart, who by then had become the director of the American Dance Festival, were in the audience. Kisselgoff reviewed the concert: "The greatest artists are the most exacting, and certainly Bala demanded no less of herself than she did of her audience and her musicians." A rarity for Balasaraswati, some of her audience left during the intermission. But "the majority, mostly young people, gave her a standing ovation. . . . Rarely have the sacred origins of Indian dance been so evident as in the brief moments of epiphany that Bala radiated in the concluding devotional dance. The sight of this exceptional performer, with eyes closed, arms raised, palms out, achieving a state of the sublime, was a revelation. By comparison, the performances we have seen here in recent years seem indecently to pander to Western audiences. . . . To say that Bala makes no concession to the audience is an understatement; the initial going could be categorized as rough."[57] Bala, in her severity after her bout in the hospital and the anxiety that surrounded her, presented a concert of such density and formality that, for some of her audience, the performance asked too much.

During the 1960s and early 1970s the audience for Bala's art grew in the United States. She gave more than two hundred programs, and word spread of the excellence of her teaching. Her brothers presented numerous performances of their own, and built powerful independent careers teaching at Wesleyan University, California Institute of the Arts, and several summer programs. By 1973, when Lakshmi was formally presented as a dancer in India, seven members of the family had taught and toured in the United States, including Brinda, Muktha, and Brinda's daughter, Vegavahini Vijayaraghavan. Three of the seven were eventually awarded the title *Sangitha Kalanidhi*; they were among the best performing artists South India had to offer. About a dozen years after Bala's performance at the East-West Encounter in Tokyo, she and her family were world renowned and well established in the United States.

Bala taught in twelve residencies between 1962 and 1981. During the 1960s she taught first at Wesleyan University, then at UCLA and the American Society for Eastern Arts at Mills College; during the 1970s and early 1980s, she taught at ASEA at Mills College, CalArts, the University of Washington, the Center for World Music in Berkeley, the American Dance Festival at Connecticut College and Duke University, and finally again at Wesleyan. Her earliest residencies were presented in academic settings where many of her students were nonprofessional dancers. The residency at CalArts in 1972 was her first in North America in a professional performing artist environment; two residencies at the American Dance Festival in 1977 and 1978 furthered the exposure of professional artists to Bala.

Balasaraswati's tours and residencies were of various durations. The longest, in 1965 and 1974, lasted about six months each. Between trips to the United States, Bala and Lakshmi lived a simple life in Madras in the home Bala had built in Kilpauk in 1964. There, Balasaraswati continued her distinguished career as a performer and teacher. Although she was now world famous, Bala's life was in many ways uncomplicated, and certainly free of the trappings often associated with fame.

The only distinction Bala tried to communicate was that she was a professional performing artist. Whatever else she was, she wanted her work to be understood as crafted by the principles and conventions of a great tradition. She did not *represent* the hereditary tradition of bharata natyam; she *was* the hereditary tradition.

SANGITHA KALANIDHI

In 1971 Ranganathan and Viswanathan bought a house together in a new housing development in the high desert north of Los Angeles. It was their first experience with home ownership. When the Sylmar earthquake struck in February 1971, the same event that had necessitated the relocation of CalArts, the foundation of Ranga and Viswa's new home cracked — a problem that could be fixed, unlike the damage to many of the homes built on neighboring hillsides. Ranga had stretched out on the floor of the living room watching television and fallen asleep. Luckily, when the earthquake struck in the early morning, the sliding glass door next to him fell out rather than in, shattering on the concrete patio outside the door. About two hours after the earthquake, having cleaned up the broken glass and dishes in my own home, I drove to the area where Ranga and Viswa lived. At the bottom of the hill on which their house was built, Ranga was standing propped up on his crutches. I had never, in the more than three years I had known him, seen him walk more than short distances; he was half a mile from home. When I asked him what he was doing, he told me, "If I'm going to die, I want to take a walk first." He climbed into my car and we drove together up to the house. Six months later fires swept up the canyons, lighting the summer sky at night — something else none of us had witnessed before.

By 1973 Viswa and his wife, Kumari, had two children, Jayasri and Kumar, both born in India. Ranga and his British wife, Edwina, had one son, Sudhama, born in Los Angeles; a second son, Arun, was born in Berkeley in 1974. Bala was close to all of her brothers' children, although differences in Bala and her siblings' child-rearing approaches were sometimes a source of tension, as seems to be the case in many families. In order to stay clear of potential disagreements, Bala maintained a somewhat detached relationship. The challenges confronting Ranganathan's and Viswanathan's families were not always well understood by the numerous students and admirers who populated their homes, as they did Bala's home in Madras. Both Kumari and Edwina faced the adjustments of integrating their lives and families with the rapidly and dramatically shifting face of American culture, and with the roles that their husbands played in that evolution. Their four children grew up in the midst of the attention and recognition their charismatic fathers drew from the students, scholars, and artists who were constantly present.

Bala had been focused on teaching Lakshmi since 1965. She presented Lakshmi in a formal *arangetram* early in 1973, at the Madras home of Lak-

Ranganathan, Los Angeles, early 1970s. Photo by Jan Steward.
Courtesy of the photographer.

shmi's half sister, the daughter of R. K. Shanmukham and his first wife. In the summer of 1973, Bala, Lakshmi, and Bala's ensemble, including Ranga and Viswa, taught and performed in a residency at the Center for Asian Studies at the University of Washington in Seattle, where they had been previously in 1968. On July 29, Lakshmi had her first concert in the United States, with Bala, Viswa, Ranga, Ramiah, Ramadas, and L. Shankar. Bala gave a concert at the University of Washington on August 16, and at the University of California at Berkeley on September 6.

Before leaving Seattle Bala received a letter from M. S. Subbulakshmi, informing Bala that she would be honored that December by the Madras Music Academy, where she had contributed so much, with the title of *Sangitha Kalanidhi*. Bala's childhood friend wrote: "Our joy cannot be described in words. The music world is being honored this year now that you [will] . . . preside over the Academy Festival. . . . God has been kind to grant our prayers that you should be honored this year. We eagerly expect your arrival back home. Meanwhile, our daughter, Radha, joins both of us in extending our greetings to you and to Lakshmi." The choice became controversial for some, however; detractors claimed that Bala was a dancer and not a musician.

Bala stayed with her brothers in California for the month preceding performances in October at the Smithsonian Institution in Washington, D.C., and at Town Hall in New York. After returning to Madras, Bala performed in Calcutta on December 18. On December 21 the secretary of the Madras Music Academy, T. T. Krishnamachari, for whom the auditorium of the Music Academy is named, sent a special message that was printed in the program for the 47th conference, commenting on the basis for the selection of Balasaraswati as president-elect of that year's conference. "More than her own heritage in both music and dance," he stated, "she has by her ability in exposition and improvisation revived an art which was well-nigh dead by the 20s of this century and the movements against the various experts in the art. . . . It was Srimathi Balasaraswati that revived this art and [has] given it status. . . . Srimathi Balasaraswati has demonstrated that professionalism in bharata natyam is the *sine qua non* for its survival. The Madras Music Academy must recognize this [and] help create an atmosphere of professionalism in this great and superb art that legend has given us."

Bala's opening address at the inauguration ceremony on the evening of the 21st was read by Lakshmi and interpreted in *abhinaya* by Bala. "Her demonstration that morning was [such] a memorable one [that] the huge [gathering at the] Music Academy Hall, packed to capacity, gave her one of the greatest ovations I have ever witnessed," Leela Shekar remembered.[1] The audience included more than twenty of Bala, Ranga, and Viswa's foreign students and friends who had traveled from Japan, the United States, and Europe. Many of this group gathered in Bala's living room on Christ-

Balasaraswati singing at home in Kilpauk, 1976. The portrait behind her is of
Vina Dhanammal. Photo by Sandip Ray.

mas Day for a festive meal; Lakshmi, having realized Christmas morning
that Bala's admirers had nowhere in particular to go that day, extended the
invitation, which was quickly broadcast. That evening Viswanathan had a
concert at the Music Academy.

"Very rarely," the citation read at her installation as conference president
began, "a few creative artists appear [whose] only concern is to identify themselves with their chosen art form. This dedication matures and ripens to
culminate in complete devotional surrender, *atma samarpana*. At this stage
a miracle happens. No longer does the artist pursue his art; instead his art
pursues him, and takes him as the right instrument. Just as the *bhakta* who
surrenders in religious devotion to the Lord, becomes a tool of the Lord, so
too the artist with his *atma samarpana* becomes the tool and puppet of his
art. Through this interaction art reveals its infinite variety of beauty in various manifestations. It ceases to be art in its final consummation but becomes
instead a blessed state of grace. In bharata natyam the one and unique artist
who attained this blessed state of experience is Balasaraswati.

"She was born into the [renowned] family of Vina Dhanammal, who
had complete mastery over all the *swaraha* [notes] and every subtle sound
shade, and sequence, *sabda* [sounds]. Her family tradition was such that

all its members stood for the highest standards demanded by music and dance and never settled for second best. Their only commitment was to the purity of art. Dhanammal's wealth of music flowed down as the pure Ganges to Balasaraswati through her mother Jayammal. It invaded the other art-form of dance too. The three essential components: *bhava, raga, tala,* met and mingled as the confluence of the three great rivers known as *Triveni Sangam* in India. That was Balasaraswati's dance. Her life-breath and living were for bharata natyam. Her thought and work were directed to the perfection of that art. Her absorption and dedication made her an artist-*yogi* par excellence.

"One can enjoy this art for its sheer beauty of expression. With knowledge of its technique one can experience more levels of delight. There are many who do not possess knowledge of the technique, pattern and structure. Yet the purity of art does not depend on these — the technical details. The true artist in all circumstances safeguards and protects the purity of his art. In this respect Balasaraswati's dedication and determination are supreme. She never compromised her fidelity to art, and, as a result, the whole world turned to her with adoration and esteem, and bowed down to it with the thought: 'Here is something great and grand!'"[2]

Her performance that year at the Academy was on December 23, with Viswanathan in the ensemble. Viswanathan's accompanists at the concert on Christmas Day included Ranganathan as well as V. Tyagarajan and V. Nagarajan — an ensemble that had performed, recorded, and taught together in the United States in the late 1960s. Tyagu and Nagu came from a family with deep personal and musical ties to Balasaraswati's family that spanned three generations. On December 28 Bala presented a demonstration of *abhinaya,* introduced by Dr. V. Raghavan. On New Year's Day she delivered a closing address and received the insignia of *Sangitha Kalanidhi,* presented by the Junior Raja of Travancore. Bala's acceptance speech, which was reviewed in the Madras papers, included a "Call for Intensive Training for Dance Students." Her appeal for advocacy of traditional bharata natyam would be her last to appear in print.

One of the students from Bala's school at the Music Academy, Ranjani Shankar, was interviewed when she was twelve years old. She was one of about twenty students who attended Bala's classes in a small annex behind the main building of the Music Academy. Apart from dancing, Ranjani said, Bala taught her to be modest, to respect people, but not to be impressed by the comments that people make. Bala insisted that her students make a wholehearted investment in dancing and "put in *bhakti* as she showed us." She stressed the importance of music and required all her students to learn music. She did not teach the students any *slokas* (Sanskrit verses); according to Ranjani, she said it would be better if they would learn *slokas* but she did not insist on it. Bala would explain the stories, the mythology on which the dances were based. "She would tell us the background of dances, so that we could understand it better."

Ranjani described how she started to attend Bala's classes, in the mid-1970s. "I joined the dance class the time she was in America." (When Bala traveled abroad, she would leave Ganesha, Kandappa's son, in charge of classes at her school.) "I had heard a lot about her from my classmates. At first I was a little scared about her. One day I came to class [after Bala had returned]. I usually came early. I saw this lady sitting there with a straight back; I knew it was Balamma. My mother confirmed this was so. It was a nice feeling that I knew such a great person, and when I got to know her, she was a very wonderful person. . . . Even when our legs were in pain and our parents would goad us to 'dance, dance,' Balamma would tell them, 'Only I know the pain they are going through.' And she would turn to us and say, 'You can sit down if your leg is paining; it doesn't matter.' That showed that she even had known those pains and understood us. There was something more special between us and we loved her, and looked up to her. I think for a person so young, it was wonderful to get that personal courage. . . ." Ranjani added that Bala's eyes were deep and knowledgeable.[3]

Leela Shekar had many opportunities to see Bala teaching at the Music Academy. Every child who has a sense of rhythm can dance, said Leela, but Bala was emphatic with her students about learning music, *raga*, and *tala*. "Even when she was conducting her dance class in the Music Academy, she was very particular. You should have seen, most of the children used to sit on her lap, the little ones that used to come. 'Balamma, Balamma,' they would shout, and would go sit on her lap. When she was conducting a class for some of the others, two children would be sitting on her lap."[4]

Bala would teach small songs she knew about Krishna. She maintained firmly, however, that young children were unable to grasp the meaning of separation of lovers. "She would say, I may teach that expression, and the child might be clever enough to portray that expression, but coming from a child of eleven or twelve, it . . . would be precocious; it won't seem natural. The girl must be at least sixteen or seventeen to portray that. So, she was very particular in choosing songs for little children. In that way . . . she was a very intuitive and conscientious teacher."[5]

Bala had developed a reputation for not teaching everyone who expressed a desire to learn from her. Bala's friend Ra Ganapati described how women would approach her, explaining what they expected to be taught. "People would always say, 'If I go to Bala, she would never teach me this, never teach me that.' . . . She [Bala] would say to me, 'Oh, you know what these people want? They want to ask me [to teach them] *Krishna ni Begane*,' you teach me *Krishna ni Begane*." Who are they to choose what I am to teach them? You say, all right, I'll come under your tutelage, you teach me. I'll stay with you a year or more, and I'll learn from you. That is different. Just come and say I'll learn "*Krishna ni Begane*." From me "*Krishna ni*," from someone else, "*Televu Virago*." What kind of teaching is that? I am not doling out songs like that.' So she refuses them, and they say, 'Bala, she is very haughty; she will never teach anybody. She has no pupils!' "[6]

Bala's student Shyamala Mohanraj worked with her for many years, and in an interview she spoke of how Bala taught *abhinaya*. "When I was a student and she was teaching expression, she would try to explain to us, when you call someone . . . when you are calling Krishna, you have to transfer yourself as Krishna's mother who is so affectionate to the child, so full of love and affection for the child. . . . You imagine Krishna is in front of you, you must call him as if you are calling a child. Bala imagined herself in the position of Yasoda and thought, 'At least for one moment, let me have the pleasure of imagining Krishna to be my son, calling him, embracing him, loving him.' . . . She said you must always keep your feet turned out and your back straight, and go down [into a plié]. The back should be straight. When it is straight, the other parts move, but the body doesn't move. When the spine is under control, the body is under control and you are under control. And that helps you to have the concentration.

"And while doing that she said it made others feel the presence of Krishna. And sometimes when she accomplished that, when she called Krishna, people would turn and look behind to see if Krishna was coming. By having the feeling, by having the concentration, you create the same feeling and concentration, pleasantness and happiness in others. She said, 'If you imagine Krishna in front of you, you can do great things.' "[7]

Bala approved of teaching dance in classes; she believed that classes developed a healthy spirit of competition. She also believed a student could begin training at any age if there was genuine talent. She expected her students at the Music Academy to study a minimum of three years. She was discouraged to realize that "many expect to master the art in three months."

T. R. Moorthy was a flute student of Viswanathan's. During the late 1960s and the 1970s he accompanied Balasaraswati's concerts, and he toured with Viswanathan in India. Moorthy once commented to me that Balasaraswati had taught him to play the flute. When I asked him what he meant, he described a moment when she reached down and gently lifted his elbow while he was playing, opening the space between his chest and his arm, giving him room to breathe. It is the position that *nagaswaram* players use, but generally not flutists other than Viswanathan. The gesture transformed his playing.

Another event that reveals the power of Bala's teaching is an anecdote related by Jayadevi Sadasivan, who attended Bala's classes at the Music Academy for a short time when she was a college student in Madras in the 1960s. Jaya recalled that she was practicing the rigorous plié position when Bala stepped up behind her and gently placed her knee against Jaya's lower spine, and her hands on Jaya's shoulders, pulling her back into the proper upright

position. Jaya never forgot the powerful sensation of Bala's touch, and she said she has never slouched since.

THE CENTER FOR WORLD MUSIC

The last undertaking by the American Society for Eastern Arts was the Center for World Music. Launched in Berkeley, California, in 1974, the Center was housed in a beautiful wooden church designed by architect Julia Morgan near the university of California campus.[8] Bala, Lakshmi, and Bala's ensemble were in residence; Ranga and Viswa remained in Los Angeles at CalArts. The program of the Center for World Music, the vision of Robert Brown, was considerably more ambitious than earlier ASEA projects. The intention was to conduct a summer session and then two semesters during the regular academic year. There were students registered from colleges and universities all over North America.

Bala was excited about the prospect of being in the program, in part because her friend, North Indian master musician Amir Khan, had agreed to be in residence during the first summer session, allowing open practice sessions of his singing. He wrote to Bala that he had no particular interest in the opportunity, but had accepted it to have the chance to be near her. He had stayed in Bala's house whenever he performed in Madras during the winter season. All of Balasaraswati's family, as well as several of her American students and scholars, anticipated this remarkable juxtaposition of Indian musical giants. However, Amir Khan was killed in a road accident on February 13, a few months before he would have left for the United States. Bala was completely distraught at the death of a friend and a great musician and deeply regretted the loss of the opportunity to work and be with him.

The faculty of the Center for World Music included *karnatic* vocalist K. V. Narayanaswamy, violinist T. N. Krishnan, and drummers Palghat Raghu, V. Nagarajan, and T. H. Vinayakaram (who joined Shakti with L. Shankar), as well as Bala's ensemble.[9] During the summer session Bala choreographed a dance drama, *Dasavatar* (*The Ten Incarnations of Vishnu*), her first group choreography since the *kuravanji* she had directed in 1950. Bala's senior students performed the dance drama; Bala had taught each dancer a role that matched her capacities, but had created no noticeable hierarchy among the variously capable and experienced group. This approach was one of Bala's great strengths: Every student felt she was receiving special and empathic instruction from Bala's heart—which she was.

Other cultural traditions represented at the Center for World Music were Japanese, Korean, Javanese, Balinese, Ghanaian, Sundanese, and new American music and dance. The center attracted many types of students. Some were musicians with cultlike followings, such as guitarists Sandy Bull and Robbie Basho. Composers Lou Harrison and Steve Reich were in residence, teaching a generation of instrument builders and protégées, including percussionist William Winant. Julie Traynor, who eventually wrote, designed, and choreographed *The Lion King* (an immensely popular Broadway musical based on an equally successful animated film), was studying Javanese puppetry. Richard Kvistad, a percussionist who traveled from Toronto for the summer, remained in the Bay Area and is today the percussionist for the San Francisco Opera. There were many others, among them some variously alienated young people seeking a sense of identity through absorption with another culture. Great artists found themselves instructing a wide variety of students—some whose objectives were anything but professional, and some who had professional careers that were permanently shaped by the experience.

Bala described teaching in the United States then: "I only go during summer, where my brothers stay," she told an interviewer. "I teach in a private institution in Berkeley. All students are the same to me. As a teacher I treat them alike. Obviously, teaching foreigners means a great deal of hard work. Their background is so different they need more attention and time than Indians to pick up the same materials. For the audiences, I find them equally responsive abroad. I have never had any problem communicating with foreign audiences."[10]

The challenges that faced Balasaraswati in teaching non-Indian students were manifold. Perhaps most difficult was that Western students had been trained to learn music and dance through notation. Their minds and memories worked differently. A mind trained to learn aurally absorbs material faster and more permanently than a mind trained with notation. Bala was distracted by any student who was taking notes rather than watching her. She wanted students to be registering and absorbing directly what she was demonstrating and explaining. "Why don't you watch me? The more you see the less I have to teach," she once exclaimed.[11]

Luise Scripps observed Bala teaching many different students in the United States, including small children. She commented, "When she taught small children, which she loved to do, she . . . would sit on the floor and speak very softly to them. And say, 'Now darling, you must do this and you must put your sweet feet this way and hold your arms,' and she was very gentle. And very carefully and slowly and softly mold them." Bella Lewitzki commented that on the occasions when she observed Bala teaching, she never heard her say "good" or "bad." "It was just amazing. She had finite answers; 'you do it this way.' Not, 'That is wrong, this is right'; or, 'This is bad and this is good' and 'the quality is lacking.' She never used the word quality. And since this woman personified quality I was fascinated with this dichotomy in the teaching. You had it there as a vehicle; as far as Bala was concerned, I would judge this to be true. The vehicle was there, it was very clear. . . . It was not that Bala did not expect things to be correct; she did. But she did not use the Western benchmark [or] standard.

"One of the things I realized, in watching her teach, was the difference in Western teaching and teaching from other countries; our vain assumption that teaching is only one thing, one way. [Her teaching] was very full of information. She gave me a lot of information she did not know she gave me." Bala did understand how much she was imparting, but she tried to let her students feel that the information they received was already in their possession. "[When] I saw another teacher from another culture repeating this, I was reminded that there are very many different ways you come at teaching. In the Western world, [touching a student] used to be a no-no; you do not invade people's privacy. But with her, yes, you push the hands back. You physically manipulate. I now do that and I've seen Donny [McKayle] do that. So I know we both do it. But I hadn't done that and I wouldn't have [if it hadn't been for Bala]."[12]

During the fall of 1974 Bala was diagnosed with cancer. The family kept the discovery quiet, and with very little notice Bala underwent surgery with a successful outcome. In the late fall Lakshmi and Bala returned to India.

The Center for World Music closed in the spring of 1975, for complex reasons, before the end of its second full semester. It would reconstitute itself with more modest but no less visionary goals, located in San Diego under Robert Brown's direction. The Center continues today, having survived the death of Robert Brown in 2005.

Bala's brother, Varadan, who had entertained guests with his imitation of *kathakali* several years previously, had died while she was in the United States, to Bala's great sorrow. Bala's relationship to her immediate family was close, in spite of the very different lives they all led. Varadan, who lived in Madras, was in frequent contact with her. He also had visited the United States, and his daughters Uma (Caroline) and Geetha (Cherie) maintained strong ties with their aunt, uncles, and cousins.

A FIRE IN THE FOREST

Ranganathan and Viswanathan returned from CalArts to rejoin the faculty at Wesleyan in the fall of 1975, and they remained there until Ranga's death in 1987 and Viswa's in 2002. In December 1975, at the end of the first semester following their return to Wesleyan, Ranga and Viswa traveled to Madras, where they stayed until May 1976.

In March 1974, before she left for Berkeley, Bala had learned that she had been elected a lifetime fellow of the Sangeet Natak Akademi, along with her childhood friend Ravi Shankar and Bombay-born conductor Zubin Mehta. In December, after she returned, she was designated honorary president with the title *Isai Perarignar* (Musical Expert) and presided over the Silver Jubilee conference of the Tamil Isai Sangam in Madras.

During the fall of 1975, Bala was notified that, in recognition of exceptional and distinguished service, the Government of India intended to honor her with the insignia of *Padma Vibhushan* (Exemplary Golden Lotus), the third degree of the award for distinguished national service. Bala had received the second degree, *Padma Bhushan*, in 1958. The announcement of the award appeared in the press on January 24, 1976, and the investiture ceremony took place at Rashapati Bhavan in New Delhi on April 2.

Lakshmi described Bala's concert in Delhi following the *Padma Vibhushan* award ceremony. Sometimes dancing "would be satisfying [for Bala] but not great," Lakshmi said; that is, Bala was not transported with every piece she performed. But Bala "would not dwell on that because she would think it would come through in some other song. . . . When she was performing in Delhi [after the award ceremony], she was doing *Kapi varnam*." Bala, Lakshmi recalled vividly, was offering a flame of an oil lamp, and Lakshmi could see that for Bala, at that moment, it was not enough. Suddenly, "She created a forest fire! The whole thing was in flames. She created a forest fire, that's how I can describe it to you. And she offered that." Bala said to Lakshmi in the intermission after the *varnam*, "I want to come to a [point] in my life where, when I have reached this level I don't want to do any *padams*, I don't want anything. I just want to be left alone." Lakshmi felt the same way after seeing her; dancing the *varnam* was enough for that day.

In September 1976 the Madras Music Academy celebrated Bala's Golden Jubilee, the fiftieth anniversary of her dancing career. This particular date has been the subject of uncertainty. Her Golden Jubilee had been noted in *The Hindu* in 1975, fifty years following her *arangetram,* and would be noted again in 1977, fifty years after her first public performance. However, on September 24, 1976, Lakshmi performed at the Music Academy, and Bala sang. *Dance* magazine noted Bala's dance anniversary in its September issue. Following the announcement in *Dance*, Bala received a note from Margot Fonteyn expressing her "deepest admiration" for Bala.[13] In a continuation of her transition from dancing to singing as Lakshmi's accompanist, Bala sang the second half of the concert Lakshmi performed at Shanmukhananda Hall in Bombay on November 24.

About this time, Kamaladevi Chattopadhyay visited Bala in Madras. She had first seen Balasaraswati dance many years before. She recalled the visit in an interview. "In my mind a dancer like Balasaraswati occurs like a rare flower that blossoms very occasionally, lighting up the surroundings with a fresh beauty that lingers long after she is no longer there. . . . I shall always cherish the first moments when I first saw her dance. I had no idea of her, except that she was a new dancer, and I watched with rapt attention and enjoyed her performance very much. . . . Many years later we got to know each other. I asked, 'Do you remember dancing at a particular place in Madras?' She said, 'I remember you were there.' I said, 'How could you know?' We had never met. She said, 'When I dance to an audience, I have great respect for every individual watching me. I feel I must give my best. But some sort of alchemy happens and I become tied into communication with a single individual — and that evening it was you. I didn't know you, yet I established some communication. Therefore, I could never forget your face or your personality, which has been with me all these years, even though I didn't know then who you were.'"[14] Years before, when Bala was a young teenager, her mother had taught her to observe every nuance of movement and behavior of the people who surrounded her, including her audience.

Satyajit Ray

There had been discussion for years about having Bengali filmmaker Satyajit Ray make a film about Bala. Ray had first seen Bala at her concert in Calcutta in 1934. The catalyst for the film project, as it finally took shape, was family friend S. Guhan, at the time finance secretary of Tamil Nadu. Guhan spoke with M. Karunanidhi, chief minister of Tamil Nadu and another great admirer of Bala's. Bala became hopeful that finally a substantial record of her dancing could be left behind. Wesleyan University had produced the only film up to that point, a short documentary of *"Krishna ni Begane Baro"* made in the 1960s. Other brief film segments had been shot, but nothing that recorded her dancing with her remarkable drummer, Kuppuswami, and nothing that left an adequate record of Bala's art.

The shooting of the film took place early in 1976. Lakshmi described the first hour of the two artists' meeting on Bala's veranda overlooking the garden at the back of her house. Satyajit Ray suggested that he film Bala in prayer, doing her daily *puja*. She refused, quietly outraged, stating as she always had that her *puja* was very private. Immediately following the disagreement about filming her prayer, Ray suggested he film her in her garden. "You want me in the garden picking flowers? Certainly!" Imitating her friend Subbulakshmi's songs from the hit film *Sakuntala*, Bala ran about the garden picking and tossing blossoms, talking to flowers, dancing along the stepping stones. "It was hilarious, actually," Lakshmi reported. "Needless to say, Ray did not include that footage."[15]

A day later Ray proposed that they shoot Bala dancing at the beach at the Shore Temple in Mamallapuram, an hour out of the city to the south of Madras. Lakshmi described how Ray stood, leaning on his camera, as he "watched Bala while she somehow managed to perform '*Krishna ni Begane Baro*' on the sand in a strong breeze. It was really captivating; she danced beautifully. When I commented that he got a jewel, he said his camera wasn't running. This was a tragedy. After that event, Bala gave Ray a dreadful time in general. She made life miserable for all of us."[16] Bala was forced to repeat the performance, a portion of which appears in the film.

The official premiere of Ray's film, *Bala*, on April 19, 1977, was presented under the sponsorship of the Government of Tamil Nadu. A review pub-

During filming of *Bala* on the beach in Mamallapuram, 1976. *From left:* Lakshmi, Balasaraswati, Viswanathan, and filmmaker Satyajit Ray. Photo by Sandip Ray.

lished after the advance screening sadly foretold what the critical response would be. "The film fails recording Bala's dance. [He] has missed [the] opportunity to record her *abhinayam*. '*Krishna ni Begane Baro*' leaves a poor impression. Ray's decision to contrast natural light and beach against the black back-drop of the *varnam* was a wrong decision. The breeze interfered with her *abhinayam*, the waves and expanse of sea, were absolutely out of place."[17]

In 1977, the Center for World Music having moved to San Diego, Luise and Sam Scripps initiated a new organization in Berkeley called Asian Traditions, under whose umbrella the Balasaraswati School of Music and Dance conducted a summer program. From May 15 to June 10, a group of Bala's senior students, of whom most had been learning at the Center for World Music, worked on another production of *Dasavatar*, the dance-drama first presented in 1974, which they performed at the end of the brief, concentrated teaching session. Lakshmi, who was beginning to dance more and more regularly, appeared in a solo concert presented by the Music Circle at Occidental College in Pomona on May 28, 1977. Ravi Shankar was in the audience. Graphic artist and photographer Jan Steward wrote of the concert: "Pundit Shankar expressed his delight to see Lakshmi for the first time. 'Pure joy,' he said. 'When Lakshmi's exquisite *abhinaya* was accompanied by Bala's singing, it was the purest joy. I experienced the incredible happiness

Balasaraswati teaching Lakshmi in 1976. Photo by Sandip Ray.

which is the gift of great art. The eyes of the dancer and the musician [Bala] often met. Their arts are blended into a totality greater than individual accomplishments can achieve. To see this family sharing their great individual gifts was not only thrilling, it was a revelation."[18]

The American Dance Festival

The American Dance Festival has its roots in Bennington College in Vermont, which was opened in 1932 with Martha Hill as chair of its dance program. The Bennington Summer School of the Dance opened in 1934, a vision of founder Hill and the initiation of an effort to move American modern dance outside of New York.[19] Martha Graham, Doris Humphrey, Charles Weidman, and Hanya Holm each taught for a week that summer. Over the succeeding years the great names in modern dance taught and presented premieres at the prestigious summer school. In 1939 the school did its residency at Mills College, where Merce Cunningham was a student, José Limón premiered a five-part solo, and John Cage presented a percussion concert. In 1947 the school was conducted for the first time as the American Dance Festival at Connecticut College, a private school in New London. Charles Reinhart became director of the American Dance Festival in 1969.

In 1977 Charles Reinhart invited Bala to the festival in New London. "At the American Dance Festival, we very rarely included anything but modern dance, except when it is someone of such quality, like Bala." Bala, Lakshmi, Ranga, Viswa, Ramiah, and Ramadas were in residence at the festival. Certain students chose to work exclusively with Bala in a separate program, and Bala's demonstrations, performances, and teaching also were woven into the rest of the festival. "So that was a very, very special time for us," Reinhart recalled. "It gave me an opportunity to know Bala personally, something I have cherished all my life. . . . It was a relationship well worth waiting for.

"I am not saying I am an expert. The quality of her dancing is above the actual dance itself. And anybody who is interested in dance can recognize that quality. When I could see that quality — you know, your heart goes into stop position and you just hold your breath — that's what I thought of her dancing. . . . I think the audiences in this country have not had a problem [recognizing greatness] no matter what the art form or how unusual it is. They have been able to recognize the greats, whether it's Kabuki or whatever. . . . When a Bala comes along — some of the intricacies of the dance movements might be lost to them — [but] her genius came soaring across those floodlights like a sledgehammer! Boom, it hits you! . . . Boom, there it is. . . . Well, of course, it was Bala, it wasn't the art form, that's what I think was so important. And it's so incredible because you think one of those artists comes along maybe every hundred years, but then, when I see her daughter Lakshmi dance, again I start to hold my breath and I realize, my God, it's going from one generation to the next. And that's very unusual, and spectacular."[20]

During the summer of 1977, Bala and Lakshmi lived in Middletown, near Ranga and Viswa, and the ensemble made the one-hour commute by car on the five days each week that they taught in New London. The session, which ran from June 25 to August 6, included a lecture-demonstration on June 29. Anna Kisselgoff wrote about the demonstration in the *New York Times* on July 1: "Balasaraswati, India's great classical dancer, is also one of the supreme performing artists in the world. It is difficult to write about her without falling into superlatives, and her performance in New London, Connecticut, Wednesday night leaves the reviewer, again, in the same happy quandary." Bala performed a concert at the end of the program on August 6. Kisselgoff had observed earlier that year: "Like all fine, classically-based artists, she insists it is the orthodoxy of traditional discipline which gives the fullest freedom to the individual creativity of the dancer. The idea that tradition is a base for creativity has been a chief tenet of [Lincoln] Kirstein and George Balanchine. No one makes the spiritual roots of bharata natyam clearer than Bala herself."[21]

At the end of the summer, Bala heard that Martha Graham was not well and wanted to pay her respects to the great dancer. Charles Reinhart arranged a meeting at Graham's elegant East Side apartment in Manhattan. Her manager, Ron Protas, remained nearby while the two women chatted. Martha Graham sat at Bala's feet, resting her head on Bala's knee. Much of

Balasaraswati visiting Martha Graham in New York City, 1977.

the talking was by Graham, who was voicing her complaints about "students today" and how things ought to be. Bala said little but shook her head, indicating gentle empathy.

In the autumn, back in India, Bala stayed quietly at home in Kilpauk. Many nights she would be unable to sleep, and would sit restlessly in her narrow bed, one leg folded over the other at the knee, and read. Bala had become at times a prisoner of her own fame. She yearned to be able to dance when she chose — and not to dance when she chose not to. She liked to be alone. Among other writing, she mused over the work of Ramakrishna, the ascetic and *yogi*-philosopher of Vedanta, engrossed in his message of boundless and doctrine-free perception of the divine. That winter Bala made a trip to the Thanjavur District, to be among the profusion of temples that she seemed to know like old friends. When she visited these ancient places, she would be greeted by headmen (the Brahmins who had the decision-making responsibility and the material and spiritual management of the temple) with simplicity and utmost respect. Some of these temples sit at the side of small country roads, and some on the banks of the many small rivulets and larger branches of the Kaveri and its tributaries. The 1977 trip turned out to be the last of her visits to her ancestral home.

In the courtyard of the art museum in the palace in Thanjavur, near the famed Sangitha Mahal (a music hall built in the early nineteenth century) where her ancestors performed, there was a cluster of stone statues that Bala

Balasaraswati and Lakshmi singing at the housewarming for Viswanathan's new home in Middletown, Connecticut, 1978. They are listening to Ranganathan's drum solo.

loved. These had been moved to Swathi Mahal (the museum in the palace complex) from the small temple dedicated to Siva in the form of Airavateswara that Bala visited on this trip, in the village of Dharasuram. The figures portray Siva, who had assumed the rags and emaciated form of a beggar and ascetic, the mendicant Kankalamurthi, encountering on a forest pathway the wives of seven ascetics, *rishis*. The *rishis*, in their arrogance, had failed to recognize him, enamored with their own earthly accomplishments as recluses. The sculptures depict Siva revealing to the sages the essence and pervasiveness of his power through his seduction of their wives. The seven *rishis'* wives, beautiful young women, are captured in the moment of submission and innocent passion, an exquisitely sculpted impression of *Sringara*.

In April 1978 Lakshmi performed under the auspices of the National Centre for Performing Arts, then under the direction of Narayana Menon, at Tejpal Auditorium in Bombay where Bala had performed twenty years earlier. In a review in the *Times of India*, a headline declared, "Delectable Abhinaya by Lakshmi," and the review stated that "she looks the spitting image of Bala in her youth." Lakshmi was accompanied by Bala, Ramiah,

Ramadas, flutist Hariharan, and Josepha Cormack, an American student of Viswanathan's who was learning at that time with Bala. I accompanied Lakshmi on the *mridangam*. I had first performed with her in 1974 while we were at the Center for World Music.

The sixtieth birthday is a momentous passage for a Hindu, a time of transition to a meditative life. As she had for many years, Bala celebrated her birthday on May 13 by cooking and offering food to the poor in her neighborhood, a gesture well known and anticipated by her neighbors. There was a Madras Corporation housing area several blocks away, and in the other direction at one end of her street was a cluster of small houses once inhabited by the butlers in service to the colonial garden homes in the area but now home to families who welcomed the gift of a meal. M. S. Subbulakshmi, who lived several houses away in the same street in Kilpauk, sent her old friend a birthday gift. Bala donated a large brass bell to the Kapaaliswara Temple in Mylapore, Gauri Ammal's temple. Bala's name was inscribed as donor, and the bell is in the temple today.

In 1978 the American Dance Festival moved from New London to a new home at Duke University in Durham, North Carolina. About a dozen of Bala's students from around the country attended the session. Bala and Lakshmi were again invited for the summer, along with Ranga, Viswa, and Ramiah. Ranga and Viswa were joined by their families. The families settled into two apartments on the edge of the Duke campus. A few days after their arrival in early July, Bala suffered a heart attack and was admitted at Duke University Medical Center. Examination showed no damage from the heart attack, but Bala was in a testy mood as she recovered. Some of the medical center's senior staff tried to be supportive, but they quickly recognized that Bala should be left to her family and friends. Bala's family, Luise Scripps, and Charles and Stephanie Reinhart did their best to bolster her spirits. Charles Reinhart commented to Luise Scripps, on whose head a considerable burden had fallen, that one day she would look back at the summer with fond memories. Whether or not she did, the Scrippses' relationship with the American Dance Festival continued; ADF offers an endowed teaching chair in Balasaraswati's name each summer as well as an award in Samuel H. Scripps's name.

The residency went forward despite Bala's illness. Lakshmi assumed Bala's teaching schedule, assisted by Luise Scripps; developed and presented a demonstration; and performed a concert without Bala's direct involvement. Lakshmi's enthusiasm for the task that fell to her was consistent with the commitment of a professional family. In spite of Bala's considerable physical discomfort, as the transfer of responsibility to her daughter took place, Bala did all she could to enable Lakshmi. It was a difficult time for both women, because Lakshmi was demonstrating not only her capacity but also her need and determination to achieve independence — and the entire family was witness to the process. Lakshmi performed at Page Auditorium at Duke on July 2, 1978.

Bala's health improved quickly, and in late August and September Bala and Lakshmi were back in Berkeley for a short residency, again under the auspices of Asian Traditions. Lakshmi performed at University of California at Berkeley and several other places while Bala continued to gain strength. Lakshmi and the ensemble participated in the Congress on Research in Dance's East/West Encounter in Hawaii, for which Bala was able to sing. Lakshmi read Bala's closing address before the international assembly of leading dance experts. After returning to the East Coast, Lakshmi gave her first performances in New York at New York University on September 22 and 23, accompanied by Bala, Viswa, Ranga, and Ramiah. On October 4 Bala danced for the first time since her heart attack three months earlier.

The Scripps family's support of the arts continued in other ways, but the year 1978 saw the end of the era of the American Society for Eastern Arts and the programs it created. With the exception of two summers at Wesleyan University, this was the last of the opportunities for intensive cross-cultural immersion that had been one of the gifts of the Scripps family. It was an appropriate time for the change, but saddening to those who recognized what was taking place. Bala and Lakshmi returned to India late in October, and Ranga and Viswa continued at Wesleyan.

A Rare Orchid

At home in India once more, in November 1978, Bala received an honorary Doctor of Literature degree, the title of *Desikottama*, from Santiniketan in Bengal at the Viswa Bharati University Convocation. This was a return to the site of her first performance in the north more than four decades earlier. S. Krishnan observed in an article he wrote for *Aside* magazine how Bala conserved strength for those things interesting to her, such as "for playing dice, which she still does with demonic fervor with her daughter, Lakshmi, around whom her life revolves, reciprocally. Their communication extends well beyond the customary communion between parent and child, generated by instinct, empathy, symbiosis, augmented by familiarity, routine and body language.... For a person of her eminence she is astonishingly accessible. Anyone with [the least] excuse could see her without much difficulty.... To Lakshmi her mother is a rare orchid, a magnificent artiste and a work of art at the same time, given into her care to cherish and protect, a destiny for which she is grateful, accepts cheerfully, and fulfills with aplomb.... On that relatively free day when not more than one or two people, relatives, foreign students, are staying in the house — and unthinkable they should want for anything—Lakshmi sees to everything, always making sure that mother is free and secure and relieved from the details of daily life."[22]

Balasaraswati and Lakshmi, Kilpauk, 1978. Photo by Pasricha Anivash.

Later that year, Bala accepted the idea of someone being allowed close enough and trusted adequately to assist Lakshmi in her care. Muni Pal Baliah, the son of an old friend, the well-known Tamil comedic actor T. S. Baliah, moved into Bala's house. Bala continued her teaching.

It is impossible for me to continue from this point in the narrative without describing my personal entry into the story. I had been a student of Balasaraswati's family, and had become close to the entire family. I also had come to know Lakshmi, at first through my constant relationship with her uncles, and then through our performances together, beginning at the Center for World Music, and at the annual meeting of the Society for Ethnomusicology in San Francisco. In 1978 Lakshmi and I became engaged. This was a time of tremendous challenge for Bala, and for all of us. Bala had no reason to fear that Lakshmi might desert her, but she did feel threatened by that thought as well as by a sense of loss of control. And although Bala had always been accessible, generous, and kind to me, she had concerns about Lakshmi's marrying me. But Lakshmi and I were married, with Bala's consent and blessing, in February 1980. Bala's friend M. S. Subbulakshmi sang for the event, and embraced her colleague and sister of fifty years.

In the summer of 1980 Bala was in residency at Wesleyan University under the aegis of Asian Traditions. Jon Higgins had become the director of the Center for the Arts at Wesleyan, and Ranga and Viswa continued to teach there. Bala performed a concert of *abhinaya* with Lakshmi, Ranga, Viswa, and Josepha Cormack. Lakshmi danced and Bala sang at Wesleyan and at Dartmouth College. During that summer it was announced that Bala had been honored with the title *Kalaimamani*, a music award from the Tamil Nadu state government.

On November 13, 1980, Lakshmi's and my son, Aniruddha, was born. Bala's life took on a new brightness. She was fascinated by Ani's very early interest in the sound of singing, and she would sit and gaze at him as she quietly sang simple pieces. The following year, when we were at Wesleyan for the summer, Ani would sleep on the floor while his mother and grandmother taught. The process of learning through exposure and absorption continued to another generation.

Asian Traditions sponsored Balasaraswati's last residency at Wesleyan University's Center for the Arts from July 1 to August 14, 1981. Lakshmi performed throughout the northeastern United States. Bala made a recording of her singing, accompanied by Ranga and Viswa, for the private label 1750 Arch Street, funded by musician and philanthropist Thomas Buckner, in a studio owned by Mark Levinson. Levinson was a bassist and student of North Indian music, whose name is associated with audio equipment and a recording studio. Bala decided not to complete the editing of the recording.

During that summer on July 29, 1981, Viswanathan, who had been divorced from his first wife, Kumari, several years before, married Josepha Cormack. On the day of the ceremony, Bala decided that she would stay at home. She wanted, she said jokingly, "to watch a real wedding"—the televised marriage of Charles and Diana, the Prince and Princess of Wales. In fact, someone had to stay behind to watch Ani.

It was fitting that Bala's last residencies in the United States were at Wesleyan. A lot had changed over the years since her stay in 1962. The university environment had changed, and the American student had changed. When Bala first toured, she was like a wondrous light. She represented something entirely fresh. In the twenty interceding years, numerous cultures and their practitioners had been "discovered." Balasaraswati was certainly recognized as a global star, but the American audience had become more jaded. Americans, and much of the modern world, had become consumers of "world music," and some of the magic was lost. Bala had made her contribution, but she was doubtful about what impact she had had.

In December 1981, after her return from her last residency in the United States, Balasaraswati was elected president of the Conference of the Indian Fine Arts Society in Madras and honored with the title *Sangitha Kala Sikhamani*, Crown Jewel of Musical Art. (This was the same organization that honored Bala when she was fourteen.) The effects of Bala's years of struggling with her health now etched her face. Ra Ganapati described: "I was once told she had been ailing for some two or three months. When I went to see her and asked her 'How are you?' she laughed, saying, 'The auto-man arrived—all the luggage was ready to take; all of a sudden, at the last moment the luggage was not put in the auto. But, even now they are outside, still there on the veranda.' That's all she said."[23]

DEVI KARUMARI AMMAN

As Bala's inclination inward became more pronounced, and as she acknowledged that her world had changed for good, she became freer. She taught Lakshmi and played with Ani. She spent time in meditation, and she looked forward eagerly to every visit to Devi Karumari Amman's shrine in Thiruverkadu. The temple was refuge for Bala, and a place where she could trust what she heard and saw. Shakti, Devi Karumari Amman, was her *guru*; although the medium sometimes counseled Bala in ways that she resisted, there was no questioning of the guidance she received, no negotiation. A visit to Devi Karumari Amman's temple was an equalizer: Bala was treated the same as the poor and disenfranchised and the same as the wealthy and powerful who were in attendance. At the temple Bala had no need to be guarded or watchful of those around her, mistrustful of flattery and ingratiation. She was able to be at ease—and free of the need for Lakshmi's intermediation.

Navaratri

On the occasion of Ani's first and second birthdays, Bala and Lakshmi distributed an individual parcel of sweets and new clothes for each of the *pujaris* (those who performed the *puja*) and others who had found refuge in the temple. In 1983 Bala decided that she wanted to sponsor a celebration at the temple of the festival of *Navaratri*, which coincided with Ani's birthday that year. In temples and homes in many parts of India, people celebrate each of the nine nights of *Navaratri*, sometimes with performances of music and dance. *Navaratri* in Thiruverkadu had always been very simple—limited by what could be financially afforded by the family on whose property the small shrine was located.

In the early 1980s the shrine at Thiruverkadu was empty of people most of the time. Located in the midst of a country family compound, the simple enclosure around the image of Devi Karumari Amman was protected by a roof that kept the earthen floor relatively dry and shaded. A large tree grew in the rough courtyard, where Punnyakoti Swamigal, Devi Karumari Amman's medium at the time, often would be sitting when Bala arrived. Sometimes Bala came to the temple unscheduled and unannounced. At other times there would be large crowds and set times for Shakti's manifestation.

Bala asked Punnyakoti to arrange the musicians for each night so that the sort of musicians and what they played would be certain to be well suited to the spirit of the celebration and enjoyable for most of the devotees who would attend the festival. Punnyakoti chose local *nagaswaram* players.

On one of the nine nights, Ani stood up and unexpectedly started to dance while the musicians played a popular song called *"Neela Vanna Kanna Va Va."* Although Ani does not remember it, children from Punnyakoti's family still recall the event — because their father scolded them afterward for "having achieved nothing in their short, misdirected lives when a three year-old child was able to dance."[24] This was the meaning of tradition, Punnyakoti explained, when a young child danced so effortlessly.

Always a Teacher

Bala remained dedicated to her Indian students, and Lakshmi enabled her to provide all of them with their *arangetrams*. On December 1, 1983, Bala's last student, Bhuvaneswari, performed. Bala had continued to teach Lakshmi with increasing depth, she herself having reached the relationship to the art she yearned for. She no longer needed to dance, she said; Lakshmi was dancing.

Music historian N. Pattabhi Raman and dancer Anandhi Ramachandran wrote of their impression of Bala in an interview at her home. "Bala had started talking freely. Conversation with her is a great experience in itself. She may not be on the stage, but her mind dances still, nuanced thoughts take shape as in her *abhinaya*, aided by snatches of singing and vivid facial and hand gesture which punctuate her speech. She offers excerpts from various *padams*. Remaining seated in a chair, she mimes a few phrases of sequences. She recalls the poetry of Tayumanavar. She talks about the *Pranava mantra* [a prayer]. She recalls the talents of various dancers of the past. She refers to her health problems. The *bhava* of her singing, the emotions displayed through delicate gestures, the images described by her long, tapering fingers all create a sense of wonder in us."[25]

When Bala watched Ani dancing, those present could observe on her face a transformation, a look of complete absorption; she understood her grandson's need to dance as a toddler. Bala had an extraordinary capacity to retain what she heard. When she was five or six years old she heard the musician and music teacher Vishnu Digambar Paluskar sing.[26] Paluskar had set to music Mahatma Gandhi's favorite *bhajan*, *"Vaishnava Janato."* Ra Ganapati remembered, "She could reproduce the exact way he sang, *'Raghupati Raaghava Rajaaraam,'* in the same tune as the master sang. . . . Even when she put her grandson Aniruddha to sleep, she would recite *'Ram Ram Ram'* the way Vishnu Digambar did. There was nothing sophisticated about it, you see, that was Bala, sublimity in simplicity."[27]

Bala seemed to be coming to terms with something about herself, through

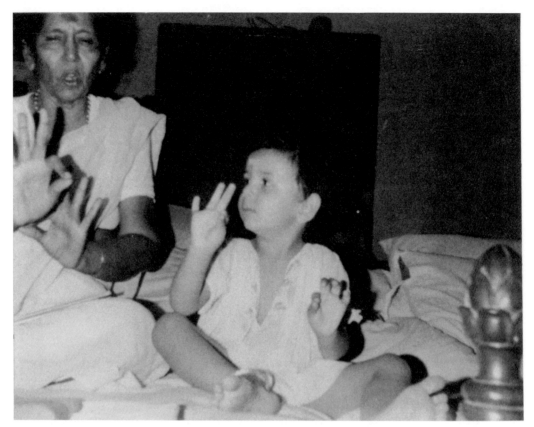

Balasaraswati with her grandson, Aniruddha Knight, Madras, 1983.
Photo by Douglas Knight.

singing for Ani and watching him dance. Bala and Lakshmi discussed the possibility that Ani might choose a career as a musician and dancer and the implications of Ani being the first male dancer in the family. Bala had expressed specific reservations about men dancing certain styles of bharata natyam that either borrowed technique from *kathakali* or that were self-consciously imitative of feminine qualities. But certainly she had no fundamental objection to male dancers, and she was a great admirer of several.

Balasaraswati's old friend Kamaladevi Chattopadhyay remembered her last visit with Bala: "She had been ill a long time and did very little dancing, and as we spoke, she said, 'I have a dancer who is going to perform for you,' and she lifted up her grandchild and put him on the table. She began to sing and the little child started dancing. One could see a deep measure of pleasure and satisfaction in her eyes. This was a totally different picture of her as a grandmother, taking pride and pleasure in the family, in that little child whom she hoped would carry on her great tradition. I would like to keep that memory with me as a last token of our friendship."[28]

Lakshmi remembered, "Yes, my son is much like Bala was when young.

Bala said she was just like him at two or three years old, dancing all day long, whenever she had the chance. Bala felt he might become a dancer." Lakshmi continued, "I will wait and see if he truly wants to become an artist; it is for him to decide."[29] Ani, interviewed when he was seven, said, "Balamma was strict with students. Her hands and feet were strong and she could still dance. She never stopped dancing; her feet kept patterns in her sleep. She was the greatest dancer in the world."[30]

"My mother taught me so many things," said Lakshmi. "Respect for art and for anything one endeavors, to maintain one's principles no matter what the cost. This thought was ingrained in her. She was unique, a supreme being to me. I understood her as an artist and as a person and I am truly grateful that I was capable of understanding her as both. I could comprehend the artist on stage as well as the mother and friend. When one enters the stage one should do one's best. She had to fight to prove how wonderful the art is. How could we forget how she was transformed while performing—and moved the audience! How dancer and audience became one!"

DUSK

Bala's blood sugar levels became more and more erratic and increasingly un-responsive to treatment. In late January 1984 she became gravely ill, and she lost consciousness at home on January 29. Lakshmi, Ani, Muni, and I were there. That day we all hoped that Bala would recover, as she had before. But her loss of consciousness deepened, and it was evident that there was little chance Bala would recover at home in Kilpauk. We arranged for her to be taken to Lady Willingdon Nursing Home the next day, where she faded into a coma. We notified Ranga, Viswa, and Luise Scripps in the United States.

Bala remained unconscious except for an event a few days before she passed away. The medium from the temple at Thiruverkadu, Punnyakoti Swamigal, had been at another function in Madras city; suddenly, as Shakti, he announced to his entourage a change in plans. He appeared unexpectedly at the hospital, still as Shakti. Bala awoke when Shakti appeared. Lakshmi was with Bala. "Having been in a comatose state for more than a week, she regained consciousness, and uttered the name 'Karumari.'"[31] She lost con-sciousness again.

Ranga, Viswa, Jody, and Luise Scripps traveled from the United States, and by February 3 all four had joined us. Lady Willingdon Nursing Home was a modest two-story colonial hospital, and Bala was upstairs in a room at the top of a wide staircase that began near the entrance. Lakshmi and I had taken a few minutes to talk with each other and were outside as the light quickly faded just after sunset. There was a shout from Bala's room, and we rushed up.

It was dusk on *Ratha Saptami*, a sacred day in the Hindu calendar. The

Mahabharata—one of two main Hindu oral epic poems, a "history"—describes the battle on this day when Drona, the great sage of the ancient clan, died, impaled on a bed of arrows on the battlefield of Kurukshetra. Luise Scripps recalled the moment from her perspective: "As [Lakshmi and Douglas] left for the hospital, Lakshmi told little Ani to take Viswa, Jody and me to the small Ganapati temple near the house." Ganapati is the brother of Murugan. "It was dusk. We followed the child to the neighborhood shrine he frequented with his grandmother. We followed the three-year old through the temple compound obeying his unspoken instructions; here *namaskarams*, offerings there. . . . We three were silent, numbed by [Ani's] presence. We reached the house only to hear [from Muni that] Bala had passed away while we were guided through this small temple. Bala was gone."[32]

We arranged to have Bala returned home. That night the house was milling with family and close friends. In the morning, the street outside the house was a sea of people, many faces that I, at least, had never seen. There was a four-foot-high stone wall that enclosed Bala's property at the front, and the crowd in the road stretched from one side to the other, and as far up the street as I could see from the front veranda—in one direction toward the orphanage that had been St. George's Anglo Indian Higher Secondary School, where the son of Raja Serfoji II of Thanjavur was educated, and in the other toward the butlers' quarters where some of the families Bala had fed every year on her birthday lived. A van arrived, red lights on top, forcing its way through the crowd. Two men emerged from the van and carried into the house a massive floral wreath. The wreath was in the shape of the great arch of cosmic flame, representing Illusion, which surrounds the dancing Nataraja; Nataraja Himself was not there. The wreath was placed at Bala's feet. It had been sent by one of Bala's admirers, Indira Gandhi.

The conventions practiced after a death vary from house to house, and even from occasion to occasion within a family. The eldest female in Bala's extended family, Vedamommie, who was the wife of Bala's first cousin Shankaran and grandniece of Balasaraswati's teacher's mentor, Pakkiria Pillai, assumed the responsibility for making certain that things were done properly over the next ten days. First, the house was prepared and then opened to family, friends, and admirers for a final goodbye. Hundreds of people slowly made their way past Bala's body in the living room, its doors opened into the garden.

The men in the family proceeded to the cremation ground where they completed Bala's last ceremony. The women remained in the house. Several days later a meal was offered that included favorite foods of Bala's, sweet and savory dishes that she had been denied for years. Before those gathered were invited to eat, servings of each dish were set out on a banana leaf, a

Balasaraswati, 1972. Photo by Jan Steward. Courtesy of the photographer.

feeding for the crows that are everywhere in India. Vedamommie and some of the others called "caw, caw" to attract the crows. It is said that the crows will not touch the offering if the soul of the departed is not pure. Someone placed the leaf on the roof over the passage between the dining room and the kitchen. There was jostling among us, a feeling of anticipation of change about to happen. Although the belief is that the crows will not come if the food is being watched, somehow someone kept an eye out and announced they had fed.

Bala was free.

Acknowledgments

There are many who have contributed in one way or another to the perpetuation of Balasaraswati's legacy. The dance world owes a debt to all of them. Without the record and memory of this great artist and her family, the traditional hereditary arts of South India would be less understood and valued.

Luise Scripps, an American student of Balasaraswati's for more than twenty years, invested her personal effort, commitment, and family financial resources for more than three decades as an advocate for Balasaraswati's teaching and performance in North America and Europe. Her husband, Samuel Scripps, was also a friend, advocate, and patron who substantially enabled the art and life of Balasaraswati and her family. Mrs. Scripps managed the collection and preservation of the repository of materials that document the history of a professional performing family of international distinction — a history that would otherwise have been lost to the vagaries of recollection and the redefinition of what happened.

A major contributor to the modern history of *karnatic* music is Bala's cousin T. Shankaran. His recollections of Balasaraswati's life and career represent many years of effort and careful documentation. Bala's brother T. Viswanathan, a music scholar of international reputation, also contributed invaluable resources and insight. Other family members also collaborated. Balasaraswati herself, although usually disinclined to talk much about herself and her art, delivered beautiful addresses on several occasions; her friend S. Guhan compiled and created English translations of these addresses, from which I have quoted extensively. These translations were in part subsequently published by the Sruti Foundation in a small book entitled *Bala on Bharatanatyam*. Videographer Smita Shah conducted a large number of interviews during the 1980s; these, too, have proven a rich source of first-hand recollections and observations of Bala and her artistry.

I am indebted to many people for their direct support and collaboration with me in the research and writing of this biography. Vegavahini Vijayaraghavan, T. Brinda's daughter, is now the senior musician in the Vina Dhanammal family and has brought that perspective to bear in many hours of conversation. Musicologist B. M. Sundaram, born to the same professional community as Balasaraswati's family, devoted several months of his time in Thanjavur and contributed generously from his great fund of carefully researched knowledge. Two pioneering American scholars of South Indian performing arts, Robert Brown and Harold Powers, both friends of Balasaraswati's, encouraged me long before I had begun this project. Others who have read the manuscript at various stages and contributed valuable information, insights, and suggestions include Kapila Vatsyayan, Charles Capwell, Charles Reinhart, Daniel Neuman, Matthew Allen, Davesh Soneji, and David Gere.

Copyeditor Jay Howland's months of meticulous work on the structuring and refinement of the manuscript provided a sensitive, expert, and disciplined perspective on this story and the language I used to tell it for which I am tremendously grateful. Staff at both Wesleyan University Press and University Press of New England have contributed with great patience, particularly Suzanna Tamminen who believed in this project from the start and supported me in it for several years, and

Amanda Dupuis, who managed the production of the book. Richard Hendel has brought his visual imagination and sense of order to its design.

As she came to her own understanding of the complex circumstances in which Balasaraswati's biography is historically and currently cast, Susan Ames Williams has been a collaborator and constructive critic. She has devoted many hundreds of hours to the organization and production of the manuscript, and at the end of the project, provided much needed stamina.

I have drawn on interviews with Balasaraswati's fellow artists, friends, and critics, and have quoted from some of the numerous reviews Balasaraswati received between 1933 and 1981. Some of these interviews and reviews have been translated from several Indian languages into English. Charles Perrier, now Dance Division librarian at the New York Public Library, transcribed many hours of interviews, and proofed and edited their translations. The work of several photographers has been included in this book, and they are credited in the list of illustrations following the contents page. Jan Steward deserves particular acknowledgment for her devotion to the subject of this book, as well as the photographs she has contributed to it. Additional thanks are due to the representatives of the several libraries, archives, and organizations that have provided material; I am grateful in particular to Norton Owen, Jacob's Pillow Dance Festival Director of Preservation, and to James Nye, Bibliographer for Southern Asia at the University of Chicago Library. My thanks also to Magnum Studios for their responsiveness to my son Aniruddha's search for the surviving work of photographer Marilyn Silverstone and for their efforts to recover and preserve that work.

The LEF Foundation in Cambridge, Massachusetts provided the initial seed funding for work on the book done in the United States and India during 2002. A Humanities Fellowship from the Asian Cultural Council funded research in India in 2003. A Guggenheim Fellowship supported work in India and the United States in 2003 and 2004. The Guggenheim Foundation also provided a subvention to Wesleyan University Press in support of the publication of this book. The value of the advocacy and encouragement I received from these organizations and the individuals who represent them has extended well beyond the generosity of their financial support.

I began working with Lakshmi Knight on this biography about a year before she succumbed to illness in 2001. Since then, several of the friends who contributed their perspective and knowledge to this project have also passed on: Balasaraswati's brother T. Viswanathan (2002); Robert Brown (2005); Bala's cousin T. Muktha (2007); Harold Powers (2007); Medha Yodh (2007); and Samuel Scripps (2007). I have missed their wisdom and suggestions, and I remember them with deep regard and appreciation.

My son, Aniruddha, knows Bala's story from members of his maternal family, particularly his mother. Across the challenging boundary of son and father, he has quietly impressed his understanding on mine. Since his mother stopped performing, he alone, as it has turned out, has had the determination to continue learning and performing the combined art of music and dance of Balasaraswati's family style. This is what Bala, Lakshmi, and I had hoped would happen, while knowing there was no real way to influence that outcome.

The following brief biographical sketches should serve two principal purposes. Some are offered as a convenient reference for readers who wish to refresh their understanding of certain figures whose names recur in the text. Others supply information about persons who were in some way significant to Balasaraswati or her family, but whose identity or accomplishments are not explained in the narrative because such explication would distract from the flow of Bala's story.

Indian names are transliterated variously, as are many Indian language terms. For more on these differences and how I have dealt with them I refer the reader to the notes on translation and transliteration that follow the Preface.

Names in Hindu South India follow several different systems, but may include a given name, subcaste, place of origin, guild, or (in the case of a musician) instrument or performance practice. In an attempt to make the names listed in this Appendix more meaningful to readers unacquainted with these systems, I have used punctuation marks to indicate these distinctions. Brackets [ ] indicate place of family origin, as in [Thanjavur] Viswanathan. Parentheses ( ) indicate the subcaste or community with which a family is associated, as in Kandappa (Pillai). And curly brackets { } indicate a guild, occupation, or instrument, as in {Vina} Dhanammal. Following are brief descriptions of the several subcaste or community names that appear in this Appendix.

Chettiar (also Chetty and Shetty, among other spellings)   *A South Indian, primarily Tamil community historically identified with agriculture and trade.*

Diksitar   *A Tamil Saivite Brahmin community who have been the traditional managers of the Siva Nataraja Temple in Chidambaram.*

Ghosh   *A Hindu Bengali surname.*

Iyengar (also Ayyangar)   *A subcaste of primarily Tamil Vaishnava Brahmins.*

Iyer (or Ayyar, Aiyar, Ayer or Aiyer; also called Sastri or Sarma)   *A name given to Brahmins of Tamil or Telugu origin.*

Khan   *An honorific title attached to a family name in parts of North India.*

Menon   *A title bestowed upon the Nairs of Cochin by its king. Menons traditionally assisted the court as generals, commanders, administrative officers, and governing officials.*

Mudaliar   *A Tamil name that means "first citizens" or "first ones" and is used by a* velalar *subcaste.*

Naidu (sometimes spelled Naicker)   *A community associated largely with trading and found primarily in Tamil Nadu, Andhra Pradesh, and Karnataka.*

Pillai   *A name mostly used by people of the* velalar *caste among the population of Tamil descent.*

Reddy (also spelled Reddi, among other variants)   *A primarily Telugu community associated with governmental administration and ownership of land.*

Sastri   *A name of a Brahmin community.*

With a few exceptions, I have listed Indian names alphabetically by given name, rather than by name indicating place, family, professional occupation, or chosen musical instrument (e.g. Abiramasundari [Thanjavur], not [Thanjavur] Abiramasundari.) Non-Indian names are listed in alphabetical order following the convention of placing surname before given name.

Abhiramasundari, [Thanjavur] (1918–1973)　*Known as Abhirami, she was a karnatic violinist, the granddaughter of Vina Dhanammal, younger sister of Brinda and Muktha, and a student of Papa Venkataramiah Iyer. Abhirami and her cousin Balasaraswati were close; Abhirami married Bala's paternal cousin. She played for the vocal concerts of her sisters Brinda and Muktha, and also for Balasaraswati's* abhinaya *concerts, beginning in the late 1930s.*

Annaswami (Sastri) (1827–1900)　*A South Indian composer who taught Vina Dhanammal's mother, Sundarammal. He was the adopted nephew and disciple of Syama Sastri. A Telugu and Sanskrit scholar, he composed* varnams *and* kritis.

Azhagiyasingarayya (ca.1870–unknown)　*Vina Dhanammal's first* vina *teacher.*

Baldas (Naidu) (ca. 1860–unknown)　*A blind* vina *master. Also known as Baladas, Balakrishna Iyer, Balakrishna Naidu, or Padam Baldas. He learned from Vina Gauri Ammal and taught Kshetrayya* padams *to Vina Dhanammal.*

Bani Bai (ca. 1919–present)　*An eminent* harikatha *exponent and a friend of Balasaraswati's family.*

Bhanumathi, [Kumbakonam] (ca.1925–present)　*A hereditary bharata natyam dancer and Balasaraswati's contemporary. She first learned from Papanasam Vadivelu Nattuvanar and became a leading disciple of Pandanallur Meenakshi Sundaram Pillai.*

Brinda, [Thanjavur] (1912–1996)　*A* karnatic *vocalist, Balasaraswati's cousin, and the eldest daughter of vocalist Kamakshiammal and S. S. Soundarajan. She and her younger sister, Muktha, both disciples of Naina Pillai, gained eminence for their vocal duets. Brinda first learned singing from her mother; studied* vina *with her grandmother Vina Dhanammal; and learned singing from Dhanammal and her aunt Lakshmiratnammal. She taught vocal music at the Government Music College, Madras, and in 1968 in the United States. Her awards included the 1965 SNA Award for Karnatic Vocal Music, and in 1976* Sangitha Kalanidhi *from the Madras Music Academy. Her daughter is the senior surviving musician in the family, Vegavahini Vijayaraghavan.*

Brown, Robert E. (1927–2005)　*An ethnomusicologist who is sometimes credited with coining the term "world music." Brown started his doctoral studies at* UCLA *as a piano major in 1953. After Mantle Hood began teaching at* UCLA *the following year, Brown switched to ethnomusicology and became Hood's first teaching assistant. Brown received his doctorate in ethnomusicology from* UCLA *after doing research with Balasaraswati's brother Ranganathan. He began teaching at Wesleyan University in 1961. Brown's world music programs, as well as others', were built on the concept of bimusicality, which was an innovative approach to music education at the time. It proposed that students, after acquiring competence in the music of their native culture, become "bimusical" by studying*

with master musicians from another culture and acquiring competence in the
musical performance and theory of that culture also.

Chandrasekharan, K. (unknown–1988) *A lawyer, scholar, art critic, and*
passionate connoisseur of the arts, and outspoken advocate of Vina Dhanammal's
family. He wrote articles on the performing arts and, notably, reviews of
Balasaraswati's concerts. He wrote often about one of her first concerts in 1933.

Chattopadhyay, Kamaladevi (1903–1988) *One of the most influential Indian*
women of the twentieth century. She was a social activist, a freedom fighter, a
leader in the fight for the dignity of women's rights and the causes of India's
artisans and hereditary artists. She was vice chairman of the Sangeet Natak
Akademi in the 1950s and chairman of the Sangeet Natak Akademi from 1977 to
1982. Kamaladevi was a long-standing friend of Balasaraswati's and an advocate
for her career.

Chidambaranatha, T. K. (Mudaliar) (1882–1954) *A Tamil scholar and music*
expert. Called "T. K. Chidambaram" and "T.K.C.," he was one of the founding
members and a leader of the Tamil Isai (Tamil Music) movement, which
promoted songs in Tamil (in addition to Telugu). He had initially favored the
movement to abolish dancing but changed his views after seeing Balasaraswati
perform in 1933.

Chinnayya (1802–ca. 1867) *One of the brothers of the Thanjavur Quartet. A*
composer of sabdam.

Chinnayya (Naidu) (dates unknown) *From Andhra Pradesh. Balasaraswati*
studied abhinaya, *Telugu, and the* puranas *with him in the early 1930s.*

Coomaraswamy, Ananda K. (1877–1947) *An art scholar and prolific writer*
whose provocative works on Indian and Southeast Asian art have affected the
thinking of East and West. From 1917 until his death in 1947, he was a research
fellow in Oriental art and curator of the Indian collection at the Museum of Fine
Arts, Boston.

de Zoete, Beryl (1879–1962) *An English ballet dancer, dance ethnologist, and*
critic. In the field of dance, she taught eurhythmics, investigated Indian dance
and theatre traditions, and collaborated with Walter Spies on a book called
Dance and Drama in Bali *(1937). In 1953 she published* The Other Mind:
A Study of Dance in South India.

(Diksitar), Mutthuswami (1776–1835) *A composer of* kritis, *mostly in Sanskrit.*
He was the teacher of the Thanjavur Quartet and guru *of the great bharata*
natyam dancer Thiruvallur Gnanam. He was the son of Ramaswami Diksitar
and grandfather (and adoptive father) of Subbarama Diksitar.

Ellappa (Mudaliar), [Kanchipuram] (dates unknown) *A cousin of* mridangam
player T. Kuppuswami Mudaliar. After the death of Kandappa Pillai, Ellappa
became nattuvanar *for Bala's ensemble, and performed with her from 1941 to*
1957. At Bala's insistence, he also taught his own dance students.

Ganapati (Sastri), Bharatam (dates unknown) *Nineteenth-century nattuvanar*
and teacher of Vina Dhanammal's grandmother Kamakshi Ammal.
Contemporary of composer Patnam Subramania Iyer.

Ganapati, Ra (dates unknown) *A journalist for* Kalki *magazine who was introduced to Balasaraswati by a cartoonist for* Kalki, *C. Swamanathan (Saama), in 1960. Ra Ganapati became a close friend of Balasaraswati's and collaborated in the writing of many of her public addresses. He later provided the family archive with extensive notes from his conversations with Balasaraswati.*

Ganesha (Pillai), K. (1924–1988)   *A* nattuvanar *and son of Kandappa Pillai. Though his father never formally trained Ganesha, Jayammal and Balasaraswati tutored him in* nattuvangam *after Kandappa died. He began to perform with Balasaraswati in 1958, replacing Ellappa Mudaliar. Ganesha Pillai taught Balasaraswati's students in Madras and the United States, and accompanied her on European and u.s. tours. His compositions for dance were said by some to be more intricate and complicated than his father's but showed the same unwavering adherence to the rules of musical form.*

Gauri Ammal, [Mylapore] (1890–1971)   *A dancer attached to Kapaaliswara Temple in Madras. A contemporary of Jayammal, she was trained by Nattuvanar Nallur Manuswami; her mother, Doraikannammal; and Nellaiappa Nattuvanar and his son Kandappa. She studied vocal music with Ariyakkudi Ramanuja Iyengar; amassed an extensive repertoire of* padams; *and, like her most famous pupil, Balasaraswati, was recognized for singing while dancing. She taught many male and female dancers, including Ram Gopal, Rukmini Devi, and students at Kalakshetra, among others.*

Gauri Ammal, [Vina] (ca. 1840–unknown)   *A noted* vina *player. Born in Udaiarpalaiam, she taught Baldas Naidu.*

(Ghosh), Haren (unknown–1946)   *A dance impresario from Calcutta. He was urged by Uday Shankar to present Balasaraswati at North Indian venues including Calcutta in 1934 and music conferences in Benaras and Muzzafarpur in 1936. Bala later referred to Ghosh as an ideal impresario, and they became good friends. He was accidentally killed during the Hindu-Muslim riots of 1946 in Calcutta, one year before the partition of India at Independence in 1947.*

Gnanasundaram, [Kanchipuram] C. P. (1931–unknown)   *A singer trained by Balasaraswati. He performed in Balasaraswati's ensemble in the 1960s and 1970s. A victim of leprosy, he was barred from travel in the United States because he bore the visible scars of leprosy on his hands. His affliction never concerned Balasaraswati.*

Gopal, Ram (1912–2003)   *A Bangalore-born "Oriental dancer." He learned from Meenakshi Sundaram Pillai, Kunju Kurup, Ellappa Mudaliar, Mylapore Gauri Ammal, and others. At La Meri's invitation he first appeared in the United States in 1938.*

Govindarajulu, Modarapu (1888–1935)   *Balasaraswati's father and a member of a prominent Telugu-speaking* dubash *shipping family in Madras. Members of Govindarajulu's family were advocates of Vina Dhanammal's music.*

Govindaswami (early twentieth century)   *A* mridangam *player trained by Kandappa Pillai for bharata natyam. He was one of Balasaraswati's drummers during the 1920s and early 1930s.*

Govindaswamy (Pillai), [Malaikottai] (1879–1931)   *An eminent South Indian violinist who considered Vina Dhanammal his guru. Dhanammal regarded Govindaswamy as an unrivaled connoisseur, able to learn from every type of* music. He was active, as early as 1910, with the Tyagaraja festival in Thiruvayaru. Consistent with social prejudices of the time, he maintained a lifelong aversion to Jayammal's plan to have Balasaraswati trained as a dancer.

Guhan, S. (1932–1998) *A distinguished civil servant, economist, and writer on a variety of subjects, including* karnatic *music and dance. During his career Guhan held positions with the Indian Administrative Service and the World Bank and served as the finance secretary of Tamil Nadu. Guhan's writing covered wide-ranging subjects that included international economic relations, economic development in Tamil Nadu, poverty alleviation, caste discrimination, the Kaveri River, and Balasaraswati. He and his wife, Shanta, were close friends of Balasaraswati and her family. Guhan's translations of Balasaraswati's addresses have been extensively quoted in this biography.*

Higgins, Jon B. (1939–1984) *An American ethnomusicologist and musician, a student of Ranganathan, Viswanathan, and Balasaraswati. He acquired considerable fame in India during the 1960s and 1970s as a singer of* karnatic *music, and he continued to perform until his accidental death. He taught at York University in Toronto, and was a member of the music faculty and the director of the Center for the Arts at Wesleyan University.*

Kamakshiammal, [Thanjavur] (1892–1953) *The youngest of Vina Dhanammal's four daughters Kamakshiammal learned music with Vina Dhanammal and Kanchipuram Naina Pillai and was taught violin. Her daughters, Brinda, Mukta, and Abhiramasundari, were distinguished musicians.*

Kannuswami (Pillai), [Baroda] (1864–1923) *A* nattuvanar, *he was a descendant of Sivanandam of the Thanjavur Quartet, teacher and uncle of Kandappa Pillai. He was the father of K. Ponniah Pillai and the grandfather of K. P. Kittappa Pillai.*

Kerkar, Kesarbai (1892–1977) *A Hindustani vocalist who received the Sangeet Natak Akademi Award in 1953, among other distinctions. She was an ardent admirer of Balasaraswati's dancing and singing.*

Khan, Abdul Karim (1872–1937) *A North Indian khyal singer of great distinction. He was from Gwalior and was a palace musician in Baroda. He and Balasaraswati's family admired each other enormously. His style directly influenced Balasaraswati's singing.*

Khan, Ali Akbar (1922–2009) *A leading North Indian instrumentalist and primary disciple of his father, Ustad Allauddin Khan. Ustad Ali Akbar Khan and Balasaraswati first met in Calcutta in 1934 and remained friends and mutual admirers. He appeared with Balasaraswati at Vikram Samvat Festival in Bombay in 1945 and at the Edinburgh Festival in 1963, and he taught and toured with the American Society for Eastern Arts from 1965 to 1967. He was director for many years of the Ali Akbar College of Music, which he founded in Marin County outside of San Francisco.*

Khan, Amir (1912–1973) *A leading exponent of North Indian khyal style singing and a close friend and admirer of Jayammal and Balasaraswati. Deeply impressed with his unique style, Balasaraswati introduced Ustad Amir Khan to the Madras audience. Bala said that he was her* manasika guru *(personal guide), although she was never his student.*

Kittappa (Pillai), K. P. (1913–1999)   *A nattuvanar, son of K. Ponniah Pillai, a member of the Thanjavur Nattuvanar family. He began his career as a singer and became a distinguished and much-respected teacher of bharata natyam. He performed* nattuvangam *for Balasaraswati's production of the* kuravanji Sarabendra Bhoopala *in 1950.*

Krishnamachari, T. T. (1899–1974)   *An industrialist and a finance minister of India. He is considered one of the architects of modern India. Krishnamachari was a secretary of the Madras Music Academy and an admirer of Vina Dhanammal's family style of music and of Balasaraswati's dance. The Music Academy auditorium is named after him.*

Krishnamurthy, R. (1899–1954)   *A freedom fighter, writer, journalist, satirist, critic, and connoisseur of the arts who wrote under the pen name "Kalki" and helped found* Ananda Vikatan *in 1940. With his friend T. K. Chidambaram Mudaliar and Balasaraswati's partner, R. K. Shanmukham, R. Krishnamurthy spearheaded the Tamil Isai movement.*

Kshetrayya (1595–1680)   *An ecstatic composer of Telugu padams. His padams were among the jewels of Balasaraswati's family repertoire and had been at the heart of Padam Baldas's legacy.*

Kumaraswami, Sarojini (1924–1995)   *A singer, student of Jayammal's, and younger sister of Leela Shekar. She performed with Balasaraswati for years, including performances at the Edinburgh Festival in 1963.*

Kuppuswami (Mudaliar), T. (1905–1989)   *Balasaraswati's* mridangam *player. Initially trained in tavil, he was then tutored by Kandappa Pillai to accompany Balasaraswati. A singer for other dancers, Kuppuswami performed* mridangam *only with Balasaraswati. His style influenced two generations of drummers, including Palghat Mani Iyer, Palani Subramaniam Pillai, Palghat Mani Iyer, T. K. Murthy, T. Ranganathan, and Palghat Raghu. In 1971 he became the only drummer for dance to receive the President's Award presented by the Sangeet Natak Akademi.*

Lakshminarayana (Sastri), Vedantam (dates unknown)   *A master of a style of dance known as* kuchipudi. *He taught Balasaraswati for two years during the late 1940s, and numerous other dancers subsequently.*

Lakshmiratnammal, [Thanjavur] (1888–1940)   *The second eldest of Vina Dhanammal's four daughters, known within the family as "Chinnakutti" ("little dear one"). She studied singing with her mother, Madurai Krishna Iyengar, and Naina Pillai. She studied* khyal *style of Hindustani music with Abdul Karim Khan. Lakshmiratnammal sang duets with elder sister Rajalakshmiammal, and with younger sister Jayammal sang for Mylapore Gauri Ammal. Her son was music historian T. Shankaran.*

Lascelles, George, 7th Earl of Harewood (1923–present)   *Lord Harewood is a devoted and enthusiastic supporter of the arts, especially opera. In the course of his career he has served as director of the Royal Opera House, Covent Garden; musical director and then chairman of the board of the English National Opera from 1986 to 1995; artistic director of the Edinburgh, Leeds, and Adelaide Festivals; and managing director of the English National Opera North.*

La Meri (1898–1988)   *An American "ethnic" dancer, born Russell Meriwether*

Hughes. *After her initial dance training in Texas, she traveled worldwide,
studying and performing various interpretations of Asian and European
dance forms. In 1940, with dancer Ruth St. Denis, she founded the School of
Natya in New York. Among her dance creations was a "bharata natyam-style"
interpretation of* Swan Lake.

Maharaj, Birju (1938–present) *A leading* kathak *dancer of the Lucknow* gharana
*(a Hindi term for an approach to performance that is associated with an extended
family, named for a city from which that family originated). Son of the acclaimed
Achchan Maharaj, who was the first male performer of traditional dance seen by
Balasaraswati and who died in 1947, the young Birju absorbed much from his
father. After his father's death he was trained by his uncle Shambhu Maharaj,
also a noted exponent of* kathak.

Meenakshi Sundaram (Pillai), [Pandanallur] (1869–1952) *Regarded by many as
the most eminent* nattuvanar *of his generation. A descendant of the Thanjavur
Quartet, grandson of Ponniah, son of Suryamurti Nattuvanar, also the father-
in-law and maternal uncle of K. Ponniah Pillai. He trained many hereditary
dancers, including Pandanallur Jayalakshmi and the Kalayani Daughters
(Jeevaratnammal and Rajalakshmiammal). He taught several* nattuvanars,
*including Chokalingam Pillai and Kandappa Pillai. Several nonhereditary
performers also learned from him, including Rukmini Devi, Ram Gopal, Shanta
Rao, and Mrinalini Sarabhai.*

(Menon), V. K. Narayana (1911–present) *A musicologist and arts executive.
The former general director of All India Radio, secretary of the Sangeet Natak
Akademi, and president of the National Centre for the Performing Arts,
Bombay, he was knowledgeable about* karnatic, Hindustani, *and Western
music and knew many notable artists. He was the author of* Balasaraswati, *a
30-page book, with photos by Marilyn Silverstone, published to coincide with
Balasaraswati's appearance at the 1963 Edinburgh Festival.*

Muktha, [Thanjavur] (1916–2007) *Daughter of Vina Dhanammal's youngest
daughter, Kamakshiammal. Muktha was trained within her family by her
mother, her aunt Lakshmiratnammal, and her grandmother, and as a young girl
studied with Naina Pillai in Kanchipuram. She occasionally sang for her cousin
Balasaraswati's performances. She received the Sangeet Natak Akademi Award
in 1973, and her teaching was acknowledged by the Madras Music Academy with
the title "Kala Acharya."*

Muthulakshmi (Reddy) (1886–1968) *One of India's first female physicians, a
social reformer, and member of the Madras Legislature.*

Naina (Pillai), [Kanchipuram] (1889–1934) *A singer who was a leading musician
in his generation. His given name was Chittoor Subramania Pillai. He was
noted in particular for his rhythmic prowess. He presented Balasaraswati in her
arangetram in Kanchipuram in 1925. A lifelong friend of Vina Dhanammal and
members of her family, Naina Pillai taught Vina Dhanammal's daughters, as
well as Balasaraswati's cousins Brinda and Muktha.*

Narasimhulu, S. (1923–unknown) *A staff artist for All India Radio and a gifted
vocalist. He was Balasaraswati's student and began performing with her in 1961. He
accompanied her during her first tours in Europe and the United States in the 1960s.*

Nellaiappa {Nattuvanar} (1854–1905)   *The father of Kandappa Pillai. A grandson, through marriage, of Ponniah of the Thanjavur Quartet, he trained many dancers. He was* nattuvanar *for Mylapore Gauri Ammal.*

Pakkiria (Pillai), {Konnakkol} (1857–1937)   *An esteemed rhythm master. Kandappa Pillai's mentor, he began his career as a* tavil *player, then began to specialize in the art of rhythmic vocalization. His maternal aunt was the wife of Sivanandam of the Thanjavur Quartet. His daughter was married to Meenakshi Sundaram Pillai's son Muthiah.*

Panchanada (Iyer), [Sathanur] (dates unknown)   *Also known as Panju Iyer or Pallavi Panchu Iyer, he was a disciple of Suddamaddalam Tambiappa Pillai, who was a disciple of Mutthuswami Diksitar. His disciples were Thirupambaram Nataraja Sundaram Pillai, Thirukodikaval Krishna Iyer, and Vina Dhanammal, to whom he taught Mutthuswami Diksitar's compositions.*

Ponniah (1804–1864)   *A* nattuvanar, *the second of the Thanjavur Quartet. A disciple of Mutthuswami Diksitar, Ponniah was a palace musician at Thanjavur, Travancore, and Mysore. His second daughter was the mother of Nellaiappa, the father of Balasaraswati's teacher Kandappa Pillai. Many of Ponniah's compositions were in Balasaraswati's repertoire.*

Ponniah (Pillai), K. (1887–1945)   *A composer of music for bharata natyam. Son of Baroda Kannuswami Nattuvanar, Ponniah taught music at the University of Madras and at Annamalai University in Chidambaram. He was named* Sangitha Kalanidhi *by the Music Academy. His sons were K. P. Kittappa Pillai and K. P. Sivanandam Pillai.*

Radhakrishna (Naidu), N. (ca. 1910–ca. 1970)   *An All India Radio clarinet artist who also played for Balasaraswati's concerts. His playing was known to be lyrical, mellow, supportive, and sensitive to the intricacy of the Dhanammal family style.*

Raghavan, V. (1908–1979)   *A Sanskrit scholar and historian of music and dance. Originally from Thiruvarur, Dr. Raghavan wrote and edited many books and articles on both music and dance. He was a strong supporter of Balasaraswati. He served as secretary of the Madras Music Academy and was music historian in charge of editing its journal. He received the* Padma Bhushan *in 1962 and was elected a fellow of the Sangeet Natak Akademi in 1964. In 1953 he helped establish a dance school for Balasaraswati at the Music Academy. Balasaraswati and Dr. Raghavan wrote a book in Tamil on bharata natyam published in 1959.*

Rajalakshmiammal, [Thanjavur] (ca. 1885–1957)   *Eldest daughter of Vina Dhanammal. She first learned music first with Patnam Subramania Iyer and then with her mother. She was a singer, with her sister Lakshmiratnammal, for Mylapore Gauri Ammal.*

Rajaratnam (Pillai), T. N. (1898–1956)   *An undisputed master of the* nagaswaram. *An admirer of Vina Dhanammal's style of music, Rajaratnam was particularly fond of Jayammal's singing. Although Vina Dhanammal normally disliked the loud outdoor* nagaswaram *and* tavil *band, for her, Rajaratnam's music was the sole exception. His manner of playing* raga alapana *set the trend for many twentieth-century vocalists such as Semmangudi Srinivasa Iyer and G. N. Balasubramaniam.*

Ramanayya (Chettiar), {Jalatarangam} (1887–ca. 1960)   *Performer of the*
jalatarangam (a set of tuned porcelain cups struck with curved bamboo sticks)
and a well-known Madras arts patron. He and his brothers Subramaniam
and Chengalvaraya were members of a wealthy merchant family. Ramanayya
Chettiar and his family were patrons and close friends of Jayammal,
Balasaraswati, and their family.

Ramanuja (Iyengar), [Ariyakkudi] (1891–1967)   *A popular* karnatic *vocalist and a*
student of V. V. Srinivasa Iyengar of Ramnad. Ramanuja Iyengar was a Mysore
palace musician, and he approved Jayammal's decision to have Balasaraswati
trained in dancing. An admirer of Vina Dhanammal's style, he learned
several padams *from her. He taught music to Mylapore Gauri Ammal. He was*
influential in creating the contemporary concert format, and he received the title
Sangitha Kalanidhi from the Madras Music Academy in 1938 and the Sangeet
Natak Akademi Award in 1952.

Ramiah (Pillai), K. (1938–present)   *A violinist who learned* nattuvangam *from*
K. Ganesha Pillai and Balasaraswati. He began performing with Balasaraswati
during the 1970s.

Ranganathan, [Thanjavur] (1925–1987)   *One of Balasaraswati's brothers, known*
by many as Ranga. A master of the mridangam, *his style of playing reflected the*
refinement of his grandmother, Vina Dhanammal, and his experience as an
accompanist of both karnatic *music concerts and bharata natyam. He studied*
with Kandappa Pillai, Palani Muthaiah Pillai (a younger contemporary
of Vina Dhanammal), and Mutthaiah Pillai's son Palani Subramaniam Pillai.
Ranganathan accompanied leading concert musicians, notably his brother
T. Viswanathan and Ramnad Krishnan. He was Balasaraswati's only drum
accompanist outside of India. For twenty years he was on the music faculty at
Wesleyan University, where he was the university's first Artist in Residence,
beginning in 1963. He also taught at California Institute of the Arts and in several
programs including those sponsored by the American Society for Eastern Arts.

Rao, Maya (1928–present)   *A kathak dancer, a nonhereditary disciple of Shambhu*
Maharaj, and a writer on dance.

Ray, Satyajit (1921–1992)   *A renowned filmmaker who first saw Balasaraswati*
dance in 1934 at the All Bengal Music Conference. In 1976 he filmed a
documentary on Balasaraswati, released in 1977.

Reinhart, Charles (1930–present)   *Since 1968 Reinhart has been president and*
director of the American Dance Festival, now conducted at Duke University. His
late wife, Stephanie Reinhart, was co-director from 1993 to 2002. He began his
career in the arts in the mid-1950s and was at various times a producer, manager,
festival director, and consultant. He has managed several major dance companies,
including the Paul Taylor Dance Company. In 1996, he and his wife were
named co-artistic advisers for dance to the Kennedy Center. In 2002 the French
government honored Reinhart with the Commandeur dans l'Orde des Artes et
des Lettres.

Scripps, Samuel H. (1927–2007)   *A lighting designer and arts patron. A man of*
wide interests, Scripps became a devoted friend and admirer of Balasaraswati
and her family in 1962. He and his wife, Luise, founded the American Society for

Eastern Arts in 1965, and Asian Traditions in 1975, to foster awareness of Asian arts, artists, and their disciplines. Scripps was an active participant in various theaters and theatrical projects, and a benefactor worldwide of dance, theater, and the fine arts. He was a major contributor to the restoration of the Globe Theatre in London.

Shankar, Ravi (1920–present)   *A musician, composer, and sitar virtuoso. Ravi Shankar, the youngest brother of Uday Shankar, was a student of Ali Akbar Khan's father, Allauddin Khan. He and Balasaraswati first met in 1932 and remained friends.*

Shankar, Uday (1902–1977)   *India's first internationally recognized contemporary dancer/choreographer. He saw Balasaraswati dance at Gana Mandir, Madras, while touring India for the first time in 1933, and became a lifelong friend and admirer.*

Shankaran, [Thanjavur] (1906–2000)   *An elder cousin of Balasaraswati who learned music from his mother, Lakshmiratnammal. He was the assistant station director for All India Radio in Baroda, Trichy, and Vijayawada. After retiring from government service in 1961, Shankaran was director of the Music College of Tamil Isai Sangam, Madras, until 1985. He published numerous articles on music, dance, and the history of the performing arts in South India and was a major contributor to the collection of materials that is the basis for this biography.*

Shanmukham (Chetty), Ramaswami Kannuswami (1892–1953)   *An industrialist, economist, statesman, and first finance minister of India. A Tamil scholar and activist, R. K. Shanmukham was one of the founders of the Tamil Isai Sangam. He was Balasaraswati's partner.*

Shawn, Ted (1891–1972)   *An American dance pioneer and one of the creative leaders of what is now called modern dance. He hosted Balasaraswati's first U.S. concerts at Jacob's Pillow Dance Festival in 1962.*

Shekar, Leela (ca. 1920–present)   *A singer, the older sister of Sarojini Kumaraswami, who learned music from Jayammal. Leela Shekar occasionally sang for Balasaraswati's performances, including during a U.S. tour in 1965.*

Sivanandam, K. P. (Pillai) (1917–2003)   *A performer of the* vina *and the last descendant of his generation of the Thanjavur Nattuvanar family. He was the half brother of K. P. Kittappa Pillai and son of K. Ponniah Pillai. He was a recipient of the title* Sangitha Kalanidhi *from the Madras Music Academy in 1992.*

Srinivasan, [Thanjavur] (1916–1972)   *Balasaraswati's eldest brother, known as Seenu.*

Subbarama (Iyer), [Vaidisvarankoil] (1839–1906)   *A composer of Tamil* padams. *The Vina Dhanammal family is the major repository of these compositions, and many were in Balasaraswati's repertoire.*

Subbaraya (Sastri) (1803–1862)   *A composer and musician and a student of all three of the "Musical Trinity," including his father, Syama Sastri. Although Subbaraya Sastri composed relatively few* kritis, *his work is a treasured part of Vina Dhanammal's family legacy.*

Subbarayar, [Dharmapuri] (dates unknown)   *A famous nineteenth-century composer of* javalis *and a close friend of Vina Dhanammal. Balasaraswati knew many of his compositions.*

Subbulakshmi, M. S. (1916–2004)   *An internationally famous* karnatic *vocalist*
and a lifelong friend of Balasaraswati's.

Subramania (Iyer), [Patnam] (1845–1902)   *A composer and performer; the first teacher of Rajalakshmiammal, Vina Dhanammal's eldest daughter.*

Subramaniam (Pillai), [Palani] (1909–1962)   *A* mridangam *player from a* tavil *lineage. He was T. Ranganathan's teacher and a friend of Balasaraswati's family.*

Swaminatha (Pillai), [Thirupambaram] Nataraja (1898–1962)   *An influential and eminent South Indian flutist from a* nagaswaram *legacy. He was T. Viswanathan's teacher, and in 1953 he received the title* Sangitha Kalanidhi *from the Madras Music Academy.*

Syama (Sastri) (1762–1827)   *A composer and musician from Thanjavur. Syama Sastri was the eldest of the "Trinity" of* karnatic *music. Many of his compositions are in the Vina Dhanammal family repertoire.*

Tagore, Rabindranath (1861–1941)   *An internationally recognized writer of modern India. He was winner of the Nobel Prize and poet laureate of India. Tagore's family founded Santiniketan in Bengal in the mid-nineteenth century. He admired Balasaraswati and her music and dancing, among many other performing artists and traditions.*

Thanjavur Quartet (early nineteenth century)   *Dance teachers, musicians, and composers in the court of Thanjavur. Four brothers, Chinnayya (1802–ca. 1867), Ponniah (1804–1864), Sivanandam (1808–1863), and Vadivelu (1810–1847). All four were disciples of Mutthuswami Diksitar, and they are credited with the codification of the modern traditional format of* bharata natyam. *Of the four, only Ponniah and Sivanandam had children. Among Ponniah's descendants are Pandanallur Meenakshmi Sundaram Pillai and Nellaiappa Pillai; Nellaiappa's son Kandappa Pillai and grandson Ganesha were nattuvanars for Balasaraswati. Sivanandam's descendants included Baroda Kannuswami Nattuvanar and his son K. Ponniah Pillai, Kandappa Pillai's teachers, and K. P. Kittippa Pillai. Balasaraswati's repertoire included most of the Quartet's compositions.*

Tyaga (Iyer), [Muthialpet] (1845–1917)   *Like his father, Vina Kuppayyar, Muthialpet Tyaga Iyer was a composer of many* tana varnams *that he taught to Jayammal and her sisters. He was a friend of Nellaiappa Nattuvanar and Vina Dhanammal.*

Tyagaraja (1767–1847)   *A composer who, along with his contemporaries Mutthuswami Diksitar and Syama Sastri, formed the "Musical Trinity" of* karnatic *music. Tyagaraja composed hundreds of devotional songs, many of them in praise of Lord Rama.*

Vatsyayan, Kapila (1928–present)   *A scholar and dance ethnologist. Dr. Vatsyayan is the author of numerous articles and sixteen books on Indian dance, art, and architecture. She was the director of the Indira Gandhi Memorial Trust in New Delhi and is a consultant to the Government of India and a member of Parliament.*

Viswanathan, [Thanjavur] (1927–2002)   *A flutist, vocalist, teacher, and ethnomusicologist. He was Balasaraswati's youngest brother and accompanied her in concerts internationally. He learned with his mother, Jayammal, and then with T. N. Swaminatha Pillai. In 1988 Viswanathan received the title of* Sangitha Kalanidhi *from the Madras Music Academy, and in 1992 he was named as the first National Heritage Fellow from India by the National Endowment for the Arts in Washington, D.C. He was head of the music department at the University of Madras, an assistant professor at Wesleyan University, and taught at California Institute of the Arts. He was in several programs including those sponsored by the American Society for Eastern Arts.*

Notes

PREFACE (pages xvii–xxii)

All notes designated as personal communications, transcriptions of recorded interviews, and other references provided without date or source are contained in an archive of material that is in the private ownership of Aniruddha Knight, collected by family members and contributing scholars between the late 1930s and the present.

1. I have learned the South Indian tradition of music from several members of Balasaraswati's family since the 1960s, and I have been taught and coached by several musicians from outside of the family. Balasaraswati's brother Ranganathan taught me the *mridangam* (the double-headed barrel drum) for nine years. Balasaraswati's drummer T. Kuppuswami Mudaliar tutored me in *mridangam* accompaniment of bharata natyam for several months in 1977–1978 and for several more months between 1980 and 1982. I learned *mridangam* for one year with M. N. Kandaswami Pillai, and was coached for several months by Karaikudi R. Mani. Balasaraswati and T. Viswanathan taught me about music, and music with dance. My initial encouragement came from Robert Brown and Richard Winslow, members of the music faculty at Wesleyan University.

2. "Servant of God."

CHAPTER I: FROM THE HEART OF THE TRADITION (pages 1–16)

1. I am indebted to musicologist B. M. Sundaram for this perspective.

2. Paraphrased from Kapila Vatsyayan, *Traditional Indian Theatre* (New Delhi: National Book Trust, 1980), 113.

3. Vatsyayan, *Traditional Indian Theatre*, 111.

4. Matthew Harp Allen, "The Tamil Padam" (Ph.D. dissertation, Wesleyan University, 1992), 52.

5. The term bharata natyam appeared in a review in a newspaper as early as 1931, referring to the traditional dance practice that became known as *sadir* in 1936. In 1931 the dance form later referred to as *sadir* was the only style of bharata natyam performed; it would be close to five years before the "renaming" of the tradition would occur, and the distinction between *sadir* and bharata natyam was made.

6. S. Seetha, *Tanjore as a Seat of Music* (University of Madras, 1981), 100.

7. Musicologist B. M. Sundaram has documented the genealogies of more than one hundred hereditary families known to have included performers for more than one generation during the twentieth century. Anthropologist Milton Singer claimed there were several hundred hereditary families.

8. Seetha, *Tanjore*, 88, 115. S. Seetha (a scholar who was previously head of the Music Department at the University of Madras) suggests that with the introduction of musical practices from the northern state of Maharashtra, *Hindustani* music and musical forms became popular in Thanjavur.

9. B. M. Sundaram, personal communication with the author, Thanjavur, 2004.

10. B. M. Sundaram, personal communication with the author, Thanjavur, 2004. "Maybe this is our Kamakshi," he commented. There is no way to know with complete certainty. The name Kamakshi prefaced by the name of place of origin, Thanjavur, does not irrefutably mean she was Balasaraswati's ancestor. Balasaraswati confirmed her family's presence in Kerala, stating in her convocation address at the Music Academy in 1973: "It is known that my great-great-grandmother Kamakshi Ammal danced in the court of Thiruvanantapuram." Thanjavur Nilapatti, a close friend of the family known within the family as "Grandma Nila," was outstanding among the dancers of Kamakshi Ammal's generation. In an interview years later she complimented Kamakshi Ammal's "high" style of dance—and commented that Balasaraswati, when she was a young girl, resembled Kamakshi Ammal.

11. Jayammal, interviewed by T. Viswanathan, Government of India Census of India 1961. These dancers included Salem Meenakshi, Radha Annamalai, Thirukazhukundram Janaki, and Aramvavil Nagaratnam.

12. Vanita, "Whispertime," *Women's World* (Delhi), October 25, 1953.

13. V. Sriram, *Carnatic Summer: Lives of Twenty Great Exponents* (Chennai: East/West Books, 2004). In a short biographical sketch of Balasaraswati's cousins T. Brinda and T. Muktha, Sriram mentions that Bala's great-grandmother Sundarammal was adopted. Adoption was common when there was no surviving female offspring to learn the family practice. Whether Sundarammal was adopted is a matter of disagreement, although Vegavahini Vijayaraghavan, T. Brinda's daughter, also states her understanding that Sundarammal was adopted by Kamakshi Ammal. T. Muktha agreed, stating that Sundarammal was adopted from a Brahmin family.

But Chinnayya Naidu, a dance teacher who taught Bala in 1932, offered a clue that seemed to connect Bala's dancing to that of Bala's great-great-grandmother Kamakshi. Naidu had been close to Bala's family for several decades, and looking at Bala curiously while watching her dance, he said to Jayammal, "This small one resembles your great-grandmother." Be that as it may, Balasaraswati and Viswanathan both commented that nothing could be said about the family practice before Vina Dhanammal's lifetime. As far as the family is concerned, their *parampara* begins with Dhanammal. The point is that it is the musical legacy that constitutes the hereditary practice. Whether Sundarammal was adopted may never be known, but the direct musical heritage she inherited and perpetuated within the family is what is important to the family.

14. This was communicated to the author in 2005 by the current owner of the house.

CHAPTER 2: MADMAN AT THE GATE (pages 17–59)

1. T. Shankaran, interviewed by T. Viswanathan.

2. F. Max Müller, *Ramakrishna: His Life and Sayings* (New Delhi: Rupa & Co., 2006), 24.

3. Ra Ganapati, in privately communicated notes on conversations with Balasaraswati.

4. K. Kalpana and Frank Schiffer, eds., *Madras: The Architectural Heritage* (Chennai: Indian National Trust for Art and Cultural Heritage, 2003), 23.

5. Eugene Irschick, *Dialogue and History: Constructing South India, 1795–1895* (Berkeley: University of California, 1994), 17, citing Davidson Love, *Vestiges of Old Madras* (London, 1913).

6. Amanda J. Weidman, *Singing the Classical, Voicing the Modern* (Durham, NC: Duke University Press, 2006), 16.

7. Lakshmi Subramanian, *From the Tanjore Court to the Madras Music Academy: A Social History of Music in South India* (New Delhi: Oxford University Press, 2006), 41.

8. S. Muthiah, *Madras Discovered* (New Delhi: Affiliated East-West Press, 1992).

9. R. Krishnamurthy, *Ananda Vikatan* (Madras), August 20, 1933.

10. Ananda K. Coomaraswamy, *The Dance of Shiva* (New York: Sunrise Turn, 1918; New York: Noonday Press, 1971), 54.

11. Ibid., 56.

12. Ibid., 57.

13. Beryl de Zoete, *The Other Mind: A Study of Dance in South India* (London: Victor Gollancz, 1953), 32–33.

14. T. Shankaran, in a letter to Lakshmi Knight, May 17, 1990.

15. Ibid.

16. Balasaraswati is not being self-effacing here. She is comparing herself to the *sanyasis* and *yogis* she admired so much.

17. S. Guhan, comp. and ed., *Bala on Bharatanatyam* (Madras: The Sruti Foundation, 1991), 9–10.

18. Personal communication from Vegavahini Vijayaraghavan.

19. Alain Danielou, *Hindu Polytheism*, Bollingen Series LXXIII (New York: Bollingen Foundation, 1964), 253–257.

20. T. Shankaran, in a letter to Lakshmi Knight, May 17, 1990.

21. This translation by Shankaran reveals his own idiosyncrasies with English.

22. A ritual dance sequence that has been adopted into the reconstructed version of bharata natyam. It was not performed on stage by hereditary dancers.

23. Mylapore Gauri Ammal, in an interview with T. Shankaran, 1971.

24. P. Jayalakshmi, interviewed by T. Shankaran, June 1, 1989.

25. de Zoete, *The Other Mind*, 17.

26. T. Shankaran, interviewed by T. Viswanathan, July 1989.

27. Guhan, *Bala on Bharatanatyam*, 18.

28. N. Pattabhi Raman and Anandhi Ramachandran, "T. Balasaraswati: The Whole World in Her Hands," Special Issue, *Sangeet Natak: Journal of Sangeet Natak Akademi* 72–73 (April–September 1984), 15.

29. Ibid.

30. "Kornad" *saris* were manufactured in Koranadu, Mayuram.

31. Radha Sarma, "The Presence of Dhanammal," Masters Remembered, *Indian Express* (Delhi), July 28, 1979.

32. Lakshmi Knight, interviewed by Luise Scripps.

33. Sarma, "The Presence of Dhanammal," *Indian Express*, July 28, 1979.

34. Name of a *raga* or musical mode.

35. The brothers of the Thanjavur Quartet were sent to Mutthuswami Diksitar for musical training.

36. The *vina* teacher, Azhagiyasingarayya, was a *Sathara Vaishnava* — a member of a community who prepare the offerings of flowers in Vaishnavite temples.

37. Indira Viswanathan Peterson refers to them as the primary scripture of Tamil Saivism in her book, *Poems to Siva: The Hymns of the Tamil Saints* (Princeton, NJ: Princeton University Press, 1989).

38. S. Y. Krishnamurthy reported in an interview with Smita Shah that Vina Dhanammal learned *"Tanayuni"* in *Bhairavi raga* from him, and taught him *"Dasaradhe"* in *Todi raga* in return.

39. It was generally remembered by older family members how pieces came into the family repertoire; however, much of that information was not documented.

40. Vegavahini Vijayaraghavan, in conversation with the author, February 14, 2006.

41. T. Viswanathan, in an interview with Luise Scripps, 1988.

42. Savitri Rajan, in an interview with T. Shankaran.

43. Sarma, "The Presence of Dhanammal," *Indian Express*, July 28, 1979.

44. Ibid.

45. Ibid.

46. T. Shankaran, in an audiotape, January 6, 1989.

47. For further details of the family lineage, see T. Viswanathan and Matthew Harp Allen, *Music in South India: The Karnatak Concert Tradition and Beyond: Experiencing Music, Expressing Culture* (New York: Oxford University Press, 2004), 89.

48. T. Brinda would later teach T. N. Swaminatha Pillai several Tyagaraja *kritis*.

49. T. Viswanathan, in personal communication with the author.

50. T. Shankaran, in personal communication with the author.

51. The musician, Hayagreevachar, was actually from Karnataka. T. Viswanathan, in a group conversation with Lakshmi Knight, Matthew Allen and the author, September 1988.

52. *Balasaraswati* by Wesleyan University; *Bala* by Satyajit Ray.

53. Viswanathan was India's first recipient of this honor from the National Endowment for the Arts.

54. T. Viswanathan, in group conversation, September 1988.

55. Viswanathan, in personal communication with the author.

56. Guhan, *Bala on Bharatanatyam*, 18.

57. Interview of Bella Lewitzki and Donald McKayle by Luise Scripps at the American Dance Festival, Duke University, June 13, 1994. Bala had just turned fifty-three.

58. A group dance performed in a circle, with intricate synchronized movement and striking of sticks.

59. The three are Patnam Subramania Iyer, Thiruppanandal Pattabhirama Rao, and Dharmapuri Subbarayar.

60. Another example of this is the gift from Syama Sastri's son to Kamakshi Ammal, the *kriti* *"Charanu, charanu."*

61. Jayammal, interviewed by T. Viswanathan, Government of India Census, 1961.

62. T. Shankaran, in an audiotape, recorded January 6, 1989.

63. Swaminatha Pillai, who was born in 1898, was the eldest of the three sons of Thirupambaram Natarajasundaram Pillai. All three sons were trained by their father to be *nagaswaram* players, like their father. Swaminatha Pillai, after several years of training on the *nagaswaram*, began a career as a vocalist of the *karnatic* concert repertoire. He began to experience problems with his voice, and started to teach himself to play the bamboo transverse flute, imitating the inflection and dynamics of the voice, creating a unique style of playing. His single student of this style was Viswanathan.

64. Guhan, *Bala on Bharatanatyam*, 17.

65. T. Shankaran, *Sruti Magazine* 60/61 (September 1989), 48.

66. Radha Annamalai, interviewed by T. Shankaran, 1985. Radha Annamalai was the daughter of Rajalakshmi of the Kalyani Daughters, the first hereditary artists to perform at the Music Academy.

67. T. Shankaran, interviewed by T. Viswanathan.

68. Guhan, *Bala on Bharatanatyam*, 17.

69. B. M. Sundaram, personal communication, 2005.

70. A version given by Roshen Alkazi in an interview with Smita Shah.

71. A version given by K. P. Kittappa Pillai in an interview with T. Shankaran, January 7, 1989.

72. Ibid.

73. Radha Annamalai, in an interview with T. Shankaran. Her aunt Jeevaratnammal was Kandappa Pillai's student. Radha Annamalai reported that Kandappa Pillai was living in their home while he taught Jeevaratnammal and that Bala came there for classes.

74. It is notable that during a period when the traditional practice was in decline, Kandappa — one of many dance teachers at that time — taught eighteen girls in a class at home, all from the hereditary community. This is more than the number of students he later taught at the Uday Shankar Performing Arts Centre in Almora.

75. Mani Mann, *Femina* (Delhi), August 28, 1964.

76. Narayana Menon, *Balasaraswati*, International Cultural Centre (Delhi), 1961.

77. B. V. K. Sastri, in an interview with Smita Shah.

78. Maya Rao, *Illustrated Weekly of India* (Delhi), June 3, 1962.

79. Bani Bai, in an interview by G. Sulochana, December 1987.

80. "Presentation of SNA Awards," *The Statesman* (Delhi), March 28, 1955.

81. Lakshmi Knight, in personal communication with the author.

82. T. Viswanathan, in an interview with Luise Scripps, July 18 and 19, 1988.

83. S. V. Vasudev, "Balasaraswati Was Goddess of Dancing," *Times of India* (Delhi), February 10, 1984. In the article, a memorial after Balasaraswati's death, Vasudev was quoting from an unpublished interview with Balasaraswati.

84. Balasaraswati recalled each piece she had performed, including the *pada varnam* "Danike," the *padam* "Nidirayil," a *jatiswaram* in *Kalyani raga*, and a *tillana* in *Mandari raga*.

85. During the course of her career, Balasaraswati identified five concerts that she described as her "five best." These included her *arangetram*, and were spread

through the earlier part of her career; all have been identified in the text of this book. From the perspective of the spectator, we might presume her best concerts were those that met with the greatest acclaim or in which great musical and dance challenges were met. But I believe I am right (particularly given that she included her first program at the age of seven in this highly exclusive group) that she was referring to the experience *she* had as she performed, the joining of the individual and the Infinite, the joining of the *jeevatma* and *paramatma* that Lakshmi refers to in her description of *"Ninni Joochi"* in Chapter 5. Balasaraswati referred to the experience on several occasions, including in her Presidential Address at the Tamil Isai Sangam in 1975: "On some occasions and in some measure, dance and music have enabled a deep experience of the presence of God." This was what made a concert great for Balasaraswati.

86. S. Krishnan, "Bala: Autumnal Years," *Aside* (Madras), April–May 1979.

87. Including *"Suntasepu," "Ella Arumaihalum"* in *Todi,* *"Nidirayil"* in *Pantuvarali,* and *"Bala Vinave"* in *Kamboji.*

88. Lakshmi Knight, in an interview with Luise Scripps.

CHAPTER 3: RENAISSANCE (pages 60–99)

1. Theosophy was a Greek term meaning "wise and divine things," implying a mystical association with the divine. It was not a philosophical system. The word appeared again in early Christian writings, with the same implications of mysticism. The term "theosophy" was used during the seventeenth century to denote Christian occultism, and came to be associated primarily with the writings and thinking of German Christian mystic Jacob Boehm, who had a revelation of the non duality between humans and God. Boehm's work influenced a number of German philosophers and theologians of the nineteenth and early twentieth centuries.

The word was brought into current usage in the nineteenth century when borrowed by Helena Blavatsky to designate her religious philosophy, Theosophy, a belief that all religions represent attempts by man to seek or perceive the absolute. Although there are references to a "conversion" to Theosophy as early as the 1880s, it was in fact a newly rationalized ideology with few advocates at that time. Since then the Theosophical Society has attracted several million members world-wide, but it has never achieved nor sought the status of a religion.

2. Stephen Prothero, *The White Buddhist: The Asian Odyssey of Henry Steel Olcott* (Bloomington: Indiana University Press, 1996), 63–104.

3. Ibid.

4. Eugene F. Irschick, *Politics and Social Conflict in South India: The Non-Brahman Movement and Tamil Separatism 1916–1929* (Berkeley: University of California Press, 1969), 1–88.

5. Weidman, *Singing the Classical,* 117.

6. This legislation was eventually passed in 1947.

7. Attributable in part to S. Muthiah, *The Hindu,* December 17, 2007. See also T. J. S. George, *MS: A Life in Music* (New Delhi: HarperCollins, 2004), 127–128.

8. E. Krishna Iyer, "Renaissance of Indian Dance and Its Architects" in Indian Fine Arts Society Souvenir, 1948; reprinted in *Rasamanjari* (Delhi), August 1997.

9. Doris Humphrey, *The Art of Making Dances*, ed. Barbara Pollack (Princeton, NJ: Princeton Book Company, 1987), 168.

273
Notes

10. This composition from the concert music repertoire was adopted by some traditional practitioners several decades before it became popular in the revised style of dance.

11. Mylapore Gauri Ammal, interviewed by T. Shankaran, 1971.

12. G. Sulochana is the last surviving daughter of Soudaravalli Ammal, who was dedicated to the temple at Thiruvarur.

13. Bhanumathi, in an interview with T. Shankaran. Concerning dance that was current in 1990, Bhanumathi said that "today, dancers perform to please the audience. There is a big difference between our old *pada varnams* composed by our ancestors and these new ones. Now they sing so many types of non-traditional songs, both good and bad, to please the public. . . . Currently dance is performed too quickly; [it] should be in a decent tempo."

14. Maya Rao, *Illustrated Weekly of India*, June 3, 1962.

15. Seetha, *Tanjore*, 144.

16. Balasaraswati, Keynote Address, Congress on Research in Dance, Honolulu, August 1978.

17. The Quartet had been in the Thanjavur court with musicians from Europe who played instruments that included the clarinet as well as the violin.

18. Some have claimed that the seating of the musicians was an innovation introduced by Rukmini Devi, but there are photographs and reviews documenting the change in the early 1930s before Rukmini Devi began performing.

19. At about the same time as the drum solo was dropped from the dance concert format, it was adopted as part of the music concert format and remains as a standard element today.

20. Guhan, *Bala on Bharatanatyam*, 14–15.

21. Sally Banes, *Dancing Women: Female Bodies on Stage* (London and New York: Routledge, 2001), 38–39.

22. G. K. Seshagiri (writing as Bhava Raga Tala), *Sound and Shadow*, April 15, 1933, 24.

23. Reprinted in *Sruti* 8, June 1984.

24. Iyer, "Renaissance of Indian Dance," *Rasamanjari*.

25. Leela Shekar, in an interview with Ra Ganapati, recorded by Smita Shah.

26. Davesh Soneji, in communication with the author, July 25, 2007.

27. Guhan, *Bala on Bharatanatyam*, 19.

28. T. Viswanathan, in an interview with Luise Scripps, 1988.

29. C. P. Ramaswami Iyer, *The Mail* (Madras), August 15, 1928.

30. *Journal of the Madras Music Academy* 2, 1933, 78. This is claimed as one of the early usages of the term *bharata natyam*. There is also an imprecision to the use of the name *nautch*; certainly there was a clearly defined difference between nautch and a more modest art form of dance one hundred years before. For a comparative account, see Julia Maitland, *Letters from Madras* (New Delhi: Oxford University Press, 2003).

31. Matthew Allen, in conversation with the author, March 2007.

32. G. K. Seshagiri (writing as Bhava Raga Tala), *Sound and Shadow*, April 23, 1933, 24.

33. To the contrary, Balasaraswati was beautiful.

34. K. Chandrasekharan, "Only One Bala for Bharata Natyam," *The Hindu*, March 1, 1984.

35. This is most likely *tillana*.

36. G. K. Seshagiri (writing as Bhava Raga Tala), *Sound and Shadow,* August 27, 1933, 62–64.

37. The wedding referred to was in about 1932. He presented Bala in concert for the first time in 1935.

38. Guhan, *Bala on Bharatanatyam*, 20.

39. R. Krishnamurthy, *Ananda Vikatan*, August 20, 1933.

40. N. Pattabhi Raman and Anandi Ramachandran, *Journal of Sangeet Natak Akademi* 72–73, April–September 1984, 28.

41. "*Vatta thotti.*"

42. T. Shankaran in an interview with T. Viswanathan.

43. B. Rajanikantha Rao, *Kshetrayya* (New Delhi: Sahitya Akademi, 1981), 16.

44. For a discussion of the genre *padam*, see A. K. Ramanujam, Velcheru Narayana Rao, and David Shulman, eds. and trans., *When God Is a Customer: Telugu Courtesan Songs by Ksetrayya and Others* (Berkeley: University of California Press, 1994). The beautiful translations are of pieces contained within Balasaraswati's family repertoire, communicated to the authors by T. Viswanathan and Lakshmi Knight.

45. Seetha, *Tanjore*, 132.

46. Rao, *Kshetrayya*, 54.

47. Banes, *Dancing Women*, 92.

48. Marie Louise Burke, *Swami Vivekananda in the West: New Discoveries* (Calcutta: Advaita Ashrama, 1983), 66.

49. Jane Desmond, "Dancing Out the Difference: Cultural Imperialism and Ruth St. Denis's *Radha* of 1906," in *Moving History/Dancing Cultures*, ed. Ann Dils and Ann Cooper Albright (Middletown, CT: Wesleyan University Press, 2001), 260.

50. Ibid., 258.

51. Sukanya Rahman, *Dancing in the Family: An Unconventional Memoir of Three Women* (New Delhi: HarperCollins, 2001), 8.

52. Ibid.

53. The mother of French pianist Simone Barbier, known as Simikie, who became Uday Shankar's dance partner, was a member of the Paris Branch of the Theosophical Society.

54. Ninotchka Devorah Bennahum, *Antonia Merce, "La Argentina": Flamenco and the Spanish Avant-Garde* (Middletown, CT: Wesleyan University Press, 2000), 166.

55. Iyer, "Renaissance of Indian Dance," *Rasamanjari*, 15.

56. Elphinstone, a Scot, was a nineteenth-century governor of Madras.

57. R. Krishnamurthy, *Ananda Vikatan*, September 10, 1933.

58. Seshagiri, *Sound and Shadow*, August 27, 1933, 62–64. Notice that the re-

viewer refers to the "tradition of bharata natyam," then uses "*sadir*" to mean the old style of dancing in general.

59. R. Krishnamurthy, *Ananda Vikatan*, September 10, 1933.

60. She was fifteen.

61. T. Shankaran, in taped conversation with T. Viswanathan.

62. T. Viswanathan, in an interview with Luise Scripps, 1988.

63. Satyajit Ray, interviewed by Smita Shah.

64. Ravi Shankar, interviewed by Smita Shah.

65. *mora mukuta pitambara soye gala vaijayanti mala |*
brindavanamem gopacharave kali kambalivala ||

This is a refrain that occurs in many *bhajans* attributed to the female saint Mirabai.

66. T. Viswanathan, in an interview with Smita Shah.

67. Manjulika Bhadhury, the Indian dance historian, in an interview with T. Shankaran.

68. Iyer, "Renaissance of Indian Dance," *Rasamanjari*, 15.

69. Balasaraswati recalled the date of this event as 1938 in an interview with Kumkum Mathur, but other sources suggest 1936.

70. Kumkum Mathur, "Dancing Is a Joy to Me," *Patriot*, February 23, 1976.

CHAPTER 4: RECONSTRUCTION (pages 100–137)

1. Some families remain intact today.

2. Guhan, *Bala on Bharatanatyam*, 15.

3. B. M. Sundaram communicated personally to the author that it was Balasaraswati who explained to him that the "*sakhi*" in the poetry of the tradition is the "*guru.*"

4. Weidman, *Singing the Classical,* 65.

5. Rukmini Devi Arundale, in an interview by Smita Shah, 1988.

6. George Arundale, "Seeing Theosophy," *The Theosophist* 57, no. 6, March 1936. Anna Pavlova has developed in India a mythological status as a dancer that may outstrip her artistic reputation in the West.

7. This was seven years after Balasaraswati had danced her *arangetram*, and a year before her first concerts for the Music Academy, so it is likely that Kandappa Pillai was making Bala practice what she already knew.

8. This would probably place this visit in 1932.

9. Balasaraswati's lack of interest in costumes was well known.

10. Rukmini Devi Arundale, in an interview by Smita Shah.

11. R. Krishnamurthy, *Ananda Vikatan*, December 15, 1935.

12. V. Patanjali, "Balasaraswati," *Illustrated Weekly of India*, May 25, 1969.

13. T. Ranganathan, in an interview with Smita Shah.

14. T. Shankaran, in a personal letter to Lakshmi Knight.

15. Leela Shekar, in an interview with Ra Ganapati.

16. The governor or chief administrator of Cochin (now Kerala), appointed by the raja.

17. T. Shankaran, in a tape recording, January 1989.

18. Mrs. Satyavati Gopalan, interviewed by Luise Scripps, May 16, 1995.

19. Aniruddha Knight, reporting on conversations with his mother, Lakshmi Knight.

20. R. Krishnamurthy, *Ananda Vikatan*, October 15, 1939.

21. She had started to learn in Madras, and then followed Kandappa to Almora. Balasaraswati was committed to supporting her family and had to remain in Madras.

22. R. Krishnamurthy, *Ananda Vikatan*, January 7, 1940.

23. T. Shankaran, in a letter to Lakshmi Knight.

24. Meenakshi Sundaram Pillai, "Bharatanatyam," *Rukmini Devi Arundale Birth Centenary Volume*, ed. Shakuntala Ramani (Chennai: The Kalakshetra Foundation, 2004), 127–128.

25. Guhan, *Bala on Bharatanatyam*, 11.

26. Popularly known as *"Viriboni."*

27. V. Patanjali, "Balasaraswati," *Illustrated Weekly of India*, May 25, 1969.

28. Leela Shekar, in an interview with Ra Ganapati.

29. Balanagamma was a mythical heroine. When Kandappa Pillai used this endearment he showed deep fondness for Bala, and Bala never forgot his words.

30. Balasaraswati, Indian Fine Arts Society address, 1982.

31. R. Krishnamurthy, *Ananda Vikatan*, October 21, 1934.

32. T. Viswanathan, in an interview with Luise Scripps.

33. Lakshmi Knight, in personal communication with the author.

34. T. Viswanathan, in a conversation with Lakshmi Knight, Matthew Allen, and the author.

35. Kamal Muilenburg, Medha Yodh's daughter, in personal correspondence with the author.

36. Krishna Nehru Hutheesing was Prime Minister Jawaharlal Nehru's youngest sister.

37. Medha Yodh, in an interview with Luise Scripps, May 25, 1995.

38. The town was named Thirukazhukundram.

39. Roshen Alkazi, in an interview with Luise Scripps, June 21 and 29, 1990.

40. T. Ranganathan, in an interview with Smita Shah.

41. Coomaraswamy, *The Dance of Shiva*, 36.

42. Another term is *vyabhichari bhavas*.

43. S. V. Shesardri, *Shankar's Weekly*, August 18, 1963.

44. Balasaraswati, in Madras Music Academy address, December 1973.

45. Guhan, *Bala on Bharatanatyam*, 6.

46. All India Dance Festival Souvenir, for Vikram Samvat 2000, Bombay, January 18–24, 1945, ed. Champaklal G. Mody.

47. Ibid.

48. Rukmini Devi Arundale employed a lighting designer from England named Alex Elmore, a Theosophist.

49. Used as a drone instrument to supplement the stringed instrument *tambura*.

50. T. Ranganathan, in an interview with Smita Shah.

51. The head of one of four monastic orders established by a ninth-century saint, Sri Aadi Shankaracharya (788–820 CE).

52. The *sthala purana* of Thiruverkadu is a loose translation of a description given to me by the current medium at the shrine of Devi Karumari Amman.

53. *Kali Yuga* is the "age of vice" described in Hindu scriptures as the last of the four stages of development that the world goes through in the cycle of *Yugas* (ages or periods). In general, there is agreement that mankind is currently in *Kali Yuga*, a time when human civilization degenerates spiritually. The word *kali* means "discord" or "contention" but is sometimes mistaken for a name of a manifestation of the Goddess Kaali, also named Durga.

CHAPTER 5: DANCING FOR MURUGAN (pages 138–184)

1. Lakshmi Knight, recalling conversation with Balasaraswati.

2. Balasaraswati Address, Madras Music Academy, December 1973. The Tamil words for "pierce" and "pour" refer to a bee's sting.

3. Ibid.

4. T. Viswanathan, in an interview with T. Shankaran.

5. T. Viswanathan, in an interview with Smita Shah.

6. Guhan, *Bala on Bharatanatyam*, 15–16.

7. de Zoete, *The Other Mind*, 187.

8. Privately, she credited her return to dancing to Devi Karumari Amman.

9. T. Viswanathan, in an interview with T. Shankaran.

10. K. Chandrasekharan (as Natya Priya), *The Hindu*, October 23, 1949.

11. T. Shankaran, in a letter to *Sruti*, 12, October 1984.

12. Sarojini Kumaraswami suffered from kidney failure and lived the last part of her life confined to a wheelchair. In 1995 Lakshmi, Aniruddha, and I were living at Balasaraswati's house in Kilpauk, and Viswanathan visited for several months. During his visit we hosted six weeks of Friday evening concerts. Despite considerable discomfort, Sarojini attended all six concerts, weeping at times, transported to another time and place. She died the evening of Viswanathan's last concert, after her daughter-in-law had taken her home.

13. Sarojini Kumaraswami, in an interview with Smita Shah.

14. Rasikan, "*Swantantra*," Madras, January 12, 1951.

15. She was accompanied by K. Ellappa Mudaliar, *nattuvanar*; T. Jayammal and Sarojini Kumaraswami, vocalists; T. Viswanathan, flute; and T. Kuppuswami Mudaliar, *mridangam*.

16. Twenty-two years later, when the secretaries of the Academy closed the school, the amount had been reduced gradually to six thousand rupees per year.

17. R. Krishnamurthy, "The Fortunate Bharatanatyam," *Kalki* (Madras), April 23, 1953.

18. Ibid.

19. Letter from T. K. Chidambaram Mudaliar to Balasaraswati.

20. There are two examples mentioned in the text of this book: from Syama Sastri's son to Kamakshi Ammal and her daughter Sundarammal; and from Dharmapuri Subbaraya Iyer to Vina Dhanammal.

21. Roshen Alkazi, in an interview with Smita Shah, 1987.

22. Ibid.

23. Vanita, *Women's World*, October 25, 1953.

24. Charles Fabri, "Gallery of Famous Indian Dancers—VII," *The Statesman* (Calcutta), June 29, 1954.

25. This was most likely set to music by Pakkiria Pillai, Kandappa Pillai's mentor, and performed with *alarippu*, a practice introduced by Kandappa Pillai.

26. Vanita, *Women's World*, October 25, 1953.

27. Guhan, *Bala on Bharatanatyam*, 7.

28. Ibid., 16.

29. See William Dalrymple, *The Last Mughal: The Fall of a Dynasty, Delhi, 1857* (New Delhi: Penguin Books India, 2006), among others, for a description of the collapse of the Mughal court in Delhi. The courtly arts were never to return.

30. At Sundareswara Hall, with K. Ellappa Mudaliar, T. Jayammal, Sarojini Kumaraswami, S. Narasimhulu, N. Radhakrishna Naidu, and T. Kuppuswami Mudaliar.

31. T. N. Rajaratnam Pillai played the *nagaswaram*, a double-reed instrument. The music performed on the *nagaswaram* includes ritual, processional, and concert practices. The instrument has a bold sound, capable of carrying across open expanses of countryside, announcing to the surrounding population that specific ceremonies are to begin, and permitting those unable to be there to participate through the familiar sound. Traditionally the community of men who perform in the *periya melam*, the ensemble of the *nagaswaram* and *tavil* (double-headed drum), have close family connections with and are members of the same community as the *devadasi*, although the families are patrilineal. The *nagaswaram* tradition is rooted in the temple, like the performance of bharata natyam, and as with bharata natyam, *nagaswaram* performers have always been from hereditary practices and legacies. But the *nagaswaram* and *tavil* traditions did not face the same public censure and rejection as the tradition of bharata natyam did; it was more difficult to discredit the male community. T. N. Rajaratnam Pillai was one of the musicians who attended Vina Dhanammal's concerts during the 1920s and early in the 1930s. Musicians in Bala's family credit Rajaratnam Pillai with influencing the family interpretation of *raga*. Rajaratnam's fame with the South Indian audience derived from his spellbinding melodic improvisation. He was particularly famous for his interpretation of *Todi raga*, and he influenced a generation of *karnatic* musicians, not just *nagaswaram* players. By adapting the *karnatic* concert repertoire rather than the repertoire performed in temples, and by altering the sound of his instrument to be expressive of the human voice (in part by increasing the length of the instrument, thereby lowering its pitch to a male singer's register), Rajaratnam brought the temple ensemble to the concert stage. Like Kandappa Pillai, he wore a shirt when he performed, breaking with an expectation of *isai velalar* musicians that they would perform bare-chested in concert, as they would when they performed in the temple. Rajaratnam sometimes appeared in concert wearing a blazer. His performances changed the course of *karnatic* music, drawing a popular audience no *nagaswaram* player in memory had previously attracted.

32. In fact this piece is not a *padam*, but it is often referred to as one.

33. P. V. Subramaniam (Subbudu), "The Award at the Capital," *Kalki* (Madras), *Times of India* (Delhi), April 3, 1955.

34. "Presentation of SNA Awards," *The Statesman*, March 28, 1955.

35. Ibid.

36. Bala uses the term borrowed from her own tradition, *adavu*, to describe the movements of pure dance.

37. "Shambhu Maharaj," *Kalki*, April 24, 1955.

38. Dr. Kapila Vatsyayan, in personal communication to the author, July 24, 2008. Birju Maharaj was first introduced to the membership of the Music Academy by Dr. Vatsyayan.

39. Some scholars assert that it entered the repertoire of bharata natyam in the Thanjavur court as an adaptation of the Marathi dance-song form *tarana*.

40. Birju Maharaj, in an interview with Smita Shah in 1985. This interview was conducted through an interpreter in Gujarati, then translated into English by Pushpa Gupta, Librarian at the Indian Consulate in New York, in April 1987.

41. It was historically the right of a *devadasi* to perform a simple ceremony outside a temple environment that was protection from *drishti*.

42. "A Dream Come True," *Times of India* (New Delhi), March 29, 1955.

43. "Bala Enchants Delhi Audience," *The Statesman* (Delhi), March 29, 1955.

44. "A Dream Come True," *Times of India* (New Delhi), March 29, 1955. Critics would sometimes comment after seeing a concert that Balasaraswati could create illusion on the stage and that the dancer would seem to disappear. Someone once commented to Vina Dhanammal during the 1930s that her granddaughter could bring the gods to the stage. "I will have to take your word for that," she is reported to have said, "I'm blind."

45. *Hindustan Times* (Delhi), April 24, 1955.

46. Music Critic, "Bharata Natyam at its Best," *Hindustan Times* (Delhi), November 4, 1955.

47. *The Sunday Hindustan Standard* (Delhi), November 6, 1955.

48. *Shankar's Weekly*, November 13, 1955.

49. Charles Rinehart, in conversation with the author, June 2008.

50. The others in the troupe were Donald McKayle, Ellen Vanderhoeven, Robert Cohan, Linda Hodes, Stuart Hodes, Cristyne Lawsen, Helen McGhee, Bertram Ross, Ellen Segal, Paul Taylor, Matt Turney, Ethel Winter, and David Wood.

51. Donya Feuer, in a conversation with Luise Scripps.

52. Donald McKayle, in an interview with Luise Scripps. "CalArts" is California Institute of the Arts, where Balasaraswati would be in residence in the early 1970s.

53. Interview with Smita Shah, September 29, 1985.

54. Bala performed with K. Ellappa Mudaliar, T. Jayammal, Sarojini Kumaraswami, T. Viswanathan, N. Radhakrishna Naidu, and T. Kuppuswami Mudaliar.

55. Her ensemble included K. Ellappa Mudaliar, T. Jayammal, Sarojini Kumaraswami, N. Radhakrishna Naidu, and T. Kuppuswami Mudaliar.

56. "Bala Excels," *Indian Express* (Madras), December 26, 1956.

57. *Aadi* is a term of respect that refers to the "old" or "original." Aadi Ponniah Pillai was one of the Thanjavur Quartet; Ponniah Pillai was his grandson, Kandappa's cousin.

58. "The Anguish of Art," *Swarajya* (Madras), February 9, 1957.

59. Meenakshi Puri, "*Padams* and *Javalis*," *Sunday Statesman* (Delhi), April 7, 1957.

60. "Chaste Rendering of *Padams*," *Times of India*, April 23, 1957.

61. T. Shankaran, in an audiotape recording, 1989.

62. Communicated directly to the author by T. Ranganathan.

63. Kshetrayya, "*Ninnu Joochi*," translated by A. K. Ramanujam in Ramanujam, Rao and Shulman, *When God Is a Customer* (Berkeley: University of California Press, 1994), 77–78. Reprinted with permission. The poetry of the piece, among several others, was provided in Telugu from the repertoire of T. Viswanathan and Lakshmi Knight.

64. Guhan, *Bala on Bharatanatyam*, 14.

65. Roshen Alkazi, in interviews with Luise Scripps, June 21 and 29, 1990.

66. Rukmini Devi Arundale, "My Experiments with Dance," *Some Selected Speeches and Writings of Rukmini Devi Arundale* (Madras: Kalakshetra Foundation). This is a transcription of a talk given by Rukmini Devi Arundale with a dance demonstration at the Dance Seminar on April 2, 1958.

67. Maya Rao, *Illustrated Weekly of India*, June 3, 1962.

68. Chiaroscuro, *Illustrated Weekly of India*, July 15, 1962.

69. Roshen Alkazi, in an interview with Smita Shah.

70. Maya Rao, *Illustrated Weekly of India*, June 3, 1962. The article refers to the event in 1958.

71. Ibid.

72. As noted in the account of Kshetrayya's challenge in Chidamabaram in the early seventeenth century, this temple is one of the few in India that are shrines for both Siva and Vishnu, in the forms of Siva Nataraja and Govindaraja Perumal.

73. This story has been recounted numerous times by Lakshmi Knight and Ra Ganapati.

74. "Diksitar" with the final *r* is the usual term of respect used to refer to a Diksita in Tamil. Bala, unable to show that respect to this Diksita, referred to him as a "Diksitan," the final *n* denoting lack of reverence. This recollection is from Lakshmi Knight.

75. Siva and Parvati.

76. A hill shrine near Madras.

77. Daughter of the celestial Indra.

78. Lakshmi Knight, in a conversation recorded in 1992.

79. This account has been told several times by Lakshmi Knight.

CHAPTER 6: ON THE BACK OF A PEACOCK (pages 185–224)

1. Kapila Vatsyayan, in an interview with Smita Shah.

2. Ibid.

3. Lakshmi Knight in private conversation with the author.

4. Kapila Vatsyayan, in an interview with Smita Shah; Narayana Menon, in an interview with Smita Shah.

5. Achieving understanding between artist and audience cross-culturally is always a challenge. In 1974 I witnessed a performance of the Japanese theater form

Noh in Madras. The audience in Madras is accustomed to an environment that resembles the temple courtyard, where people chat, greet each other, and come and go. An announcement was made at the outset of the performance, and again during it, asking that the audience understand and appreciate the actors' expectation of silence and solemnity—like the audience reaction that Balasaraswati encountered in Tokyo in 1961. But the announcement was ineffective. Similarly, Western artists performing in India may find the casual, seemingly unenthusiastic audience response disconcertingly flat. And when Indian artists perform in the West, the audience's enthusiasm and the almost obligatory standing ovations are sometimes overwhelming—and occasionally mislead performers into thinking that the response is more unusual than it actually may be.

6. Kapila Vatsyayan, in a conversation with Lakshmi Knight.

7. T. Viswanathan, in an interview with Luise Scripps, 1988.

8. Lord Harewood, in an interview with Smita Shah.

9. Charles Reinhart, in an interview with Smita Shah.

10. Norton Owen, *A Certain Place: The Jacob's Pillow Story* (Becket, MA: Jacob's Pillow Dance Festival, 1997).

11. Jacob's Pillow Dance Festival Director of Preservation Norton Owen, in personal communication with the author, August 9, 2008. Program notes from Jacob's Pillow Dance Festival archives, courtesy of Norton Owen.

12. Ted Shawn, "Bala: First Lady of Bharata Natyam," *Span*, May 19, 1962.

13. Kapila Vatsyayan, in an interview with Smita Shah.

14. Walter Terry, *New York Herald Tribune*, August 22, 1962.

15. Wesleyan University owned American Education Publications, the publisher of *My Weekly Reader*, a magazine distributed to millions of children through elementary schools all over the United States. Xerox Corporation's purchase of AEP in exchange for Xerox stock in 1965 helped to finance several of Wesleyan's graduate programs, including the expansion of the World Music program that was started in 1961.

16. Richard Winslow, in personal communication with the author.

17. Richard Winslow, "Report of the Department of Music" (Wesleyan University, 1960–61), in "Saraswati's Journey: South Indian Karnatak Music in the United States" by Joseph Getter (master's thesis, Wesleyan University, May 1998).

18. Mrinalini Sarabhai, *The Voice of the Heart* (New Delhi: HarperCollins, 2004).

19. Merce Cunningham, in an interview with Smita Shah.

20. Allen Hughes, *New York Times*, November 25, 1962.

21. Renee Renouf, *Thought* (Delhi), May 5, 1963.

22. Narayana Menon, in an interview with Smita Shah.

23. Lord Harewood, in an interview with Smita Shah.

24. Clive Barnes, *New York Times*, August 24, 1963.

25. Narayana Menon, in an interview with Smita Shah.

26. One of these sessions was privately tape recorded.

27. Her ensemble was K. Ganesha, T. Viswanathan, S. Narasimhulu, Sarojini Kumaraswami, and T. Ranganathan.

28. Her ensemble was K. Ganesha, T. Viswanathan, S. Narasimhulu, Lakshmi Shanmukham, and T. Ranganathan.

29. Her ensemble was K. Ganesha, T. Viswanathan, S. Narasimhulu, Lakshmi Shanmukham, and T. Ranganathan.

30. After their first residency at Wesleyan University in 1962, Balasaraswati, Ranganathan, and Viswanathan all went on to teach at Wesleyan and in programs at Mills College and California Institute of the Arts. Beginning in the mid-1960s some of the leaders of the American avant-garde in music seemingly coincidentally crossed paths with Bala and her family in these settings. These included John Cage, Pauline Oliveros, Lou Harrison, Morton Subotnick, James Tenney, David Rosenboom, Alvin Lucier, and Anthony Braxton. The common thread in the teaching of this diverse group of artists was their belief in the significance of the process of making art.

31. Jean Battey, *Washington Post*, November 6, 1962.

32. The family's determination to keep Bala's ill health a secret reflected the competitiveness of their professional environment.

33. The title of secretary is the most senior position in certain organizations that do not have managing directors.

34. Narayana Menon, *The Hindu*, February 19, 1984.

35. S. Y. Krishnaswamy, "Bala: An Anniversary Tribute," *Sruti*, February–March 1985.

36. S. V. Shesardri, *Shankar's Weekly*, August 18, 1963.

37. Guhan, *Bala on Bharatanatyam*, 13.

38. On December 31, 1965, the ensemble was K. Ganesha, S. Narasimhulu, K. Gnanasundaram, Leela Shekar, N. Radhakrishna Naidu, and T. Kuppuswami Mudaliar.

39. V. Chandreshekaran, in an interview with Smita Shah.

40. This happened at a private concert at the home of M. M. Malaviya, President of the Indian National Congress in 1909, 1918, 1932, and 1933. M. M. Malaviya co-founded the Benares Hindu College with Annie Besant in 1898.

41. Her ensemble was K. Ganesha, S. Narasimhulu, K. Gnanasundaram, N. Radhakrishna Naidu, and T. Ranganathan.

42. Her ensemble was K. Ganesha, S. Narasimhulu, K. Gnanasundaram, Leela Shekar, N. Radhakrishna Naidu, and T. Ranganathan.

43. It has been said that Lakshmi moved to the United States following our marriage in 1980, leaving her mother alone in India. In truth, Lakshmi was never to leave her mother's side, despite the fact that this choice necessitated prolonged periods of separation for Lakshmi, Ani, and me. These allegations appeared in print after Lakshmi's death in 2001; she never had an opportunity to counter them. But the facts of what happened are well remembered by the author and others who have known the family well.

44. S. Krishnan, "Balasaraswati," *Aside* (Madras), 1984.

45. Lord Harewood, in an interview with Smita Shah.

46. *Indian Express* (Bombay), April 6, 1971.

47. With K. Ganesha, K. Gnanasundaram, T. Muktha, Lakshmi Shanmukham, T. R. Moorthy, and T. Kuppuswami Mudaliar.

48. *Indian Express* (Bombay), February 11, 1971.

49. Her ensemble included K. Ganesha, K. Gnanasundaram, S. Narasimhulu,

N. Radhakrishna Naidu, T. R. Moorthy, and T. Kuppuswami Mudaliar. Bala's cousin T. Muktha sang *padams*, although her name was not listed in the program notes.

50. Her ensemble was T. Brinda, S. Narasimhulu, Lakshmi Shanmukham, Jon Higgins, T. R. Moorthy, and T. Kuppuswami Mudaliar.

51. *Indian Express* (Bombay), October 31, 1971.

52. Her ensemble was T. Muktha, K. Ganesha, K. Gnanasundaram, Ramadas, N. Radhakrishna Naidu, and T. Kuppuswami Mudaliar.

53. N. M. N., "Music to Match Sublime Dance," *The Hindu,* January 7, 1971.

54. *Times of India* (Bombay), March 5, 1972.

55. Bella Lewitzki, in an interview with Luise Scripps, 1977.

56. Bella Lewitzki and Donny McKayle, in an interview with Luise Scripps at the American Dance Festival at Duke University, June 13, 1994.

57. Anna Kisselgoff, *New York Times*, September 22, 1972.

CHAPTER 7: "SOMETHING GREAT AND GRAND" (pages 225–254)

1. Leela Shekar, in "Bala As I Knew Her," a private statement written in the late 1980s.

2. Ra Ganapati, published in *Kalki* and read in Tamil at the event conferring the title *Sangitha Kalanidhi* on Balasaraswati at the Madras Music Academy, December 1973. Translated into English by P. V. Subramaniam, known as Subbudu.

3. Traditionally, learning *slokas* is a part of the training of a young person, including dance students.

4. Ranjani Shankar, in an interview with Smita Shah.

5. Leela Shekar, in an interview with Ra Ganapati.

6. Ra Ganapati, in an interview with Smita Shah.

7. Shyamala Mohanraj, in an interview with Smita Shah.

8. Julia Morgan, who was mentored by the well-known California architect Bernard Maybeck, also designed several of the distinctive wooden homes that run up the slopes of Berkeley and the Hearst Castle, which sits on a bluff above the Pacific, south of the Bay Area.

9. The staff also included Balasaraswati's *nattuvanar* Ramiah Pillai and singer Ramadas.

10. Mathur, "Bala: Dancing Is a Joy to Me," *Patriot*, 1976.

11. Notation of Indian music was introduced during the nineteenth century enabling the evolution of institutional learning. It was not a new problem, but it was becoming a more serious problem. The author was present when Balasaraswati made her comment.

12. Bella Lewitzki, in an interview with Luise Scripps, 1977.

13. Dame Margot Fonteyn, in a letter to Awards Committee, *Dance*, March 6, 1977.

14. Kamaladevi Chattopadhyay, in an interview with Luise Scripps, January 7, 1989.

15. The man who directed the Tamil film *Shakuntala* was the American filmmaker Ellis R. Dungan. Sometimes referred to in India as "Duncan," Dungan, of Irish heritage, was born in a small town in Ohio. He was a film student at the Uni-

versity of Southern California. In 1935, at the beginning of what he expected to be a long career in Hollywood, he traveled to India to visit a classmate named Mani Lal Tandon, whose family lived in Bombay. Dungan was unexpectedly offered the opportunity to direct a Tamil film in Madras. From 1936 to 1950 he proceeded to have a brilliant career in Tamil film direction, which included *Shakuntala* (1940) and other successful films, most notably *Meera,* another film that featured M. S. Subbulakshmi, released in 1945. *Shakuntala* was the first Indian commercial film to be shown in the United States, where it premiered in 1943.

Although he never learned Tamil, Dungan fastidiously vetted the script of each film he directed in translation. He introduced several famous musicians and dancers to Indian cinema, and perhaps even the idea of including the song and dance routines now typical of Indian popular films. In addition to M. S. Subbulakshmi, Dungan filmed the singing legend G. N. Balasubramanium, *nagaswaram* player T. N. Rajaratnam Pillai, and the dancer first known as "Baby" Kamala, Kamala Lakshman. He introduced the comedian T. S. Baliah, whose son Muni Pal eventually moved to Balasaraswati's home to assist in her care after she fell ill in the late 1970s. The off-and-on chief minister of Tamil Nadu, M. G. Ramachandran, debuted in Dungan's first film release. Dungan died in Los Angeles in 2001, largely forgotten on the Indian film scene, despite his remarkable contributions to Tamil film. (This account is drawn in part from S. Muthiah, "He Made MS a Film Star," *The Hindu,* January 21, 2002.)

16. Lakshmi Knight, in a recorded conversation with Luise Scripps.

17. Sunil Kothari, "Incomplete Homage to Balasaraswati," *Times of India*, April 3, 1977.

18. Jan Steward, in personal correspondence with Luise Scripps shortly after the performance.

19. Janet Mansfield Soares, *Martha Hill and the Making of American Dance* (Middletown, CT: Wesleyan University Press, 2009), 39–57.

20. Charles Reinhart in an interview with Smita Shah.

21. Anna Kisselgoff, *New York Times*, March 13, 1977.

22. S. Krishnan, "Bala: Autumnal Years," *Aside*, April 1979.

23. Ra Ganapati, in notes privately contributed to the family archive.

24. This story was related to me by Punnyakoti Swamigal's son more than twenty years after the event.

25. N. Pattabhi Raman and Anandhi Ramachandran, "T. Balasaraswati: The Whole World in Her Hands," *Journal of Sangeet Natak Akademi* 72–73.

26. In the very early 1900s, Paluskar started a music school called Gandharva Mahavidyala, one of the first music schools to challenge the traditional teacher-student relationship.

27. Ra Ganapati, in an interview with Smita Shah.

28. Kamaladevi Chattopadhyay, in an interview with Luise Scripps, January 28, 1994.

29. Lakshmi Knight, in an interview with Anita Raj Ratnam, April 1986.

30. Aniruddha Knight, in an interview with Smita Shah.

31. Lakshmi Knight, in private communication with Luise Scripps.

32. Luise Scripps, recollections in writing, 1991.

Glossary

aadi (Sanskrit) "Original" or "old." Often a term of veneration.

abhinaya (Sanskrit) Literally "to carry forward." An old art of expressive dance, using movement, facial expression, and body posture; often conveying the emotional content of an idea or line of poetry.

abhishekam (Sanskrit) Ablution, a sacred bathing symbolizing spiritual purification, a ceremony of symbolic offerings.

adavu (Telugu and Tamil) The basic unit of the movement grammar of *nritta*, or "pure" dance, varying from style to style. One version was codified and introduced by the Thanjavur Quartet.

adi tala (Tamil) A colloquial name for an eight count meter performed in *karnatic* music. Its theoretical name is *chaturasra jaathi triputa tala*.

alapana (Sanskrit) See *raga alapana*.

alarippu (Tamil) "Flowering," "bloom," or "flower bud"; the first item of dance in the traditional sequence of a concert of bharata natyam, introducing the three fundamental positions of "pure" dance choreography.

anupallavi (Sanskrit) Second section of several South Indian song forms, following *pallavi*.

arangetram (Tamil) A term combining two Tamil words to mean "climbing a platform"; the name of a ceremony in which a dance student is presented in a formal introduction before a knowledgeable audience.

acharya (Sanskrit) A teacher or master in religious matters; a founder or leader of a particular sect; or a title affixed to the names of learned persons, used sometimes to refer to the headman or most learned of *brahmins* in a particular temple.

arudhi (Tamil) Literally "limit" or "boundary." A rhythmic sequence performed in dance that signals the conclusion of a larger, more elaborately constructed "pure" dance composition. The term is used also in music to refer to a midpoint in a *tala* structure, a point in the meter of secondary stress — a resting point in the text, and often the point in the meter where an *arudhi* concludes.

atma (Sanskrit) or *atman* (Tamil) The soul or higher self.

bani (Sanskrit and Tamil) In South Indian music, a style of performance evolved by a particular performer. *Bani* is often confused with the term *parampara*, representing a family legacy. In North Indian music the term defines one of a several approaches to the art of *dhrupad* singing.

bhajan (Hindi) Any of several types of Hindu devotional songs, often sung by groups of devotees.

bhakta (Sanskrit) A devotee of God.

bhakti (Sanskrit) A personal relationship to the divine which may be expressed through music and poetry. *Bhakti* is often thought to have been founded by a seventh-century devotee of Siva from Thanjavur, Thirunakkarasar, known as "Appar," a composer of hymns in praise of Siva called *thevaram*.

bhava (Sanskrit)   Intense emotion or feeling that may be employed in a dramatic performance.

bol (Hindi)   A spoken syllable used in performance, and to represent a percussive sound created on a drum or by a dancer's foot. Applies to North Indian music and dance traditions.

charanam (Sanskrit)   Literally "foot," the term for the third section of several South Indian song forms.

charana-swara-sahitya (Sanskrit)   Several sections of composed music that follow a refrain, the *charanam*, found in the dance-song forms *pada varnam* and *swarajati*. They consist of a melody composed in solfège (*swara*) followed by the same melody composed and performed with words (*sahitya*).

chaturasra (Sanskrit)   The number four in the rhythmic and metric content of music and dance, one of the five *jaathis*. (See *jaathi*.)

chinna melam (Tamil and Sanskrit)   Dance ensemble, including dancer, dance master, and accompanying musicians.

darsan (Sanskrit)   Literally "sight" or "beholding." The term is used in reference to viewing images of the divine, as in "receiving *darsan*" or "doing *darsan*."

devadasi (Sanskrit)   "Female servant of God," a term that has been traced back to early medieval sources but came into common usage in the nineteenth century, referring to various communities of matrilineal families including performers of ritual service, music, and dance.

dharma (Sanskrit)   Law or religious duty.

dhrupad (Hindi)   A North Indian vocal genre, said by some to be the oldest of styles referred to as *Hindustani*. The solo tradition is based on poetic verse written in praise of the divine or of local royalty and patronage.

dubash (Tamil)   Derived from the Sanskrit "*dwibhasi*" meaning, literally, "two languages." The *dubash* were bilingual interpreters between the British (or other European colonizers) and the Indian community. During early eighteenth-century British occupation of India, there was a *dubash* for every major officer in the East India Company's establishment. Some *dubash* became wealthy and powerful as brokers of trade and political power between the Indian and foreign communities.

eduppu (Tamil)   The point in a metric structure where a phrase of text begins, which often does not coincide with the first count of the *tala*.

gajjai (Tamil)   Ankle-bells worn by a dancer.

ghazal (Urdu)   An ancient form of poetry of Persian origin and the basis for musical interpretation in several North Indian styles. Similar in lyrical content to the South Indian *padam*, focusing on human love, particularly the emotions of lovers in separation.

gharana (Hindi)   In *Hindustani* music and dance, from a root word meaning "family" or "house"; a style associated with an extended family, and typically named for a place of family origin.

gnanam (Sanskrit)   "Wisdom"; the knowledge of transcendence.

gopi (Sanskrit)   A "cow-herd girl," specifically referring to the young women whose unconditional devotion (*bhakti*) for Krishna is described in the *puranas* and *Gita Govinda*. Most famous of these is Radha.

gopuram (Sanskrit)   The tower, often ornate, rising above the gateway through the wall that encloses a shrine, particularly in South Indian temple architecture.

guru (Sanskrit)   Teacher, "the one who removes the darkness."

guru-sishya (Sanskrit)   The relationship between master and student.

gurukula (Sanskrit)   "The family of the *guru*," a system of transfer of knowledge from master or teacher to disciple or student.

harikatha (Sanskrit)   A nineteenth century performance practice that includes recounting of episodes from the *puranas*, philosophical discourse, and singing, performed with *abhinaya*.

hasta (Sanskrit)   "Hand"; hand gestures with meaning.

Hindustani (Hindi)   "Of Hindustan" (northern India); in relation to music, refers to northern styles as opposed to the *karnatic* system of South India.

isai velalar (Tamil)   A mid-twentieth century name of a subgroup of the *velalar* caste; the community of musicians and dancers that includes *devadasi* and *nattuvanar* families.

jaathi (Sanskrit)   "Group," one of the five basic elements of rhythm and counting of musical time. The five *jaathis* have, in the order of their traditional presentation, values of four, three, seven, five, and nine. Among other uses, the word *jaathi* refers to the number of counts, or length, of the *tala* component rendered through clapping and finger counting (*laghu*).

jalatarangam (Sanskrit)   A musical instrument consisting of several porcelain bowls, each filled with water to achieve a specific pitch when struck with a small curved bamboo stick.

jati (Sanskrit and Tamil)   A phrase of rhythmic syllables (such as *dheem*, *tha ki ta*, or *ta dhin gi na thom*) used by the *nattuvanar*, and in melody in various dance song forms. The word *jati* is also used colloquially to refer to composed sections of "pure" dance footwork.

jatiswaram (Sanskrit)   A song form originally part of the bharata natyam *margam* created by the Thanjavur Quartet; the second piece in a traditionally formatted performance. It has no lyrics but is composed of groupings of *swaras* (syllables of solfège).

javali (Kannada)   A musical form composed for bharata natyam that became particularly popular in the nineteenth century. Often composed in a lively medium tempo and expressing love in colloquial language. Some *javalis* have no *anupallavi*, but all have *pallavi* and *charanams*. Typically composed in *ragas* that would have been familiar to the nineteenth-century popular audience.

jeevatma (Sanskrit)   Soul.

kalapramana (Sanskrit)   Literally "time promise." In music, sense of rhythm or tempo. Innate mastery of rhythmic time.

karnatic (Tamil and English)   Styles of music associated with the southern region of India, often referred to as a unified "classical" style of performance and repertoire from Tamil Nadu, Andhra Pradesh, Karnataka, and Kerala.

kathak (Hindi, Urdu, Sanskrit)   A hereditary dance form designated by the Sangeet Natak Akademi as one of the several "classical" styles of India, originating in the north. *Kathak* traces its origins to nomadic bards, *Kathaks*, or storytellers who gave extemporaneous expositions of stories primarily from the *puranas*, told through *abhinaya*. The tradition may be rooted in early temple and ritual practices. It was later influenced by *bhakti* in the early medieval period, as were most performing arts traditions, and later still by the arts of the Mughal courts.

kathakali (Malayalam)   A highly stylized form of dance drama from Kerala designated as "classical," based primarily on the epic mythology of the *Ramayana* and *Mahabharata*. The actor-dancers wear mask-like make-up and elaborate costumes. Modern *kathakali* is said to have its origins in a seventeenth century codification of existing forms of dance drama presenting the stories of Rama and Krishna. *Kathakali* also shares similarities with older Sanskrit drama and local performance arts, including movements from martial arts. It was traditionally performed in temples and palaces, now presented in contemporary performing arts venues. The music performed with the dance is closely aligned with the movement and mood of the scenario and characters.

khanda (Sanskrit)   The number five in the rhythmic and metric content of music and dance; one of the five *jaathis*.

khyal (Hindi, Urdu)   A contemporary genre of *Hindustani* singing, popularized in its current form in the early eighteenth century. A *khyal* composition, consisting of several lines of poetic text, is performed variously by different performers, with only the text and the *raga* remaining the same. The texts of the compositions cover diverse topics, including romantic and divine love, the praise of patrons and the pantheon of the gods, descriptions of the seasons and times of day, and stories and attributes of Lord Krishna. The composition serves as a framework for various kinds of improvisation, and is performed with melodic (harmonium, *sarangi*, or violin) and percussion (*tabla*) accompaniment.

kirtana (Sanskrit)   A song form similar in structure to *kriti*, but historically older, originating in the late fifteenth century. The lyrics are devotional and sometimes relate to *puranic* incidents.

kolattam (Tamil)   Popularized today as a group dance often performed by children and amateur dancers. In its traditional form *kolattam* involved intricate group movements by male and female dancers of all ages, performed with music and rhythmic striking of sticks. Some traditional *kolattam* dancers still earn their living from these performances, which often occur during village festivities.

konnakkol (Telugu and Tamil)   The performance practice of vocalizing rhythmic syllables for accompaniment and solo.

korvai (Tamil)   A composed rhythmic section performed by percussionists or melodic musicians in the context of the *karnatic* music concert tradition. Its structure consists typically of a "body" with a shape, and a pattern that serves as a conclusion. Similar to the rhythmic composition for dance, *tirmanam*.

kriti (Sanskrit)   A South Indian song form refined in the seventeenth century. *Kritis* have three main segments: a *pallavi*, an *anupallavi*, and at least one *charanam*. They may also employ a variety of other melodic embellishments. The subject of the text may be religious or philosophical.

kurathi (Tamil)   The gypsy character in the dance drama *kuravanji*.

kuravanji (Tamil)   An operatic dance drama, historically primarily performed in temples in Tamil Nadu. The main theme is the love of the heroine for the deity of the temple or the local ruler. The central characters in most *kuravanjis* are a heroine and a gypsy woman (*kurathi*.)

kuchupudi (Telugu)   In its modern expression, a solo dance form that shares many elements of grammar and style with bharata natyam, and might be said to be a regional variant with specific identifiable characteristics. As a regionally distinct solo style, the form dates to the early twentieth century, and has been designated a "classical" dance form.

lasya (Sanskrit)   Gentle or lyrical dance.

lavani (Marathi)   A style of singing from the central Indian states of Maharastra and Madya Pradesh that became popular in the eighteenth century, and in the court of Thanjavur in the nineteenth century.

laya (Sanskrit)   "Movement"; in music, tempo or rhythm.

Mahabharata (Sanskrit)   One of the two great Hindu Sanskrit epics, describing a war between two families, or tribes, in prehistorical India. Retained as an oral history, the epic is the source for innumerable moral and ethical stories, and images that have fired the imaginations of South and Southeast Asians for millennia. Perhaps most famous of these stories is Krishna's ethical lecture, known as the *Bhagavad Gita*, bestowed on his friend Arjuna in the moments before a monumental war.

mandapam (Sanskrit)   The pillared hall structure found in many South Indian Hindu temples.

manikkatthar (Tamil)   A woman who had the knowledge to be able and trusted to perform *pujas* in the private shrines of patrons, a role usually filled by a *devadasi*.

Manipuri (Mayek)   A dance style performed in the northeastern state of Manipur. Although all regional dance styles now conferred with the authenticity of being "classical" are difficult to define as unified practices, Manipuri may be the most difficult to classify as a single form. It has roots confirmed to exist in early ritual practices, but its current form was codified during the eighteenth century, when both the thematic content and style of costumes were established. The presently accepted style includes a variety of local regional styles. The content of most of the repertoire and interpretive aspects of the dance style focuses on the myths and stories of Krishna and Radha.

margam (Sanskrit)   "Path," a "way" or manner of action; the sequence of pieces in the traditional concert format defined by the Thanjavur Quartet.

maya (Sanskrit)   A veil of illusion that each person must see through in order to achieve liberation of the soul. The divinity Maya governs the phenomenal universe of perceived duality superimposed on the unity of Brahman.

melam (Sanskrit)   An ensemble of dancer and musicians; also, performance.

melaprapti (Sanskrit)   An introduction to a concert of bharata natyam performed by the drummer and dancer, announcing the beginning of the performance. The convention went out of use in the early twentieth century.

misra (Sanskrit)   The number seven in the rhythmic and metric content of music and dance; one of the five *jaathis*.

mridangam (Sanskrit)   A double-headed barrel drum used in the accompaniment of bharata natyam and the *karnatic* tradition of music.

mudra (Sanskrit)   Symbolic gestures made with one or two hands. Used in pure dance (*nritta*), these gestures are specifically defined in shape but carry no meaning. Used in expressive dance (*nritya*) with facial expression, body position and comportment, and the poetic text, *mudras* express connotative meaning.

mukhavina (Sanskrit)   A double-reed instrument similar to the *nagaswaram* but shorter and an octave higher in pitch. Previously a common instrument in the musical ensemble for bharata natyam (*chinna melam*), the *mukhavina* was replaced during the early twentieth century by clarinet (introduced to India in the late eighteenth century in British brass ensembles) and the bamboo transverse flute.

muktayi-swara (Sanskrit)   A section of composed solfège that appears at the end of the first half of a *tana varnam*, following the *anupallavi*.

nadai (Tamil)   "Manner of walking," or pulses between counts of *tala*, synonymous with the Sanskrit word *gati* (gait).

nagaswaram (Sanskrit)   A double-reed instrument used in temple processional music, now found in concert performance; principal instrument of the *periya melam*.

nattuvanar (Tamil)   The conductor of the dance ensemble, performer of *nattuvangam*, and, often, a singer. Also the name affixed to some families of musicians and teachers associated with bharata natyam, as in the Thanjavur Nattuvanar family.

nattuvangam (Tamil)   A musical practice consisting of the vocalization of rhythmic syllables and a cymbal technique mirroring a dancer's footwork during sections of composed, choreographed "pure" dance.

natya (Sanskrit)   The combined arts of movement, music, and theater.

nautch (English)   An Anglicization of the Hindi word for dance, *nac*, and the Sanskrit word, *natya*. Perhaps first coined by the British in the 1830s to describe parlor entertainment, "nautch" became used indiscriminately by colonists and some Indians as a term for dancing, irrespective of regional difference or cultural origin, or religious or secular function.

nayaka (Sanskrit)   In Sanskrit dramaturgy and the repertoire of bharata natyam, the hero in a scenario involving hero, heroine, and a messenger or intermediary.

nayika (Sanskrit)   In Sanskrit dramaturgy and the repertoire of bharata natyam, the heroine.

niraval (Tamil)   Improvised melody performed within the structure of a composed poetic text; performed with *kriti* in the *karnatic* music concert program, and with *sabdam*, *varnam*, *javali*, and *padam* in the performance of bharata natyam.

nritta (Sanskrit)   "Pure" dance without connotative or narrative meaning, including footwork and positions of the body and limbs.

nritya (Sanskrit)   Expressive dance. See *abhinaya*.

odissi   Named for its region of origin, Orissa, a modern reconstruction of dance based upon a tradition of temple practice. The modern style is characterized by graceful movements and the use of *tribhanga*, the triple bends in the body used in choreography, performed by either a solo dancer or several dancers. The theme of the contemporary dance practice is primarily the myth of Radha and Krishna. Reconstructed following the departure of the British after Independence; it has now been designated as a "classical" form.

padam (Sanskrit) A song form with two or three sections of poetic verse, first composed in the fifteenth century and intended to be interpreted with dance; now sometimes performed in concerts of *karnatic* music.

pada varnam (Sanskrit) Compositional form of music intended to be performed with dance, consisting of *pallavi, anupallavi, muktayi-swara-sahitya*, and *charanam* with *charana-swara-sahitya*. First composed by members of the Thanjavur Quartet. Occupies a major, central role in the traditional concert format.

pallavi (Sanskrit) Literally "growing shoot" or "young branch"; the first line of various compositional forms. Also, a name of a performance practice, in which a line of text is composed in a rhythmic and metric structure that serves as the foundation for a variety of improvisational techniques.

parampara (Sanskrit) A particular teacher's lineage. See *bani* and *sampradaya*.

paratma (Sanskrit) The Oversoul.

periya melam (Tamil) An ensemble that includes the *nagaswaram* and *tavil* and performs temple and processional music.

prasadam (Tamil) An offering, usually edible, first placed before a deity and then distributed to worshippers at the conclusion of certain ceremonies in a temple.

prayoga (Sanskrit) A musical phrase that is characteristic of a particular *raga*.

puja (Sanskrit) Ritual performed to pray or show respect and as a means of offering love, praise, gratitude, and supplication to God. The purpose of a *puja* is to communicate with God and to maintain the relationship between the physical world and the subtle inner worlds.

purana (Sanskrit) Literally "belonging to earlier times"; the name of an ancient genre of Hindu literature, distinct from oral tradition. Primarily post-Vedic, *puranic* texts contain narratives of the history of the universe from creation to destruction; genealogies of the mythological kings and heroes, and divine characters; and descriptions of Hindu cosmology, philosophy, and geography. Each *purana* presents a view of the ordering of the world from the particular perspective of the narrator.

pushpanjali (Sanskrit) A ritual offering of flowers presented by a *devadasi* to an image of the divine. Not part of the original *margam* of bharata natyam, this offering was adopted as an invocation during the 1930s.

raga (Sanskrit) The melodic aspects of music.

raga alapana (Sanskrit) An improvised exposition of a *raga* performed in preparation for a composition in that particular *raga*.

Ramayana (Sanskrit) One of the two great Hindu Sanskrit epics. The *Ramayana* is said to have been composed about 1000 BCE and provides in its telling the rules of morality and duty that weave through the epic ordeal of its hero and heroine, Rama and his wife, Sita. Attributed to the Sanskrit poet Valmiki, oral versions of Rama's story circulated for centuries. The epic was probably first written down sometime around the first century CE. The *Ramayana* has since been told, retold, and translated throughout South and Southeast Asia. Most Hindus learn the characters and incidents of the *Ramayana* as children, and through them are taught the concepts of "right" behavior and thought.

rasa (Sanskrit)   In aesthetic theory, the flavor, taste, or essence of a work of art.

rasika (Sanskrit)   A person who is knowledgeable about and appreciative of the performing arts.

rishi (Sanskrit)   A sage, an ancient seer or shaman.

sabda (Sanskrit and Tamil)   Sound.

sabdam (Sanskrit)   The third piece in a traditionally organized performance of bharata natyam. An old form, now largely disappeared, that consists of four lines of text interspersed with four sections of rhythmic syllables sung in melody. Its performance relies heavily on the capacity of a musician to sing the improvised melodic form *niraval*, and a dancer's capacity to improvise *abhinaya*.

sabha (Sanskrit)   Organization, society, or association.

sadhana (Sanskrit)   A means by which a devotee achieves spiritual liberation.

sadir (Tamil)   Literally "beauty"; refers to the activity of dancing. The term was coined as a name for the hereditary style of bharata natyam, distinguishing it from the nonhereditary "revived" styles of dancing that emerged in the 1930s.

sahitya (Sanskrit)   Words or text.

sakhi (Sanskrit)   In Sanskrit dramaturgy and art, and the repertoire of bharata natyam, a messenger or intermediary between the *nayika* and *nayaka*; the heroine's friend or companion.

sama (Sanskrit)   The beginning of a cycle of meter.

samadhi (Sanskrit)   In Hinduism, the location of the ultimate act of asceticism, the intentional departure from the physical body. May also refer to the mausoleum of a saint or spiritual leader.

sambal (Sanskrit)   Sacred ash.

sampradaya (Sanskrit)   Sometimes translated as "community," referring to a process that reinforces cumulative knowledge of many kinds, including myth, religious and spiritual discipline, and the hereditary arts. *Sampradaya* is a system of belief or knowledge orally transmitted through a teacher, who has been preceded by generations of teachers initiated into the same system, to a student or devotee. That student or devotee in turn becomes an interpreter and teacher. Participation in *sampradaya* (which always coexists with a teacher's or family's heritage, *parampara*, and the style of a particular teacher, *bani*) ensures continuity with the past, but at the same time provides a basis for and expectation of change, the inherited knowledge becoming the source of creative gesture, particularly in the arts.

sanchari (Sanskrit)   Literally "movements of the note." Subordinate emotions conveyed through the performing arts. Sometimes used colloquially to refer to variations of *abhinaya*.

sanctum sanctorum (Latin and English)   Literally "holy of holies": the most sacred place within a sacred building such as a temple. Refers to the *garbha griha* in a Hindu temple, the shrine inside a temple complex where the main deity is installed.

Sangam (Sanskrit and Tamil)   In Sanskrit, "getting together." The Tamil *Sangams* were a series of legendary assemblies of Tamil scholars and poets that, according to traditional accounts, existed in the remote past; the third *Sangam* was said to have created the earliest existing Tamil literature. The *Sangam* legends played a significant role in inspiring political, social, and literary movements in Tamil Nadu in the early twentieth century.

sangathi (Sanskrit and Tamil)   A variation of a melody. Some *sangathis* are created by the composer of the piece; some are variations that have evolved within a particular style of performance. In the Vina Dhanammal family style, performers create numerous *sangathis* for compositions, which vary from one family member to another.

sangitha (Sanskrit)   Music.

Sangitha Kalanidhi   "Treasure of the Art of Music," an award presented by the Madras Music Academy, considered to be the highest honor bestowed on South Indian musicians.

sankirna (Sanskrit)   The number nine in the rhythmic and metric content of music and dance; one of the five *jaathis*.

sanyasi (Tamil)   One who has renounced the material world and lives a life spent in inner contemplation.

sarangi (Hindi)   A North Indian bowed instrument used traditionally to accompany *khyal* style of singing and *kathak* style of dance.

sastra (Sanskrit)   A "rule"; knowledge based on principles. *Sastra* refers to a scripture or an ancient treatise written in explanation of some idea, especially in matters involving religion or discipline.

sloka (Sanskrit)   A Sanskrit verse form; two lines of eight syllables each. In Balasaraswati's style a basis for improvisation of music and dance without meter. Traditionally a *sloka*, or its Tamil equivalent *viruttam*, appeared at the conclusion of a concert.

Sringara (Sanskrit)   The first of the nine *rasas*, "love." *Sringara* means literally "that which creates ecstasy."

sruti (Sanskrit)   Literally "hearing," but used to mean "pitch" and "intonation."

swara (Sanskrit)   A note or degree of scale in a *raga*. As a degree or position in a mode, a *swara* may also be a cluster of pitches, a micromelody based on the characteristics of a particular *raga*.

swarajati (Sanskrit)   A musical form divided into three main sections, originally structured for dance performance but adapted for the concert stage by composer Syama Sastri. Similar to the form *pada varnam*.

swara kalpana (Sanskrit)   Musical improvisation performed using solfège. *Kalpana* means "imagination."

swarupa (Sanskrit)   Literally "truth," but understood to suggest the proper shape and organization of a *raga*.

tala (Sanskrit)   The rhythmic aspect of music; derived from the Sanskrit term meaning "to strike with the hands."

talam (Sanskrit)   Pair of cymbals used in performances of *periya melam*, *chinna melam*, and *harikatha*.

tambura (Tamil)   An instrument that is a member of the lute family, used to provide a drone for the performance of music.

tana varnam (Sanskrit)   Compositional form consisting of *pallavi*, *anupallavi*, *muktayi-swara*, and *charanam* with *charana-swaras*. Similar in structure to *pada varnam* compositions for dance, *tana varnam* is intended for music concerts. Usually the first composition in a *karnatic* music performance.

tarana (Urdu, Hindi): A type of composition sung in *Hindustani khyal* in which certain words and syllables from the language of the percussionist are set to melody. The song might include a partial or complete composition for *tabla* within the body of the *tarana*. Largely disappeared from performance by the early twentieth century, the *tarana* was researched and reintroduced by the singer Ustad Amir Khan, whom Balasaraswati admired greatly. Argued by some to be the predecessor of the South Indian music form *tillana*.

tavil (Tamil)   Double-headed drum used in *periya melam* ensembles to accompany *nagaswaram*. Today the *tavil* appears in some fusion performances of music and dance.

thevaram (Tamil)   Collection of verses in praise of Siva by three Tamil poets, known as Nayanmars, who communicated their faith through these compositions. *Thevaram* continue to be sung as a hereditary practice in some temples.

thiru- (Tamil)   "Holy." A prefix in many place names, it indicates a place of veneration.

thumri (Hindi)   A name for a genre of music sometimes performed at the end of *Hindustani khyal* programs. Romantic or *Sringara* based, the theme usually concerns Radha's (or another of the *gopi* devotees') love for Krishna. This style is characterized by its sensuality, and by a less rigid interpretation of the grammar of raga than is presented with *khyal*.

tilak (Sanskrit)   A mark of beauty or auspiciousness placed on the forehead.

tillana (Tamil)   A compositional form of debated origin. Some (including Balasaraswati) claim it is a descendant of the North Indian form *tarana*; others argue it is an old South Indian form. A *tillana* is characterized by the mixture in its composition of words and drum syllables, set to music. Currently concludes a traditionally formatted concert of bharata natyam.

tirmanam (Tamil)   Literally "decision" or "end." A composition recited by the *nattuvanar* and executed in pure dance. The *tirmanam* is characterized by syllables that are performed vocally, and choreography that uses *adavus*. The structure of a *tirmanam* consists of a body with a shape or design and a concluding pattern, often a phrase repeated three times, composed with the syllables "*ta dhin gi na thom*." Similar to the *karnatic* rhythmic design *korvai*, with the addition of a short concluding rhythmic sequence, *arudhi*.

tiruppugazh (Tamil)   Literally "praise of the Lord," the name of a collection of verses composed in the fifteenth century by Arungirinathar, mostly in praise of Lord Murugan. The texts of *tiruppugazh* highlight humanity and righteous behavior in preference to ritual and the routine of worship.

trayasra (Sanskrit)   The number three in the rhythmic and metric content of music and dance; one of the five *jaathis*. *Trayasra* is often colloquially transliterated as *tisra.*

tulasi (Sanskrit and Tamil)   A basil-like plant associated with the Goddess and Vishnu, used throughout India in temple worship and for medicinal purposes, especially in *Ayurvedic* medicine.

tutti (Tamil)   A small bagpipe that was used as a drone accompaniment in the dance ensemble prior to the introduction of the *tambura* by Kandappa Pillai.

varnam (Sanskrit)   A song form in the *karnatic* tradition. A *tana varnam* is the customary opening for a concert of music; a *pada varnam* holds a central position in a dance concert. In dance compositions the lyrics are simple, allowing the dancer the greatest scope for elaboration of ideas and exhibition of the characteristics of the particular *raga.*

vidwan (Sanskrit)   A person who has knowledge. As an honorific title preceding the name of a South Indian musician, the term connotes scholarship and experience expressed in performance.

vina (Sanskrit)   A generic name for a stringed instrument used in Indian music concerts, found throughout India in several configurations, some now disappeared.

viruttam (Tamil)   A devotional verse composed in Tamil. In Balasaraswati's style, a *viruttam*, like a *sloka*, is a basis for improvisation of music and dance without meter. Traditionally a *viruttam* or *sloka* appeared at the conclusion of a concert.

vur (Tamil)   Ancestral place of origin.

Yasoda (Sanskrit)   Krishna's foster mother.

Bibliography

BOOKS

Allen, Matthew Harp. "The Tamil Padam: A Dance Music Genre of South India." Vol. I: Text. PhD diss., Wesleyan University, 1992.

Apffel-Marglin, Frédérique. *Wives of the God-King: The Rituals of the Devadasis of Puri*. New Delhi and New York: Oxford University Press, 1985.

Banes, Sally. *Dancing Women: Female Bodies on Stage*. London and New York: Routledge, 2001.

Bennahum, Ninotchka Devorah. *Antonia Merce, "La Argentina": Flamenco and the Spanish Avant-Garde*. Middletown, CT: Wesleyan University Press, 2000.

Besant, Annie. *Annie Besant: An Autobiography*. Chennai: Theosophical Publishing House, 1999. First edition 1893.

Burke, Marie Louise. *Swami Vivekananda in the West: New Discoveries*. Calcutta: Advaita Ashrama, 1983.

Chetanananda. *God Lived with Them: Life Stories of Sixteen Monastic Disciples of Sri Ramakrishna*. Calcutta: Advaita Ashrama, 2001.

Coomaraswamy, Ananda K. *The Dance of Shiva*. Rev. ed. New York: Noonday Press, 1971. First published 1918 by Sunrise Turn, New York.

———. *The Mirror of Gesture*. Cambridge, MA: Harvard University Press, 1917.

———. *The Transformation of Nature in Art*. Cambridge, MA: Harvard University Press, 1934.

Dalrymple, William. *The Last Mughal: The Fall of a Dynasty, Delhi, 1857*. New Delhi: Penguin Books India, 2006.

Danielou, Alain. *Hindu Polytheism*. Bollingen Series LXXIII. New York: Bollingen Foundation, 1964.

De Bary, William Theodore, ed. *Sources of Indian Tradition*. New York: Columbia University Press, 1958.

Desmond, Jane. "Dancing the Difference: Cultural Imperialism and Ruth St. Denis's *Radha* of 1906" in *Moving History/Dancing Cultures: A Dance History Reader*, edited by Ann Dils and Ann Cooper Albright, 256–270. Middletown, CT: Wesleyan University Press, 2001.

Devi, Ragini. *Dance Dialects of India*. Delhi: Motilal Banarsidass, 1972.

de Zoete, Beryl. *The Other Mind: A Study of Dance in South India*. London: Victor Gollancz, 1953.

Dixon, Joy. *Divine Feminine: Theosophy and Feminism in England*. Baltimore: Johns Hopkins University Press, 2001.

Eck, Diana. *Darsan: Seeing the Divine Image in India*. New York: Columbia University Press, 1998.

Fuller, C. J. *Servants of the Goddess*. New Delhi: Oxford University Press, 1984.

Gandhi, Rajmohan. *Mohandas: A True Story of a Man, His People and an Empire*. New Delhi: Penguin Books India, 2006.

Gaston, Anne-Marie. *Bharata Natyam: From Temple to Theatre*. Delhi: Manohar, 1996.

George, T. J. S. *MS: A Life in Music*. New Delhi: HarperCollins, 2004.

Guhan, S., comp. and ed. *Bala on Bharatanatyam*. Madras: The Sruti Foundation, 1991.

Hart, George L. III. *Poets of the Tamil Anthologies*. Princeton, NJ: Princeton University Press, 1979.

Higgins, Jon B. *The Music of Bharata Natyam*. New Delhi: American Institute of Indian Studies, 1984.

Humphrey, Doris. *The Art of Making Dances*, ed. Barbara Pollack. Princeton, NJ: Princeton Book Company, 1987.

Irschick, Eugene F. *Dialogue and History: Constructing South India, 1795–1895*. Berkeley: University of California Press, 1994.

———. *Politics and Social Conflict in South India: The Non-Brahman Movement and Tamil Separatism 1916–1929*. Berkeley: University of California Press, 1969.

Iyer, E. Krishna. *Personalities in Present Day Music*. 2nd ed. Chennai: Trinity Music Book Publishers, 2006.

Jackson, William J. *Tyagaraja and the Renewal of Tradition: Translations and Reflections*. Delhi: Motilal Banarsidass, 1994.

Jones, Betty True, ed. *Dance as Cultural Heritage*. Dance Research Annual XV. CORD, 1985.

Jordan, Kay K. *From Sacred Servant to Profane Prostitute: A History of the Changing Legal Status of the Devadasi in India, 1857–1947*. New Delhi: Manohar, 2003.

Kalpana, K., and Frank Schiffer, eds. *Madras: The Architectural Heritage*. Chennai: Indian National Trust for Art and Cultural Heritage, 2003.

Kersenboom, Saskia C. *Nityasumangali: Devadasi Tradition in South India*. Delhi: Motilal Banarsidass, 1998. First edition 1987.

Leslie, Julia, ed. *Roles and Rituals for Hindu Women*. Delhi: Motilal Banarsidass, 1992.

Luytens, Mary. *The Life and Death of Krishnamurti*. Chennai: Krishnamurti Foundation, 2006. First published 1990 by John Murray, London.

Maitland, Julia. *Letters from Madras*. New Delhi: Oxford University Press, 2003. First published 1843 by John Murray, London.

McKayle, Donald. *Transcending Boundaries: My Dancing Life*. London and New York: Routledge, 2002.

Menon, Indira. *Great Masters of Carnatic Music 1930–1965*. New Delhi: Indialog 2004.

———. *The Madras Quartet: Women in Karnatak Music*. New Delhi: Roli Books, 1999.

Menon, Narayana. *Balasaraswati*. Delhi: International Cultural Centre, 1961.

Miller, Barbara Stoler, ed. and trans. *The Gitagovinda of Jayadeva: Love Songs of the Dark Lord*. Delhi: Motilal Banarsidass, 1984.

Mukhopadhyay, Ashoke Kumar. *Uday Shankar: Twentieth Century's Nataraja*. New Delhi: Rupa & Co., 2004.

Müller, F. Max. *Ramakrishna: His Life and Sayings*. New Delhi: Rupa & Co., 2006. First published 1898 by Longmans, Green, Madras.

Muthiah, S. *Madras Discovered*. New Delhi: Affiliated East-West Press, 1987. Reprinted incorporating stories from "Tales of Old and New Madras" 1992. Page references are to the 1992 edition.

Nair, Janiki. *Women and Law in Colonial India: A Social History*. In collaboration with National Law School of India University, Bangalore. New Delhi: Kali for Women, 2000.

Neuman, Daniel. *The Life of Music in North India*. Detroit: Wayne State University Press, 1980.

Orr, Leslie C. *Donors, Devotees, and Daughters of God: Temple Women in Medieval Tamilnadu*. New York and Oxford: Oxford University Press, 2000.

O'Shea, Janet. *At Home in the World: Bharata Natyam on the Global Stage*. Middletown, CT: Wesleyan University Press, 2007.

Owen, Norton. *A Certain Place: The Jacob's Pillow Story*. Becket, MA: Jacob's Pillow Dance Festival, 1997.

Petersen, Indira Viswanathan. *Poems to Siva: The Hymns of the Tamil Saints*. Princeton, NJ: Princeton University Press, 1989.

Peterson, Indira Viswanathan and Davesh Soneji, eds. *Performing Pasts: Reinventing the Arts in Modern South India*. New Delhi: Oxford University Press, 2008.

Powers, Harold S. "The Background of the South Indian Raga-System." PhD diss., Princeton University, 1958.

Prasad, A. K. *Devadasi System in Ancient India: A Study of Temple Dancing Girls of South India*. Delhi: HK Publishers, 1990.

Prasad, R. C. *Early English Travellers in India*. Delhi: Motilal Banarsidass, 1965.

Prothero, Stephen. *The White Buddhist: The Asian Odyssey of Henry Steel Olcott*. Bloomington and Indianapolis: Indiana University Press, 1996.

Raghavan, V. *Splendours of Indian Dance*. Chennai: Dr. V. Raghavan Centre for Performing Arts, 2004.

Rahman, Sukanya. *Dancing in the Family: An Unconventional Memoir of Three Women*. New Delhi: HarperCollins, 2001.

Ramani, Shankuntala, ed. *Rukmini Devi Arundale: Birth Centenary Volume*. Chennai: The Kalakshetra Foundation, 2003.

———. *Some Selected Speeches & Writings of Rukmini Devi Arundale*. 2 vols. Chennai: The Kalakshetra Foundation, n.d.

Ramanujam, A. K. *The Interior Landscape: Love Poems from a Classical Tamil Anthology*. New Delhi: Oxford University Press, 1999. First published 1967 by Indiana University Press.

Ramanujam, A. K., Velcheru Narayana Rao and David Shulman, eds. and trans. *When God Is a Customer: Telugu Courtesan Songs by Ksetrayya and Others*. Berkeley: University of California, 1994.

Ramaswami, N. S. *The Founding of Madras*. Bombay: Orient Longman, 1977.

Rao, B. Rajanikantha. *Kshetrayya*. New Delhi: Sahitya Akademi, 1981.

Sadasivan, K. *Devadasi System in Medieval Tamil Nadu*. Trivandrum: CBH Publications, 1993.

Said, Edward W. *Orientalism*. New York: Vintage Books, 1979. First published 1978 by Pantheon Books.

Sambamoorthy, P. *A Dictionary of South Indian Music and Musicians.* Vol. I.
Madras: The Indian Music Publishing House, 1952.

———. *A Dictionary of South Indian Music and Musicians.* Vol. II. Madras:
The Indian Music Publishing House, 1959.

———. *A Dictionary of South Indian Music and Musicians.* Vol. III. Madras:
The Indian Music Publishing House, 1971.

———. *Great Composers Book II: Tyagaraja.* 2nd ed. Madras: The Indian Music
Publishing House, 1970.

Sarabhai, Mrinalini. *The Voice of the Heart.* New Delhi: HarperCollins, 2004.

Seetha, S. *Tanjore as a Seat of Music.* Madras: University of Madras, 1981.

Shah, Amrita. *Vikram Sarabhai: A Life.* New Delhi: Penguin Viking, 2007.

Shankar, Jogan. *Devadasi Cult, a Sociological Analysis.* Delhi: Ashish Publishing,
1990.

Shawn, Ted. *Every Little Movement: A Book About François Delsarte.* New York:
Dance Horizons, 1963.

Singer, Milton. *When a Great Tradition Modernizes: An Anthropological
Approach to Indian Civilization.* Chicago: University of Chicago Press, 1972.

———. *Structure and Change in Indian Society, the Study of Indian Society and
Culture.* Edited by Milton Cohn and Bernard S. Cohn. Chicago: Viking Fund
Publications in Anthropology, University of Chicago Press, 1968.

Soares, Janet Mansfield. *Martha Hill and the Making of American Dance.*
Middletown, CT: Wesleyan University Press, 2009.

Srinivasan, Amrit. "Temple 'Prostitution' and Community Reform: An
Examination of the Ethnographic, Historical and Textual Context of the
Devadasi in Tamil Nadu, South India." PhD diss., Cambridge University,
1984.

Sriram, V. *Carnatic Summer: Lives of Twenty Great Exponents.* Chennai:
East-West Books, 2004.

———. *The Devadasi and the Saint: The Life and Times of Bangalore
Nagarathnamma.* Madras: East-West Books, 2007.

Subrahmanian, N. *History of Tamilnad (A.D. 1565–1984).* 3rd and fully rev. ed.
Madurai: Ennes, 1984.

Subramanian, Lakshmi. *From the Tanjore Court to the Madras Music Academy:
A Social History of Music in South India.* New Delhi: Oxford University Press,
2006.

Sundaram, B. M. *Varna Swarajati.* Thanjavur: Sarasvati Mahal Library, 2002.

Thurston, Edgar. *Castes and Tribes of Southern India.* Vol. 11. Madras:
Government Press, 1909.

Vatsyayan, Kapila. *Indian Classical Dance.* New Delhi: Publications Division
Ministry of Information and Broadcasting, Government of India, 1974.

———. *Traditional Indian Theatre—Multiple Streams.* New Delhi: National
Book Trust, 1980.

Vishwanathan, Lakshmi. *Women of Pride: The Devadasi Heritage.* New Delhi:
Roli Books, 2008.

Viswanathan, T., and Matthew Harp Allen. *Music in South India: The Karnatak*

Concert Tradition and Beyond: Experiencing Music, Expressing Culture. New York: Oxford University Press, 2004.

Warren, W. H., and N. Barlow, comps. *The Church in the Fort: A History of St. Mary's.* Rev. ed. Chennai: St. Mary's Church, 2002.

Weidman, Amanda J. *Singing the Classical, Voicing the Modern.* Durham, NC: Duke University Press, 2006.

Winslow, Richard. "Report of the Department of Music (Wesleyan University, 1960–61)" in "Saraswati's Journey: South Indian Karnatak Music in the United States" by Joseph Getter. Master of Arts thesis, Wesleyan University, May 1998.

Woodruff, John. *Sakti and Sakta: Essays and Addresses.* Madras: Ganesh and Co., 1927.

Zvelebil, K. V., trans. *The Lord of the Meeting Rivers: Devotional Poems of Basavanna.* Delhi: Motilal Banarsidass / Paris: UNESCO, 1984.

REVIEWS, ARTICLES, AND MISCELLANEOUS

Balasaraswati's family and several of the family's friends and students collected and contributed articles, program notes, and other documents that are now part of the body of material retained in Balasaraswati's family. In addition to making extensive reference to many of these materials, this biography draws directly from about one hundred published reviews and articles written about Balasaraswati during and after her career. Many are attributable to dance critics and scholars who were contemporaries of Balasaraswati; about two dozen were written by staff critics and published without attribution. The following list of published articles and reviews represents a selection of the hundreds that were read in the course of my research for this book.

Abhinasi. *The Sunday Hindustan Standard* (New Delhi), November 6, 1955.

Allen, Matthew Harp. "Rewriting the Script for South Indian Dance." *The Drama Review* 41, no. 3 (1997).

Arundale, George. "Seeing Theosophy." *The Theosophist* 57, no. 6 (March 1936).

———. *The Theosophist* 57, no. 8 (May 1936).

Arundale, Rukmini Devi. *The Theosophist* 57, no. 5 (February 1936).

Balasaraswati Felicitation Committee. Program Notes (April 4, 1969).

Barnes, Clive. *New York Times,* August 24, 1963.

———. *New York Times,* October 22, 1965.

Battey, Jean. *Washington Post,* November 6, 1962.

Bharati, Shuddhananda. "Kshetrajna and the Indian Dance." *Illustrated Weekly of India,* June 12, 1960.

Bowers, Faubian. *Dance,* August 1962.

Chandrasekharan, K. (as Natya Priya). *The Hindu,* October 23, 1949.

Chandrasekharan, K. "Only One Bala for Bharata Natyam." *The Hindu,* March 1, 1984.

Chiaroscuro. *Illustrated Weekly of India* (Delhi), July 15, 1962.

Dance. October 1969.

Dance Advance Archives. http//www.danceadvance.org.

Fabri, Charles. "Gallery of Famous Indian Dancers — VII." *The Statesman,* June 29, 1954.

Fonteyn, Margot. Letter to Awards Committee. *Dance,* March 6, 1977.

Hindustan Times, November 5, 1955.

Hughes, Allen. *New York Times,* November 25, 1963.

Indian Express (New Delhi), "Dance Recital by Bala," March 29, 1955.

Indian Express (Madras), "Bala Excels," December 26, 1956.

Indian Express (Bombay), February 11, 1971.

Indian Express (Bombay), April 6, 1971.

Indian Express (Bombay), November 2, 1971.

Iyer, C. P. Ramaswami. *The Mail* (Madras), August 15, 1928.

Iyer, E. Krishna. "Renaissance of Indian Dance and Its Architects." Indian Fine Arts Society Souvenir (1948). Reprinted in *Rasamanjari* (Delhi), August 1997.

———. "Tamil Artists Who Received Awards: Balasaraswati." *Sunday Times of India,* April 10, 1955.

Journal of the Madras Music Academy II (1933).

Kalki. "Shambu Maharaj." April 24, 1955.

Kersenboom, Saskia. "Devadasi Murai." *Rasamanjari* II, no. 2 (August 1997).

Kisselgoff, Anna. *New York Times,* December 6, 1972.

———. *New York Times,* March 17, 1977.

———. *New York Times,* July 1, 1977.

Kokhar, Ashish Mohan. *Attendance: The Dance Annual of India, 2000.*

———. *Attendance: The Dance Annual of India, 2001.*

Kothari, Sunil. "Incomplete Homage to Balasaraswati." *Times of India,* April 3, 1977.

Krishnamurthy, R. *Ananda Vikatan,* August 20, 1933.

———. *Ananda Vikatan,* September 10, 1933.

———. *Ananda Vikatan,* June 17, 1934.

———. *Ananda Vikatan,* October 21, 1934.

———. *Ananda Vikatan,* December 23, 1934.

———. *Ananda Vikatan,* January 5, 1935.

———. *Ananda Vikatan,* November 3, 1935.

———. *Ananda Vikatan,* December 15, 1935.

———. *Ananda Vikatan,* October 15, 1939.

———. *Ananda Vikatan,* January 7, 1940.

Krishnaswamy, S. Y. "Bala: An Anniversary Tribute." *Sruti,* February–March 1985.

Krishnan, S. "Bala: Autumnal Years." *Aside,* April–May 1979.

———. "Balasaraswati." *Aside,* May 1984.

Mann, Mani. *Femina* (Delhi), August 28, 1964.

Mathur, Kumkum. "Dancing Is a Joy to Me." *Patriot,* February 23, 1976.

Menon, Narayana. *The Hindu,* February 19, 1984.

Mody, Champaklal G., ed. All India Dance Festival Souvenir. Vikram Samvat 2000, January 18–24, 1945.

Muthiah, S. "He Made MS a Film Star." *The Hindu* (Chennai), January 21, 2002.

———. *The Hindu,* December 17, 2007.

N. M. N. "Music to Match Sublime Dance." *The Hindu*, January 7, 1971.

Nevile, Pran. "The Nautch Girl and the Sahib." *The India Magazine of Her People and Culture* 10 (January 1990).

Parker, Kunal M. "'A Corporation of Superior Prostitutes': Anglo-Indian Legal Conceptions of Temple Dancing Girls, 1800–1914." *Modern Asian Studies* 32, no. 3 (July 1998): 559–633.

Patanjali, V. "Balasaraswati." *Illustrated Weekly of India*, May 25, 1969.

Pattabhi Raman, N., ed. "Bala: An Anniversary Tribute." *Sruti*, February–March 1985.

———. "25 in 2000." *India Today*, May 2000.

Pattabhi Raman, N., and Anandhi Ramachandran. "T. Balasaraswati: The Whole World in Her Hands." Special Issue, *Sangeet Natak: Journal of Sangeet Natak Akademi* 72–73 (April–September 1984).

Puri, Meenakshi. "Padams and Javalis." *Sunday Statesman*, April 7, 1957.

Raman, V. P. "The Anguish of Art." *Swarajya*, February 9, 1957.

Rao, Maya. *Illustrated Weekly of India* (Delhi), June 3, 1962.

Rasikan. "Swanantantra." Madras, January 12, 1951.

Renouf, Renee. *Thought* (Delhi), May 5, 1963.

Sarma, Radha. "The Presence of Dhanammal." Masters Remembered. *Indian Express* (July 28, 1979).

Seshagiri, G. K. (as Bhava Raga Tala). *Sound and Shadow*, April 15, 1933, 24.

———. *Sound and Shadow*, April 23, 1933, 24.

———. *Sound and Shadow*, August 27, 1933, 62–64.

Shankar's Weekly, November 13, 1955.

Shankaran, T. "Bala." Special Issue, *Sangeet Natak: Journal of the Sangeet Natak Akademi* 72–73 (April–September 1984).

———. "Kandappa Nattuvanar." Special Issue, *Sangeet Natak: Journal of the Sangeet Natak Akademi* 72–73 (April–September 1984).

———. "Bala's Musicians." Special Issue, *Sangeet Natak: Journal of the Sangeet Natak Akademi* 72–73 (April–September 1984).

———. *Sruti* 9 (July 1984).

———. *Sruti* 12 (October 1984).

———. *Sruti* 60/61 (September 1989).

Shawn, Ted. "Bala: First Lady of Bharata Natyam." *Span,* May 19, 1962.

Shesardri, S. V. *Shankar's Weekly*, August 18, 1963.

Srinivasan, Priya. "Bodies Beneath the Smoke." *Discourses in Dance* Vol. 4, Issue 1 (2007), 23.

Sruti, November 1983, 4–11.

Sruti 8, June 1984.

Sruti 27/28, December 1986–January 1987.

The Statesman (Delhi), "Presentation of SNA Awards," March 28, 1955.

The Statesman (Delhi), "Bala Enchants Delhi Audience," March 29, 1955.

The Statesman (Delhi), March 31, 1962.

Subramaniam, P. V. (as Subbudu.) "The Award at the Capital." *Kalki* (Madras), April 3, 1955.

Sunday Hindustan Standard (Delhi), November 6, 1955.

Swarajya. "The Anguish of Art." February 9, 1957.

Times of India (New Delhi), "A Dream Come True," March 29, 1955.

Times of India (New Delhi), "Chaste Rendering of Padams," April 23, 1957.

Times of India (Bombay), November 6, 1961.

Times of India (Bombay), March 5, 1972.

Terry, Walter. *New York Herald Tribune*, August 22, 1962.

Vanderstoel, Graeme. "A Brief History of the American Society for Eastern Arts and the Center for World Music in the Bay Area from 1963." Center for World Music (San Diego), 2004.

Vanita. "Whispertime." *Women's World* (Delhi), October 25, 1953.

Vasudev, S. V. "Balasaraswati Was Goddess of Dancing." *Times of India* (Delhi), February 10, 1984.

INTERVIEWS AND MISCELLANEOUS

About fifty interviews are part of the collection of materials I used as a historical basis for this biography. Every interview was recorded and transcribed, and I have made extensive use of these transcripts in my research. Some of the interviews were originally conducted in English, but many were conducted in a vernacular language (Hindi, Gujarati, Telugu, or Tamil) and translated.

The undated interviews listed below derive from the work of five key contributors. Video recordings made between 1985 and 1988 by Smita Shah, a videographer from Bangalore, constitute a major portion of the interviews. Luise Scripps recorded interviews with several significant figures in the 1980s and 1990s. Other recordings were made by members of Balasaraswati's family. Bala's cousin T. Shankaran, whose name is very well known among historians of *karnatic* music, recorded interviews between 1985 and 1991. Her brother T. Viswanathan, former head of the Department of Music at the University of Madras and a long-standing scholar and teacher at Wesleyan University, recorded the notes of his first interview in 1961 and continued his work into the 1990s. Lakshmi Knight also conducted interviews in the 1980s and 1990s.

In addition to the interview transcripts, written reflections on Balasaraswati were contributed to the archive during the 1980s and 1990s by several of her closest associates, particularly by journalist and philosopher Ra Ganapati and by Balasaraswati's music student and accompanist Leela Shekar.

As this book goes to press, the interviews and personal reflections, in both recorded and transcribed or written forms, remain the private property of Balasaraswati's family. One of the aims of this work is to make some of that material publicly accessible.

Alkazi, Roshen, interview with Luise Scripps, June 21 and 29, 1990.

Annamalai, Radha, interview with T. Shankaran, 1985.

Arundale, Rukmini Devi, interview with Smita Shah.

Bai, Bani, interview with G. Sulochana, December 1987.

Bhadhury, Manjulika, interview with T. Shankaran.

Bhanumathi, K., interview with T. Shankaran.

Chandreshekar, V., interview with Smita Shah.

Chattopadhyay, Kamaladevi, interview with Smita Shah.

Cunningham, Merce, interview with Smita Shah.

Damija, interview with Smita Shah.

Ganapati, Ra, interview with Smita Shah.

Ganapati, Ra, personal notes given to Lakshmi Knight.

Ganapati, Ra, personal correspondence with Lakshmi Knight, August 1, 1990.

Gauri Ammal, Mylapore, interview with T. Shankaran, 1971.

Gopalan, Mrs. Satyavati, interview with Luise Scripps.

Harewood, George Lascelles, interview with Luise Scripps.

Harewood, George Lascelles, interview with Smita Shah.

Iyer, T. L. Venkatarama, address at the opening of the Balasaraswati School, 1953.

Jayalakshmi, P., interview with T. Shankaran, 1989.

Jayammal, T., Government of India Census interview by T. Viswanathan, 1961.

Kisselgoff, Anna, interview with Luise Scripps.

Knight, Aniruddha, interview with Smita Shah.

Knight, Lakshmi, interviews with Luise Scripps on several occasions.

Krishnamachari, T. T., in an address to the Madras Music Academy, December 1973.

Kumaraswami, Sarojini, interview with Smita Shah.

Kuppuswami, T., interview with T. Shankaran.

Lewitzki, Bella, interview with Luise Scripps, 1977.

Lewitzki, Bella, and Donald McKayle, interview at the American Dance Festival with Luise Scripps, June 13, 1994.

McKayle, Donald, interview with Luise Scripps, 1999.

Maharaj, Birju, interview with Smita Shah.

Menon, Narayana, interview with Luise Scripps.

Menon, Narayana, interview with Smita Shah.

Mohanraj, Shyamala, interview with Smita Shah.

Pillai, K. P. Kittappa, interview with T. Shankaran, January 7, 1989.

Pillai, K. P. Kittappa, interview with T. Viswanathan.

Rajan, Savitri, interview with T. Shankaran.

Ranganathan, T., interview with Smita Shah.

Ratnam, Anita Raj, interview with Luise Scripps, April 1986.

Ray, Satyajit, interview with Smita Shah.

Reinhart, Charles, interview with Smita Shah.

Reinhart, Charles, interview with Luise Scripps, 1999.

Sastri, B. V. K., interview with Smita Shah.

Scripps, Luise, interview with Lakshmi Knight.

Scripps, Luise, written recollections, 1991.

Shankar, Ranjani, interview with Smita Shah.

Shankar, Ravi, interview with Smita Shah.

Shankaran, T., interview with T. Viswanathan.

Shankaran, T., letter to Lakshmi Knight dated May 17, 1990.

Shankaran, T., audiotape recorded January 6, 1989 and given to Lakshmi Knight.

Shankaran, T., letter dated January 9, 1989.

Shekar, Leela, private statement entitled "Bala As I Knew Her."

Shekar, Leela, interview with Ra Ganapati, recorded by Smita Shah.

Steward, Jan, personal correspondence with Luise Scripps.

Sundaram, B. M., interviews with the author, November 2004–January 2005 and December 2005, and several conversations between January 2006 and January 2009.

Vatsyayan, Kapila, interview with Luise Scripps.

Vatsyayan, Kapila, interview with Smita Shah.

Viswanathan, T., interview with Smita Shah.

Viswanathan, T., interview with Luise Scripps.

Viswanathan, T., recorded conversation with Lakshmi Knight, Matthew Allen, and the author, September 1988.

Yodh, Medha, interview with Luise Scripps, May 25, 1995.

Index

About the Author

Douglas M. Knight Jr. is a musician and independent scholar whose personal and artistic relationship with India and Balasaraswati's family began in the late 1960s. He has appeared in performance with Balasaraswati, her brothers Ranganathan and Viswanathan, her daughter, Lakshmi Knight, and her grandson, Aniruddha Knight. Douglas Knight has been a Fulbright Scholar and a Guggenheim Fellow as well as the recipient of other awards.

About the Driftless Series

The Driftless Series is a publication award program established in 2010 and consists of five categories:

DRIFTLESS NATIONAL, for a second poetry book by a United States citizen

DRIFTLESS NEW ENGLAND, for a poetry book by a New England author

DRIFTLESS ENGLISH, for English language poetry from an author outside the United States

DRIFTLESS TRANSLATION, for a translation of poetry into English

DRIFTLESS CONNECTICUT, for an outstanding book in any field by a Connecticut author

The Driftless Series is funded by the Beatrice Fox Auerbach Foundation Fund at the Hartford Foundation for Public Giving. For more information and a complete list of books in The Driftless Series, please visit us online at http://www.wesleyan.edu/wespress/driftless.